Shugo Chara!

2

PEACH-PIT

Translated by
Satsuki Yamashita

Adapted by
Nunzio DeFilippis and Christina Weir

Lettered by
North Market Street Graphics

KC
KODANSHA
COMICS

Shugo Chara! volume 2 is a work of fiction. Names, characters, places, and incidents are the products of the author's imagination or are used fictitiously. Any resemblance to actual events, locales, or persons, living or dead, is entirely coincidental.

A Kodansha Comics Trade Paperback Original.

Shugo Chara! volume 2 copyright © 2007 PEACH-PIT
English translation copyright © 2007, 2013 PEACH-PIT

All rights reserved.

Published in the United States by Kodansha Comics, an imprint of Kodansha USA Publishing, LLC., New York.

Publication rights for this English edition arranged through Kodansha Ltd., Tokyo.

First published in Japan in 2007 by Kodansha Ltd., Tokyo.

ISBN 978-1-61262-314-6

Original cover design by Akiko Omo.

Printed in the United States of America.

www.kodanshacomics.com

9 8 7 6 5 4 3 2

Translator: Satsuki Yamashita
Adapter: Nunzio DeFilippis and Christina Weir
Lettering: North Market Street Graphics

Contents

Honorifics Explained

Throughout the Kodansha Comics books, you will find Japanese honorifics left intact in the translations. For those not familiar with how the Japanese use honorifics and, more important, how they differ from American honorifics, we present this brief overview.

Politeness has always been a critical facet of Japanese culture. Ever since the feudal era, when Japan was a highly stratified society, use of honorifics—which can be defined as polite speech that indicates relationship or status—has played an essential role in the Japanese language. When addressing someone in Japanese, an honorific usually takes the form of a suffix attached to one's name (example: "Asuna-san"), is used as a title at the end of one's name, or appears in place of the name itself (example: "Negi-sensei," or simply "Sensei!").

Honorifics can be expressions of respect or endearment. In the context of manga and anime, honorifics give insight into the nature of the relationship between characters. Many English translations leave out these important honorifics and therefore distort the feel of the original Japanese. Because Japanese honorifics contain nuances that English honorifics lack, it is our policy at Kodansha Comics not to translate them. Here, instead, is a guide to some of the honorifics you may encounter in Kodansha Comics books.

-san: This is the most common honorific and is equivalent to Mr., Miss, Ms., Mrs. It is the all-purpose honorific and can be used in any situation where politeness is required.

-sama: This is one level higher than "-san" and is used to confer great respect.

-dono: This comes from the word "tono," which means "lord." It is an even higher level than "-sama" and confers utmost respect.

-kun: This suffix is used at the end of boys' names to express familiarity or endearment. It is also sometimes used by men among friends, or when addressing someone younger or of a lower station.

-chan: This is used to express endearment, mostly toward girls. It is also used for little boys, pets, and even among lovers. It gives a sense of childish cuteness.

Bozu: This is an informal way to refer to a boy, similar to the English terms "kid" and "squirt."

Sempai/Senpai: This title suggests that the addressee is one's senior in a group or organization. It is most often used in a school setting, where underclassmen refer to their upperclassmen as "sempai." It can also be used in the workplace, such as when a newer employee addresses an employee who has seniority in the company.

Kohai: This is the opposite of "sempai" and is used toward underclassmen in school or newcomers in the workplace. It connotes that the addressee is of a lower station.

Sensei: Literally meaning "one who has come before," this title is used for teachers, doctors, or masters of any profession or art.

-[blank]:   This is usually forgotten in these lists, but it is perhaps the most significant difference between Japanese and English. The lack of honorific means that the speaker has permission to address the person in a very intimate way. Usually, only family, spouses, or very close friends have this kind of permission. Known as *yobisute*, it can be gratifying when someone who has earned the intimacy starts to call one by one's name without an honorific. But when that intimacy hasn't been earned, it can be very insulting.

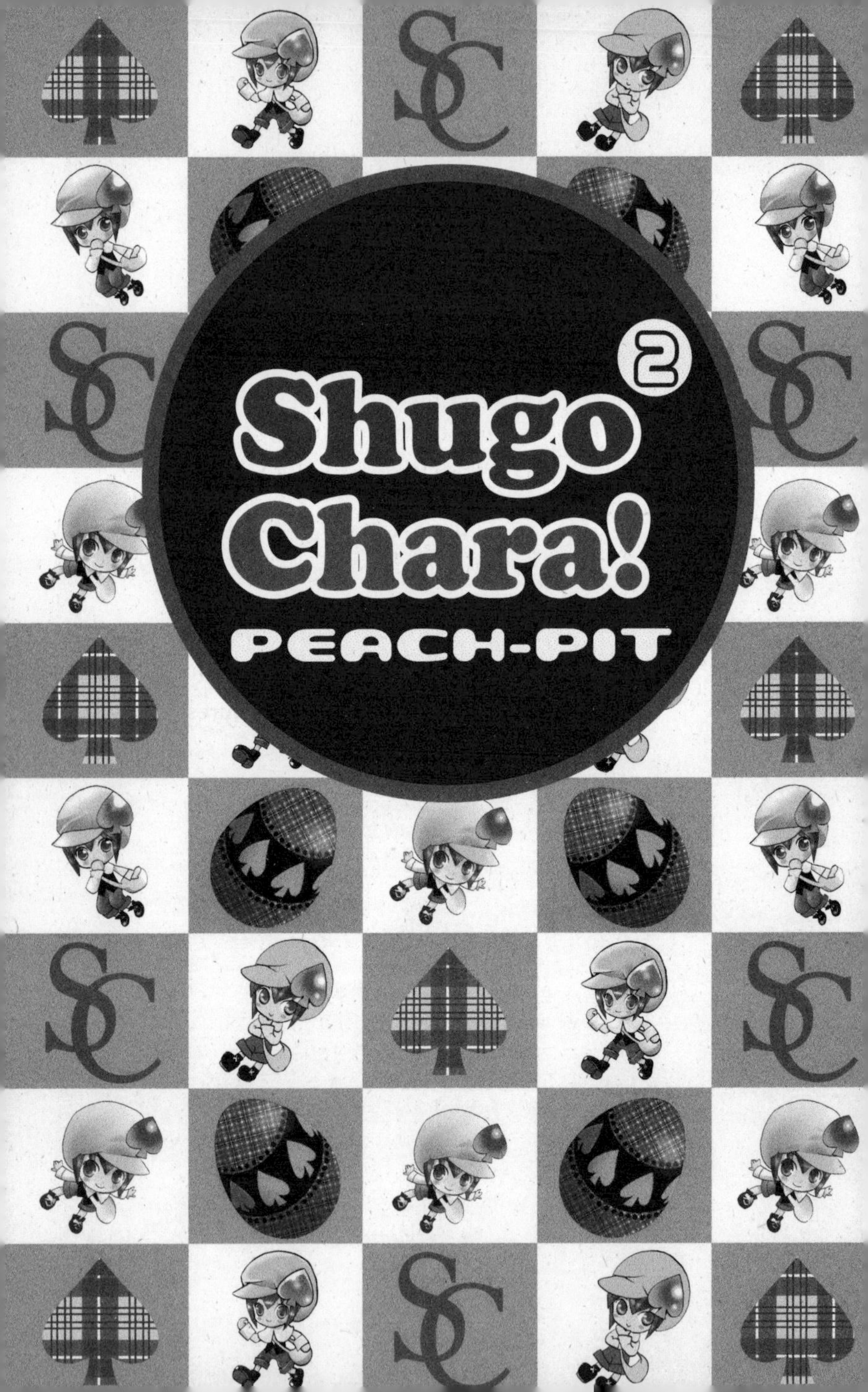
2
Shugo Chara!
PEACH-PIT

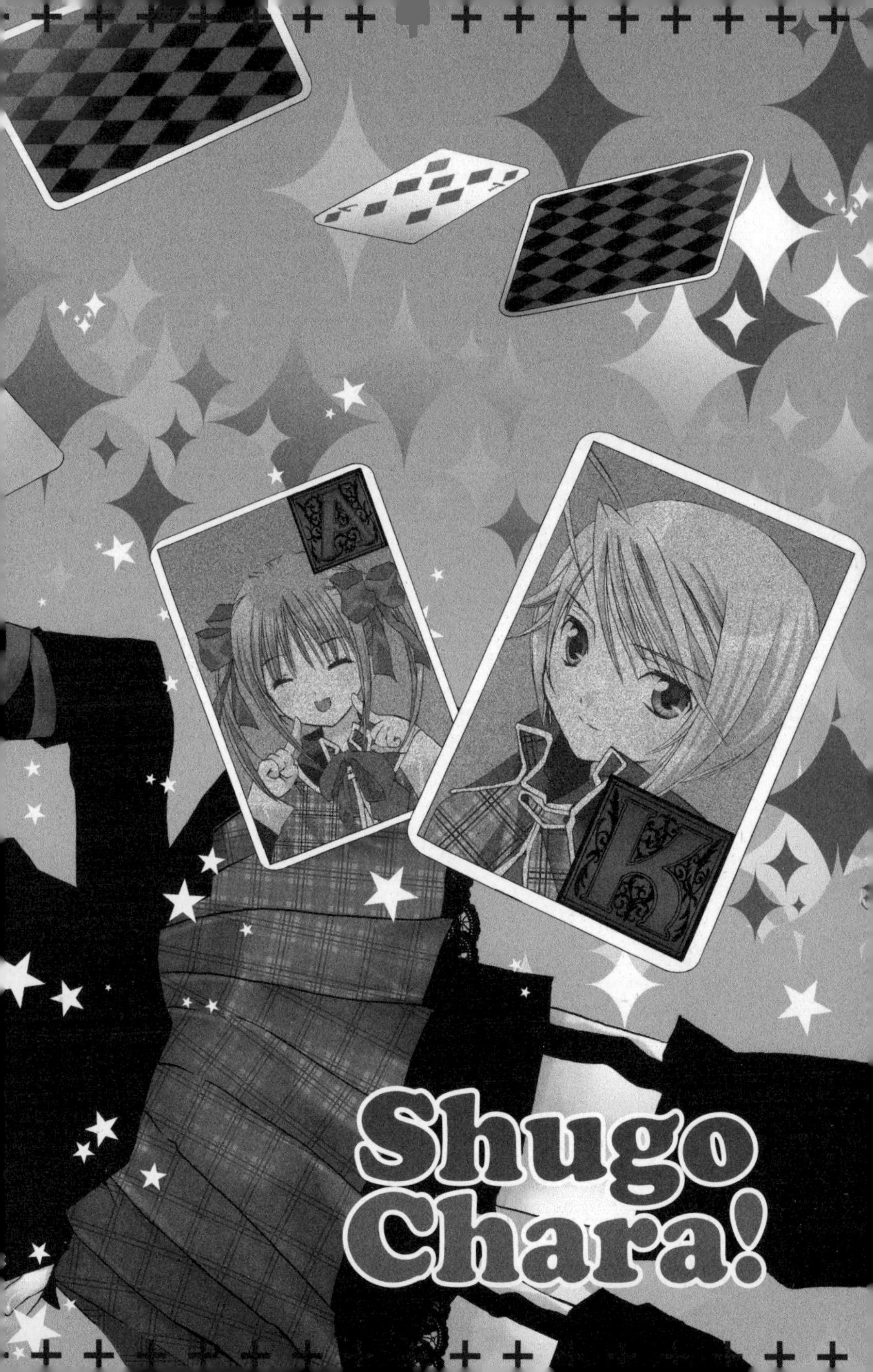
Shugo
Chara!

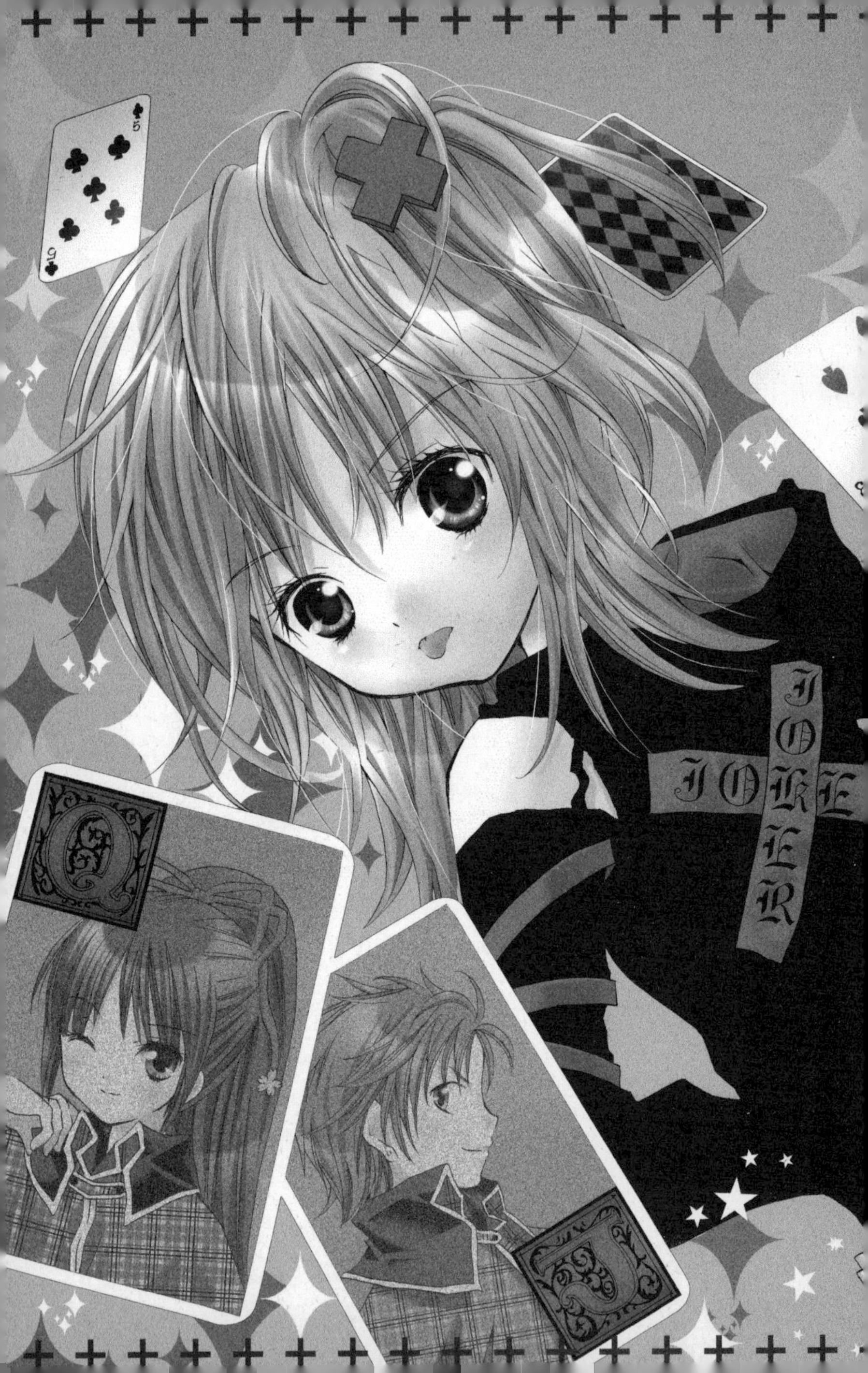
JOKER
JOKER

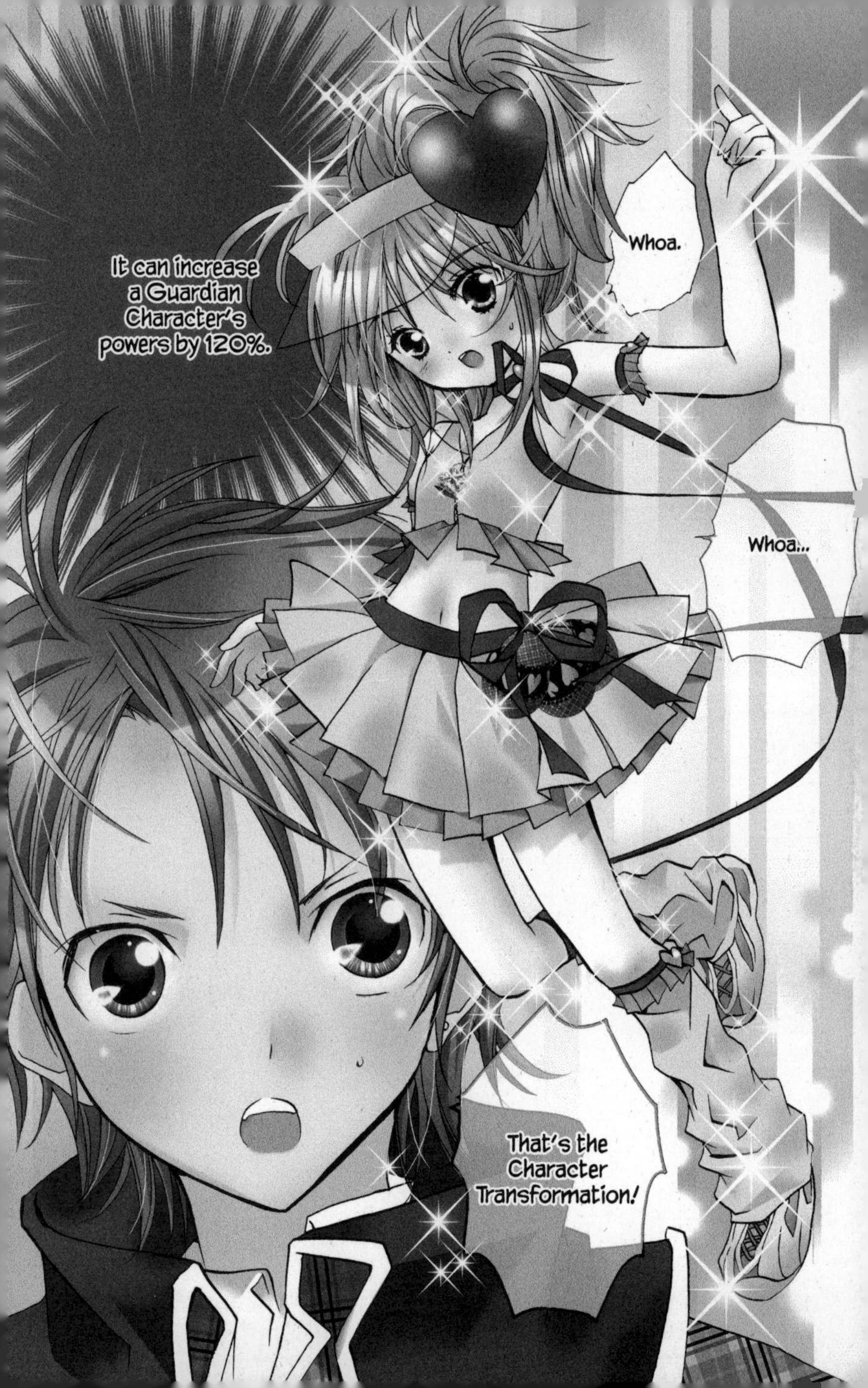
Whoa.
Whoa...
It can increase a Guardian Character's powers by 120%.
That's the Character Transformation!

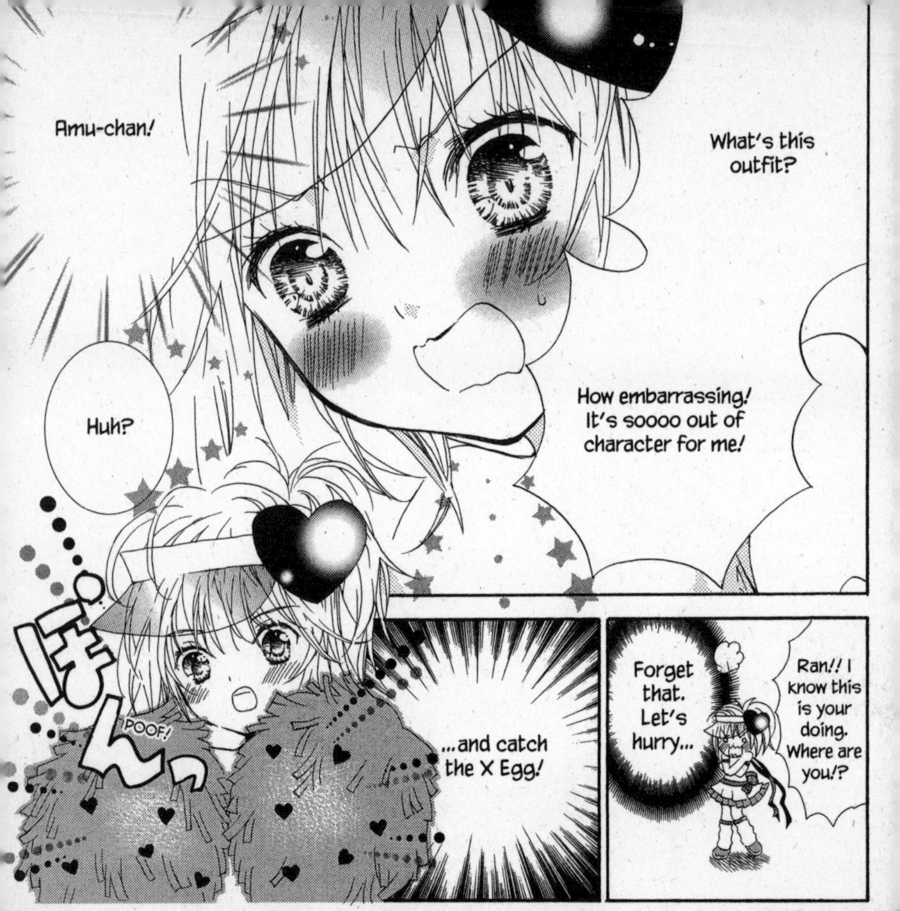

What's this outfit?
How embarrassing! It's soooo out of character for me!
Amu-chan!
Huh?
Ran!! I know this is your doing. Where are you!?
Forget that. Let's hurry...
...and catch the X Egg!
ぽんっ
POOF!

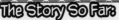

The Story So Far:

- Amu is socially awkward and has a hard time being true to her heart. One day she wished that she could change and become the person she wanted to be. And three Guardian Characters appeared!
- They each claim to be the person she really wants to be. Amu is surprised by the things they can do.
- Amu was asked to join the Guardians of Seiyo Elementary School, a group of students who each have their own Guardian Characters as well. Her first job as a Guardian was to hunt for X Eggs. But during the hunt, she underwent a Character Transformation!!

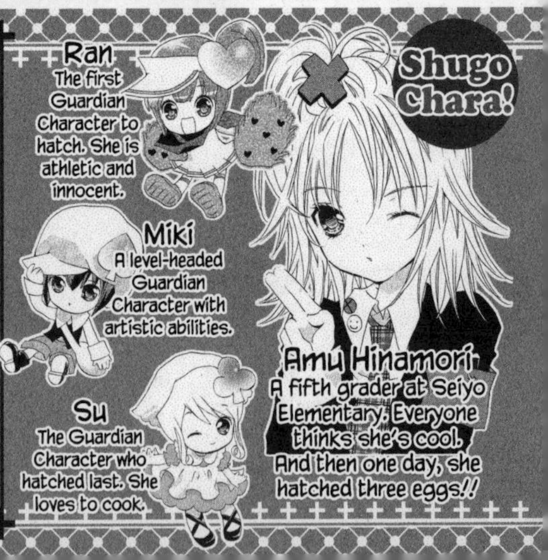

Shugo Chara!
Amu Hinamori
A fifth grader at Seiyo Elementary. Everyone thinks she's cool. And then one day, she hatched three eggs!!
Ran
The first Guardian Character to hatch. She is athletic and innocent.
Miki
A level-headed Guardian Character with artistic abilities.
Su
The Guardian Character who hatched last. She loves to cook.

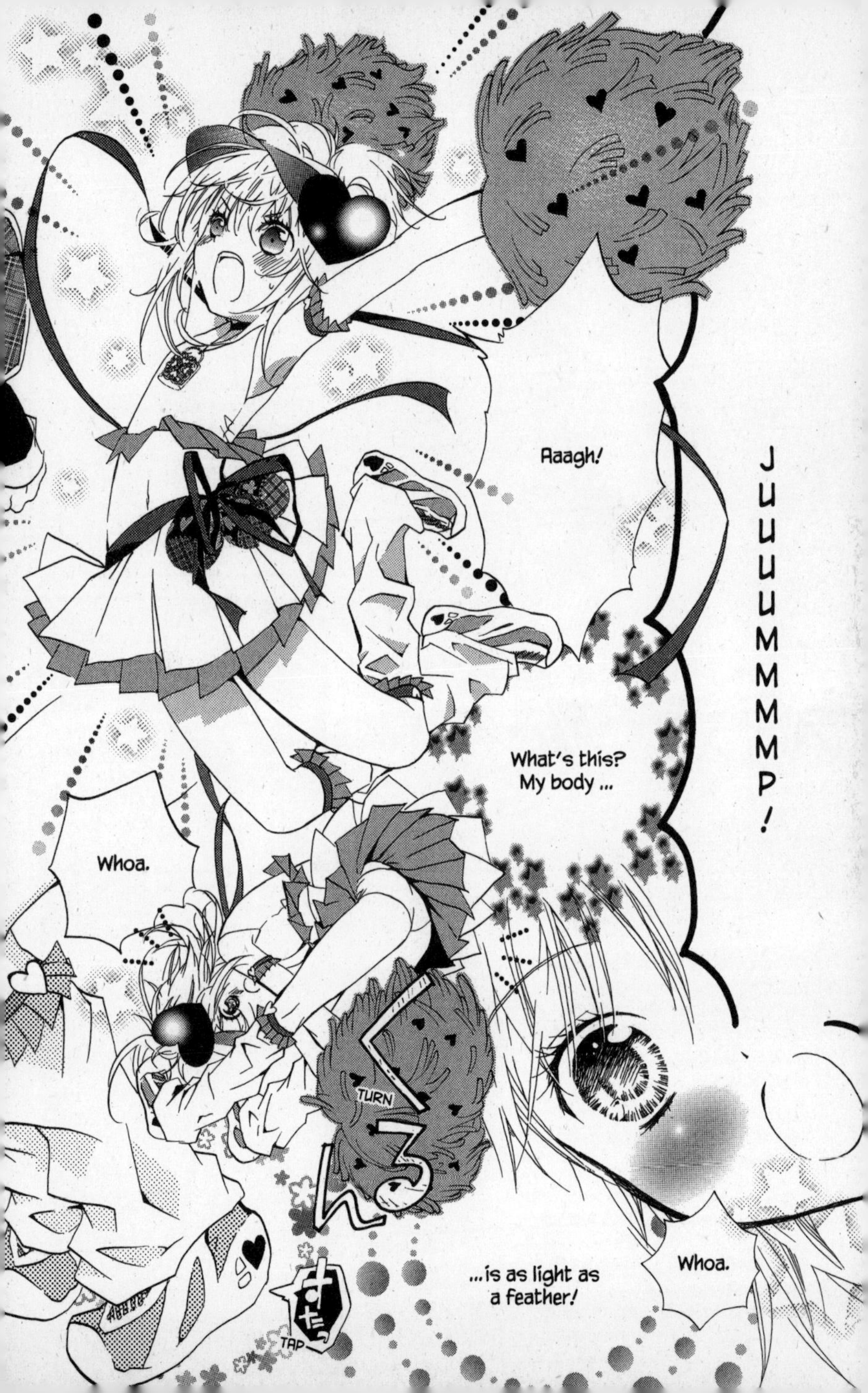
JUUUUMMMMP!
Aaagh!
What's this? My body ...
Whoa.
TURN
Whoa.
...is as light as a feather!
TAP

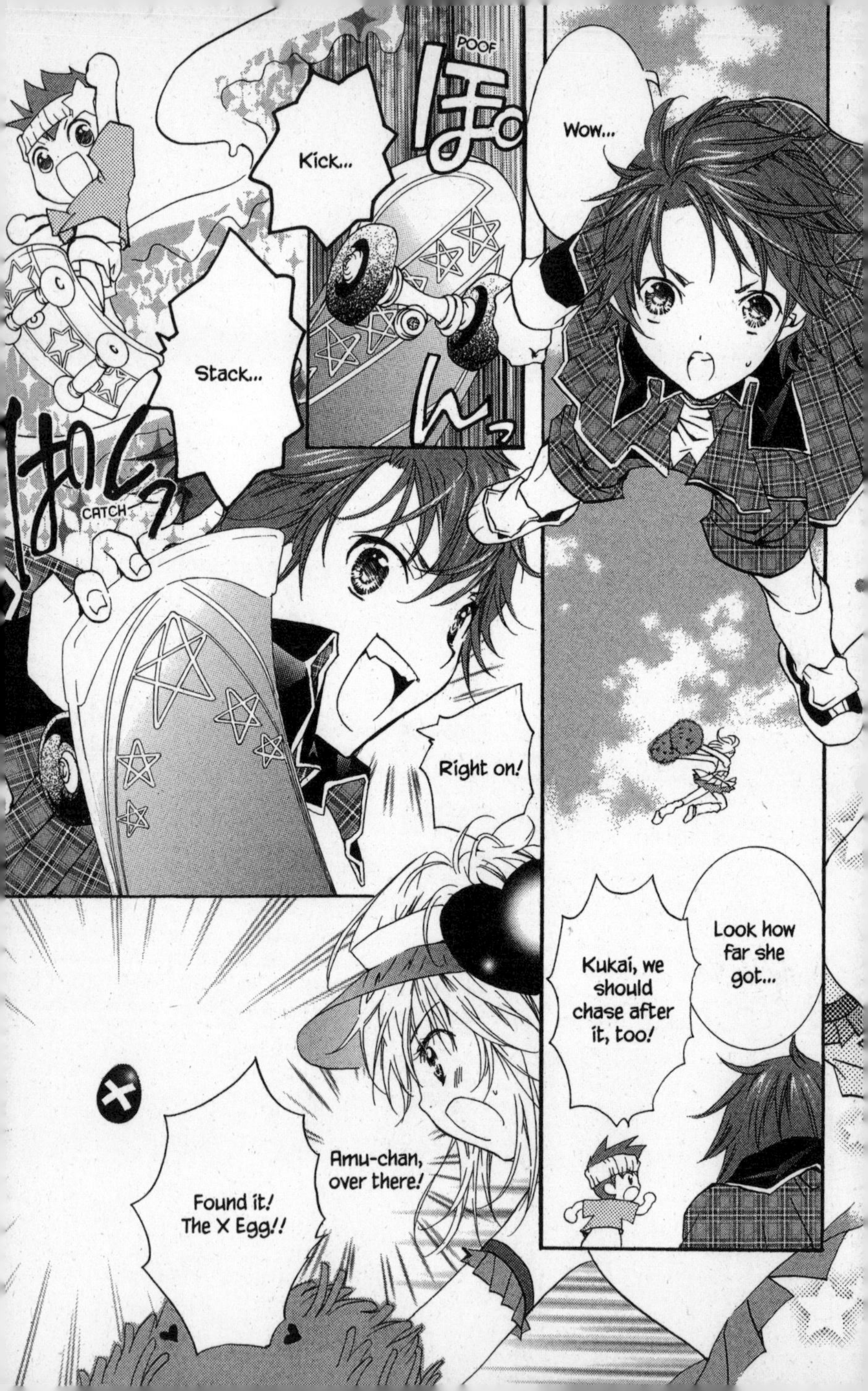

Wow...
POOF
Kick...
Stack...
CATCH
Right on!
Look how far she got...
Kukai, we should chase after it, too!
Amu-chan, over there!
Found it! The X Egg!!

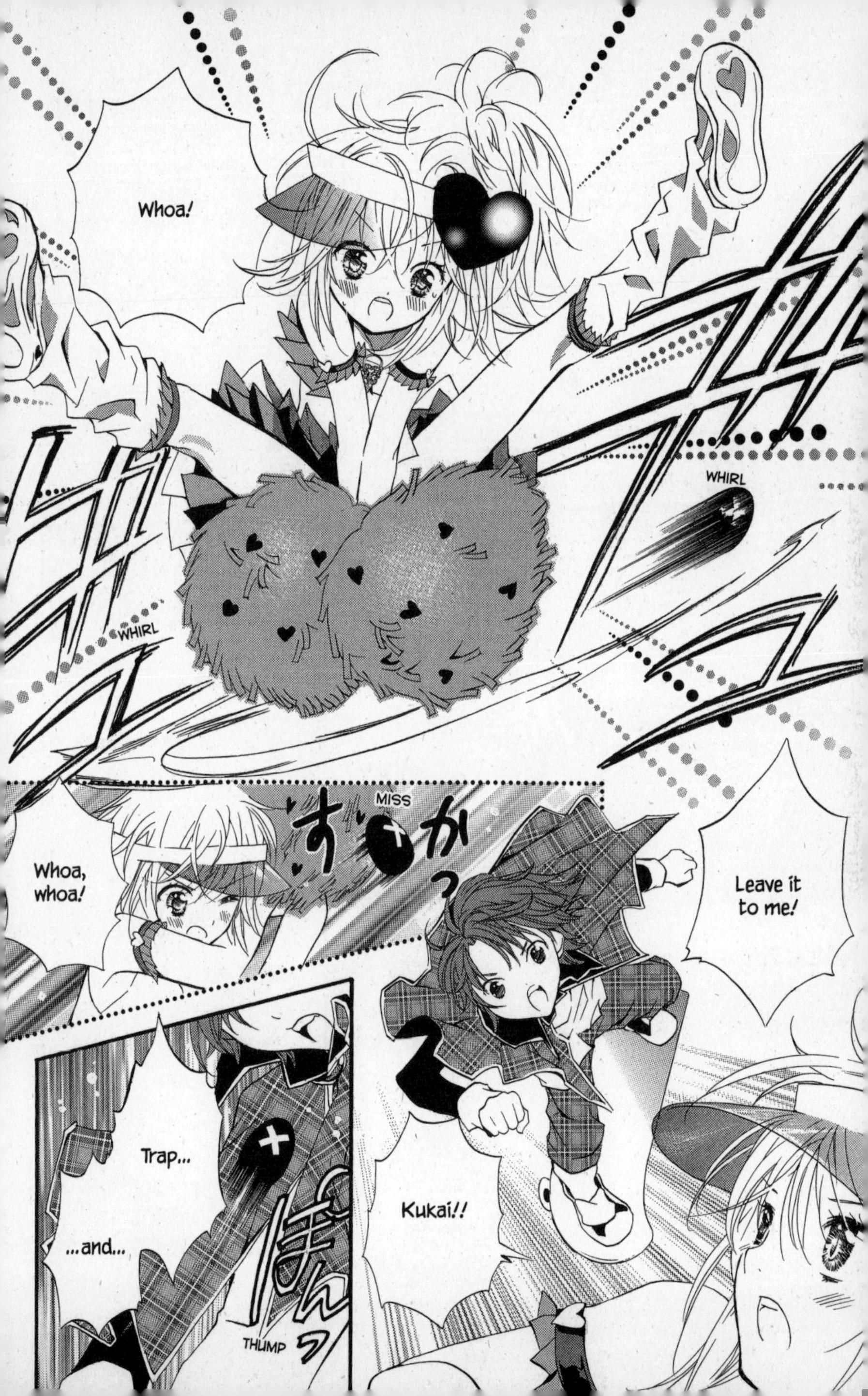

Whoa!
WHIRL
WHIRL
Leave it to me!
MISS
すかっ
Whoa, whoa!
Kukai!!
Trap...
...and...
ぽんっ
THUMP

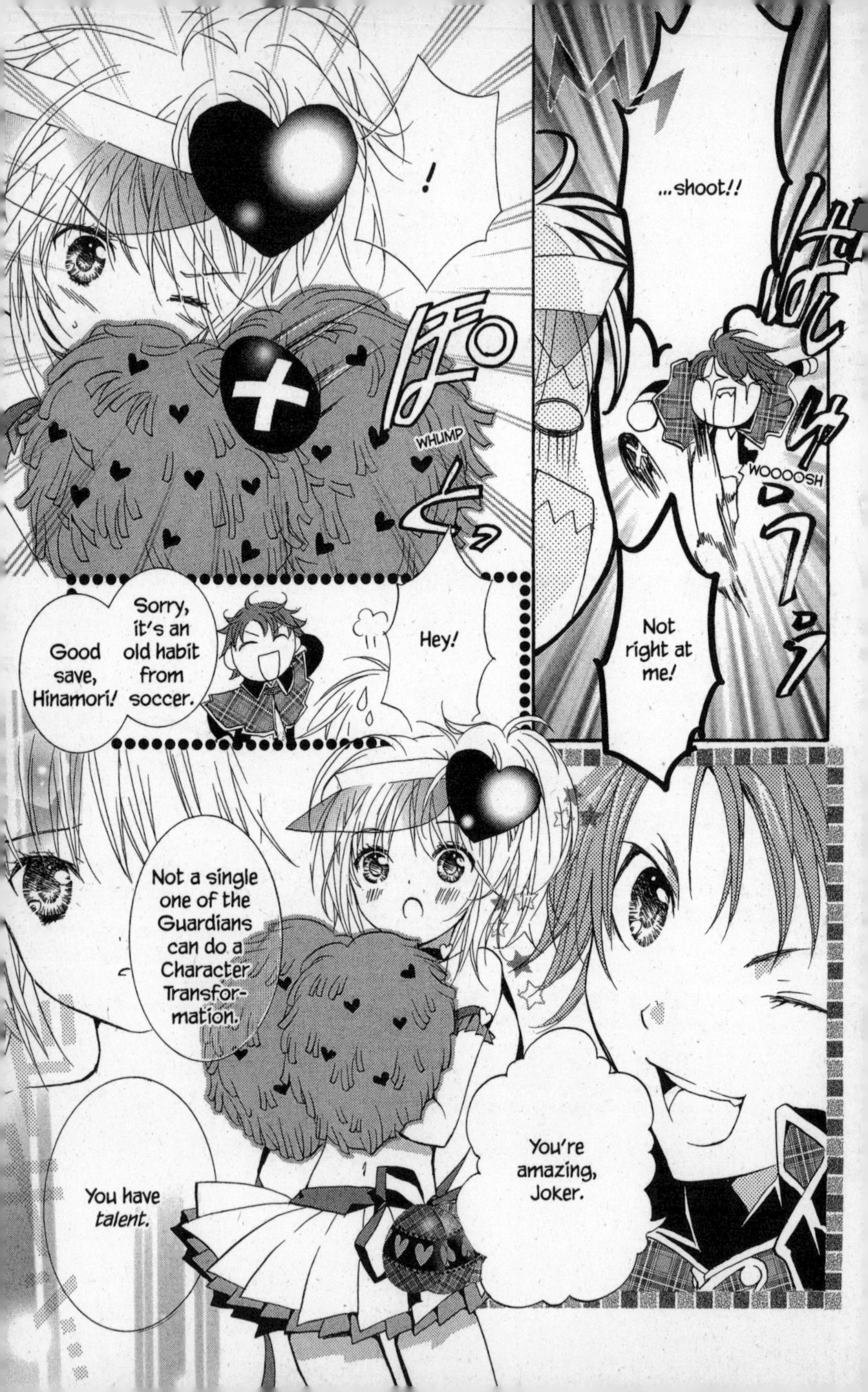
...shoot!!
WOOOOSH
Not right at me!
!
WHUMP
Hey!
Sorry, it's an old habit from soccer.
Good save, Hinamori!
You're amazing, Joker.
Not a single one of the Guardians can do a Character Transformation.
You have *talent.*

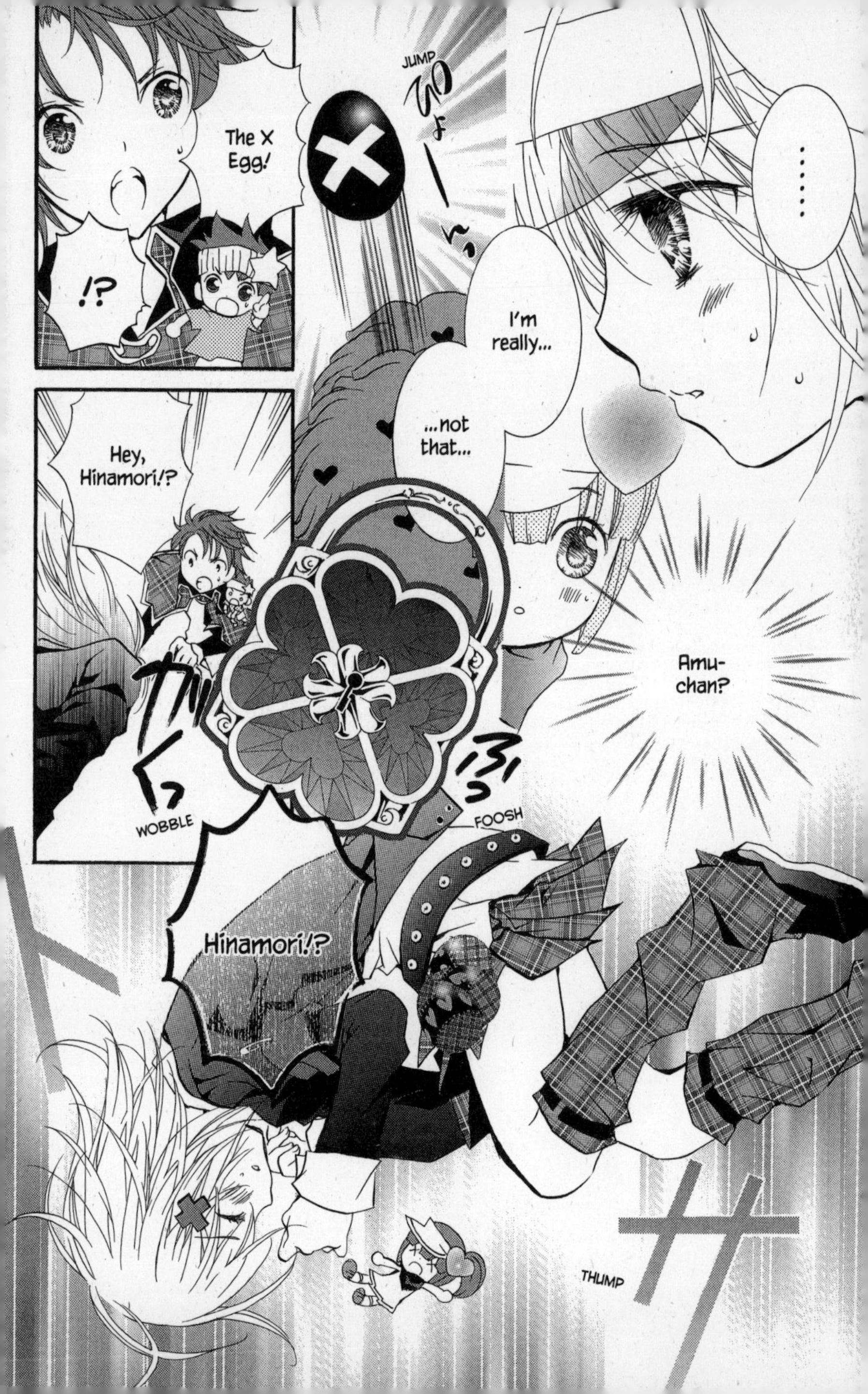

......
I'm really...
...not that...
JUMP
The X Egg!
!?
Hey, Hinamori!?
WOBBLE
Amu-chan?
FOOSH
Hinamori!?
THUMP

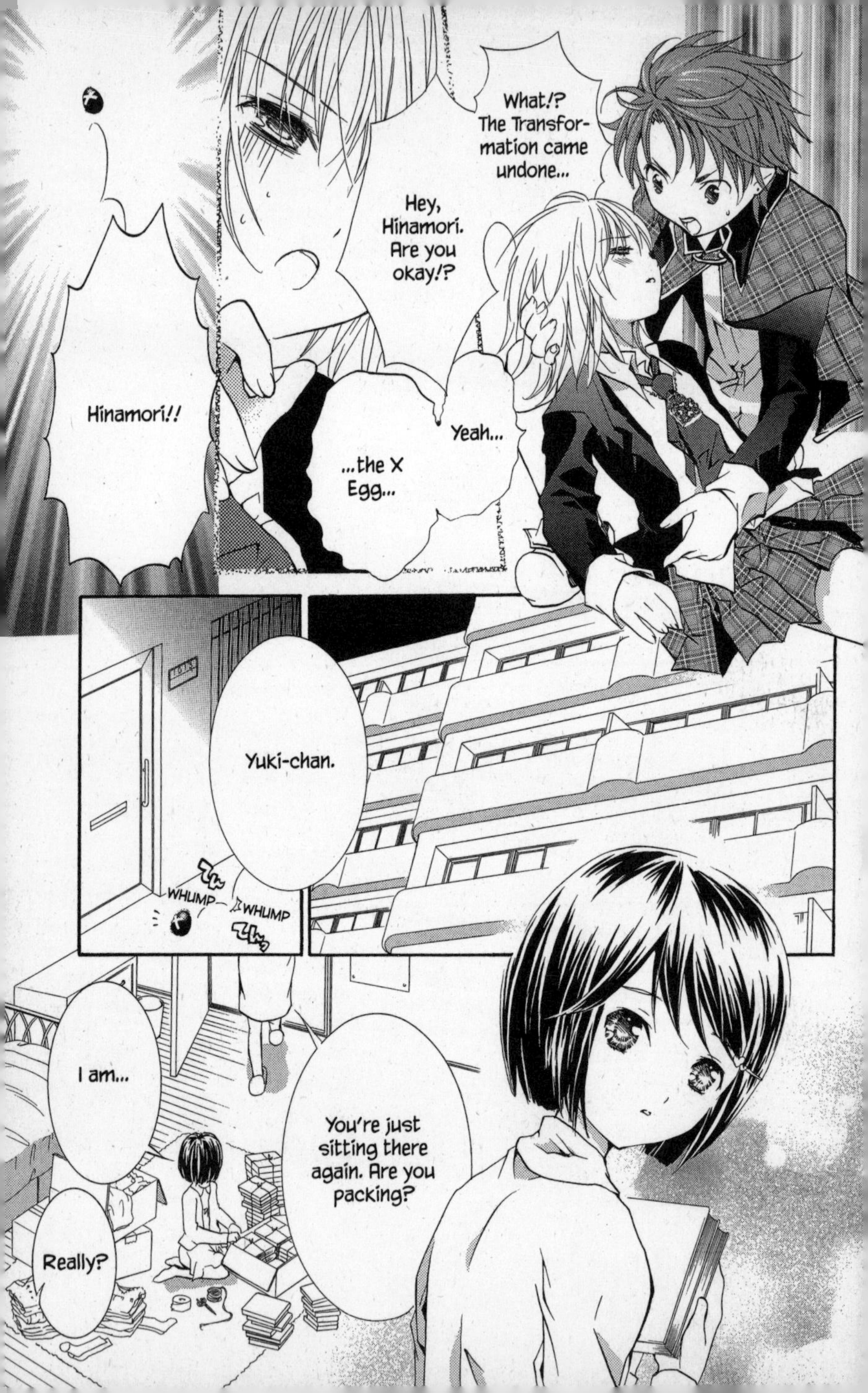
What!? The Transformation came undone...
Hey, Hinamori. Are you okay!?
Yeah...
...the X Egg...
Hinamori!!
Yuki-chan.
WHUMP
WHUMP
You're just sitting there again. Are you packing?
I am...
Really?

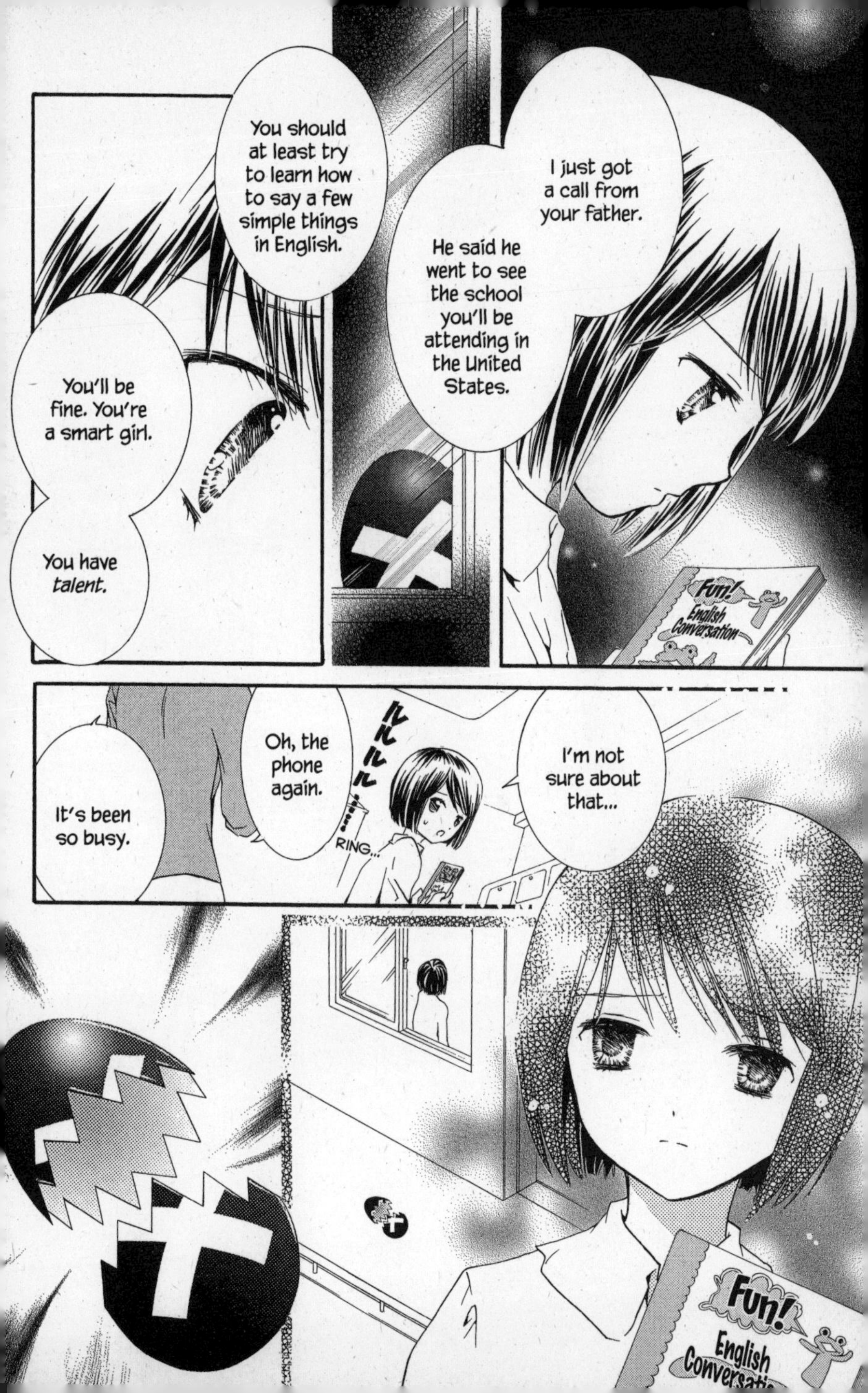
I just got a call from your father.
He said he went to see the school you'll be attending in the United States.
Fun! English Conversation
You should at least try to learn how to say a few simple things in English.
You'll be fine. You're a smart girl.
You have *talent.*
I'm not sure about that...
RING...
Oh, the phone again.
It's been so busy.

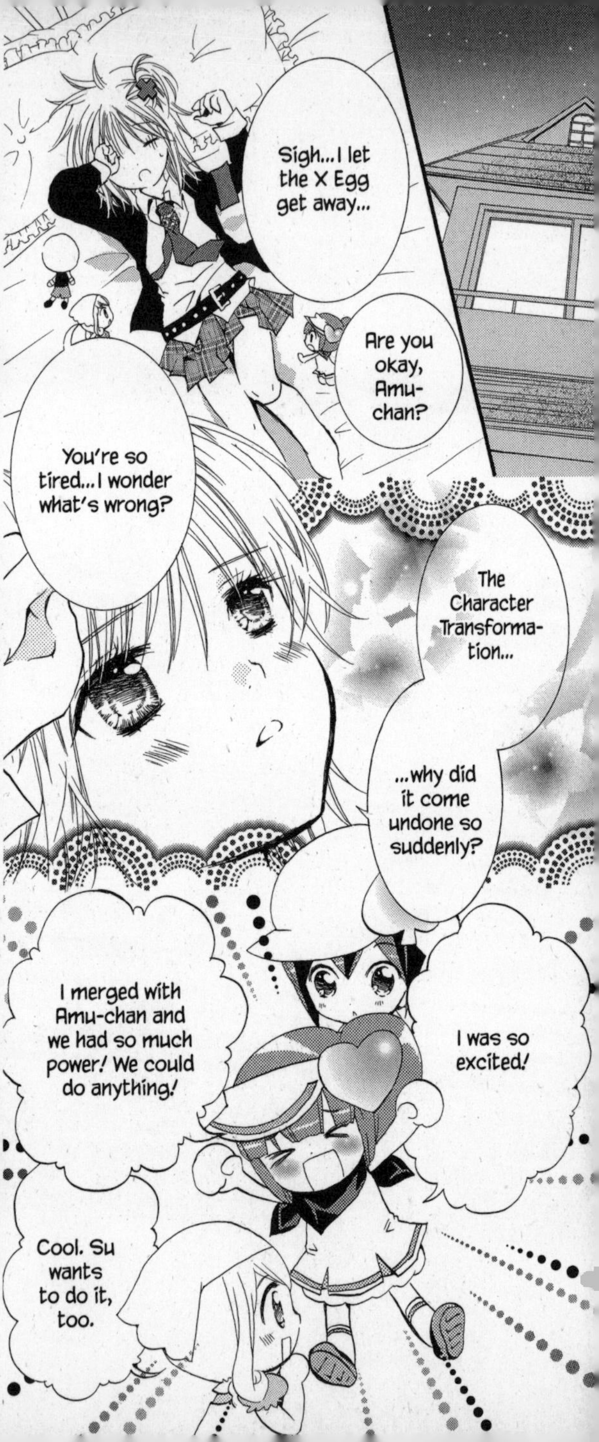

Sigh...I let the X Egg get away...
Are you okay, Amu-chan?
You're so tired...I wonder what's wrong?
The Character Transformation...
...why did it come undone so suddenly?
I merged with Amu-chan and we had so much power! We could do anything!
I was so excited!
Cool. Su wants to do it, too.

character profile

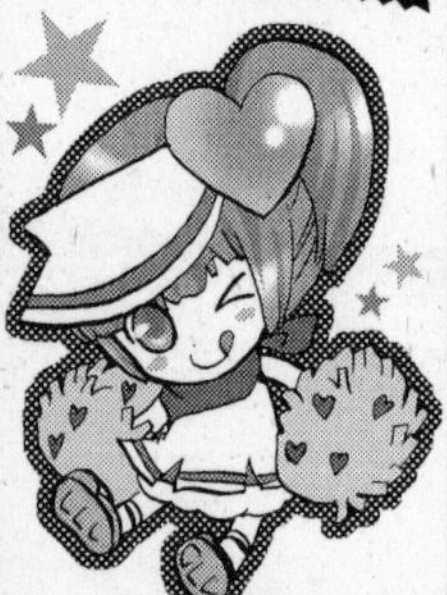

ラン

RAN

Guardian Character of: Amu
Special Skill: Cheering
Is bad at: Being quiet

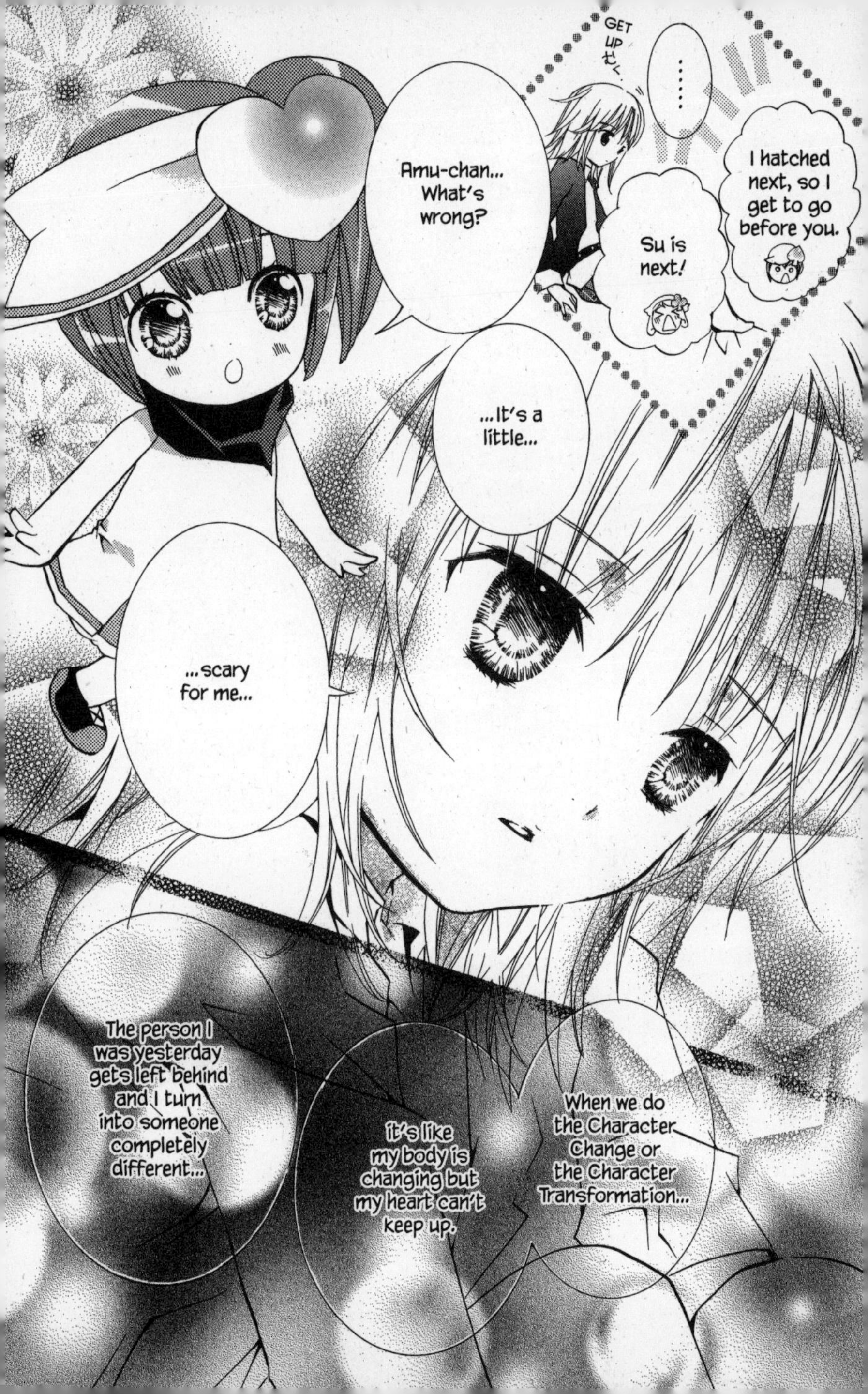
GET UP むく
......
I hatched next, so I get to go before you.
Su is next!
Amu-chan... What's wrong?
...It's a little...
...scary for me...
When we do the Character Change or the Character Transformation...
it's like my body is changing but my heart can't keep up.
The person I was yesterday gets left behind and I turn into someone completely different...

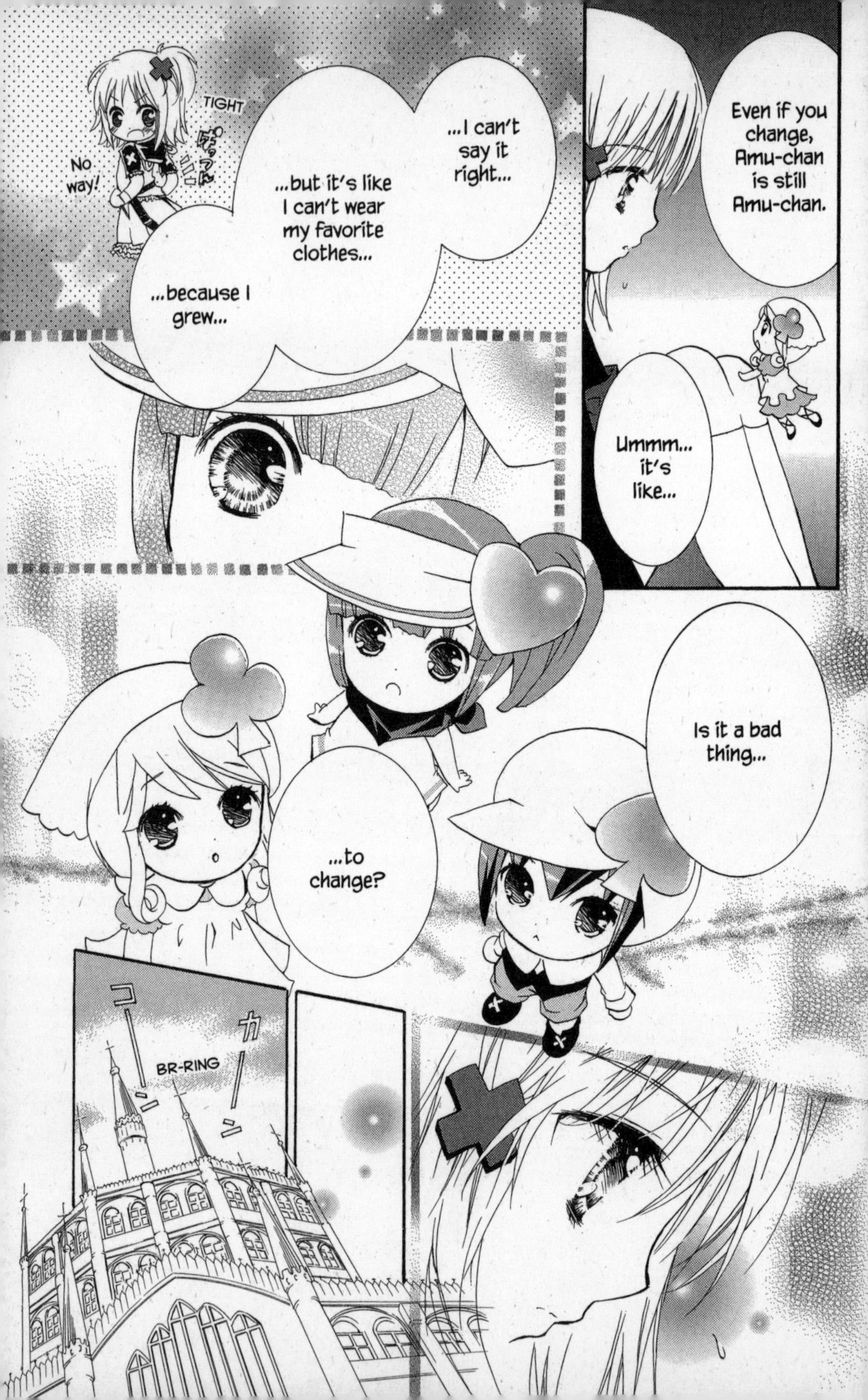
Even if you change, Amu-chan is still Amu-chan.
Ummm... it's like...
...I can't say it right...
...but it's like I can't wear my favorite clothes...
...because I grew...
TIGHT
No way!
Is it a bad thing...
...to change?
BR-RING

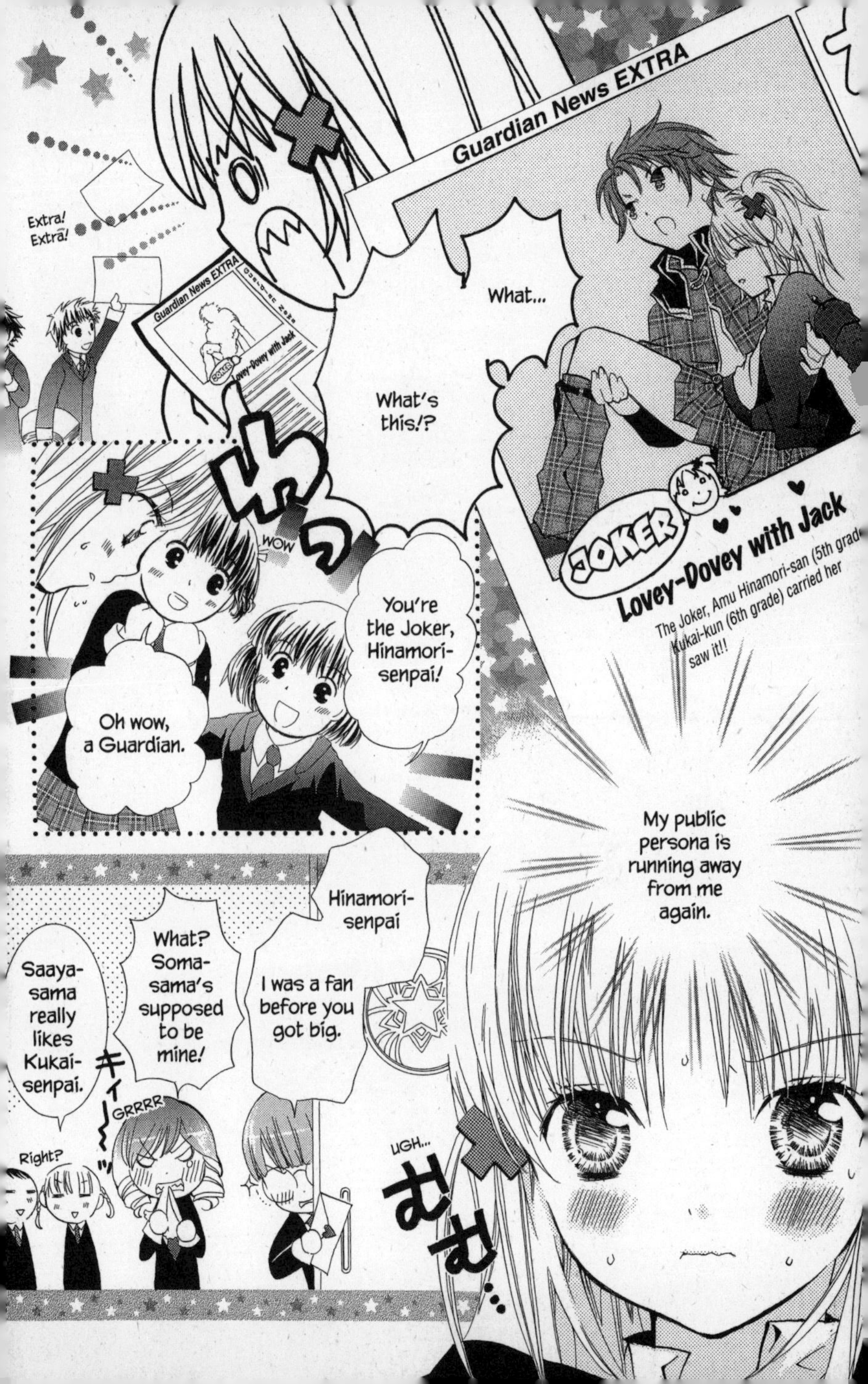
Guardian News EXTRA
What...
What's this!?
Extra! Extra!
Guardian News EXTRA
Lovey-Dovey with Jack
JOKER
Lovey-Dovey with Jack
The Joker, Amu Hinamori-san (5th grad
Kukai-kun (6th grade) carried her
saw it!!
My public persona is running away from me again.
WOW
You're the Joker, Hinamori-senpai!
Oh wow, a Guardian.
UGH...
Hinamori-senpai
I was a fan before you got big.
What? Soma-sama's supposed to be mine!
GRRRR
Saaya-sama really likes Kukai-senpai.
Right?

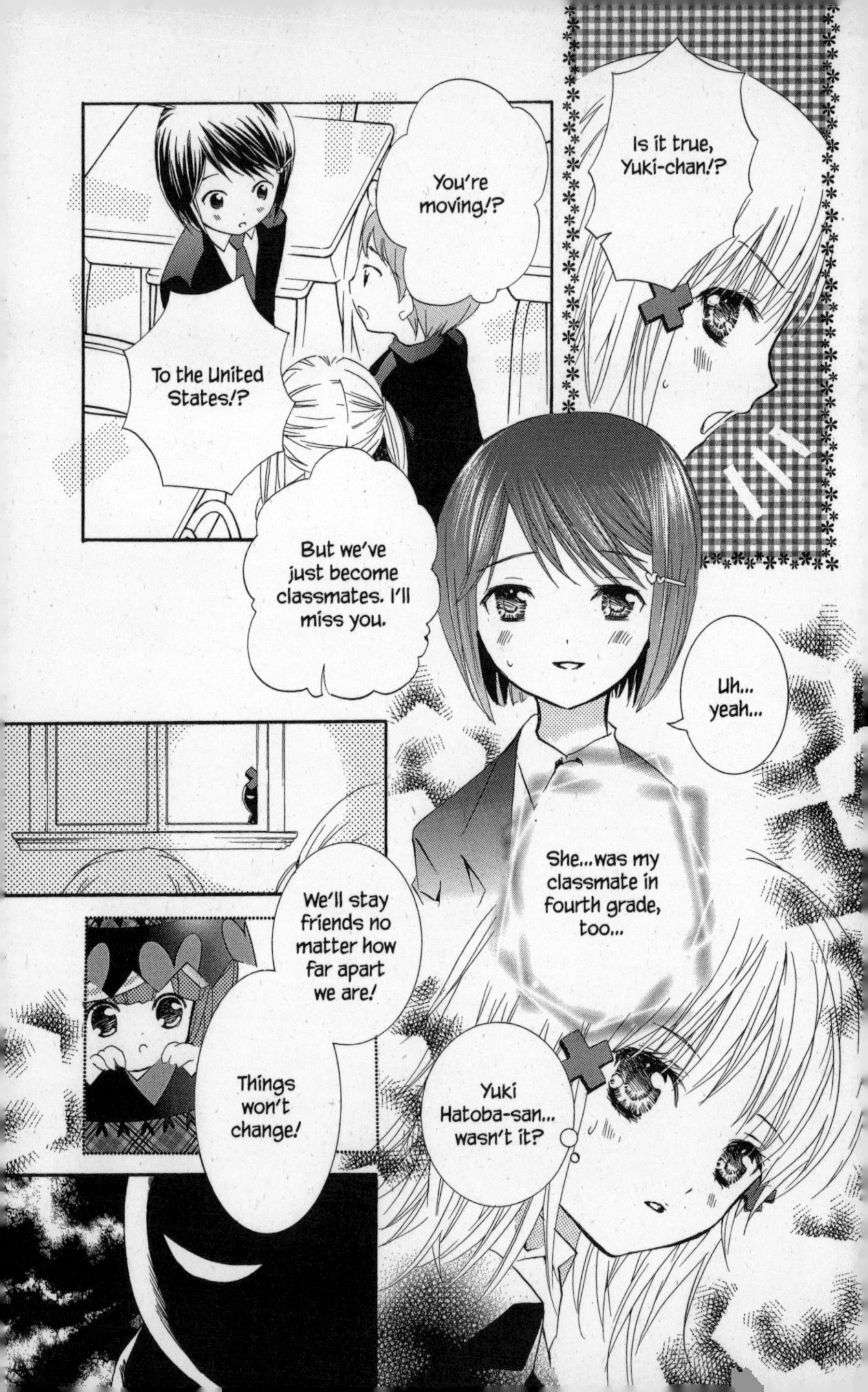

Is it true, Yuki-chan!?
You're moving!?
To the United States!?
But we've just become classmates. I'll miss you.
Uh... yeah...
She...was my classmate in fourth grade, too...
Yuki Hatoba-san... wasn't it?
We'll stay friends no matter how far apart we are!
Things won't change!

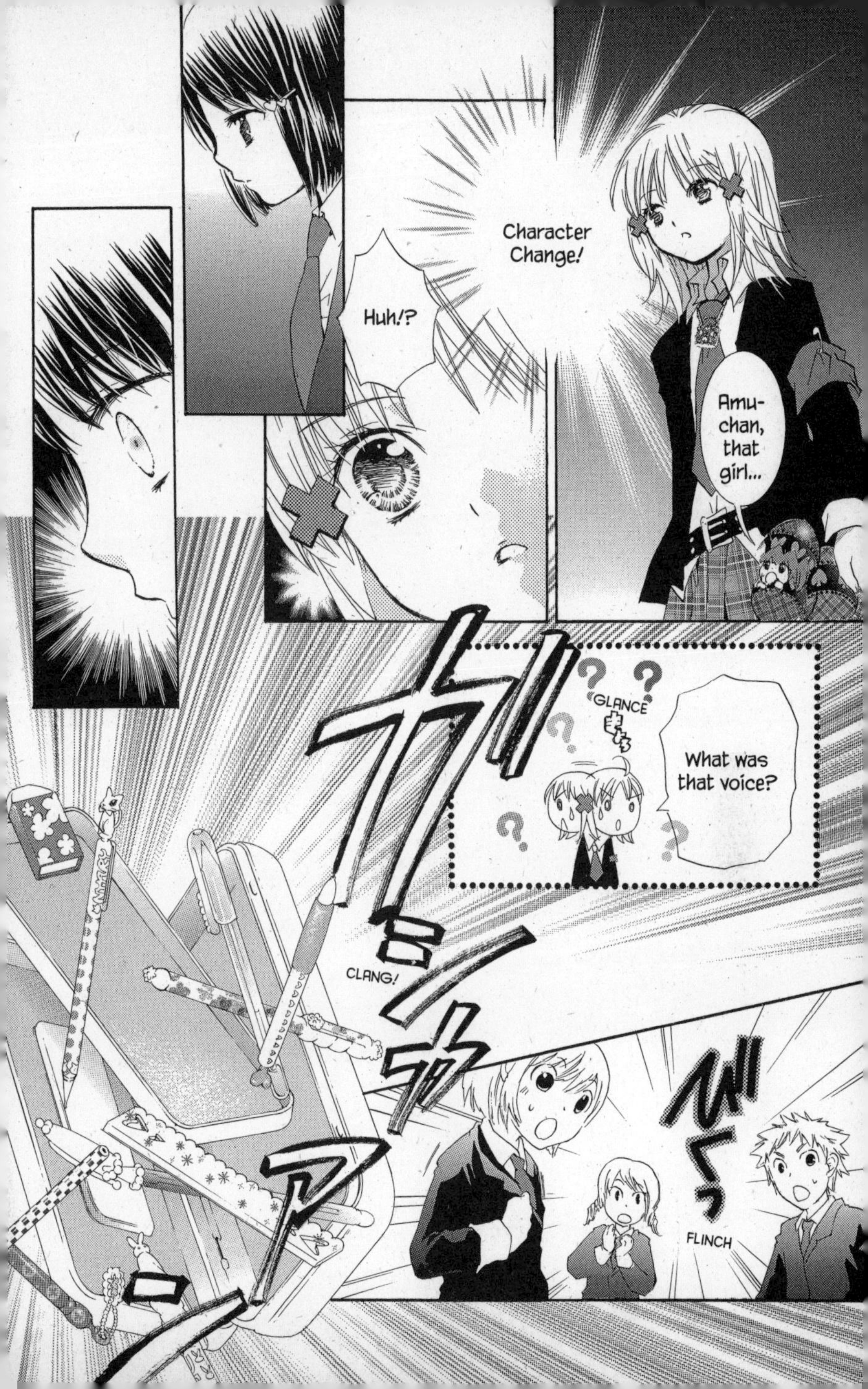
Character Change!
Amu-chan, that girl...
Huh!?
GLANCE
What was that voice?
CLANG!
FLINCH

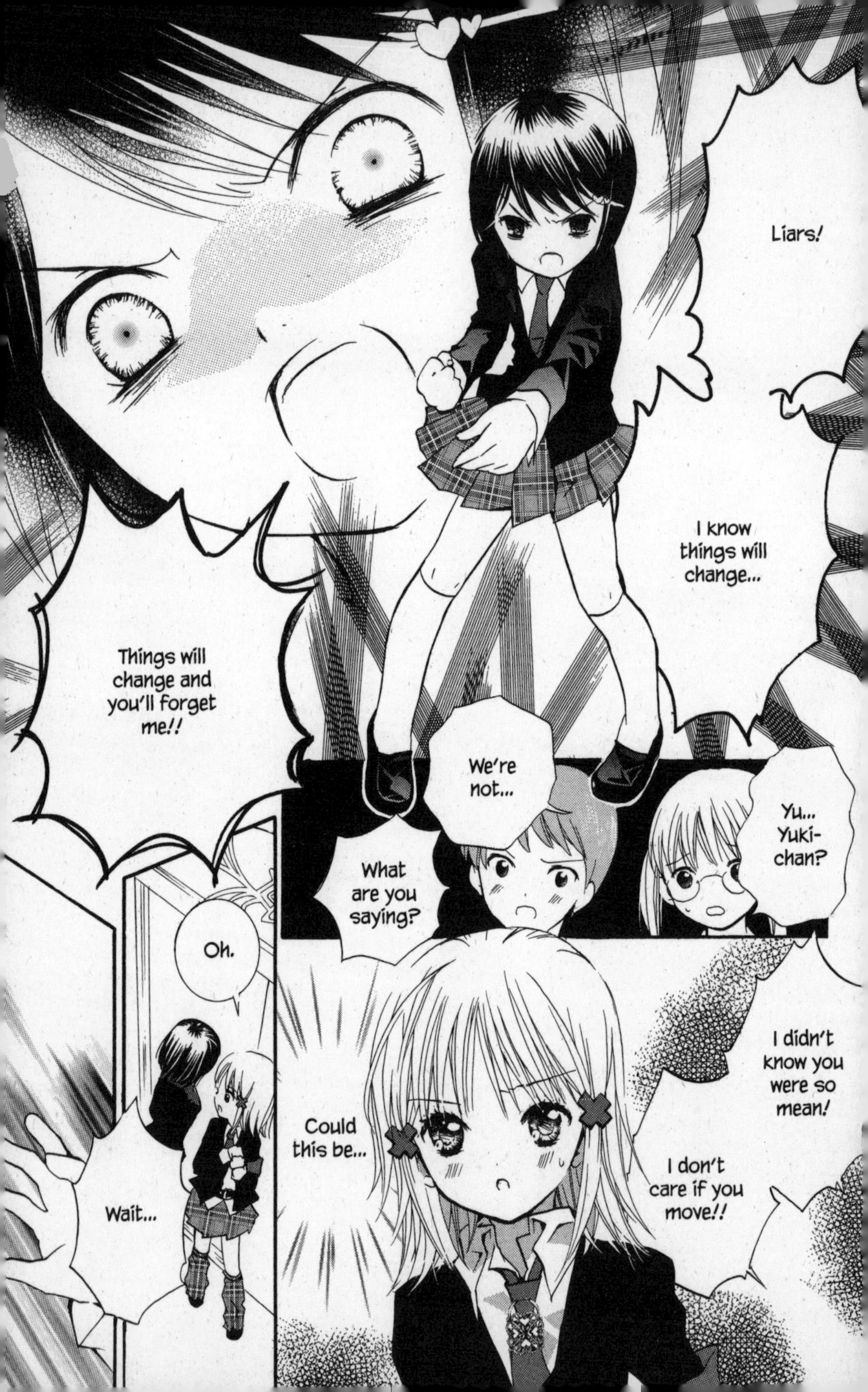
Liars!
I know things will change...
Things will change and you'll forget me!!
Yu... Yuki-chan?
We're not...
What are you saying?
I didn't know you were so mean!
I don't care if you move!!
Could this be...
Oh.
Wait...

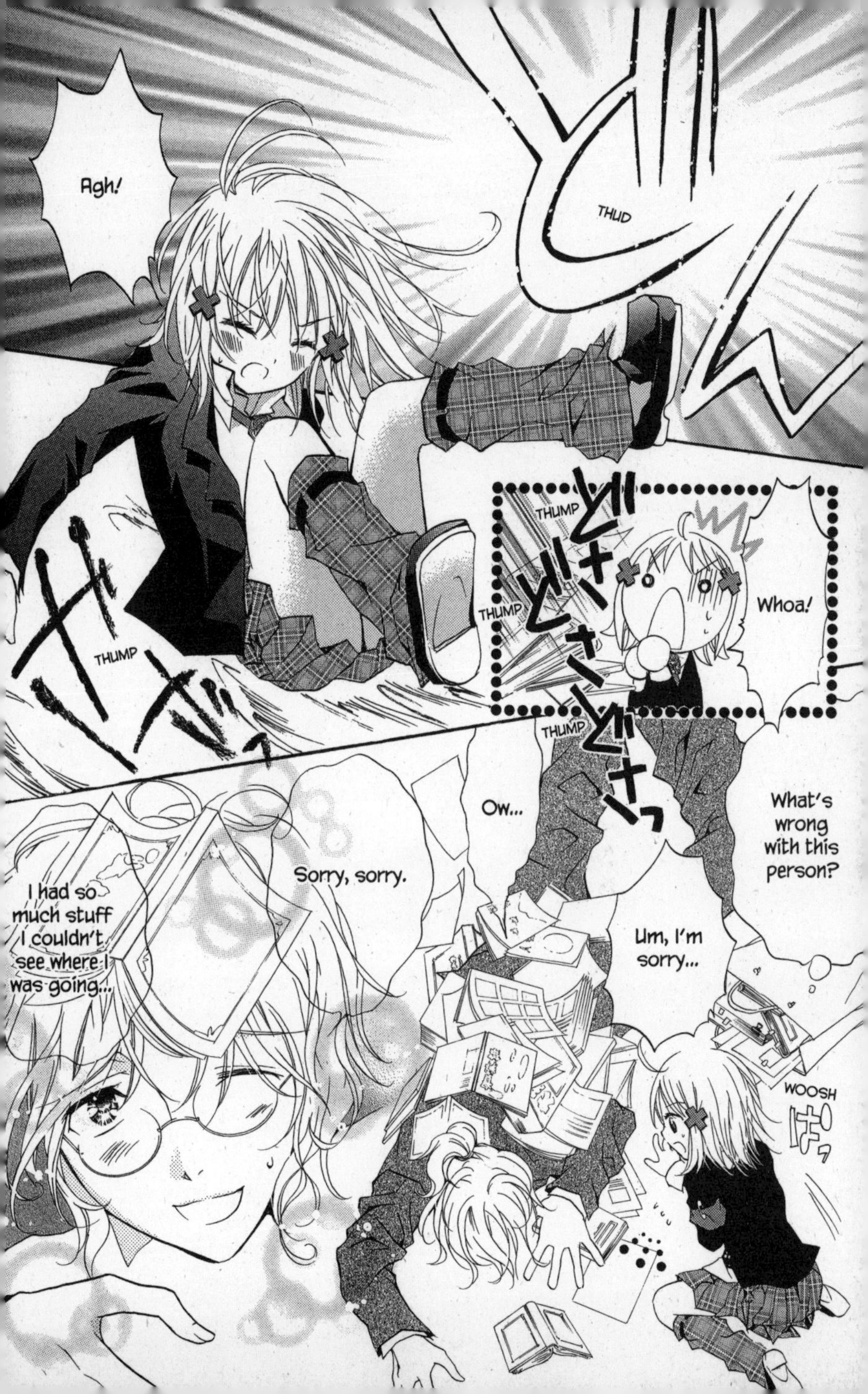
THUD
Agh!
THUMP
THUMP
THUMP
Whoa!
THUMP
What's wrong with this person?
Ow...
Um, I'm sorry...
WOOSH
Sorry, sorry.
I had so much stuff I couldn't see where I was going...

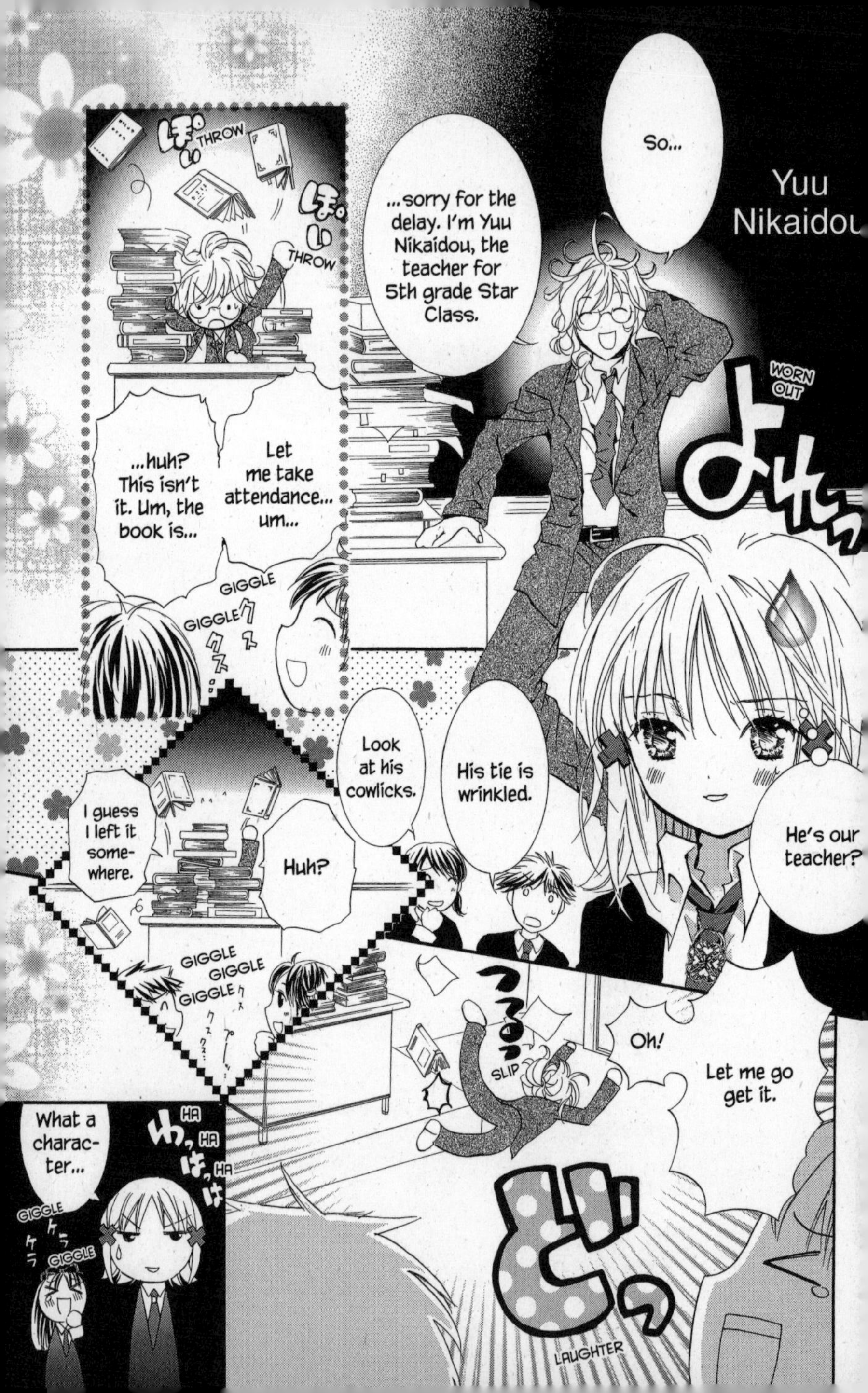
Yuu Nikaidou
So...
...sorry for the delay. I'm Yuu Nikaidou, the teacher for 5th grade Star Class.
WORN OUT
He's our teacher?
THROW
THROW
Let me take attendance... um...
...huh? This isn't it. Um, the book is...
GIGGLE
GIGGLE
His tie is wrinkled.
Look at his cowlicks.
Huh?
I guess I left it somewhere.
GIGGLE
GIGGLE
GIGGLE
Oh!
Let me go get it.
SLIP
LAUGHTER
HA
HA
HA
What a character...
GIGGLE
GIGGLE

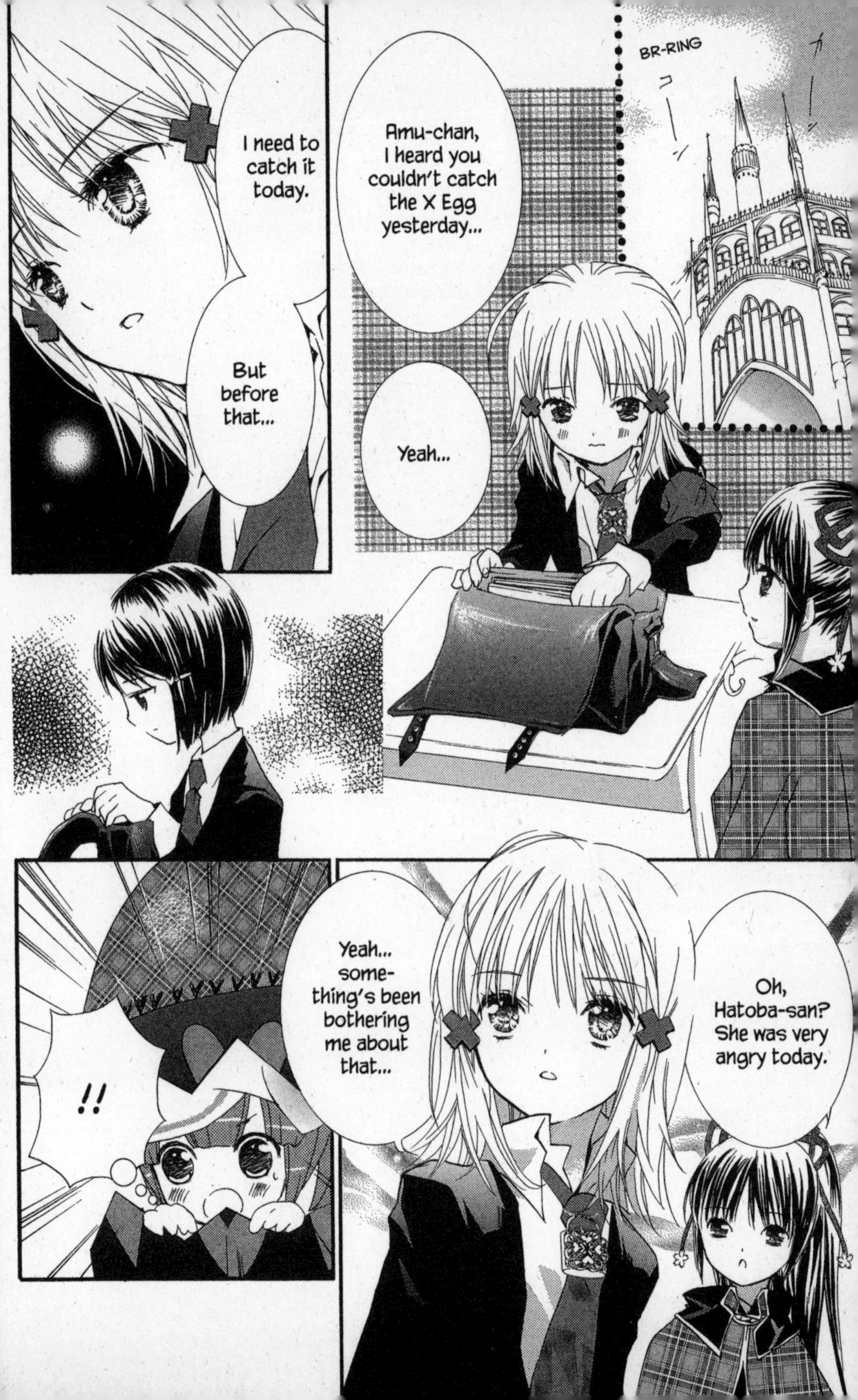
BR-RING
Amu-chan, I heard you couldn't catch the X Egg yesterday...
Yeah...
I need to catch it today.
But before that...
Oh, Hatoba-san? She was very angry today.
Yeah... some-thing's been bothering me about that...
!!

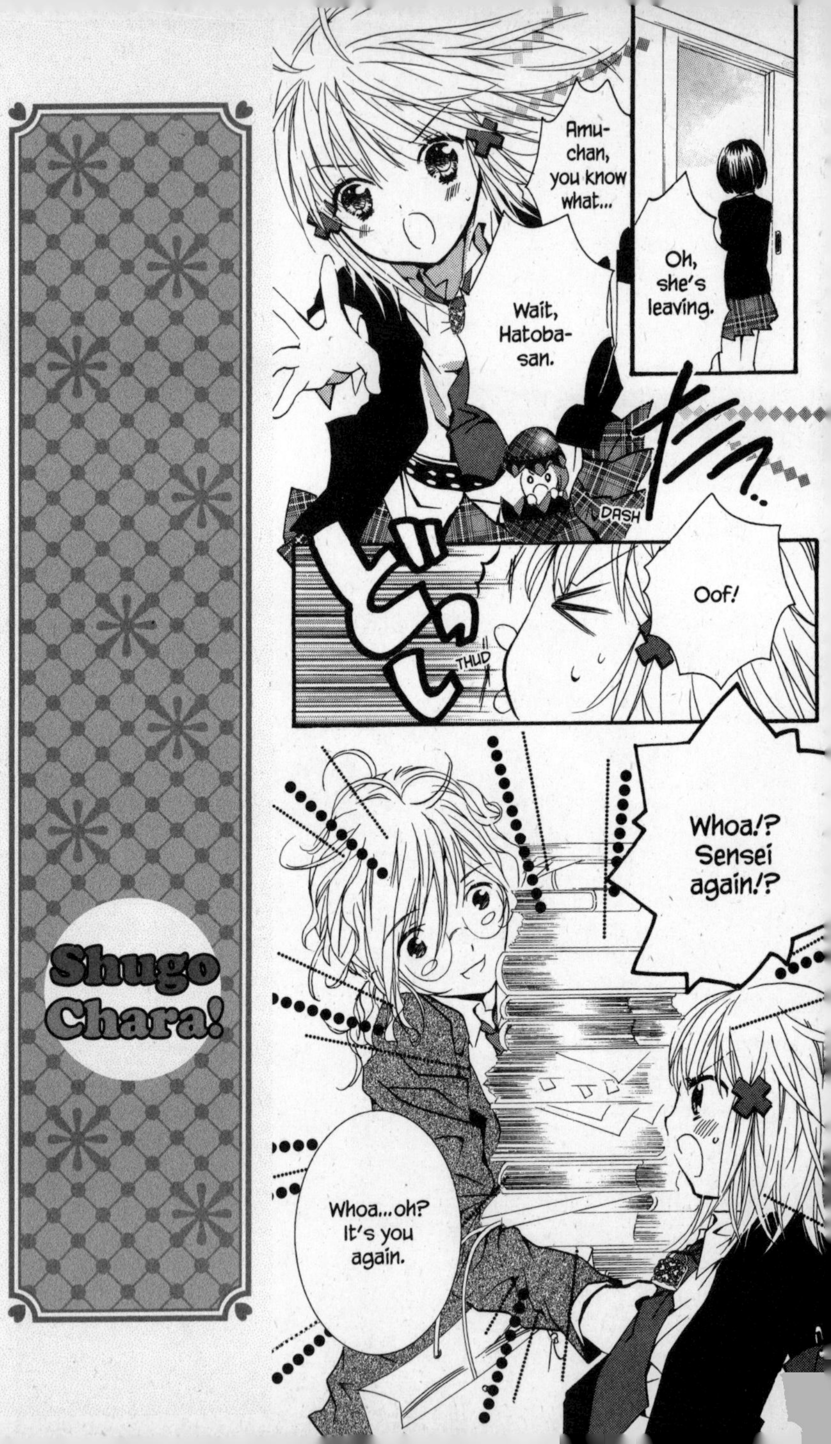
Amu-chan, you know what...
Oh, she's leaving.
Wait, Hatoba-san.
DASH
Oof!
THUD
Whoa!? Sensei again!?
Whoa...oh? It's you again.

Shugo Chara!

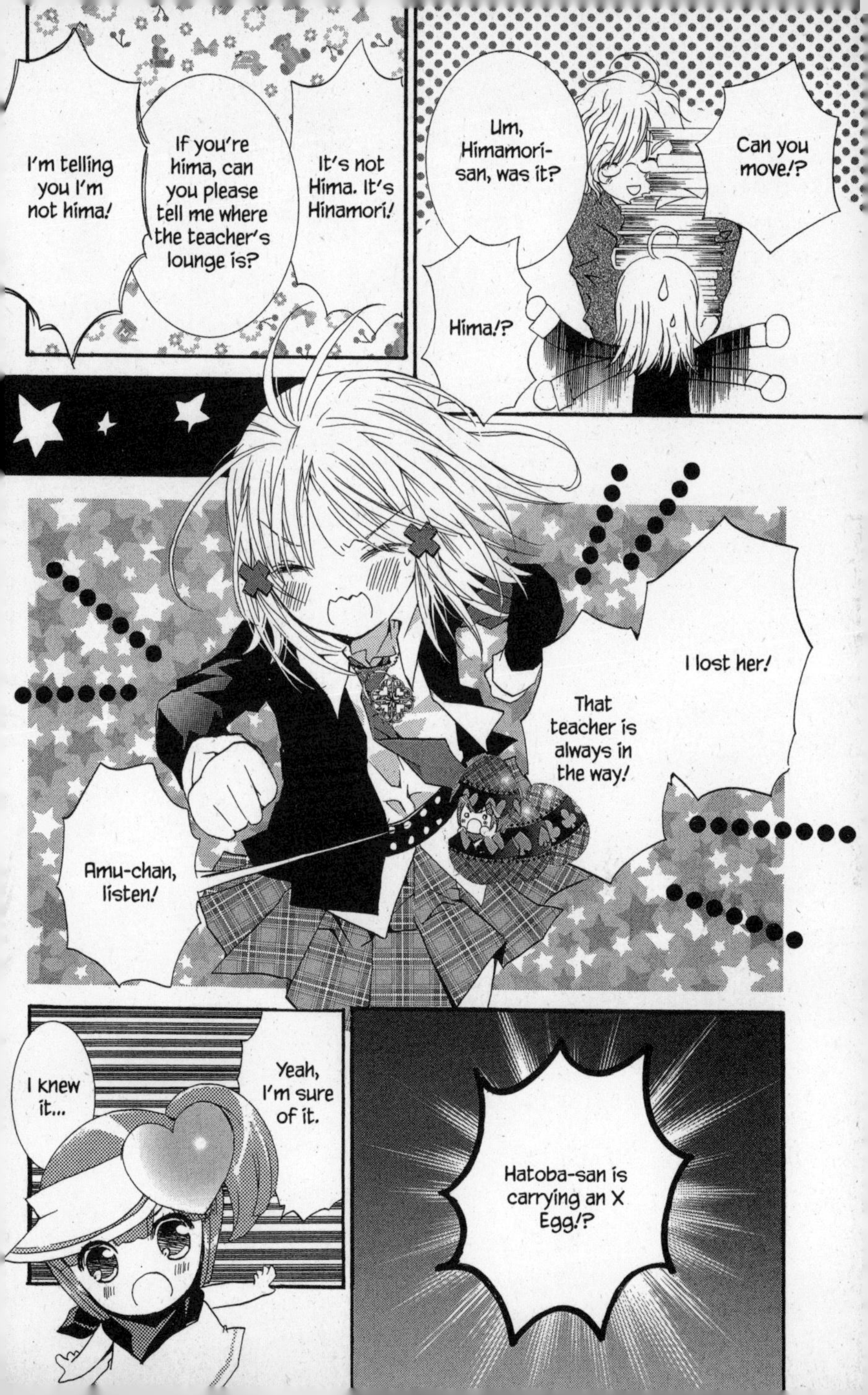
Can you move!?
Um, Himamori-san, was it?
Hima!?
It's not Hima. It's Hinamori!
If you're hima, can you please tell me where the teacher's lounge is?
I'm telling you I'm not hima!
I lost her!
That teacher is always in the way!
Amu-chan, listen!
Hatoba-san is carrying an X Egg!?
Yeah, I'm sure of it.
I knew it...

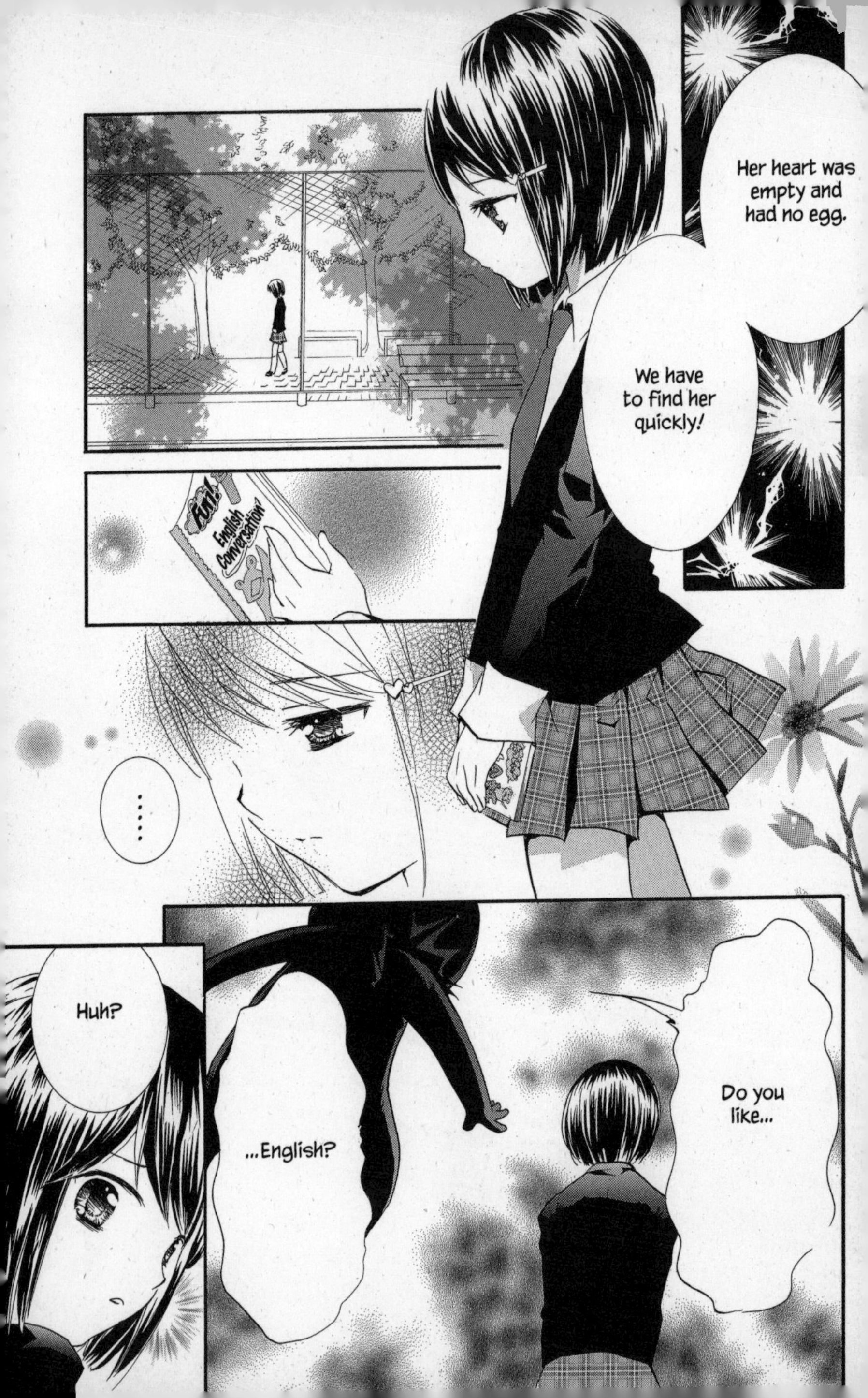
Her heart was empty and had no egg.
We have to find her quickly!
Fun! English Conversation
......
Do you like...
...English?
Huh?

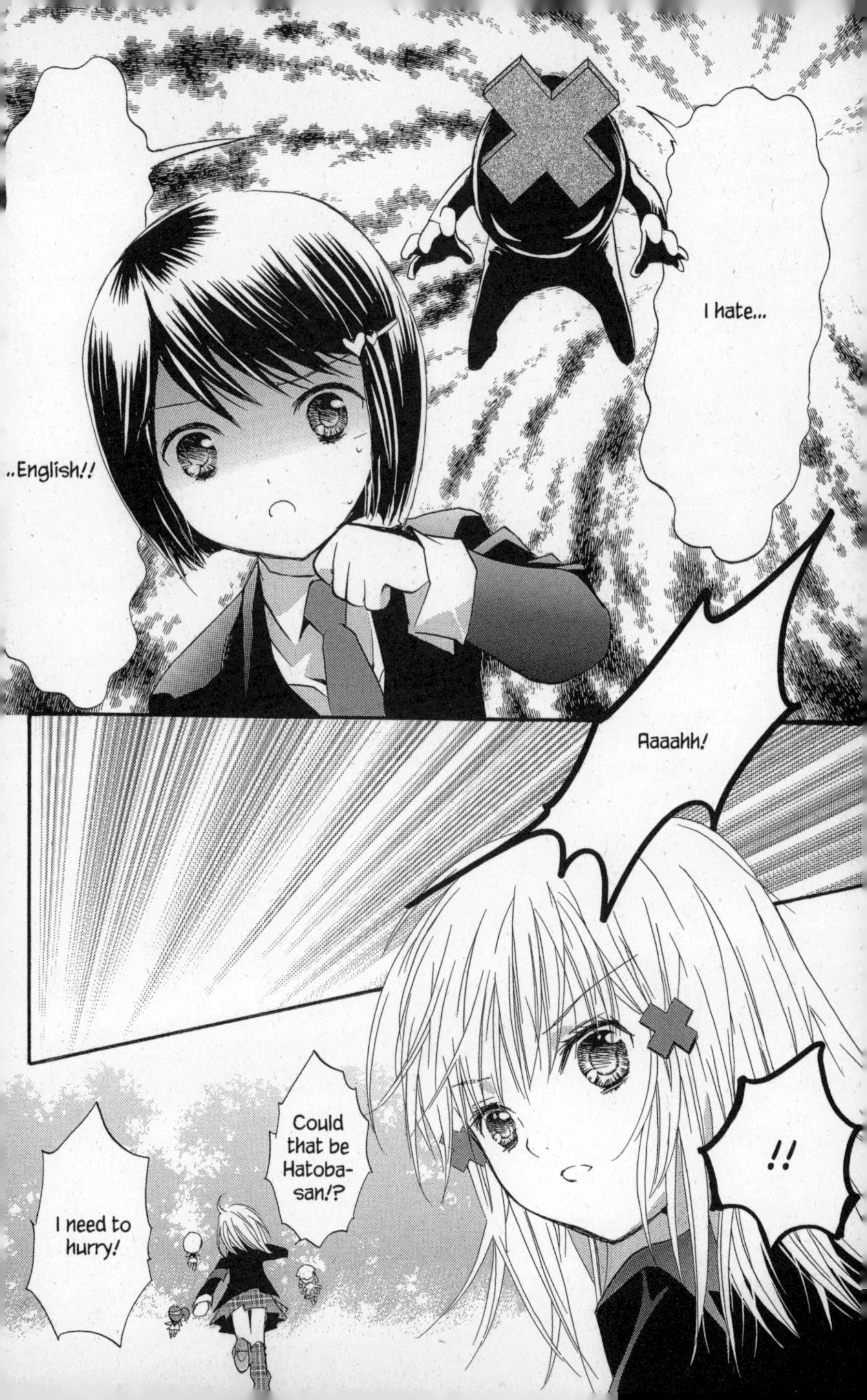
I hate...
..English!!
Aaaahh!
!!
Could that be Hatoba-san!?
I need to hurry!

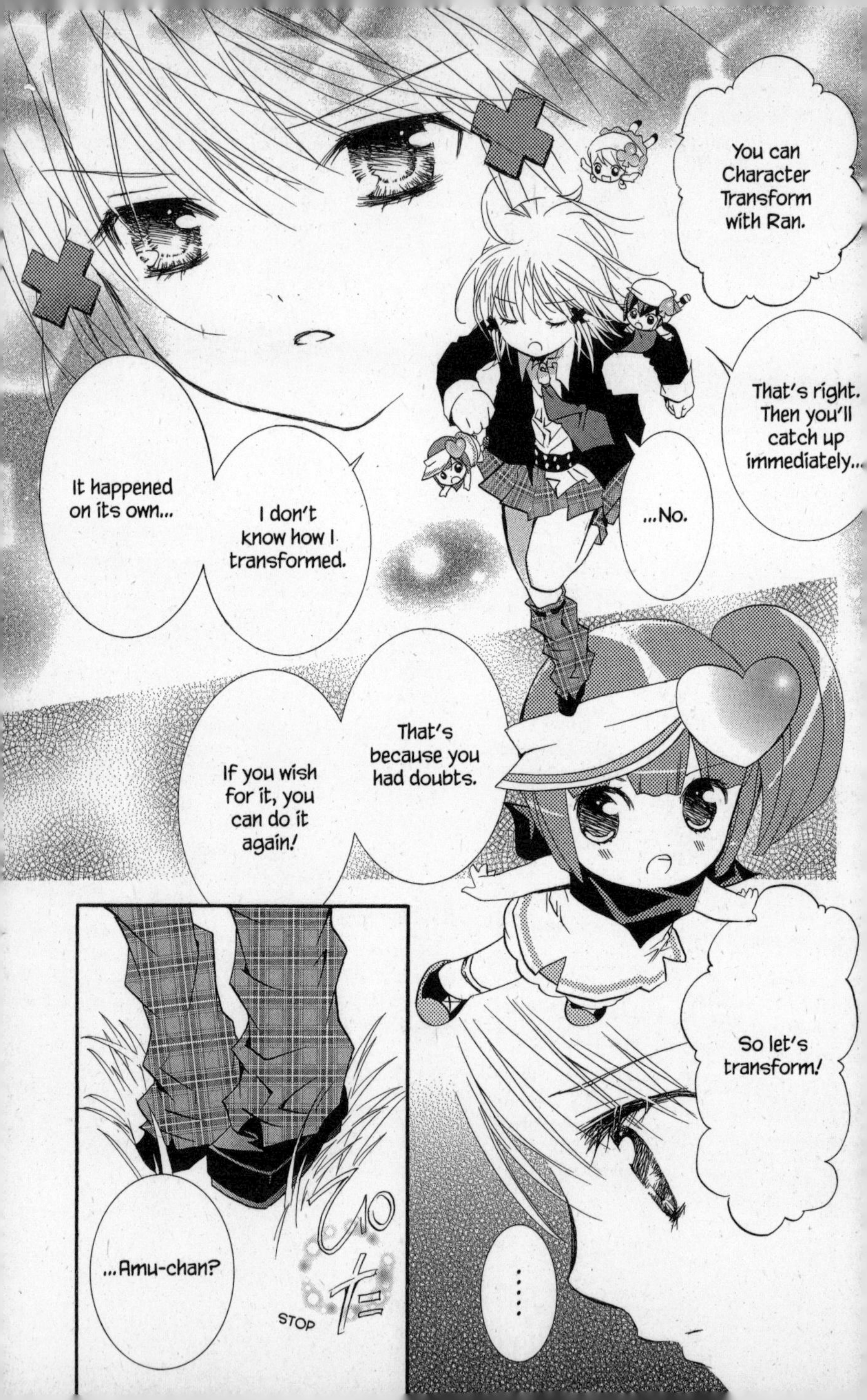
You can Character Transform with Ran.
That's right. Then you'll catch up immediately...
...No.
I don't know how I transformed.
It happened on its own...
That's because you had doubts.
If you wish for it, you can do it again!
So let's transform!
.....
...Amu-chan?
STOP

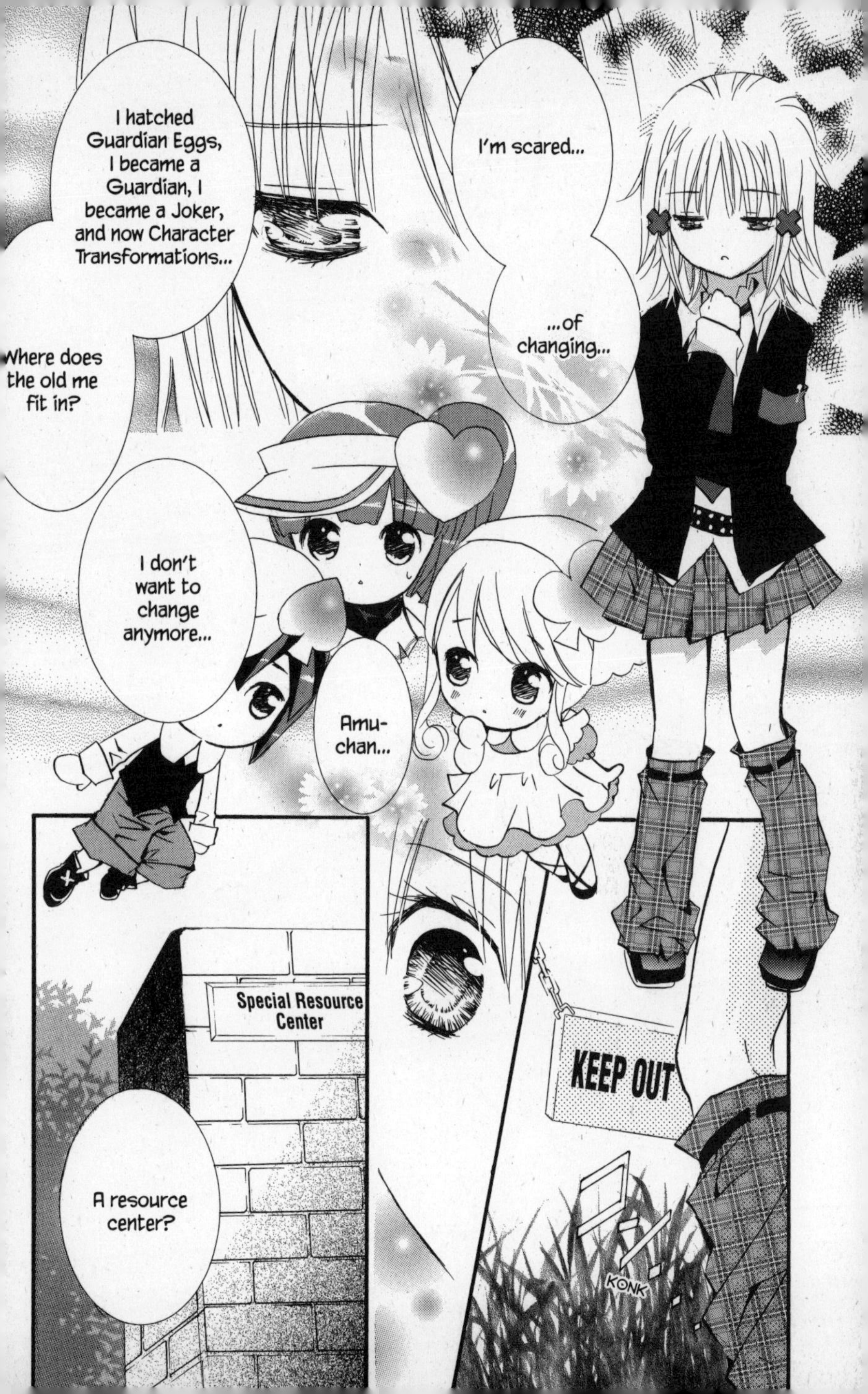
I'm scared...
...of changing...
I hatched Guardian Eggs, I became a Guardian, I became a Joker, and now Character Transformations...
Where does the old me fit in?
I don't want to change anymore...
Amu-chan...
KEEP OUT
KONK
Special Resource Center
A resource center?

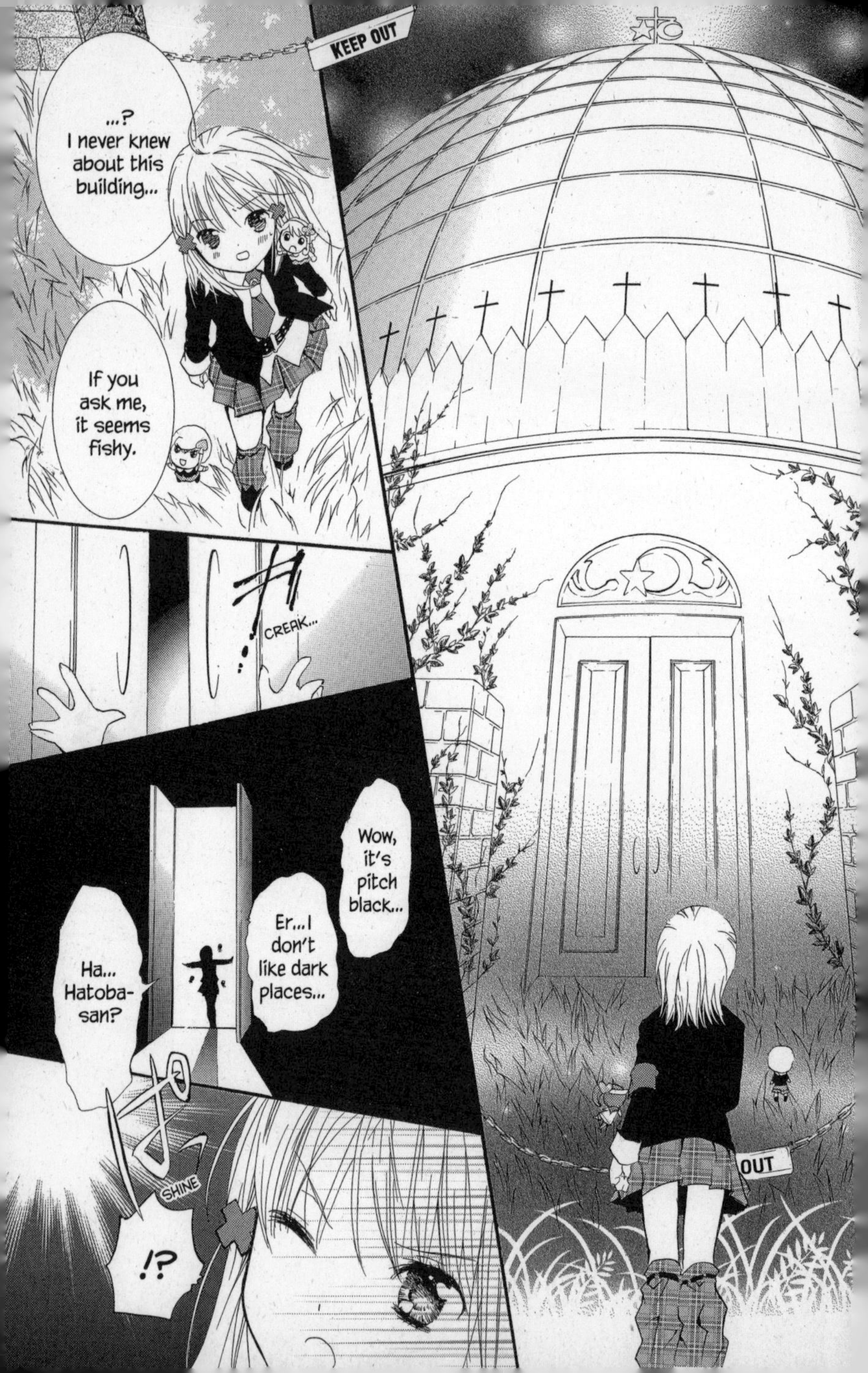
OUT
KEEP OUT
...? I never knew about this building...
If you ask me, it seems fishy.
CREAK...
Wow, it's pitch black...
Er...I don't like dark places...
Ha... Hatoba-san?
SHINE
!?

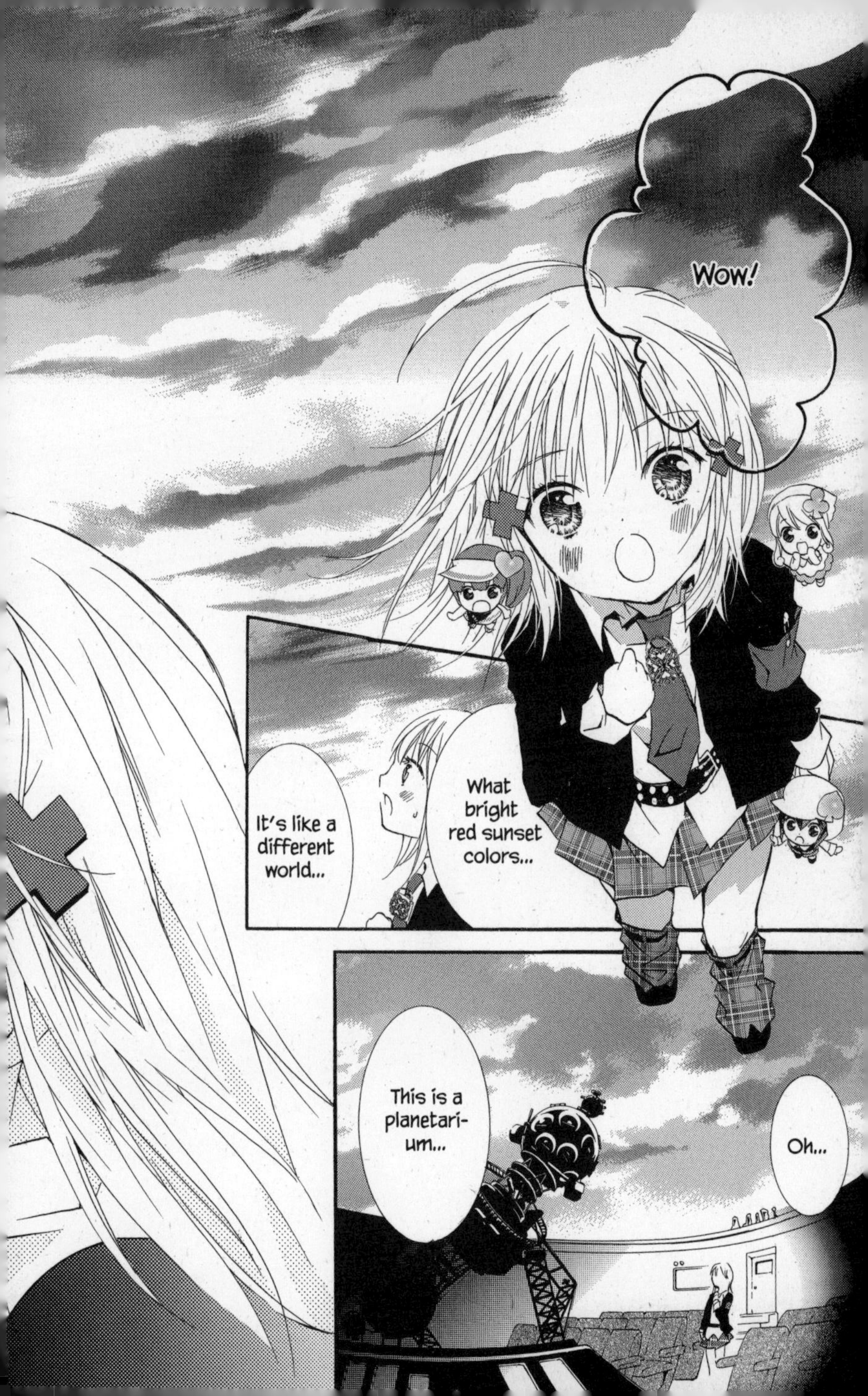
Wow!
What bright red sunset colors...
It's like a different world...
Oh...
This is a planetarium...

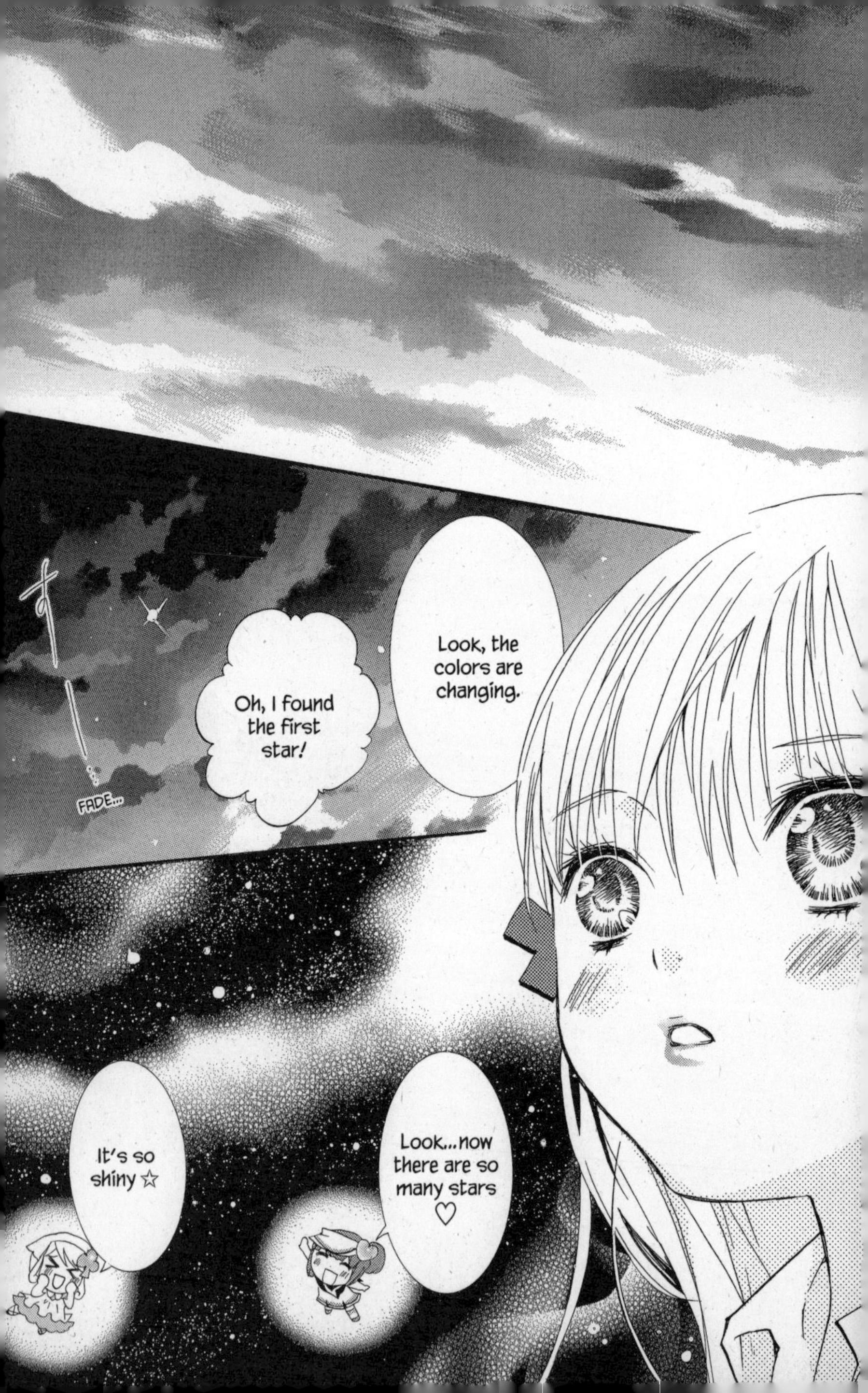
Look, the colors are changing.
Oh, I found the first star!
FADE...
Look...now there are so many stars ♡
It's so shiny ☆

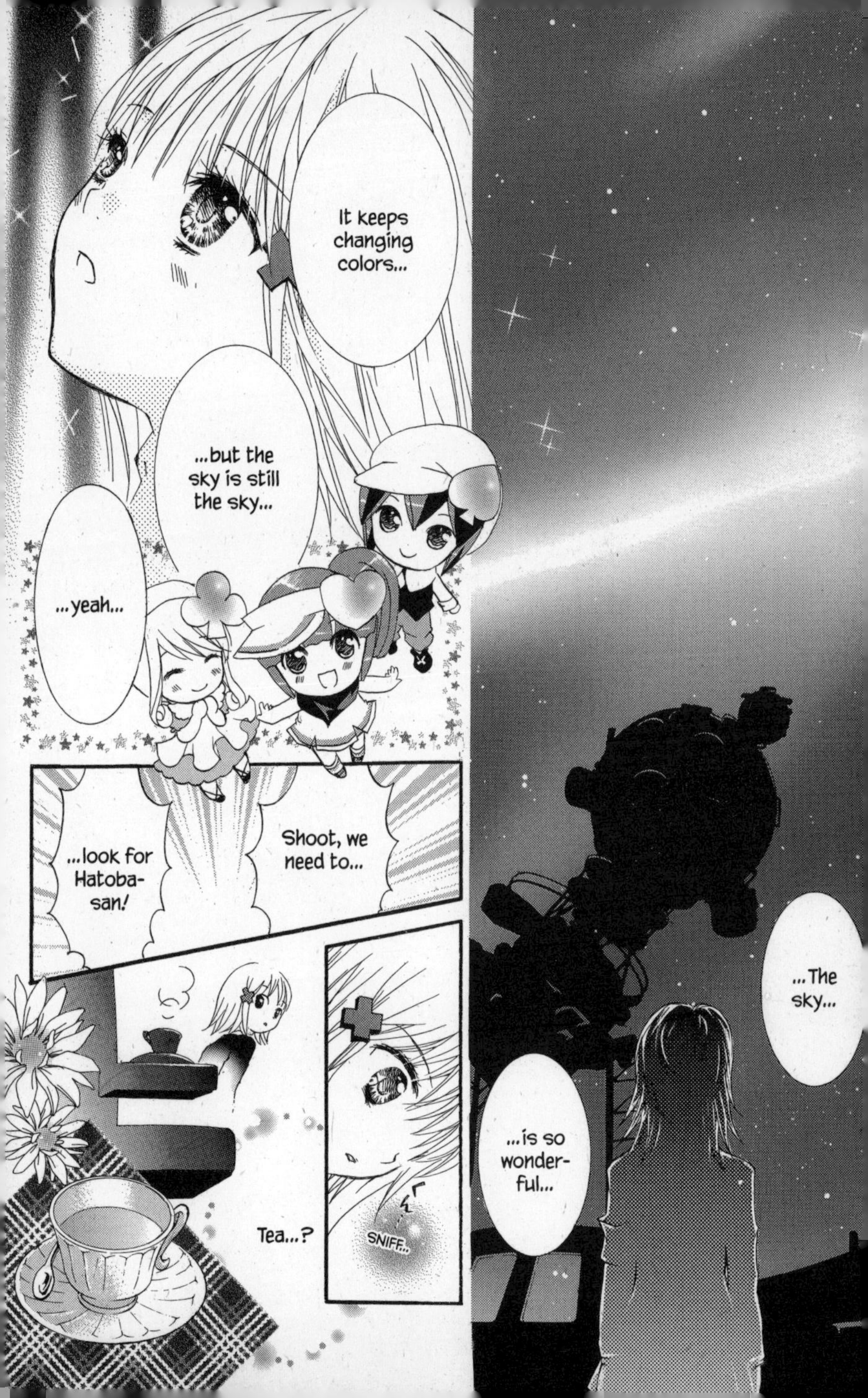
...The sky...
...is so wonderful...
It keeps changing colors...
...but the sky is still the sky...
...yeah...
Shoot, we need to...
...look for Hatoba-san!
SNIFF...
Tea...?

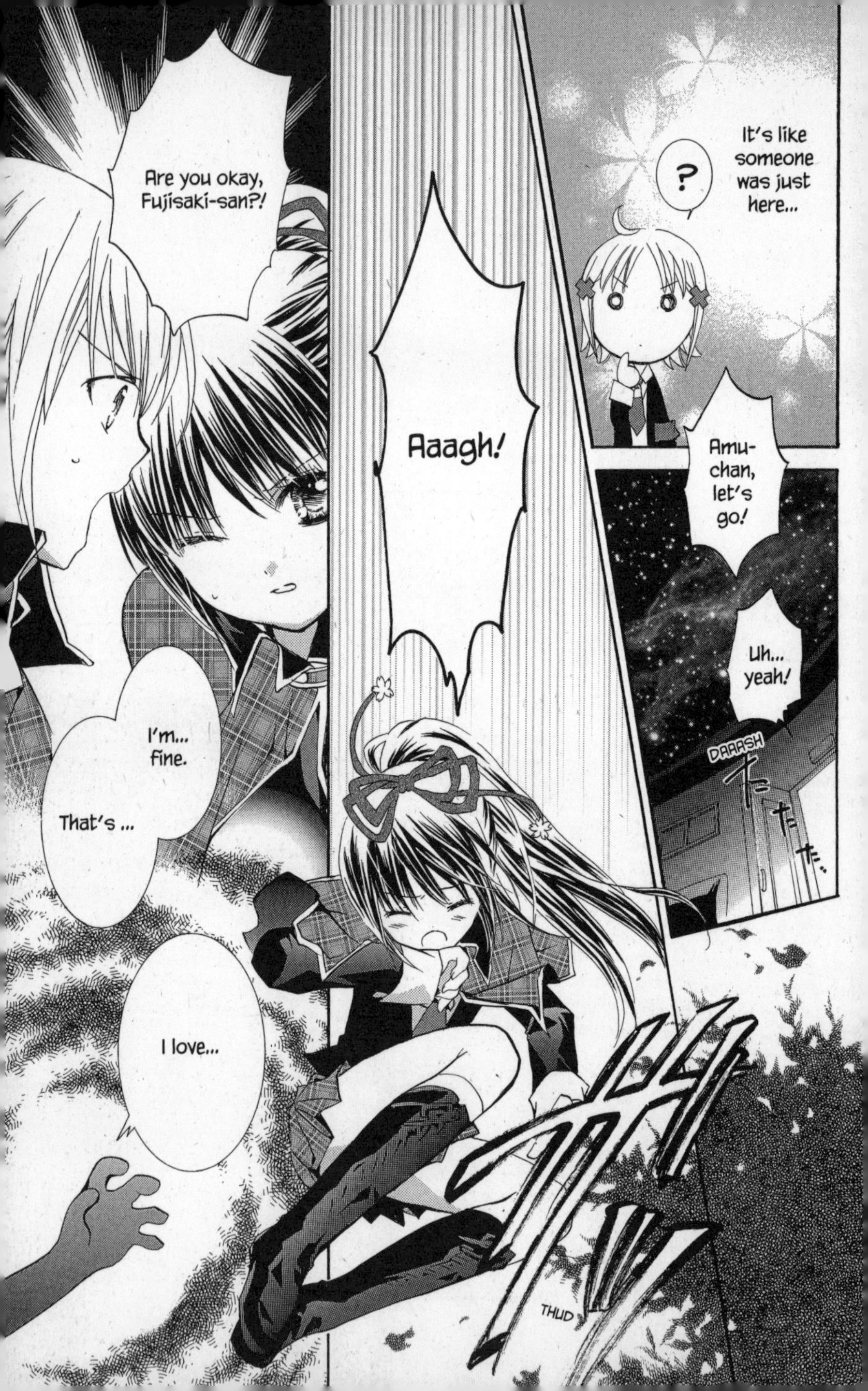
?
It's like someone was just here...
Amu-chan, let's go!
Uh... yeah!
DAAASH
Aaagh!
THUD
Are you okay, Fujisaki-san?!
I'm... fine.
That's ...
I love...

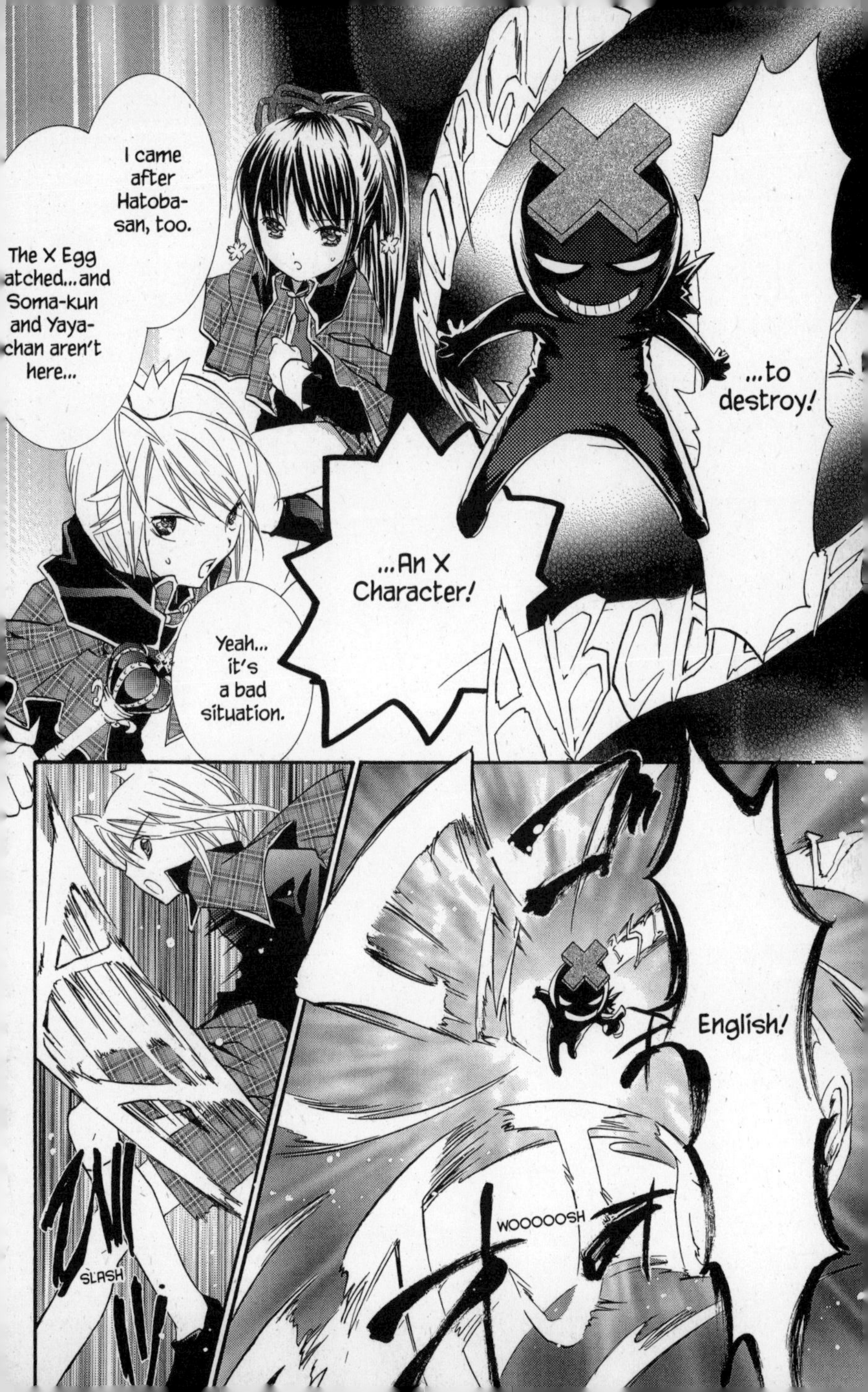
...to destroy!
...An X Character!
I came after Hatoba-san, too.
The X Egg atched...and Soma-kun and Yaya-chan aren't here...
Yeah... it's a bad situation.
English!
WOOOOOSH
SLASH

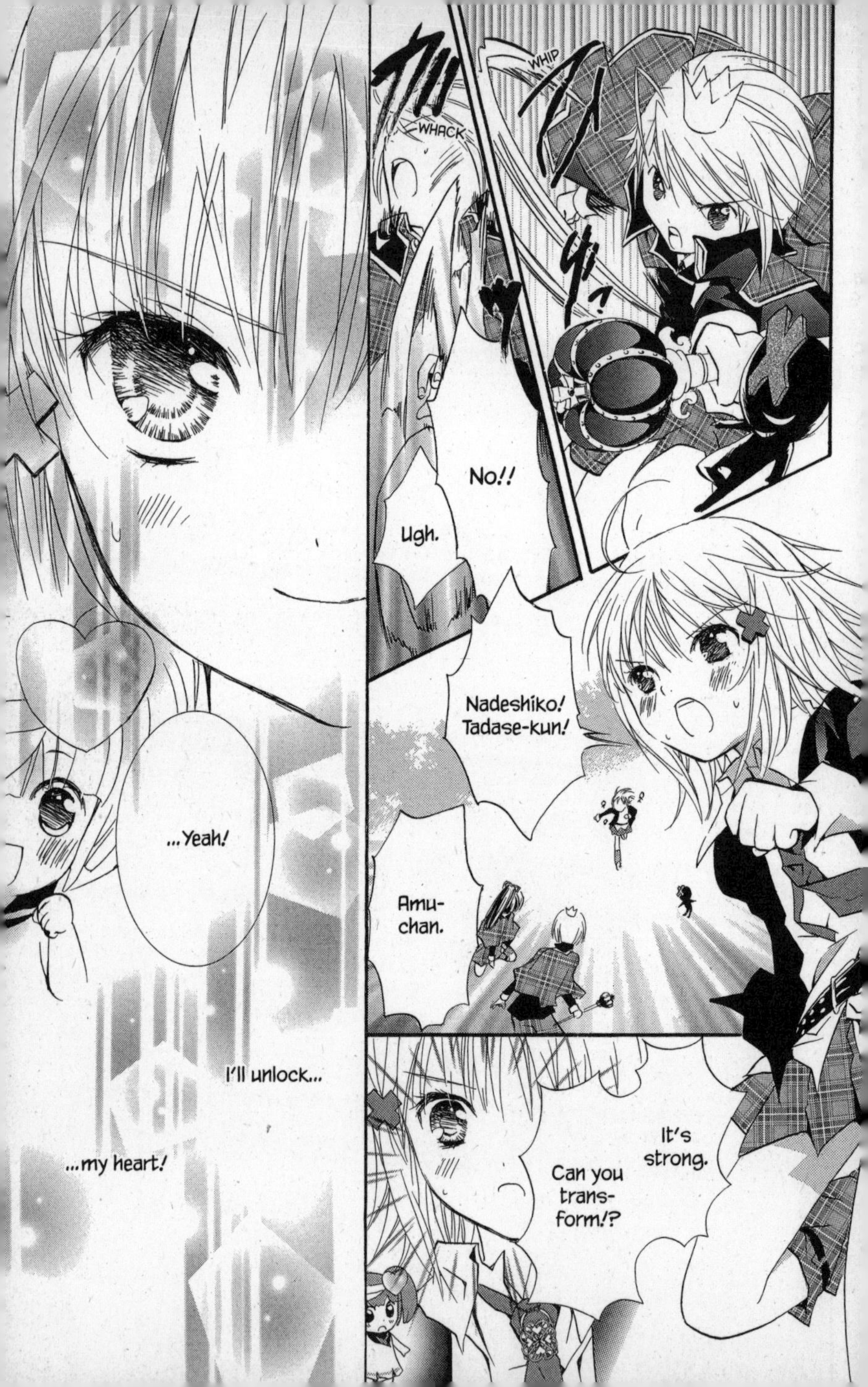
WHIP
WHACK
No!!
Ugh.
Nadeshiko! Tadase-kun!
Amu-chan.
It's strong.
Can you transform!?
...Yeah!
I'll unlock...
...my heart!

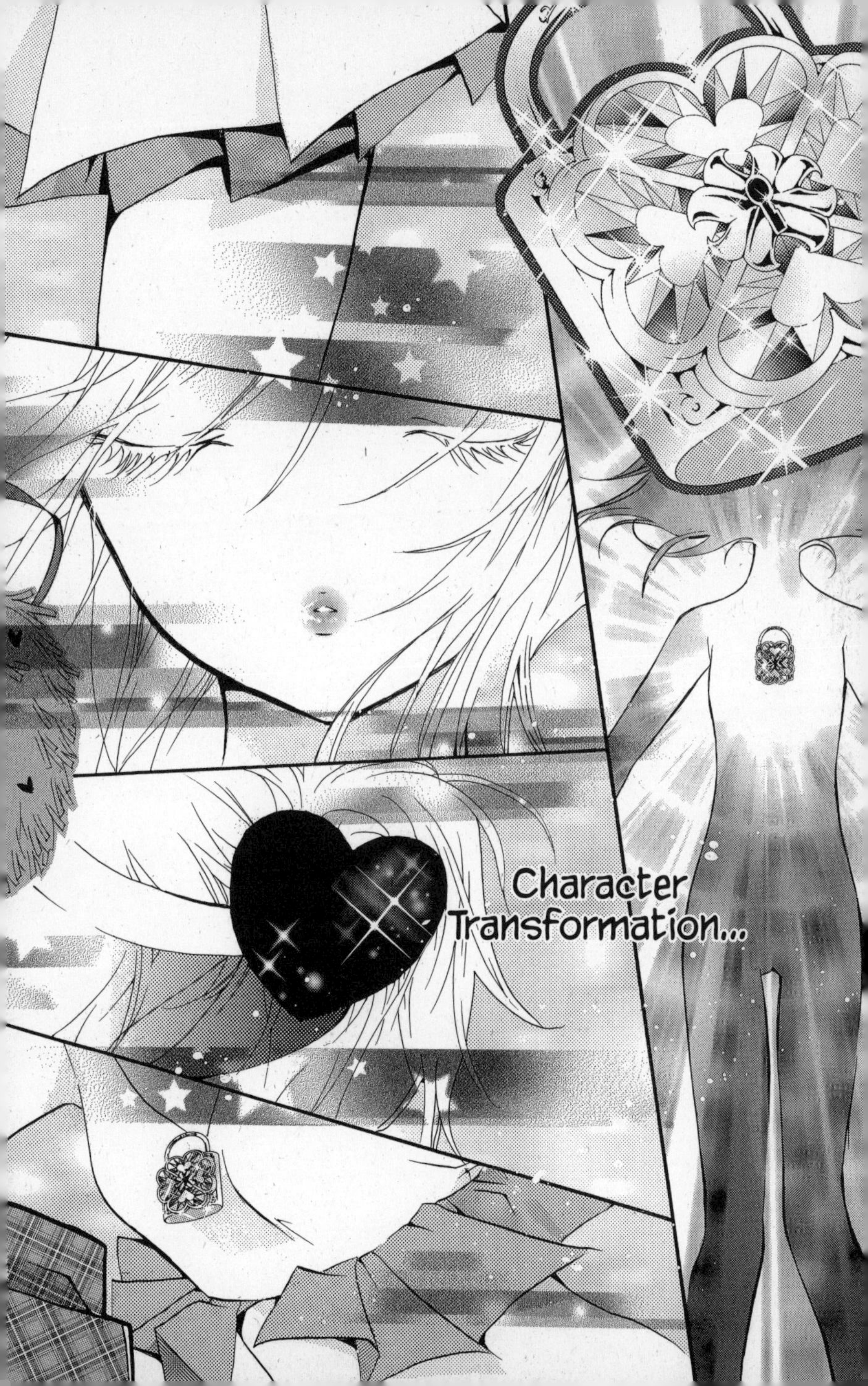
Character Transformation...

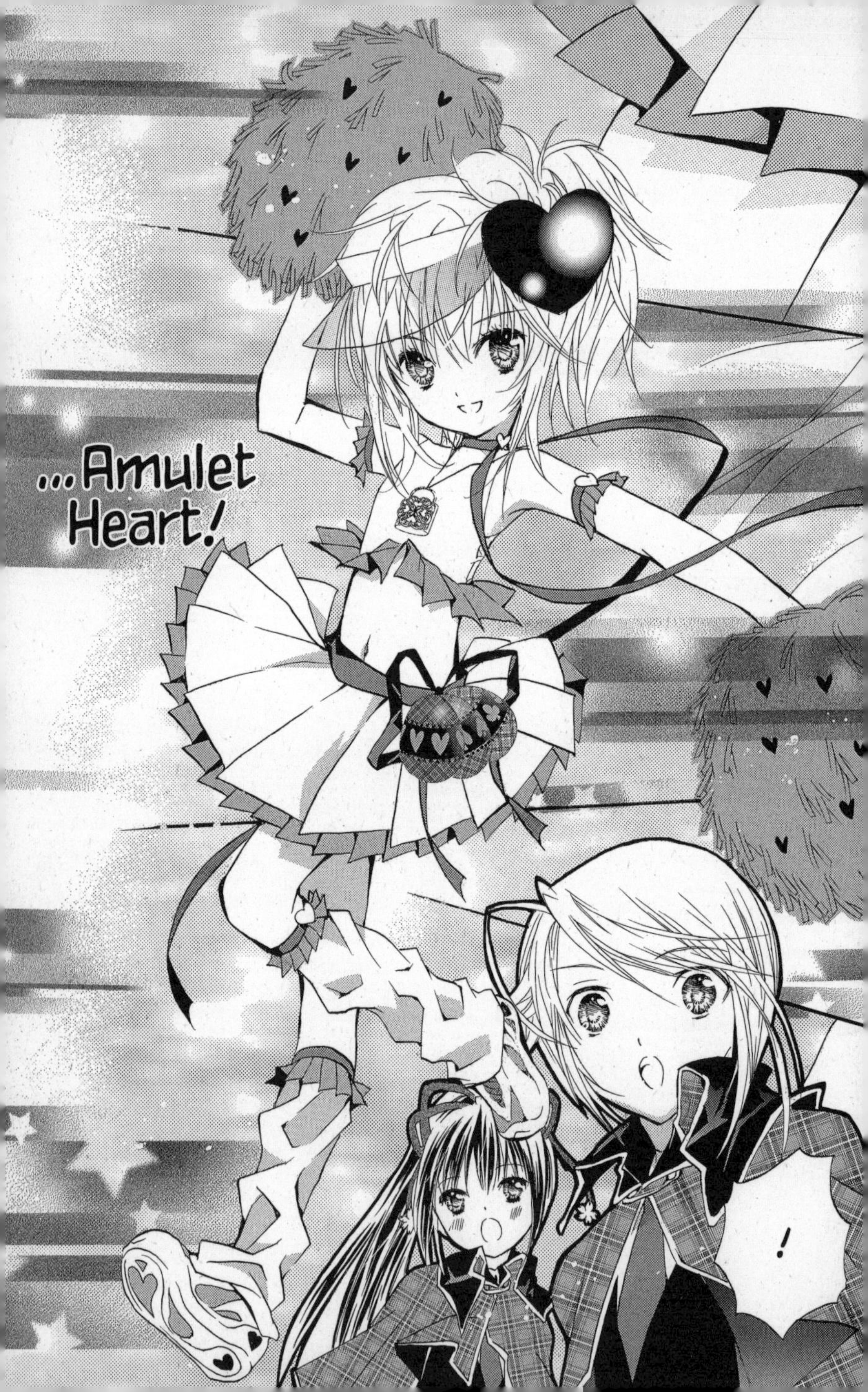
...Amulet Heart!
!

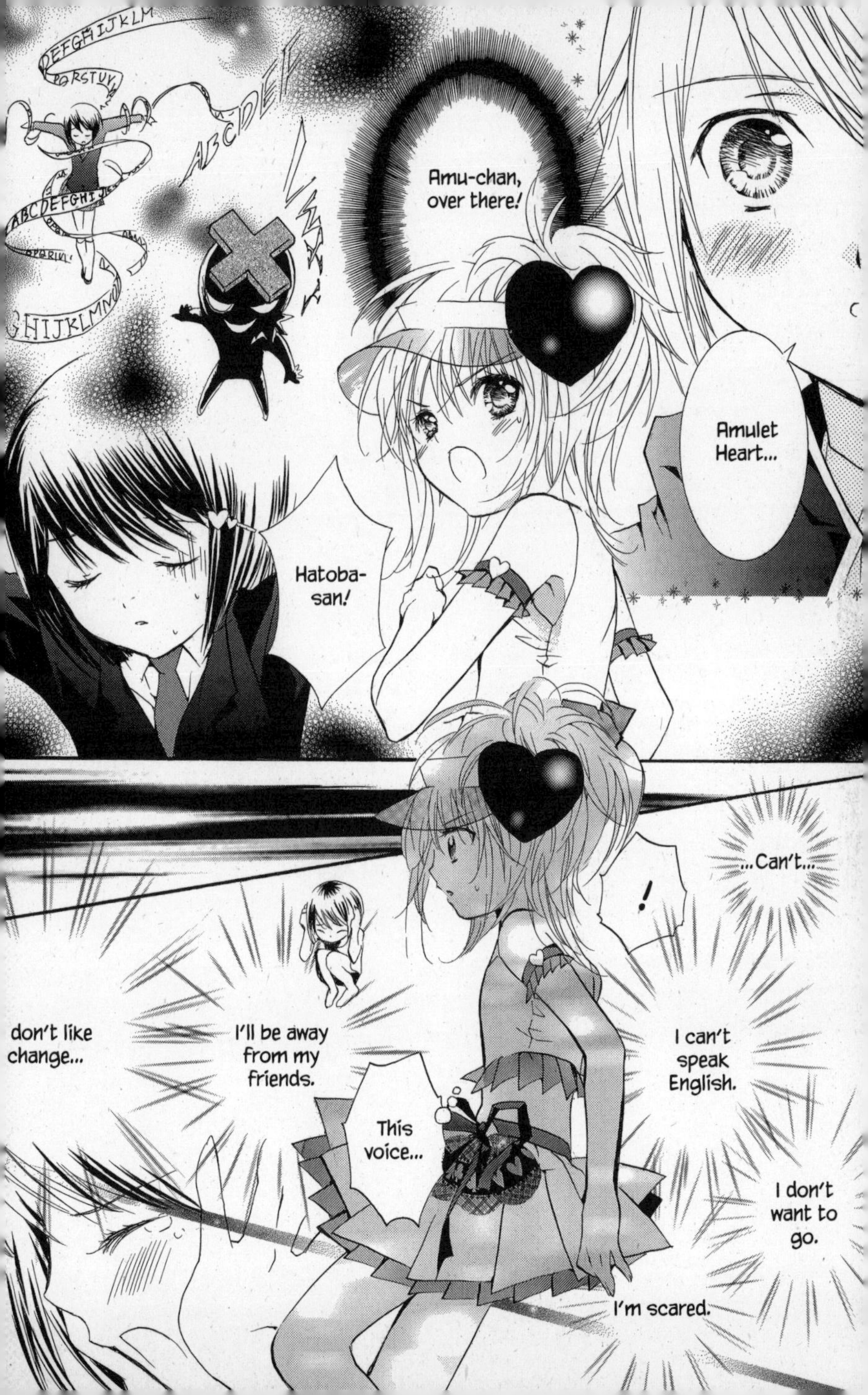
Amulet Heart...
Amu-chan, over there!
Hatoba-san!
...Can't...
!
I can't speak English.
I don't want to go.
I'm scared.
This voice...
I'll be away from my friends.
don't like change...

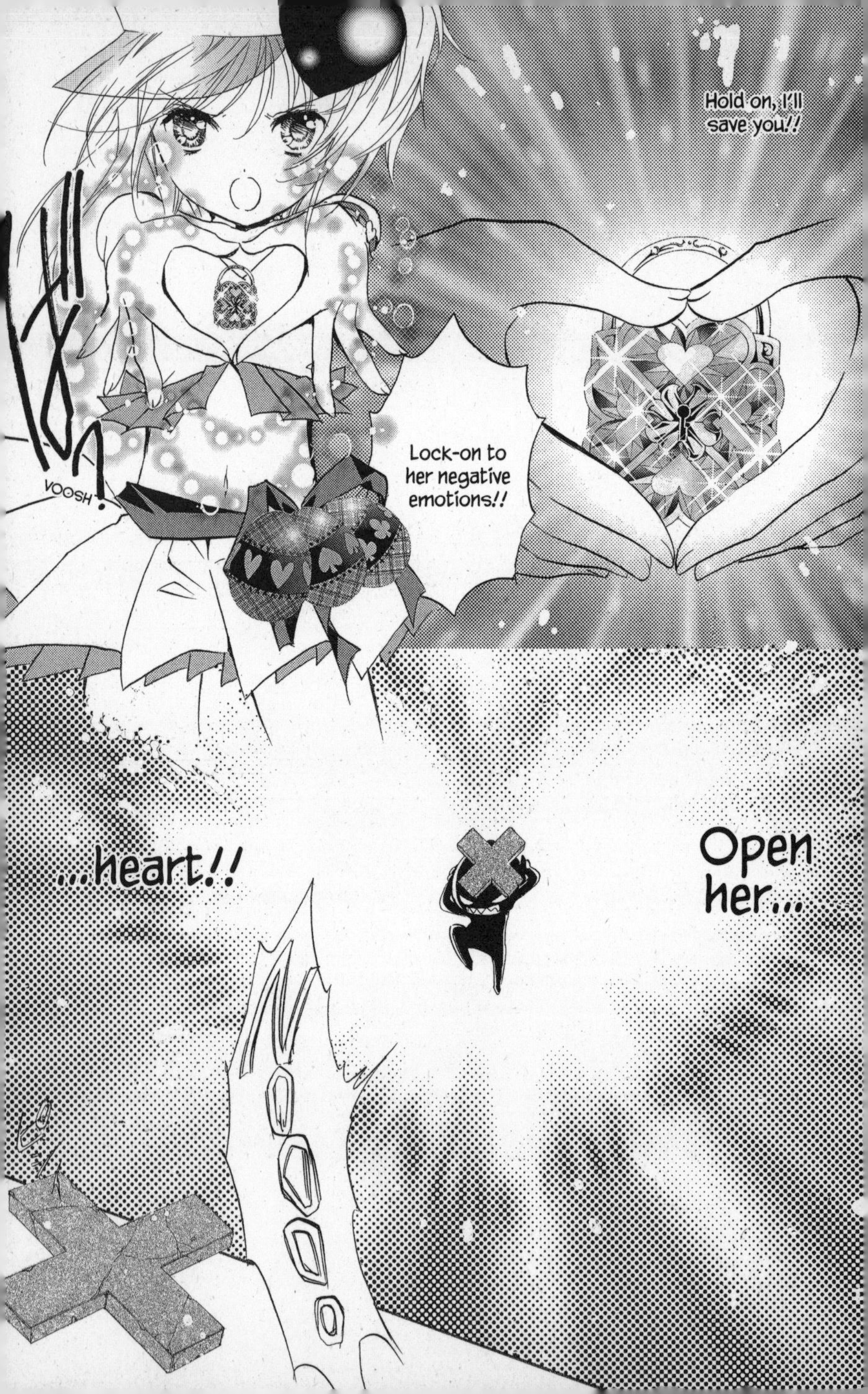

Hold on, I'll save you!!
Lock-on to her negative emotions!!
VOOSH!
Open her...
...heart!!

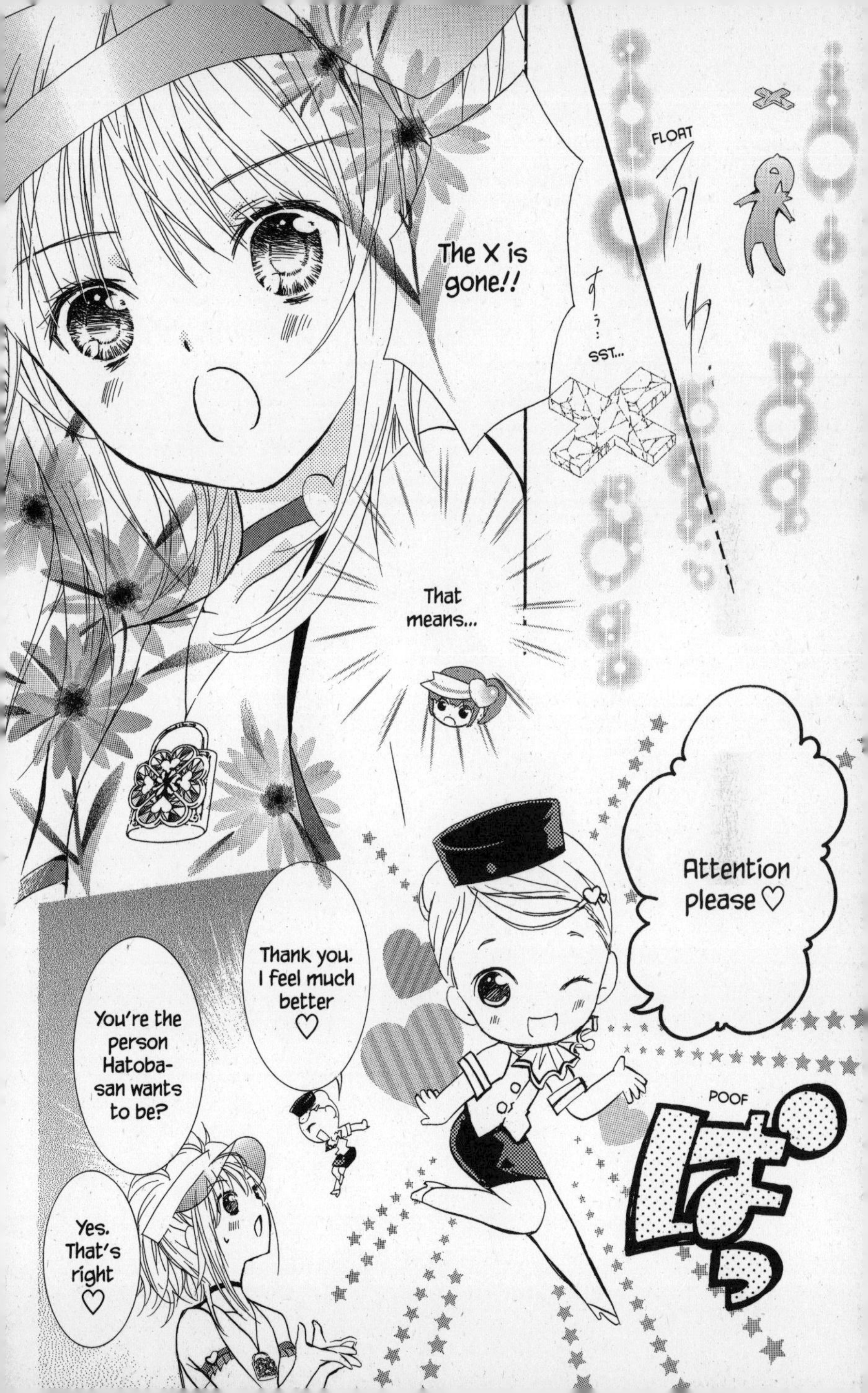
FLOAT
すぅ…
SST...
The X is gone!!
That means...
Attention please ♡
POOF
ぱっ
Thank you. I feel much better ♡
You're the person Hatoba-san wants to be?
Yes. That's right ♡

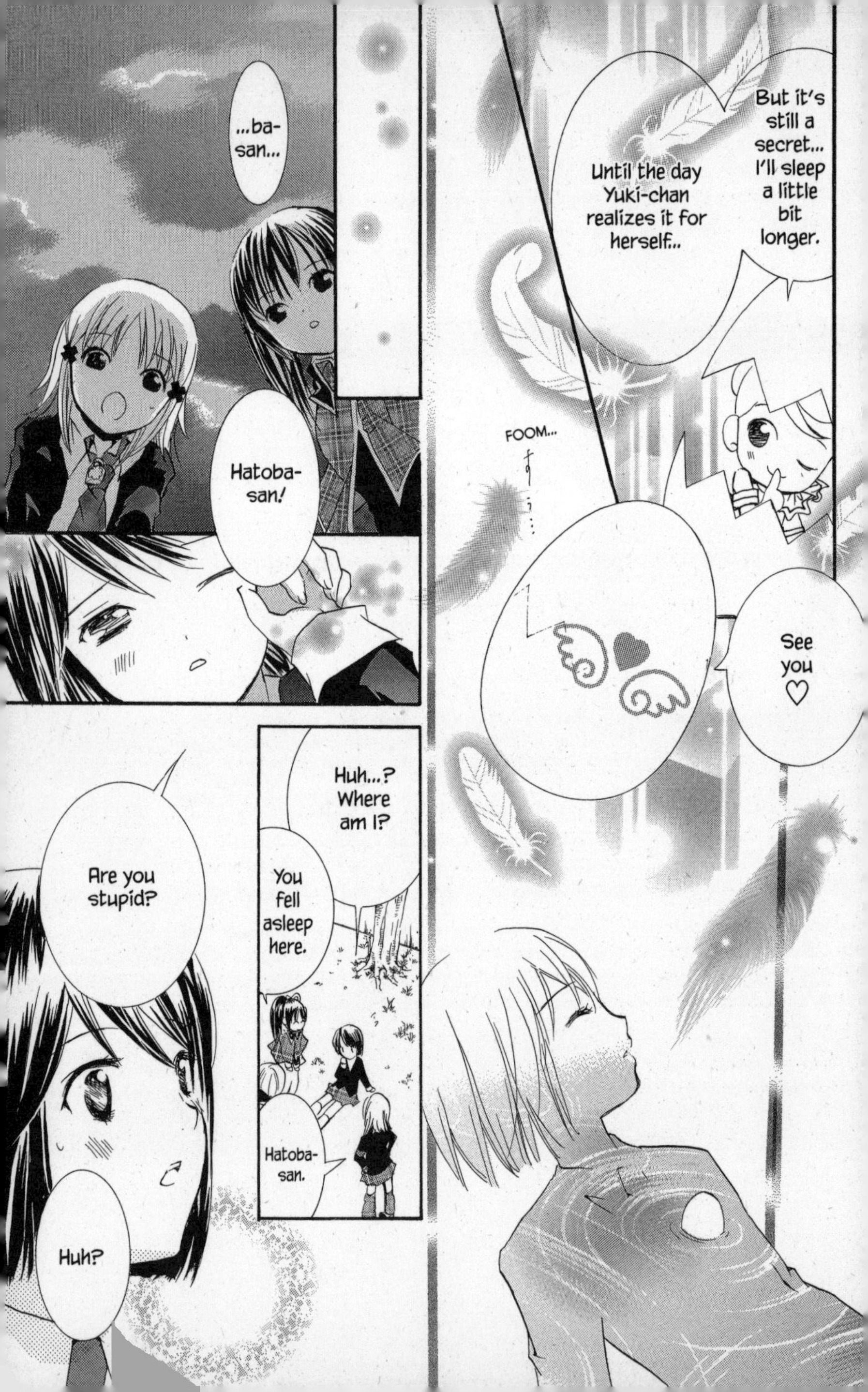
But it's still a secret... I'll sleep a little bit longer.
Until the day Yuki-chan realizes it for herself..
FOOM...
See you ♡
...ba-san...
Hatoba-san!
Huh...? Where am I?
You fell asleep here.
Hatoba-san.
Are you stupid?
Huh?

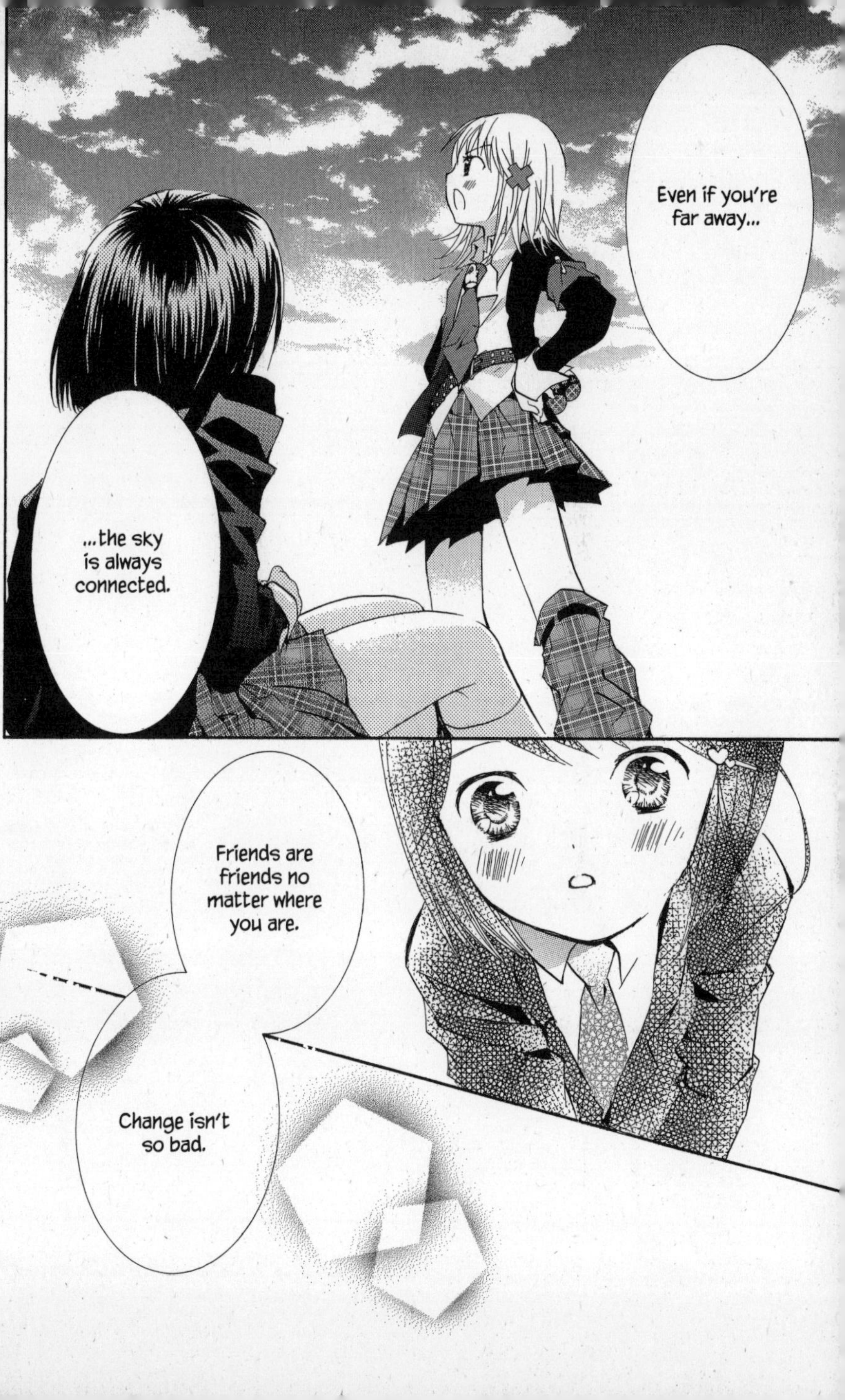
Even if you're far away...
...the sky is always connected.
Friends are friends no matter where you are.
Change isn't so bad.

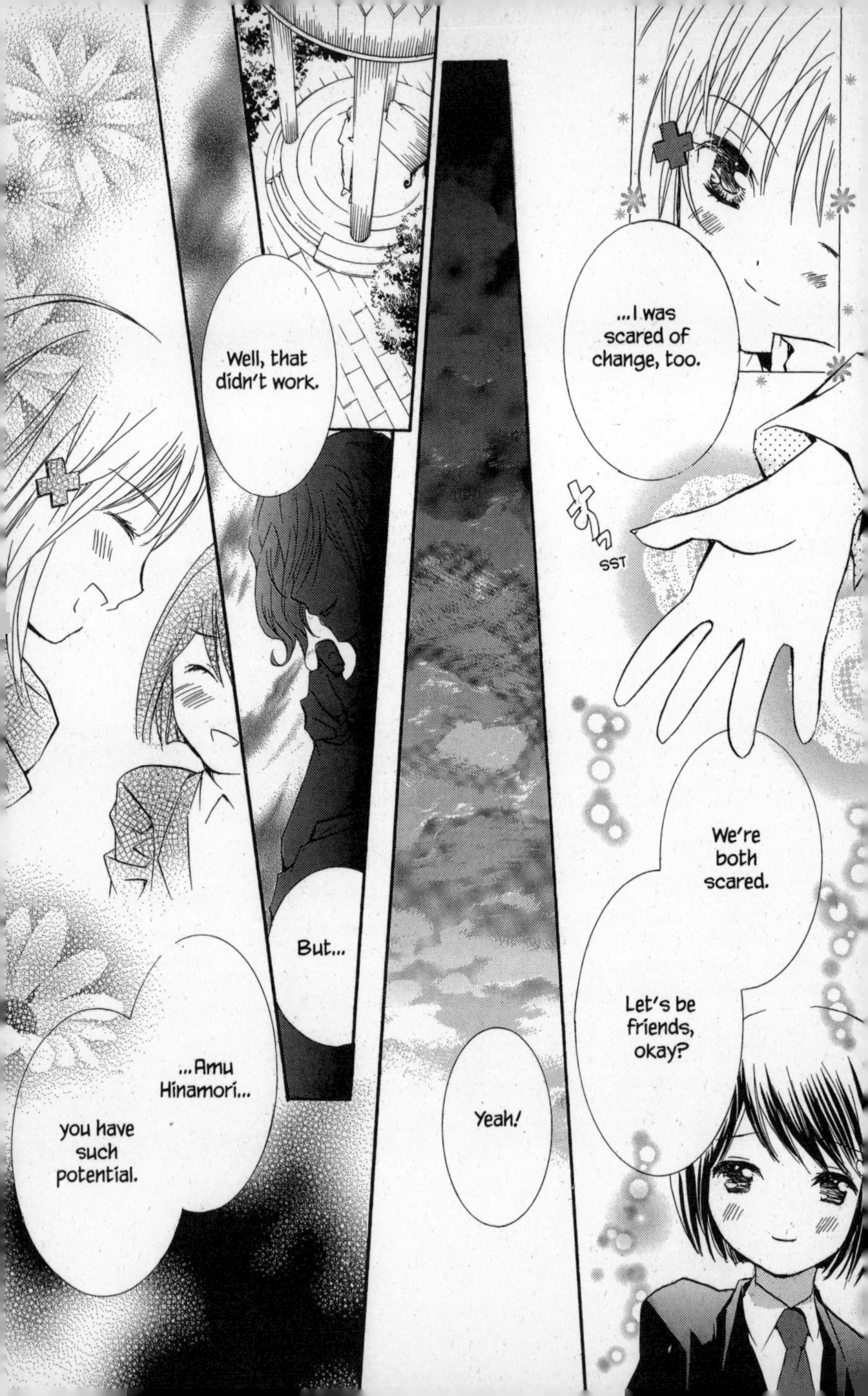
...I was scared of change, too.
SST
We're both scared.
Let's be friends, okay?
Yeah!
Well, that didn't work.
But...
...Amu Hinamori...
you have such potential.

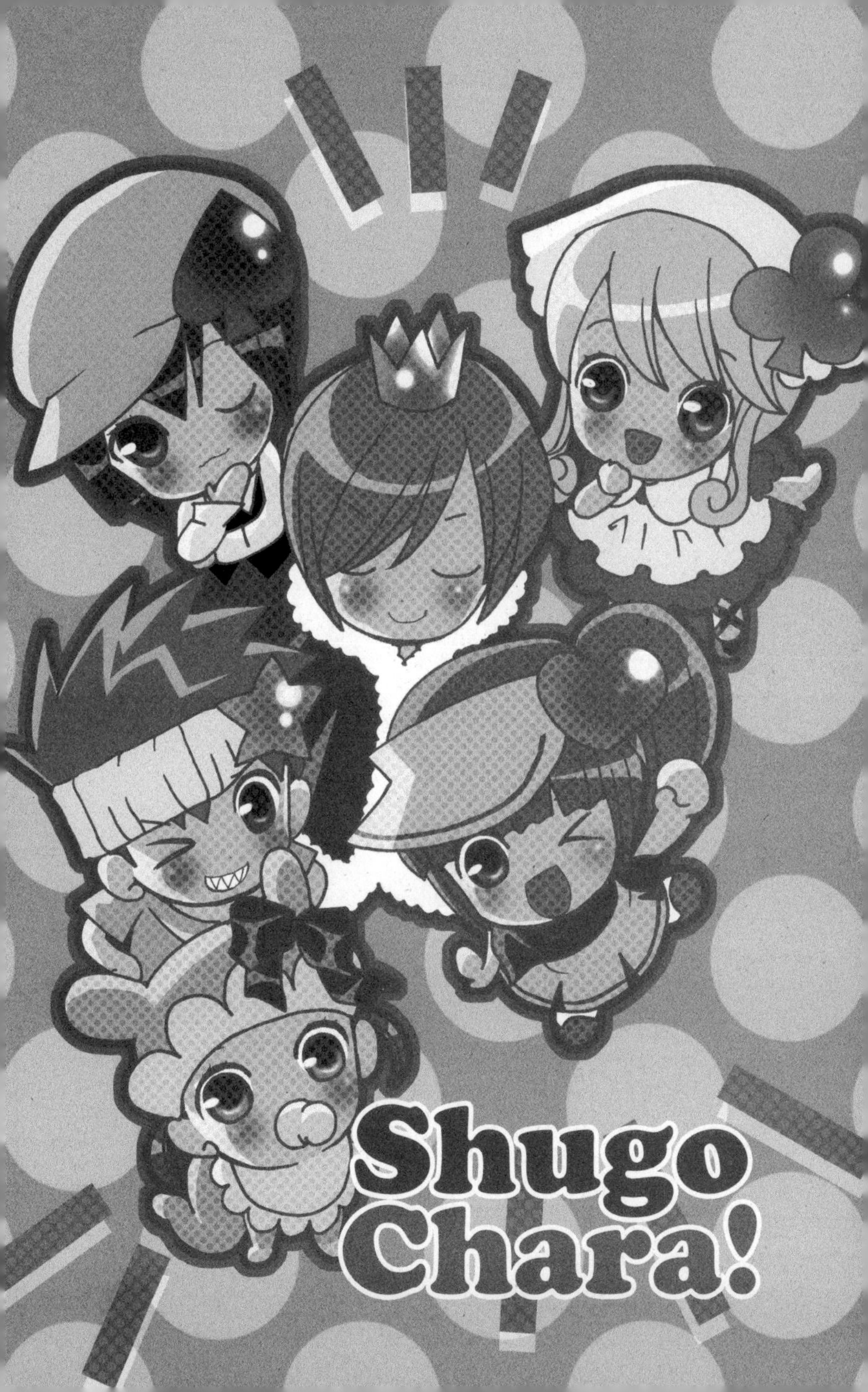
Shugo
Chara!

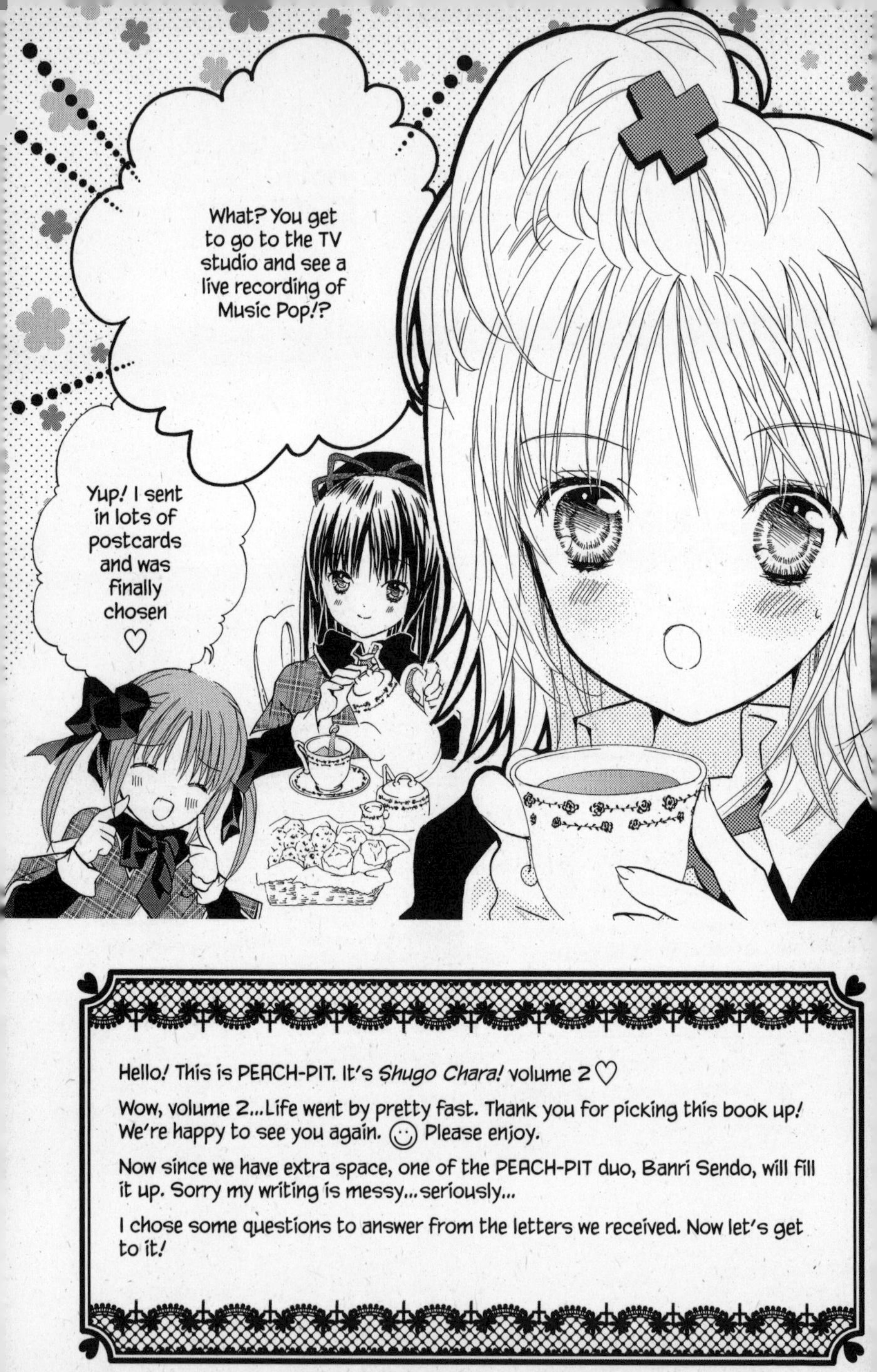
What? You get to go to the TV studio and see a live recording of Music Pop!?
Yup! I sent in lots of postcards and was finally chosen ♡

Hello! This is PEACH-PIT. It's *Shugo Chara!* volume 2 ♡

Wow, volume 2...Life went by pretty fast. Thank you for picking this book up! We're happy to see you again. ☺ Please enjoy.

Now since we have extra space, one of the PEACH-PIT duo, Banri Sendo, will fill it up. Sorry my writing is messy...seriously...

I chose some questions to answer from the letters we received. Now let's get to it!

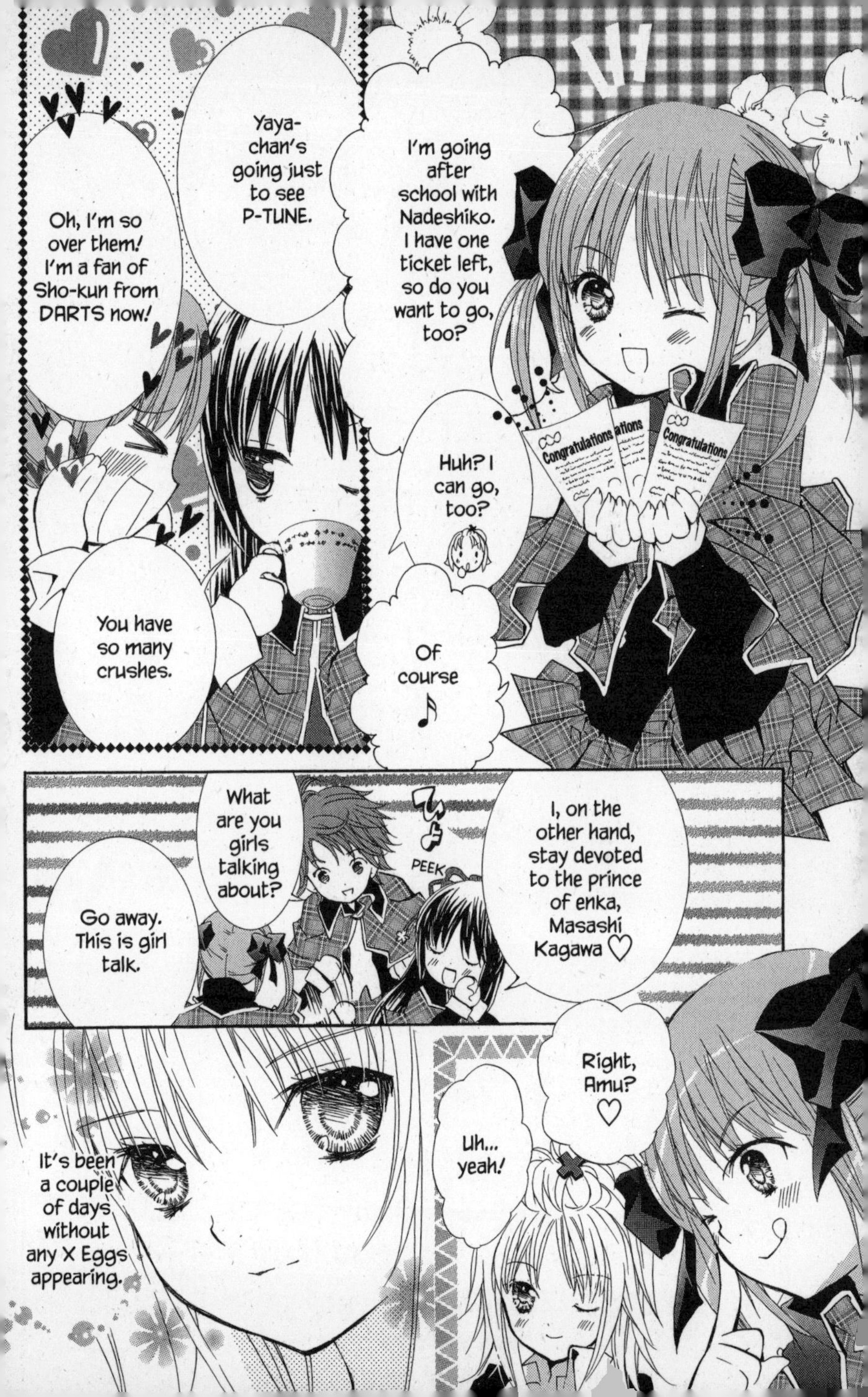
I'm going after school with Nadeshiko. I have one ticket left, so do you want to go, too?
Congratulations
Huh? I can go, too?
Of course ♪
Yaya-chan's going just to see P-TUNE.
Oh, I'm so over them! I'm a fan of Sho-kun from DARTS now!
You have so many crushes.
I, on the other hand, stay devoted to the prince of enka, Masashi Kagawa ♡
PEEK
What are you girls talking about?
Go away. This is girl talk.
Right, Amu? ♡
Uh... yeah!
It's been a couple of days without any X Eggs appearing.

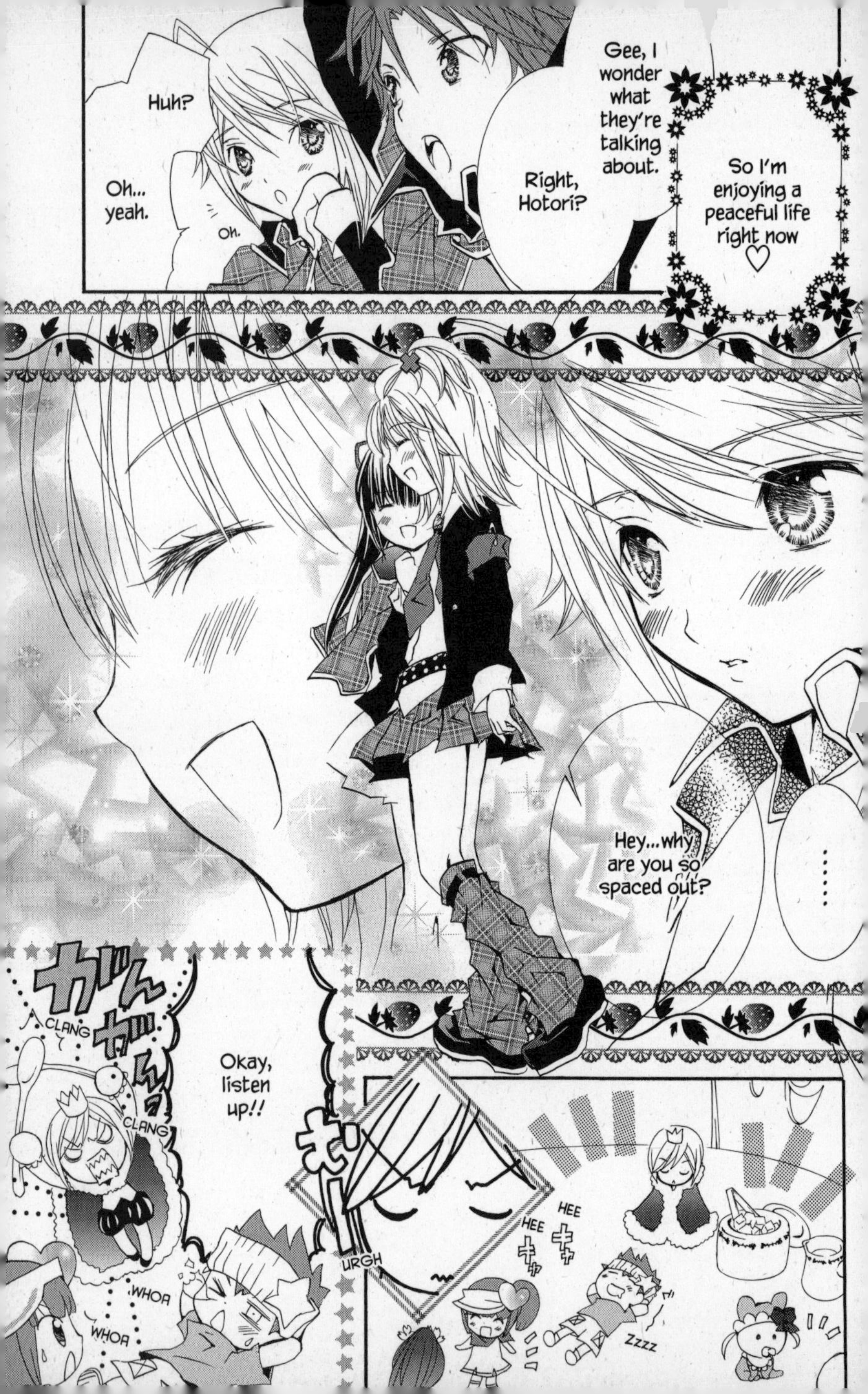
So I'm enjoying a peaceful life right now ♡
Gee, I wonder what they're talking about.
Right, Hotori?
Huh?
Oh... yeah.
Oh.
......
Hey...why are you so spaced out?
HEE
HEE
URGH
Zzzz
Okay, listen up!!
CLANG
CLANG
WHOA
WHOA

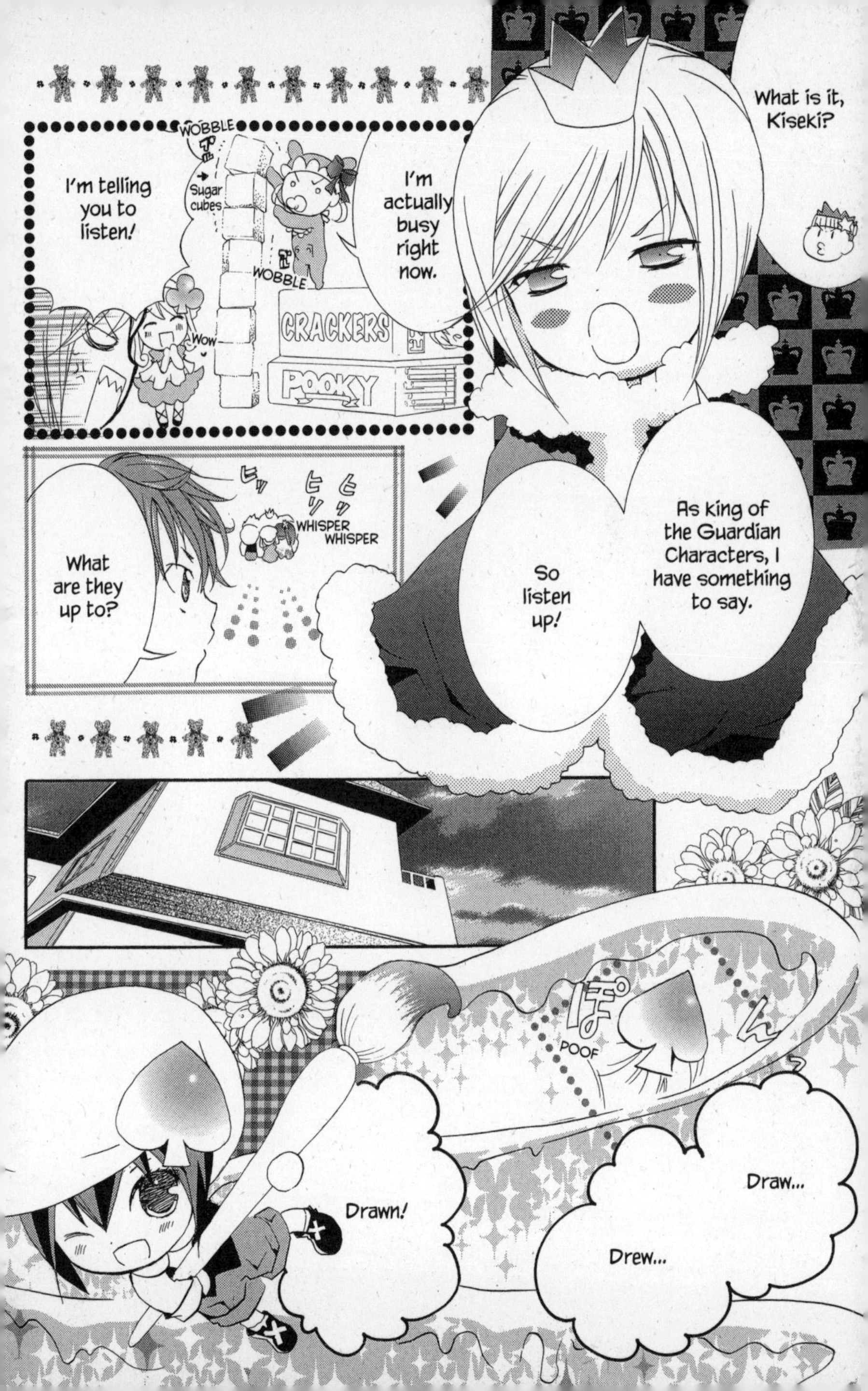
What is it, Kiseki?
As king of the Guardian Characters, I have something to say.
So listen up!
I'm actually busy right now.
WOBBLE
Sugar cubes
WOBBLE
I'm telling you to listen!
CRACKERS
POOKY
WOW
WHISPER WHISPER
What are they up to?
POOF
Draw...
Drew...
Drawn!

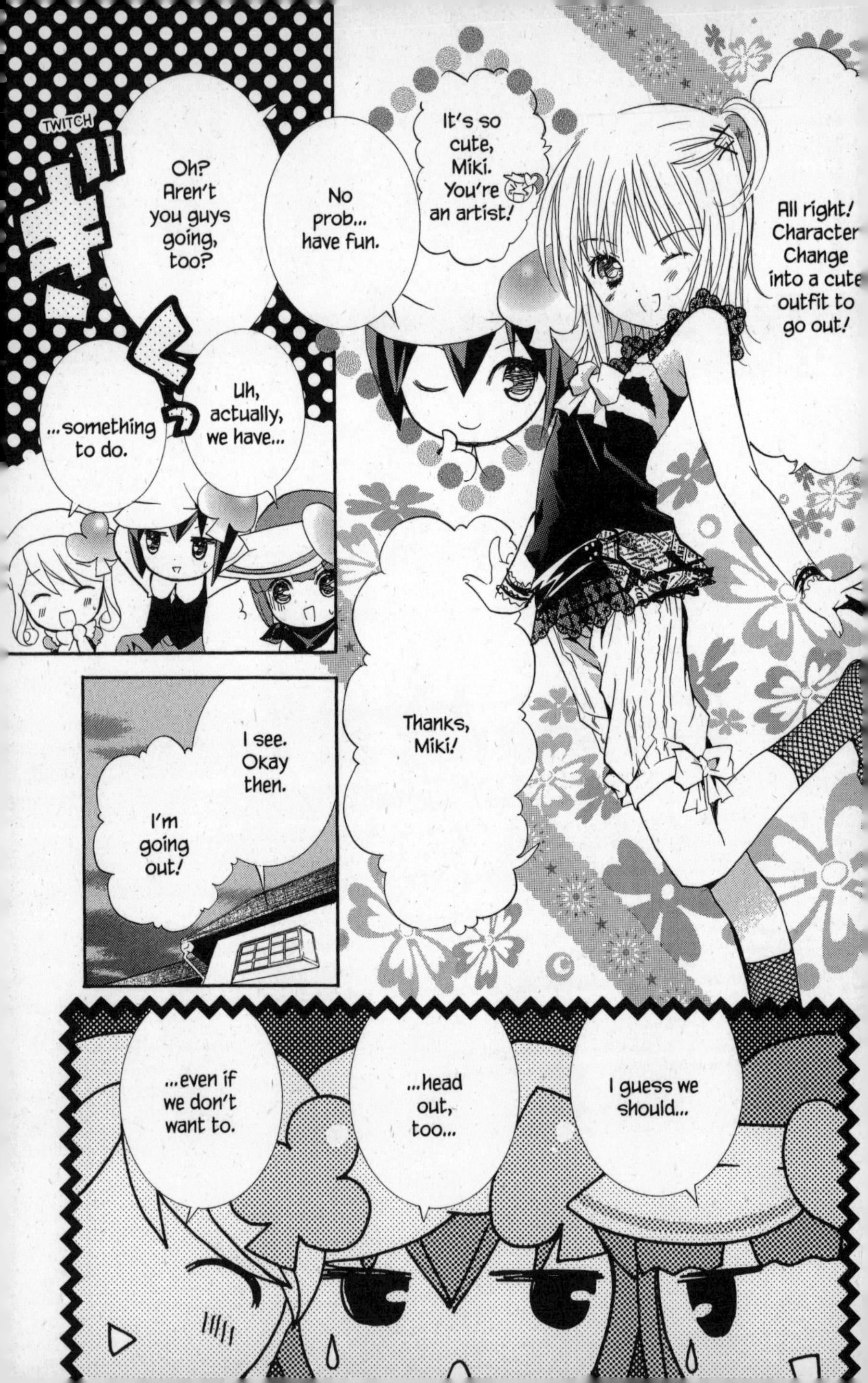
All right! Character Change into a cute outfit to go out!
It's so cute, Miki. You're an artist!
No prob... have fun.
Thanks, Miki!
Oh? Aren't you guys going, too?
TWITCH
Uh, actually, we have...
...something to do.
I see. Okay then.
I'm going out!
I guess we should...
...head out, too...
...even if we don't want to.

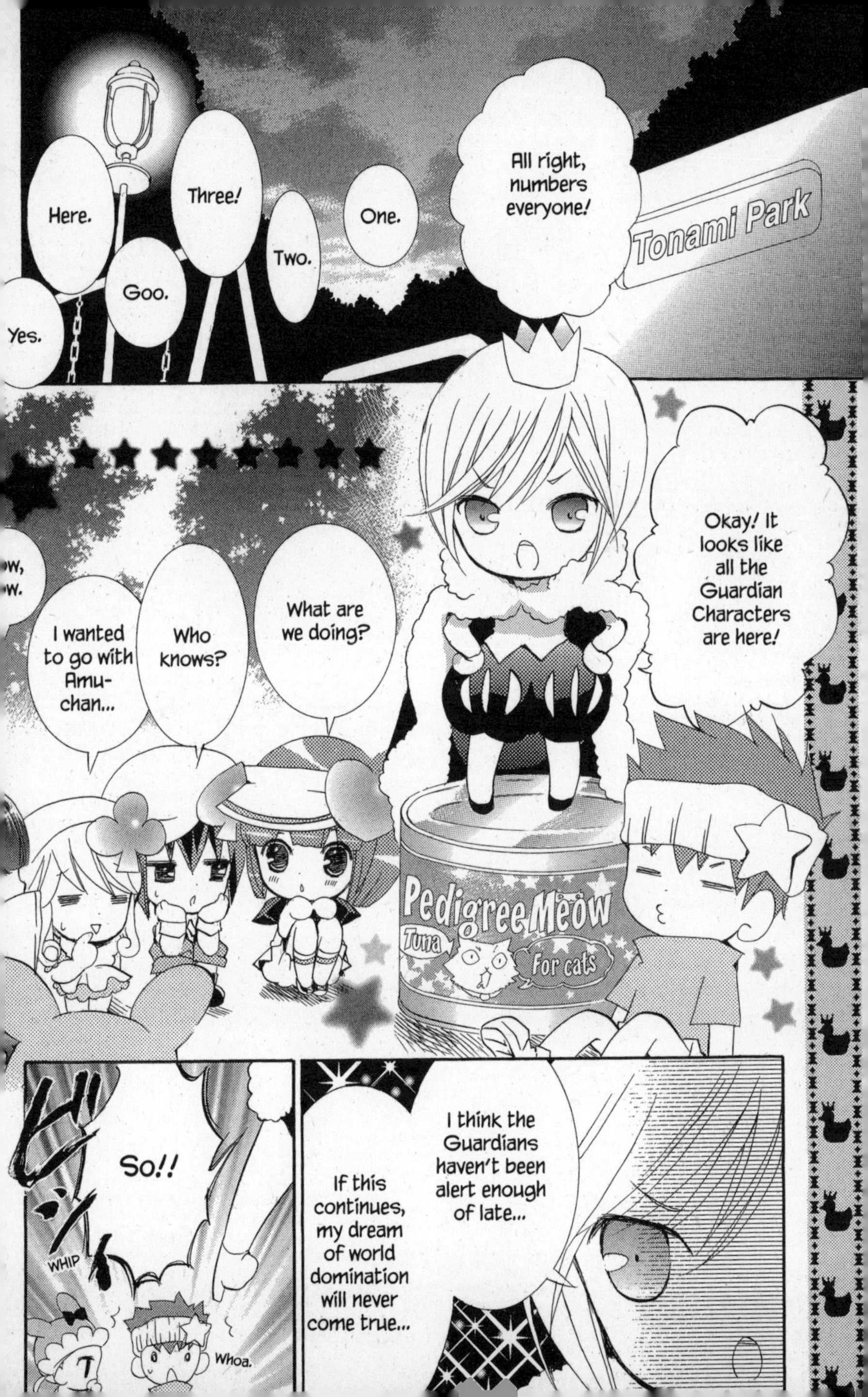
Tonami Park
All right, numbers everyone!
One.
Two.
Three!
Goo.
Here.
Yes.
Okay! It looks like all the Guardian Characters are here!
What are we doing?
Who knows?
I wanted to go with Amu-chan...
Pedigree Meow
Tuna
For cats
I think the Guardians haven't been alert enough of late...
If this continues, my dream of world domination will never come true...
So!!
WHIP
Whoa.

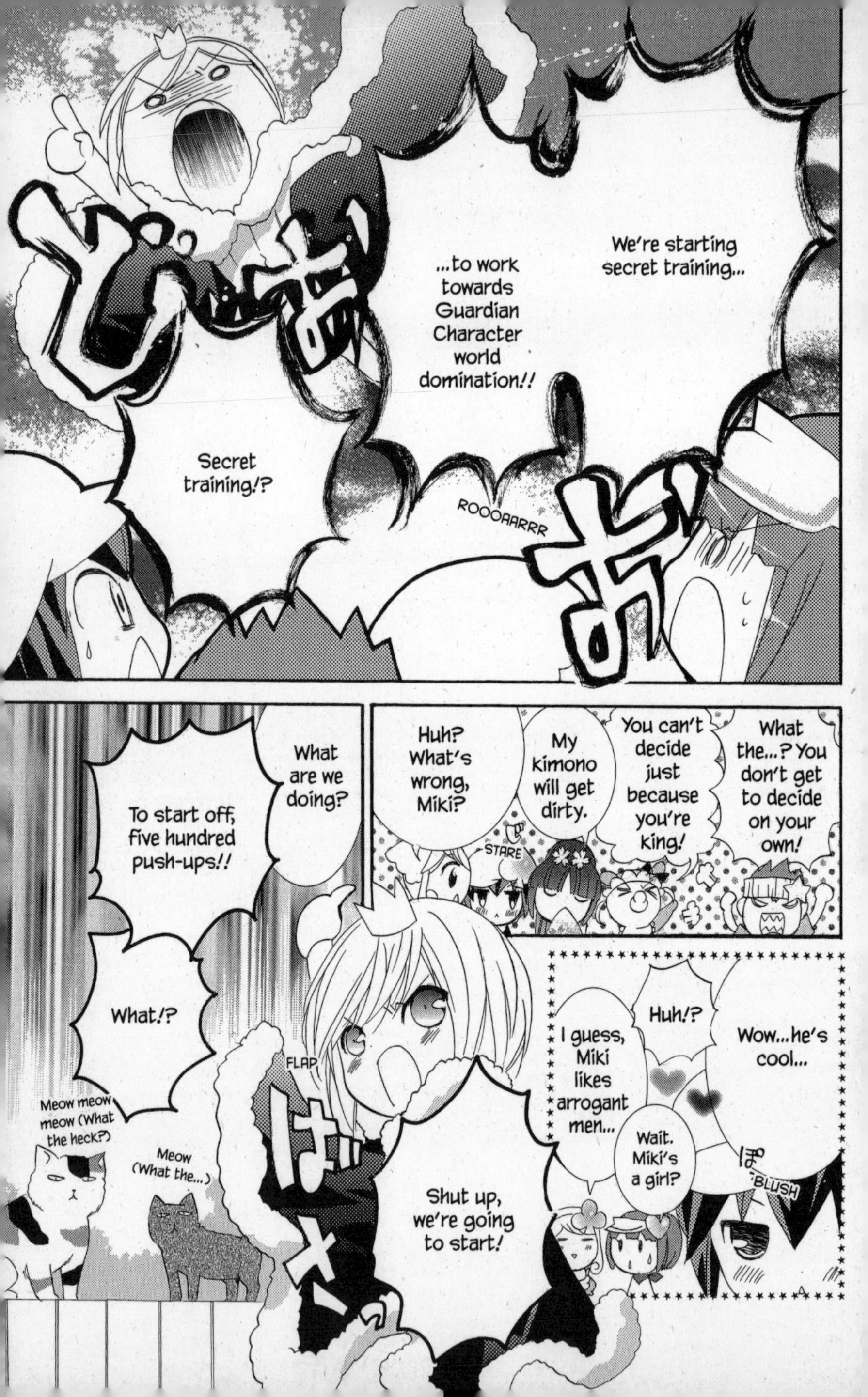
We're starting secret training...
...to work towards Guardian Character world domination!!
ROOOARRRR
Secret training!?
What the...? You don't get to decide on your own!
You can't decide just because you're king!
My kimono will get dirty.
Huh? What's wrong, Miki?
STARE
Wow...he's cool...
Huh!?
I guess, Miki likes arrogant men...
Wait. Miki's a girl?
BLUSH
What are we doing?
To start off, five hundred push-ups!!
What!?
Shut up, we're going to start!
FLAP
Meow (What the...)
Meow meow meow (What the heck?)

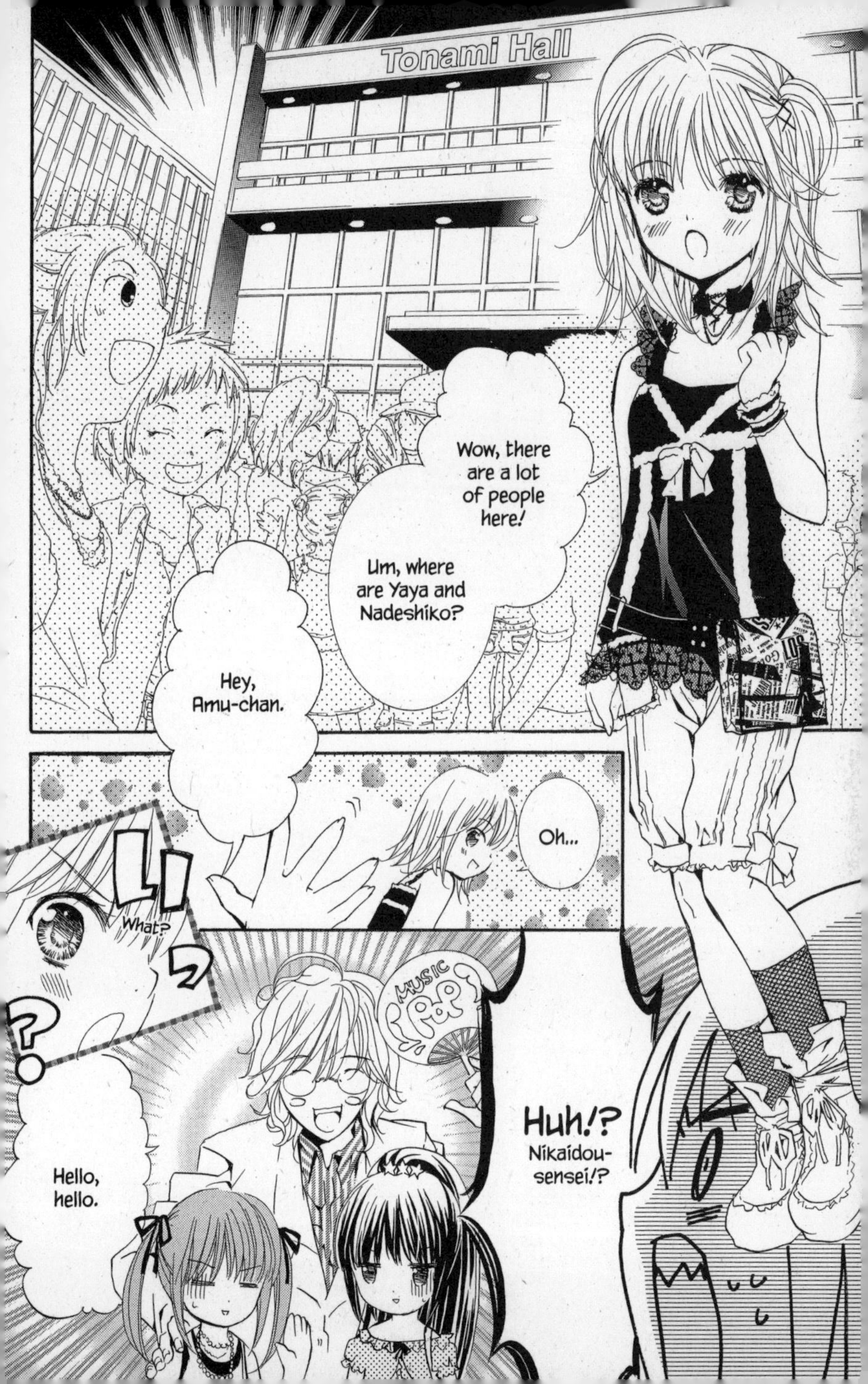
Tonami Hall
Wow, there are a lot of people here!
Um, where are Yaya and Nadeshiko?
Hey, Amu-chan.
Oh...
What?
Huh!? Nikaidou-sensei!?
MUSIC POP
Hello, hello.

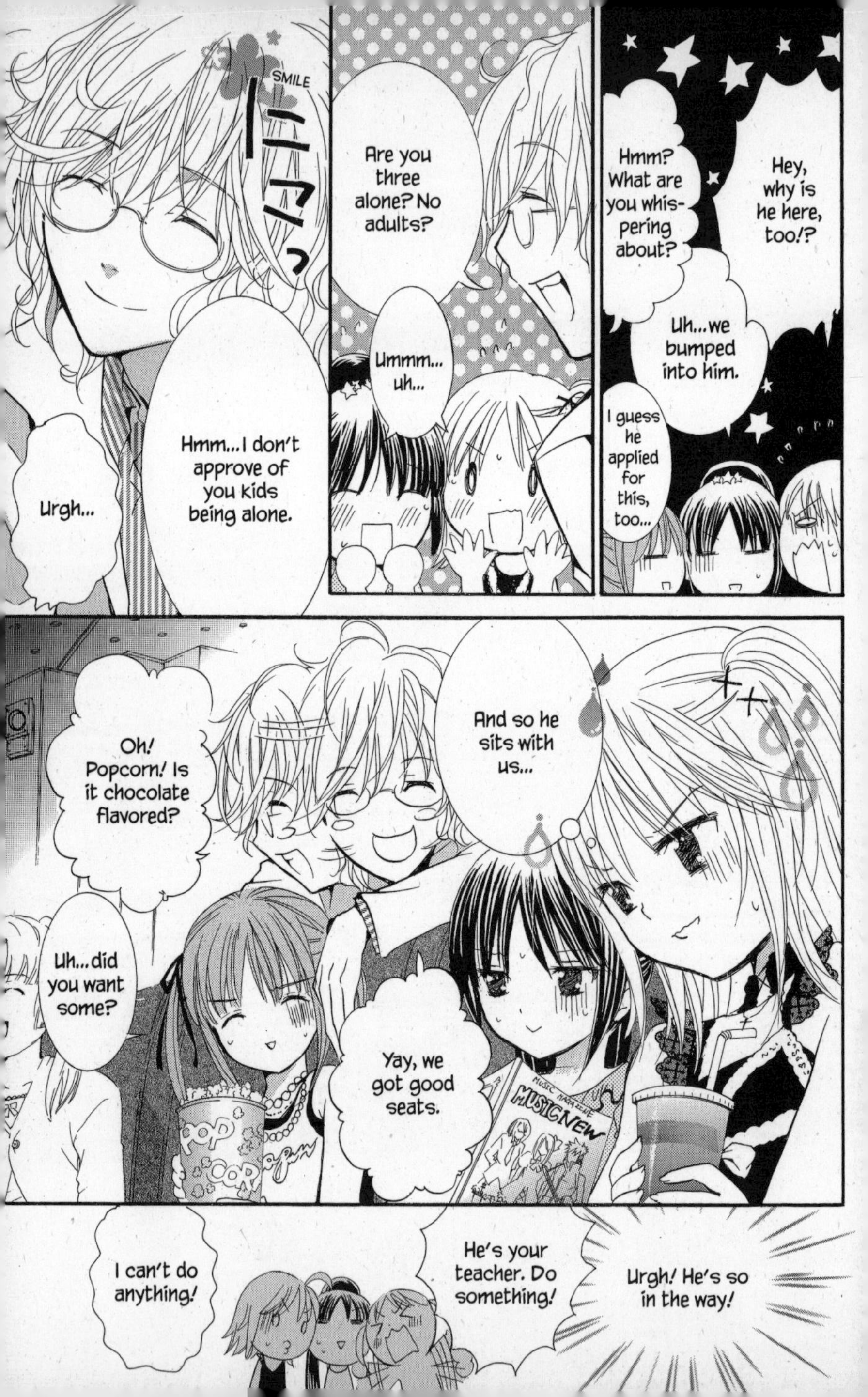
Hey, why is he here, too!?
Hmm? What are you whispering about?
Uh...we bumped into him.
I guess he applied for this, too...
Are you three alone? No adults?
Ummm... uh...
SMILE
ニコッ
Hmm...I don't approve of you kids being alone.
Urgh...
And so he sits with us...
Oh! Popcorn! Is it chocolate flavored?
Yay, we got good seats.
MUSIC NEW
Uh...did you want some?
POP CORN
Urgh! He's so in the way!
He's your teacher. Do something!
I can't do anything!

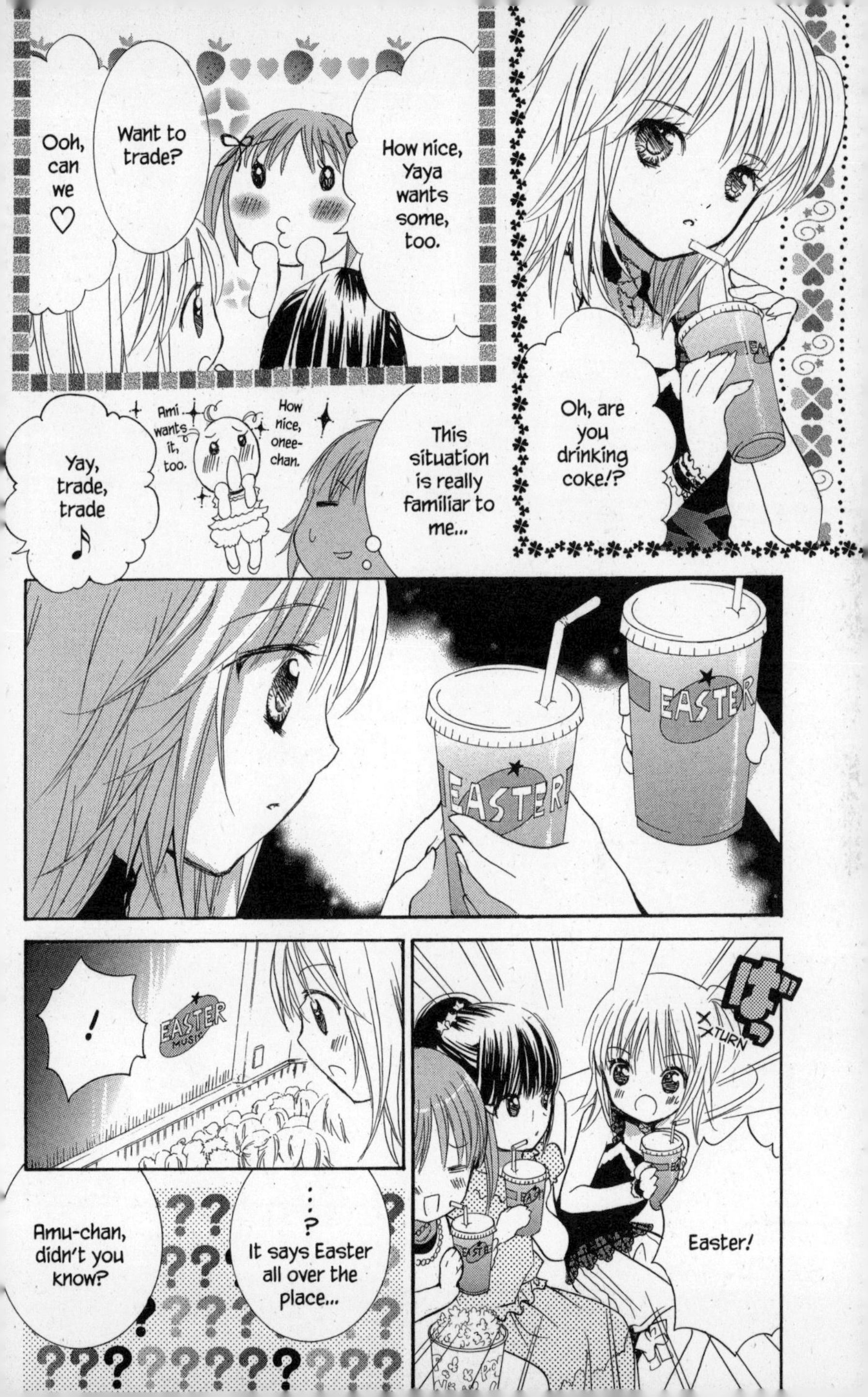

Oh, are you drinking coke!?
How nice, Yaya wants some, too.
Want to trade?
Ooh, can we ♡
This situation is really familiar to me...
How nice, onee-chan.
Ami wants it, too.
Yay, trade, trade ♪
EASTER
EASTER
TURN
Easter!
!
EASTER MUSIC
...? It says Easter all over the place...
Amu-chan, didn't you know?

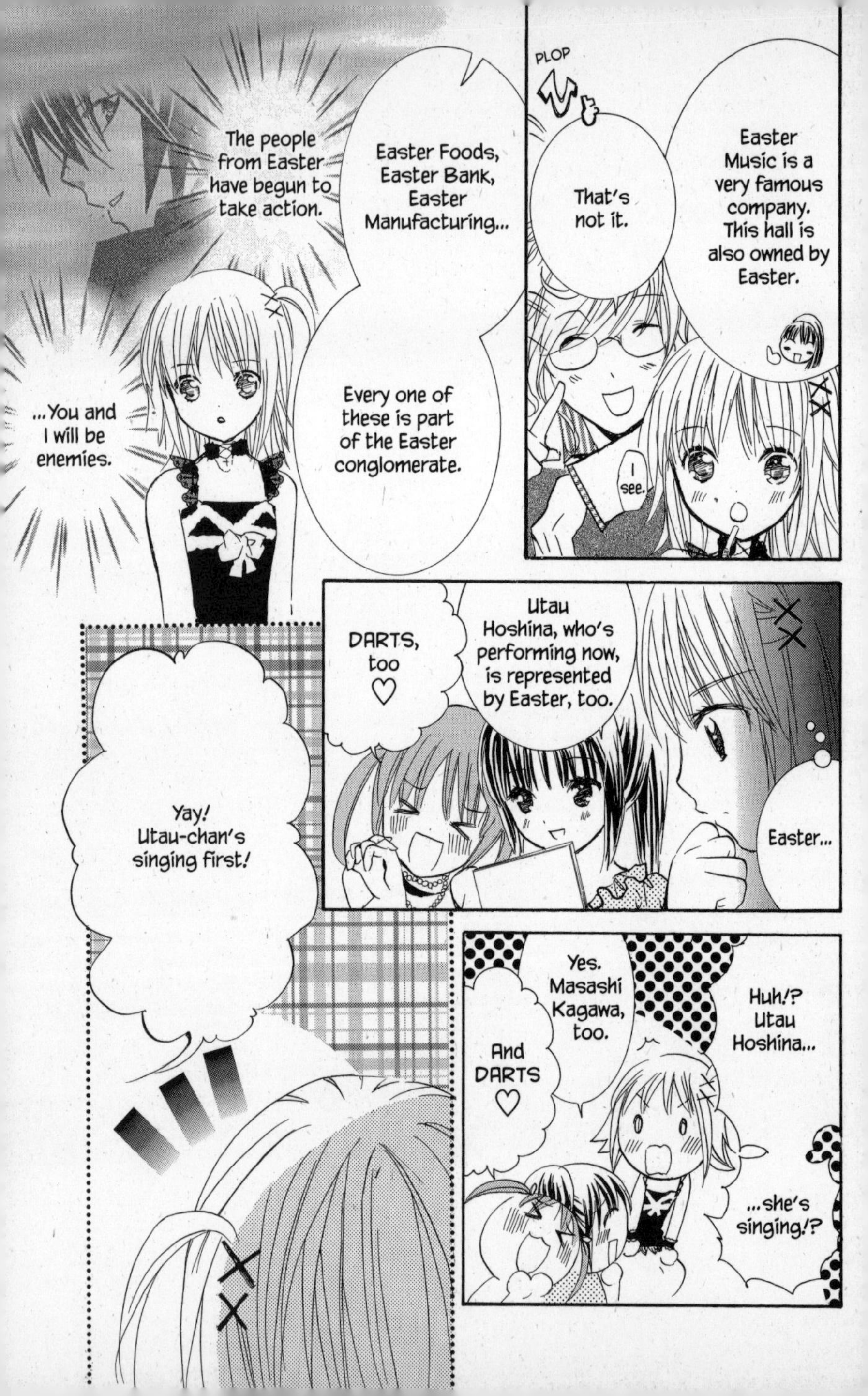
PLOP
Easter Music is a very famous company. This hall is also owned by Easter.
That's not it.
I see.
Easter Foods, Easter Bank, Easter Manufacturing...
Every one of these is part of the Easter conglomerate.
The people from Easter have begun to take action.
...You and I will be enemies.
Easter...
Utau Hoshina, who's performing now, is represented by Easter, too.
DARTS, too ♡
Huh!? Utau Hoshina...
Yes. Masashi Kagawa, too.
And DARTS ♡
...she's singing!?
Yay! Utau-chan's singing first!

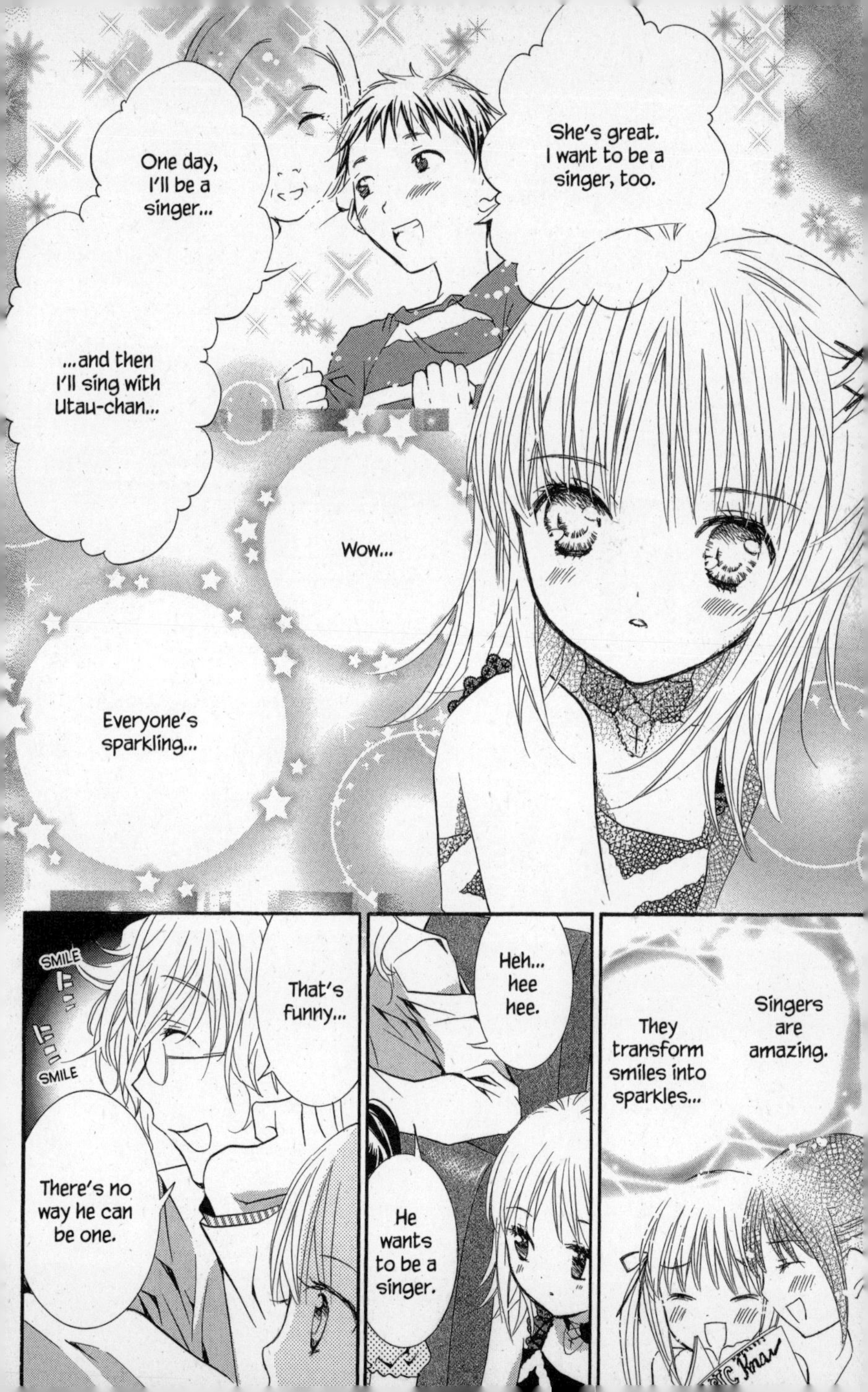
She's great. I want to be a singer, too.
One day, I'll be a singer...
...and then I'll sing with Utau-chan...
Wow...
Everyone's sparkling...
Singers are amazing.
They transform smiles into sparkles...
Heh... hee hee.
He wants to be a singer.
That's funny...
SMILE
SMILE
There's no way he can be one.

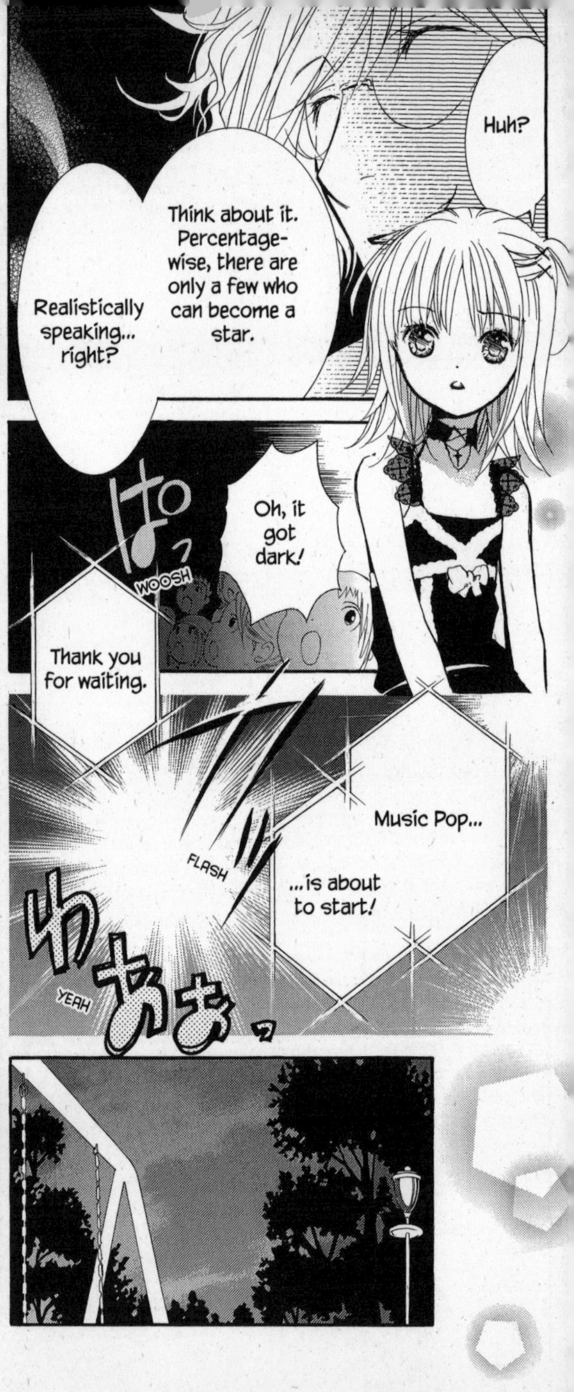
Huh?
Think about it. Percentage-wise, there are only a few who can become a star.
Realistically speaking... right?
Oh, it got dark!
WOOSH
Thank you for waiting.
Music Pop...
...is about to start!
FLASH
YEAH

character profile

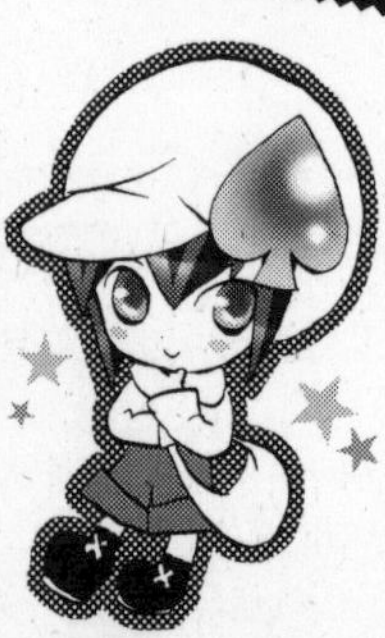

ミキ

MIKI

Guardian Character of: Amu
Special Skill: Art
Doesn't like: Being controlled

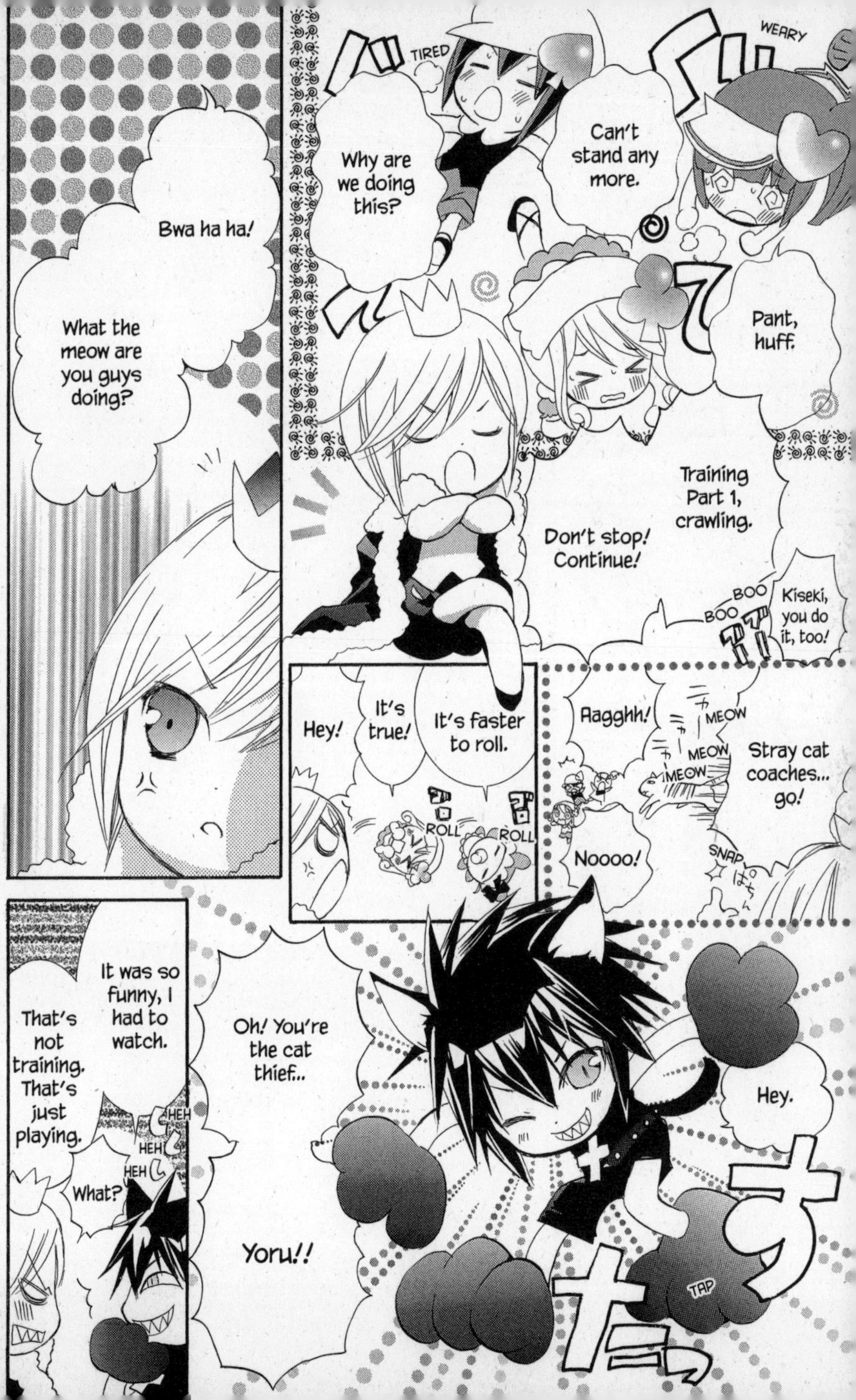

WEARY
Can't stand any more.
TIRED
Why are we doing this?
Pant, huff.
Training Part 1, crawling.
Don't stop! Continue!
Kiseki, you do it, too!
BOO
BOO
Stray cat coaches... go!
MEOW
MEOW
MEOW
Aagghh!
SNAP
Noooo!
It's faster to roll.
It's true!
Hey!
ROLL
ROLL
Bwa ha ha!
What the meow are you guys doing?
Hey.
TAP
Oh! You're the cat thief...
Yoru!!
It was so funny, I had to watch.
HEH
HEH
HEH
That's not training. That's just playing.
What?

Shugo Chara!

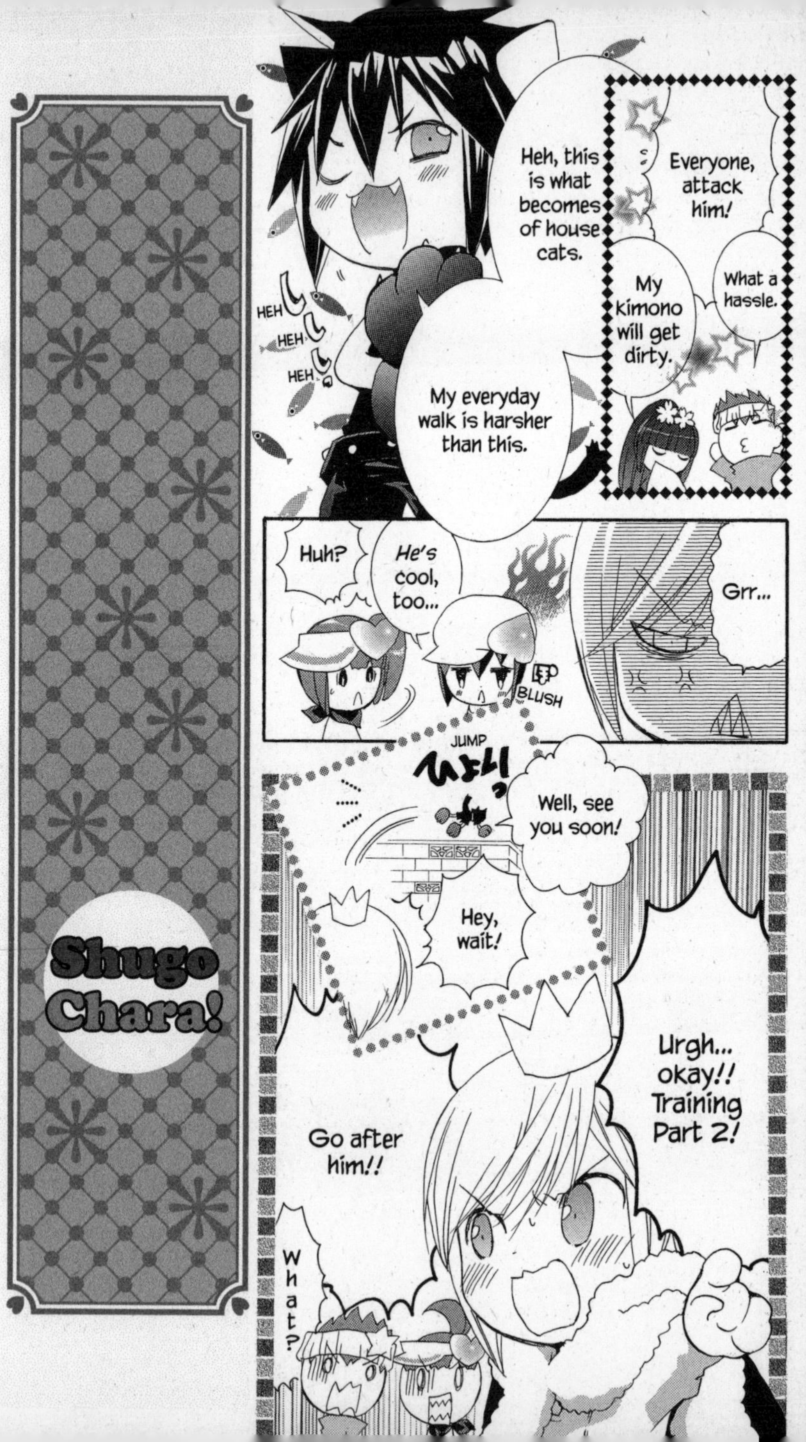
Everyone, attack him!
What a hassle.
My kimono will get dirty.
Heh, this is what becomes of house cats.
HEH
HEH
HEH
My everyday walk is harsher than this.
Grr...
He's cool, too...
BLUSH
Huh?
JUMP
Well, see you soon!
Hey, wait!
Urgh... okay!! Training Part 2!
Go after him!!
What?

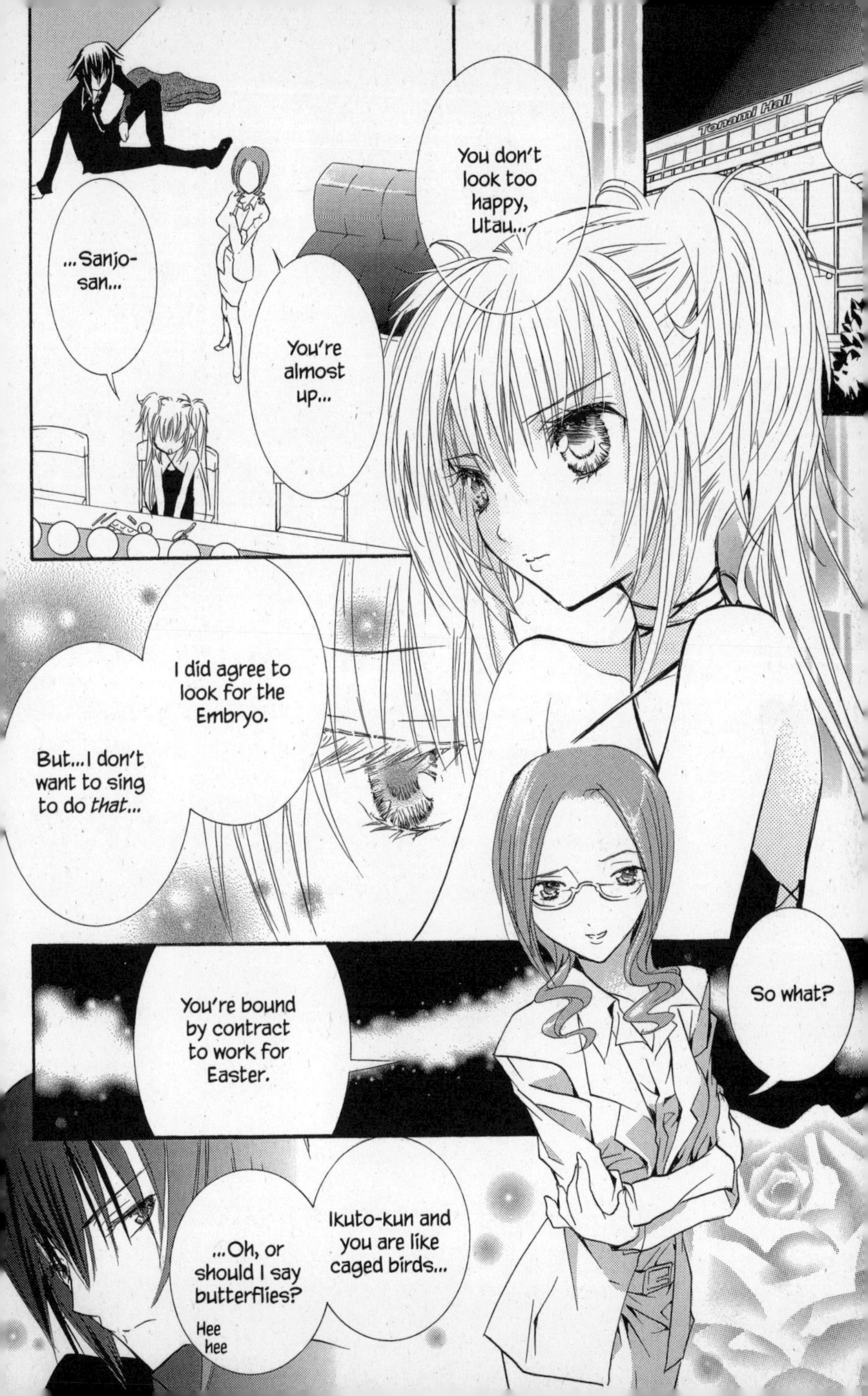
Tonami Hall
You don't look too happy, Utau...
You're almost up...
...Sanjo-san...
I did agree to look for the Embryo.
But...I don't want to sing to do *that*...
So what?
You're bound by contract to work for Easter.
Ikuto-kun and you are like caged birds...
...Oh, or should I say butterflies?
Hee hee

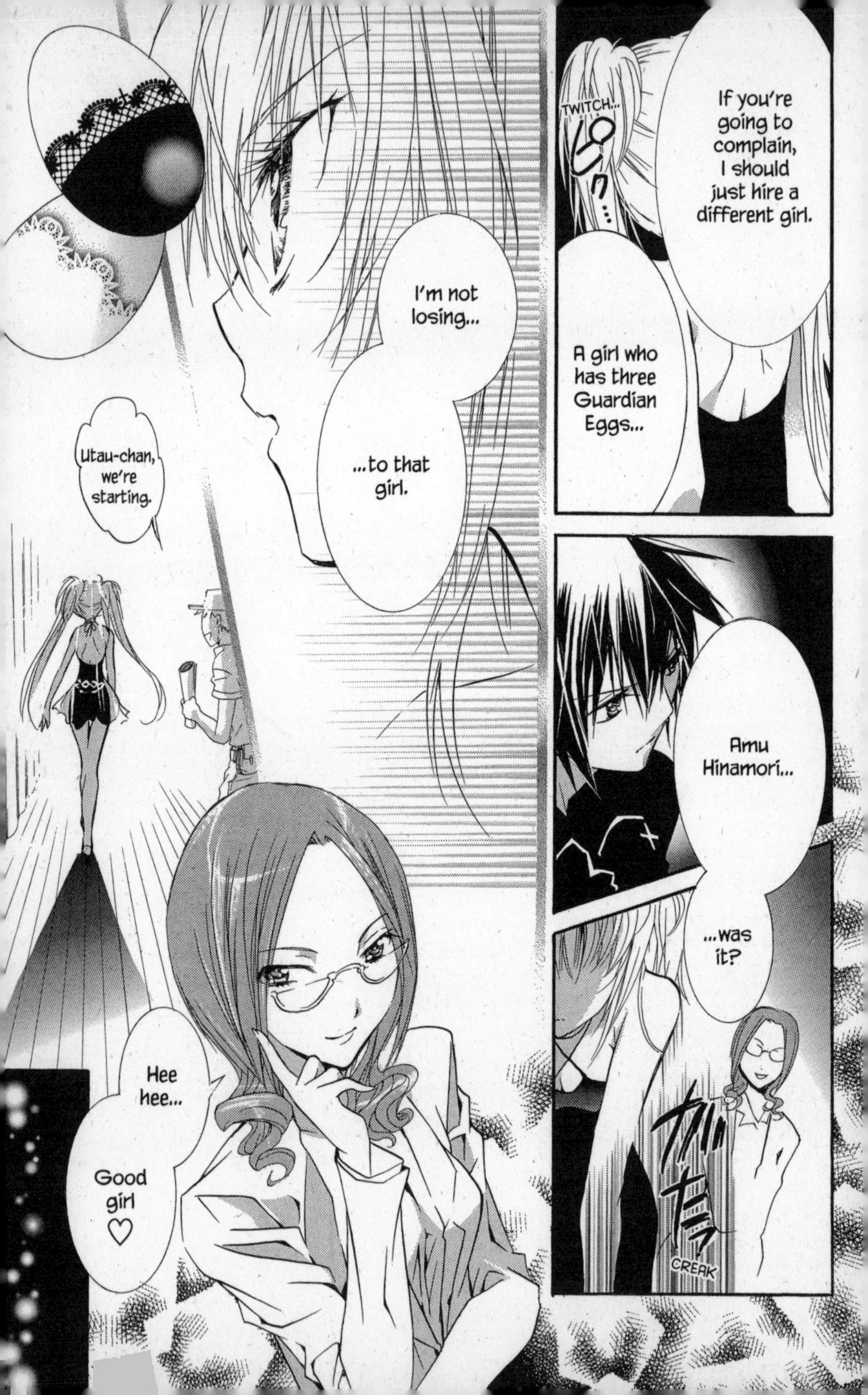
If you're going to complain, I should just hire a different girl.
TWITCH...
A girl who has three Guardian Eggs...
Amu Hinamori...
...was it?
CREAK
I'm not losing...
...to that girl.
Utau-chan, we're starting.
Hee hee...
Good girl ♡

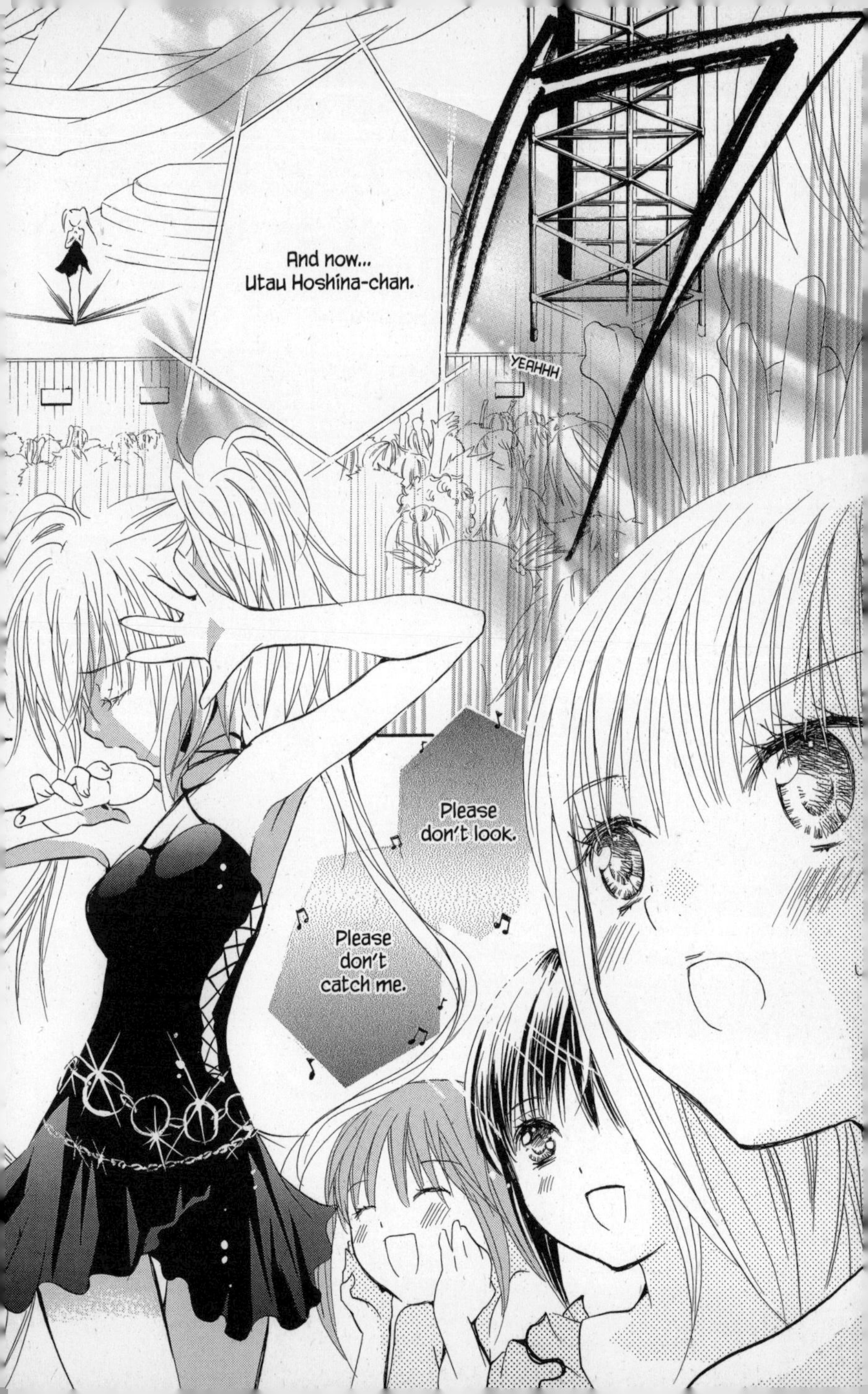
And now... Utau Hoshina-chan.
YEAHHH
Please don't look.
Please don't catch me.

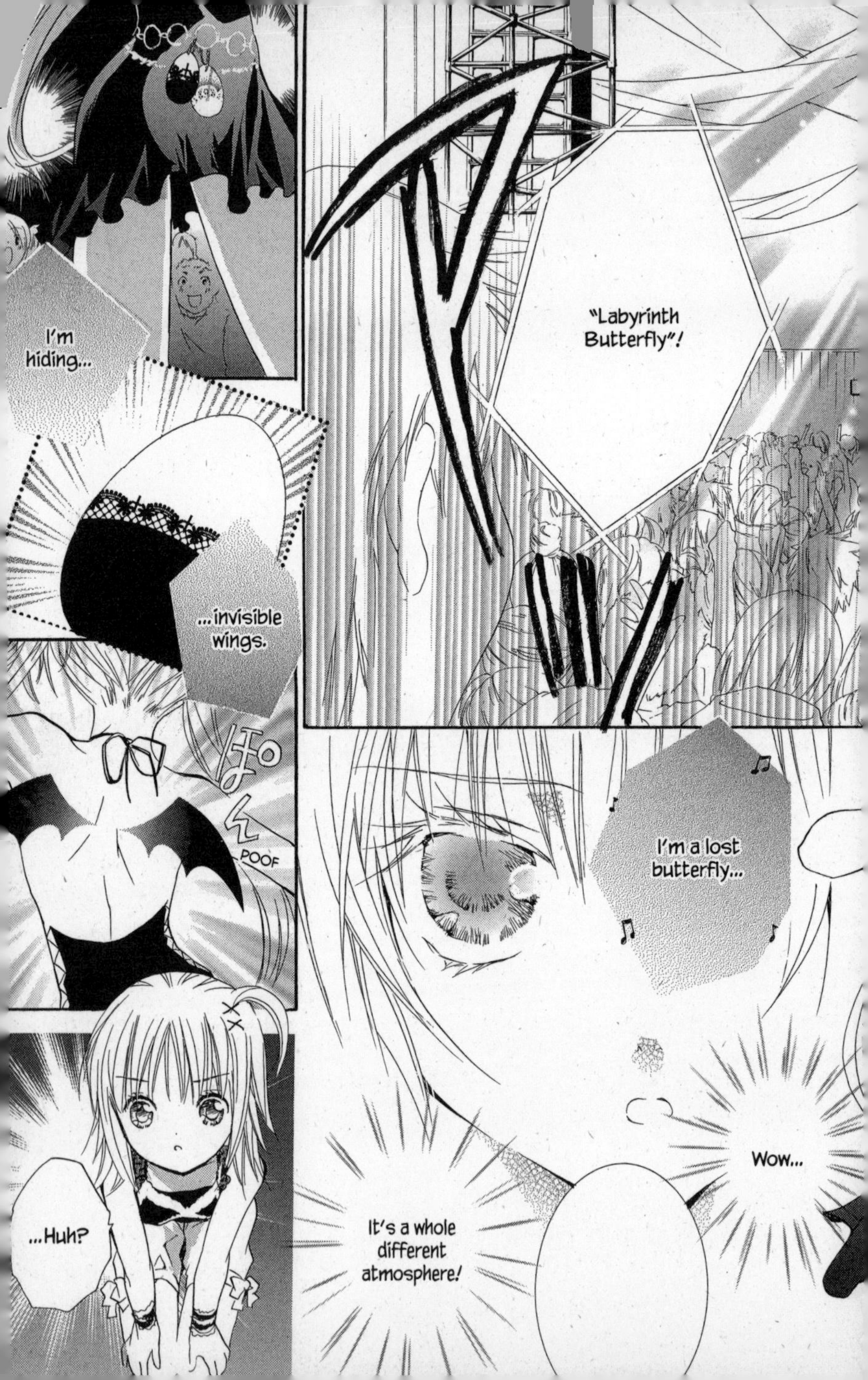
"Labyrinth Butterfly"!
I'm hiding...
...invisible wings.
ほん
POOF
I'm a lost butterfly...
Wow...
It's a whole different atmosphere!
...Huh?

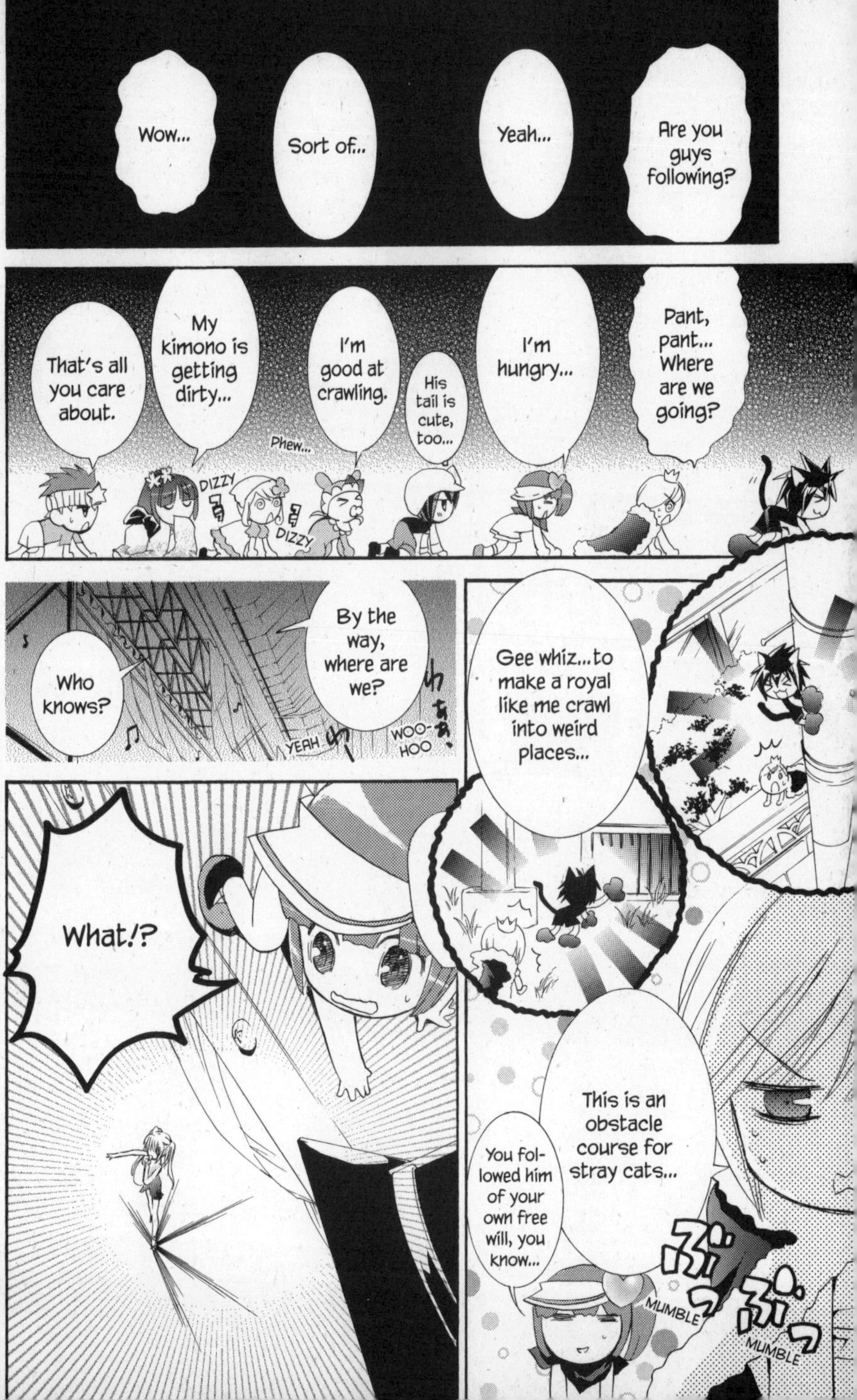
Are you guys following?
Yeah...
Sort of...
Wow...
Pant, pant... Where are we going?
I'm hungry...
His tail is cute, too...
I'm good at crawling.
Phew...
DIZZY
DIZZY
My kimono is getting dirty...
That's all you care about.
Gee whiz...to make a royal like me crawl into weird places...
This is an obstacle course for stray cats...
You followed him of your own free will, you know...
MUMBLE
MUMBLE
By the way, where are we?
Who knows?
YEAH
WOO-HOO
What!?

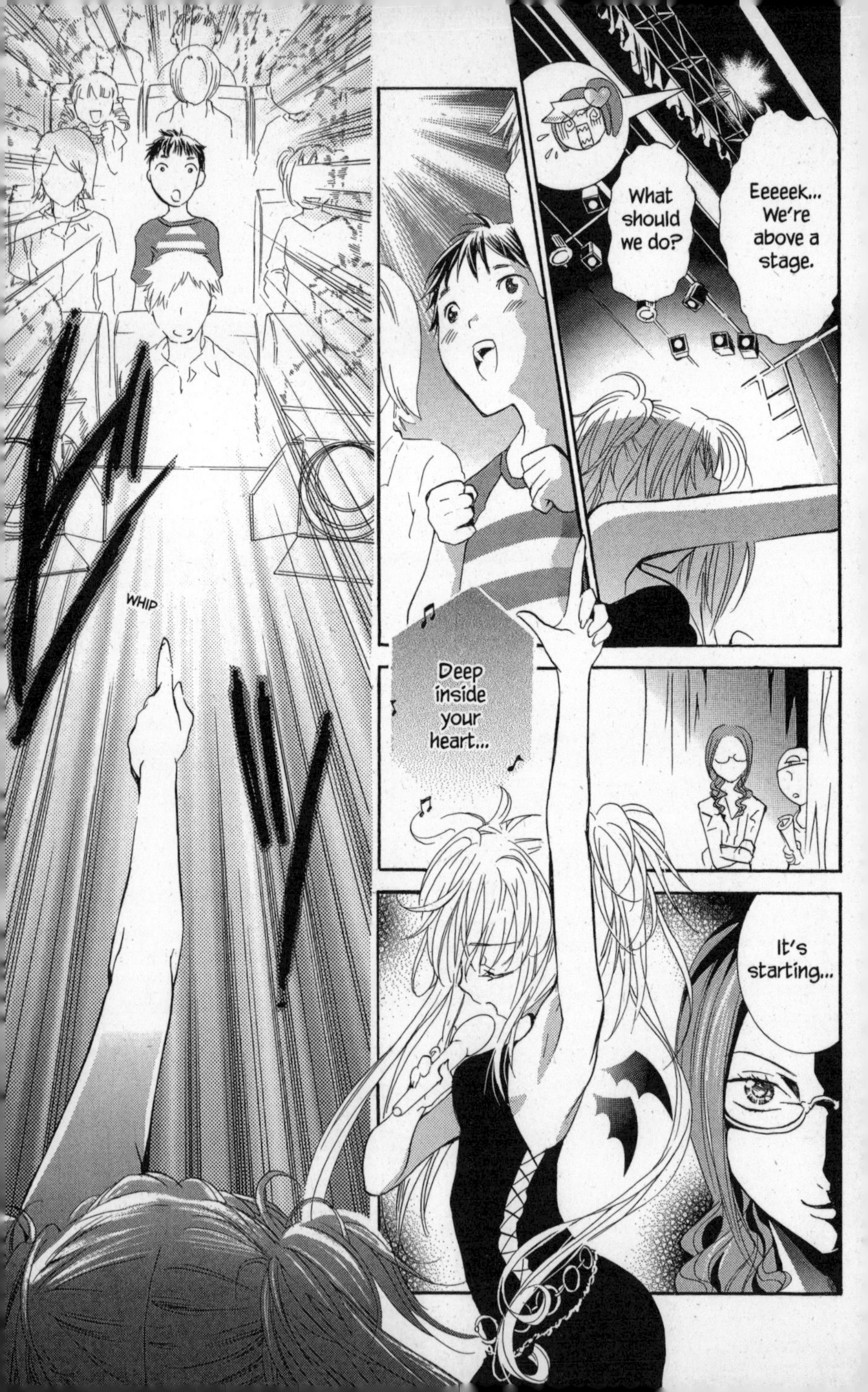
Eeeeek... We're above a stage.
What should we do?
Deep inside your heart...
It's starting...
WHIP

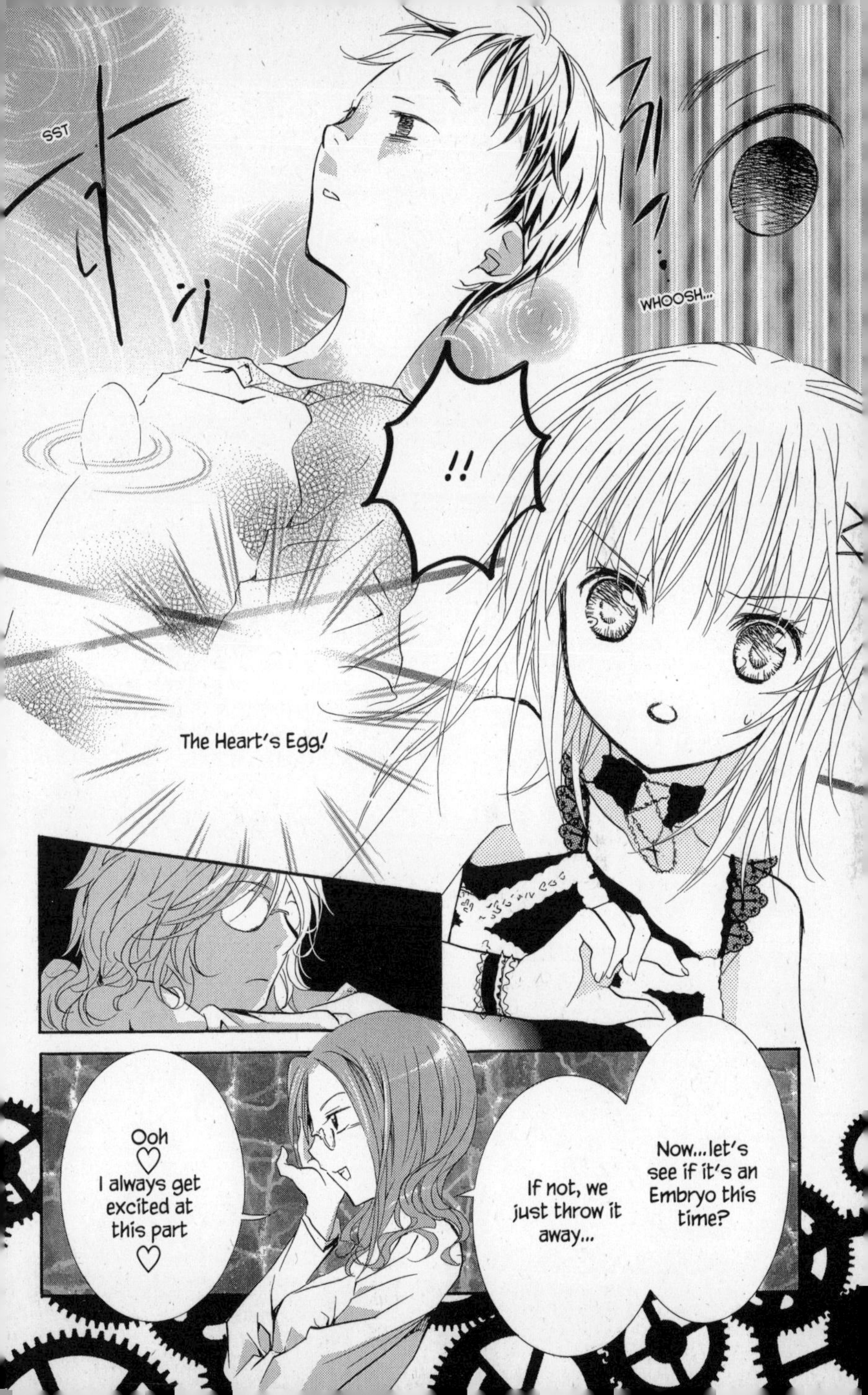
WHOOSH...
SST
!!
The Heart's Egg!
Now...let's see if it's an Embryo this time?
If not, we just throw it away...
Ooh ♡ I always get excited at this part ♡

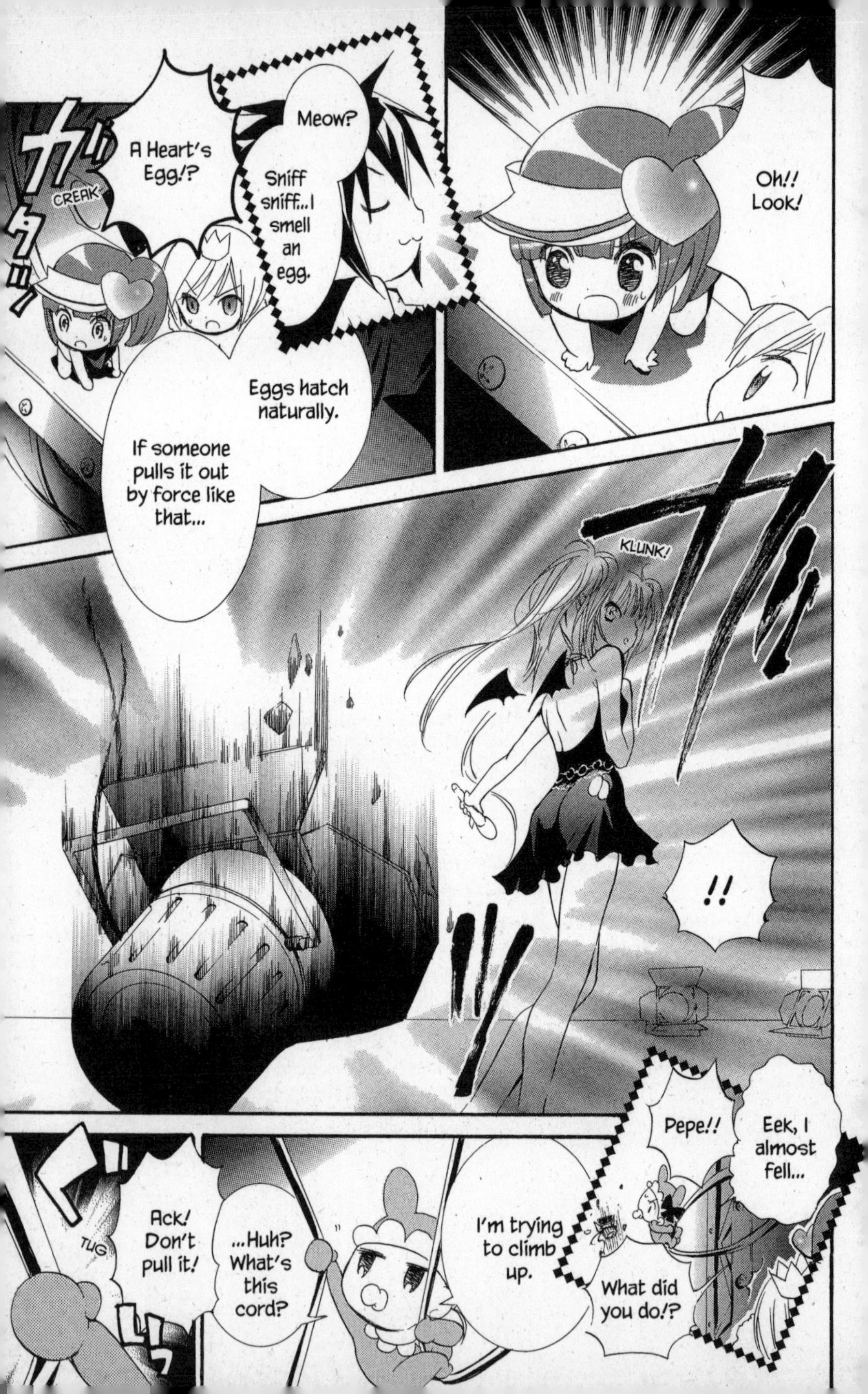
Oh!! Look!
Meow?
Sniff sniff...I smell an egg.
A Heart's Egg!?
CREAK
Eggs hatch naturally.
If someone pulls it out by force like that...
KLUNK!
!!
Eek, I almost fell...
Pepe!!
What did you do!?
I'm trying to climb up.
...Huh? What's this cord?
Ack! Don't pull it!
TUG

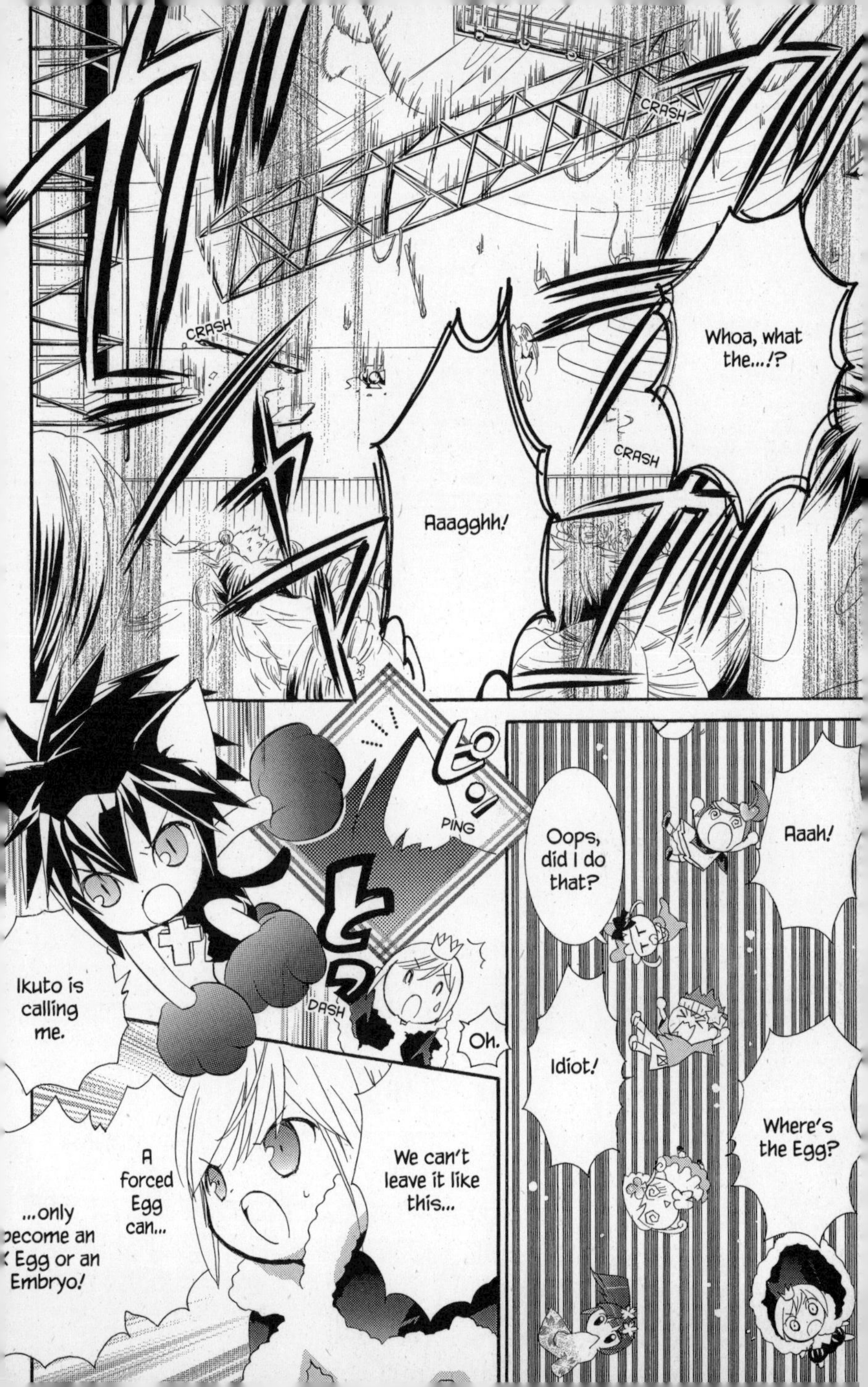
CRASH
Whoa, what the...!?
CRASH
CRASH
Aaagghh!
Aaah!
Oops, did I do that?
Idiot!
Where's the Egg?
PING
DASH
Oh.
Ikuto is calling me.
We can't leave it like this...
A forced Egg can...
...only become an Egg or an Embryo!

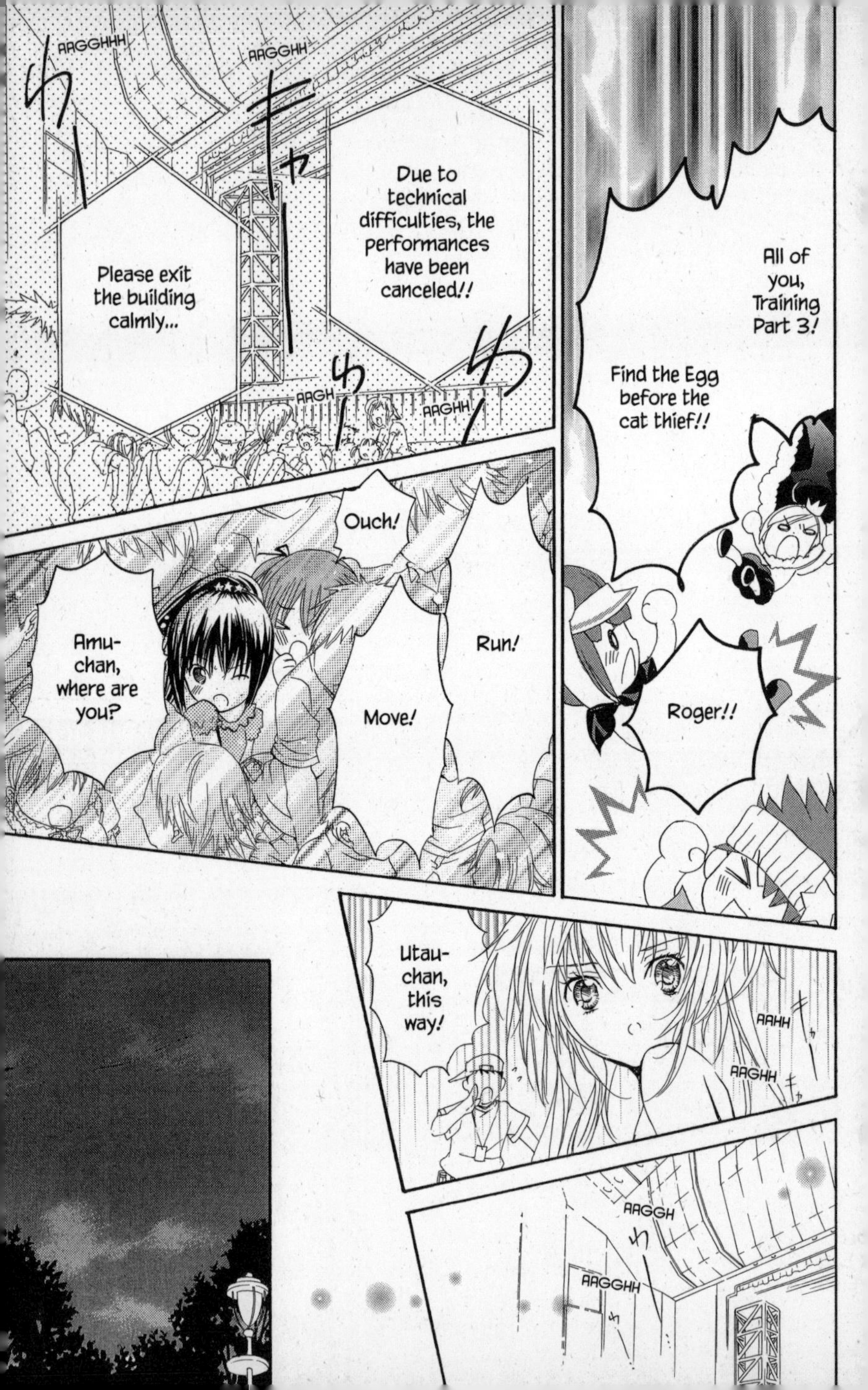
All of you, Training Part 3!
Find the Egg before the cat thief!!
Roger!!
AAGGHH
AAGGHHH
Due to technical difficulties, the performances have been canceled!!
Please exit the building calmly...
AAGHH
AAGH
Ouch!
Run!
Move!
Amu-chan, where are you?
Utau-chan, this way!
AAHH
AAGHH
AAGGH
AAGGHH

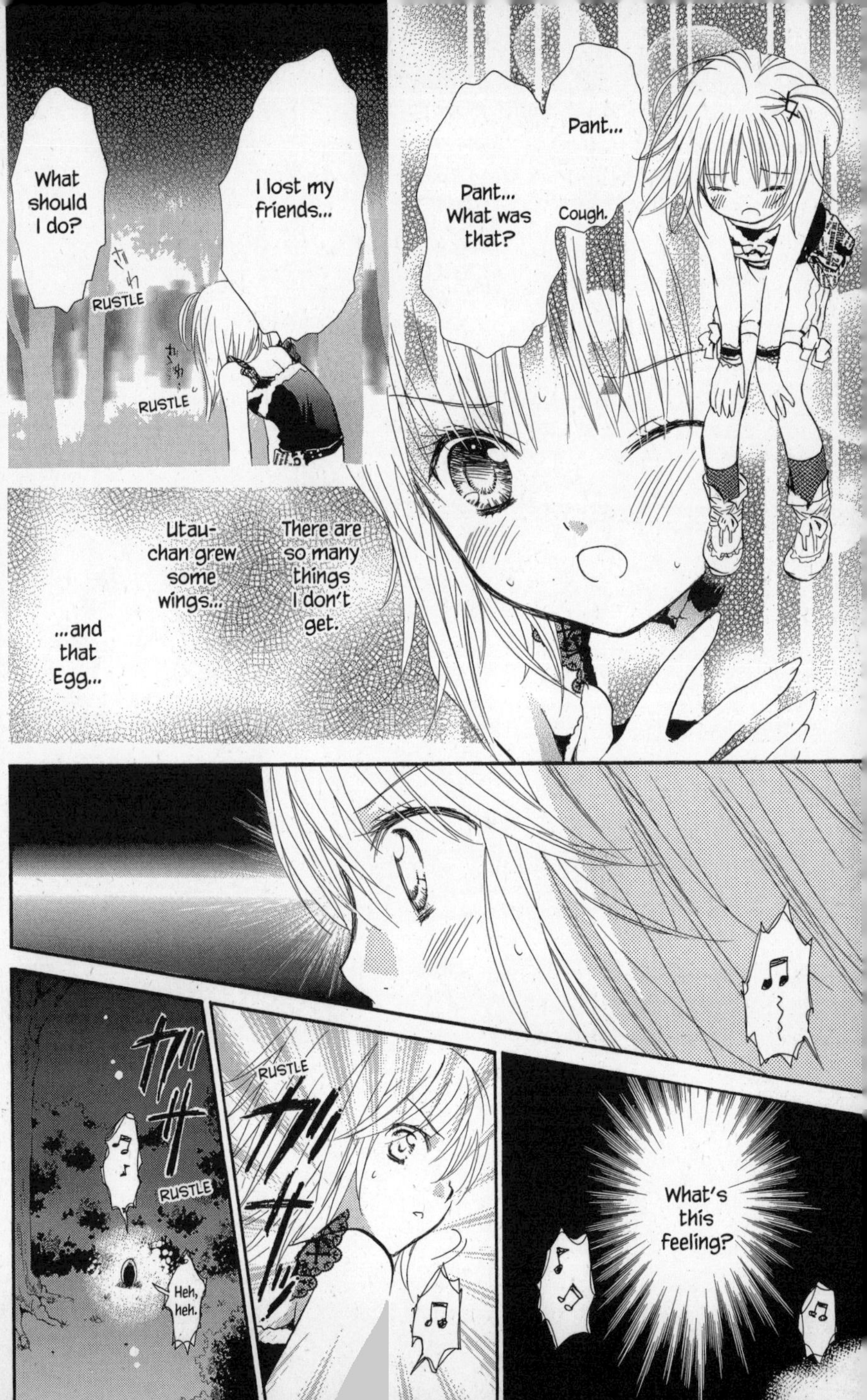

Pant...
Pant... What was that?
Cough.
I lost my friends...
What should I do?
RUSTLE
RUSTLE
There are so many things I don't get.
Utau-chan grew some wings...
...and that Egg...
What's this feeling?
RUSTLE
RUSTLE
Heh, heh.

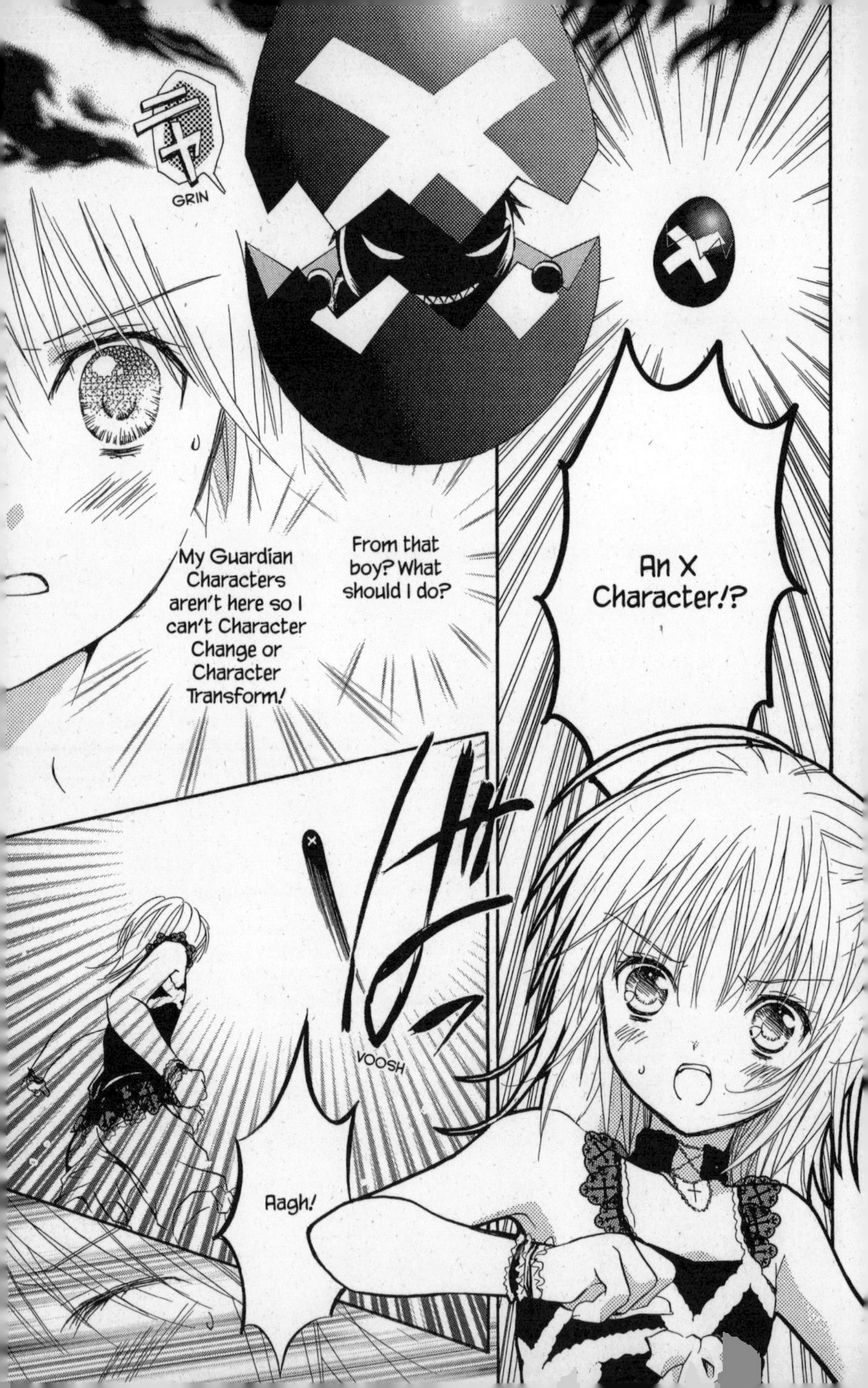
An X Character!?
GRIN
From that boy? What should I do?
My Guardian Characters aren't here so I can't Character Change or Character Transform!
VOOSH
Aagh!

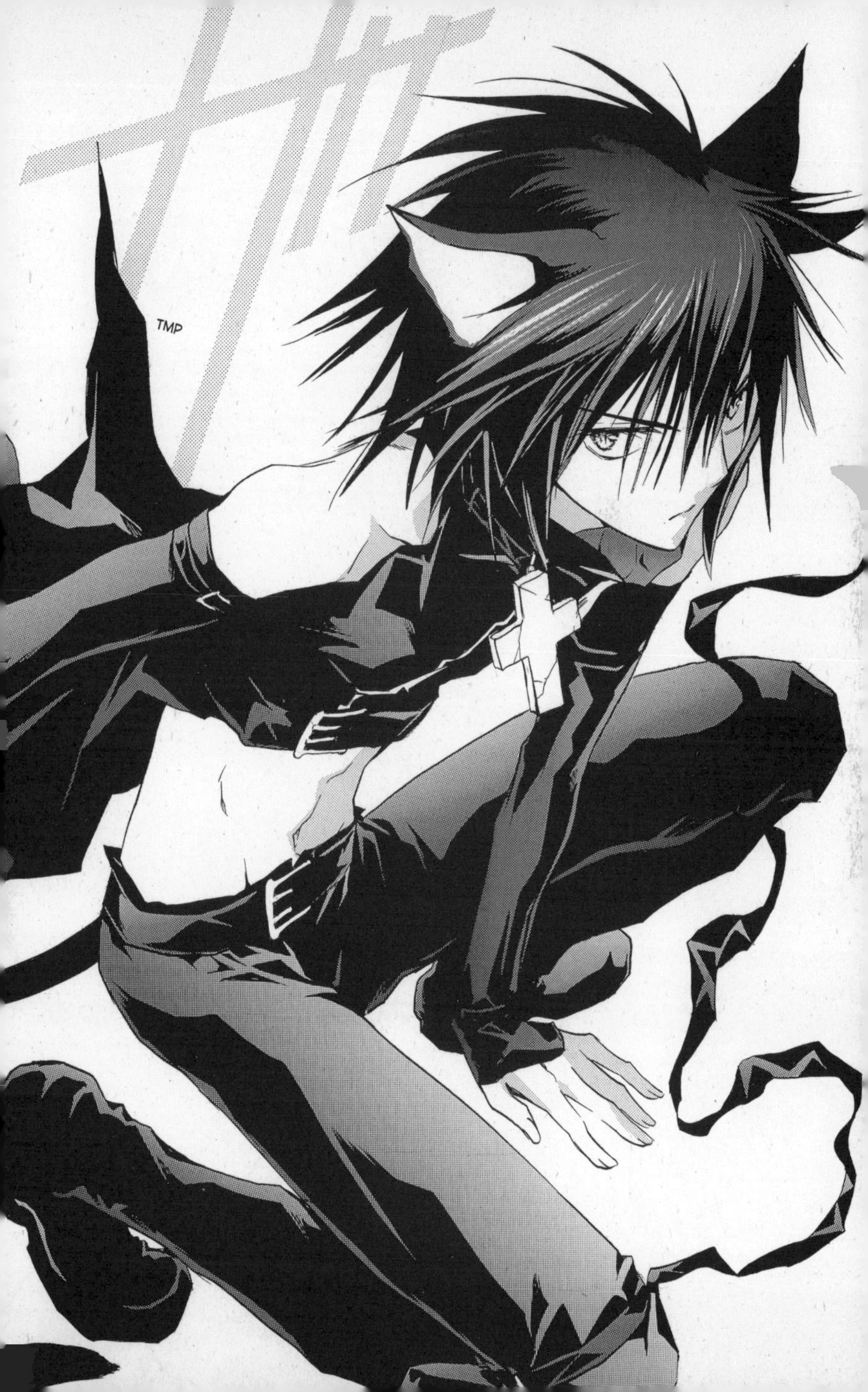
TMP

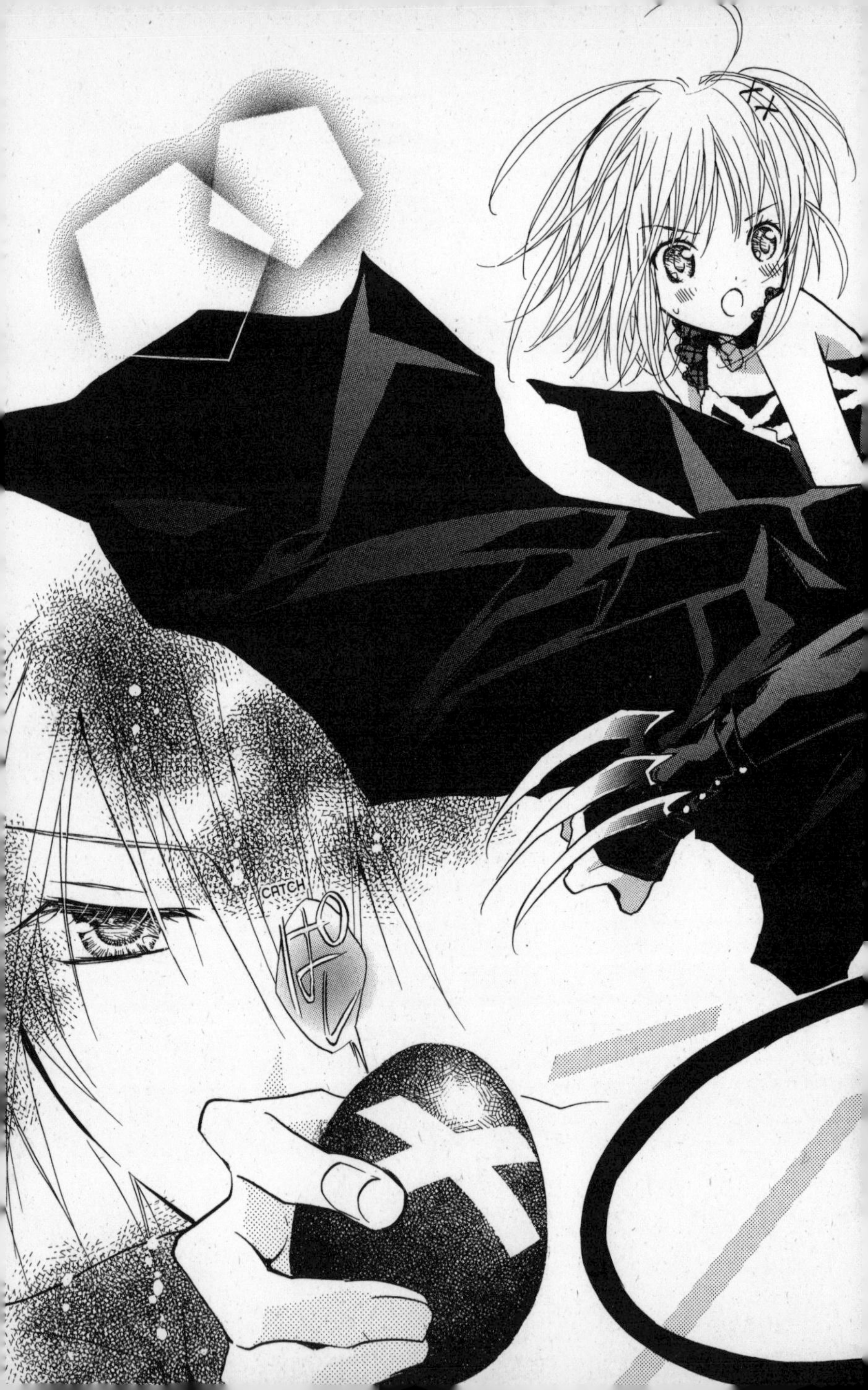
CATCH

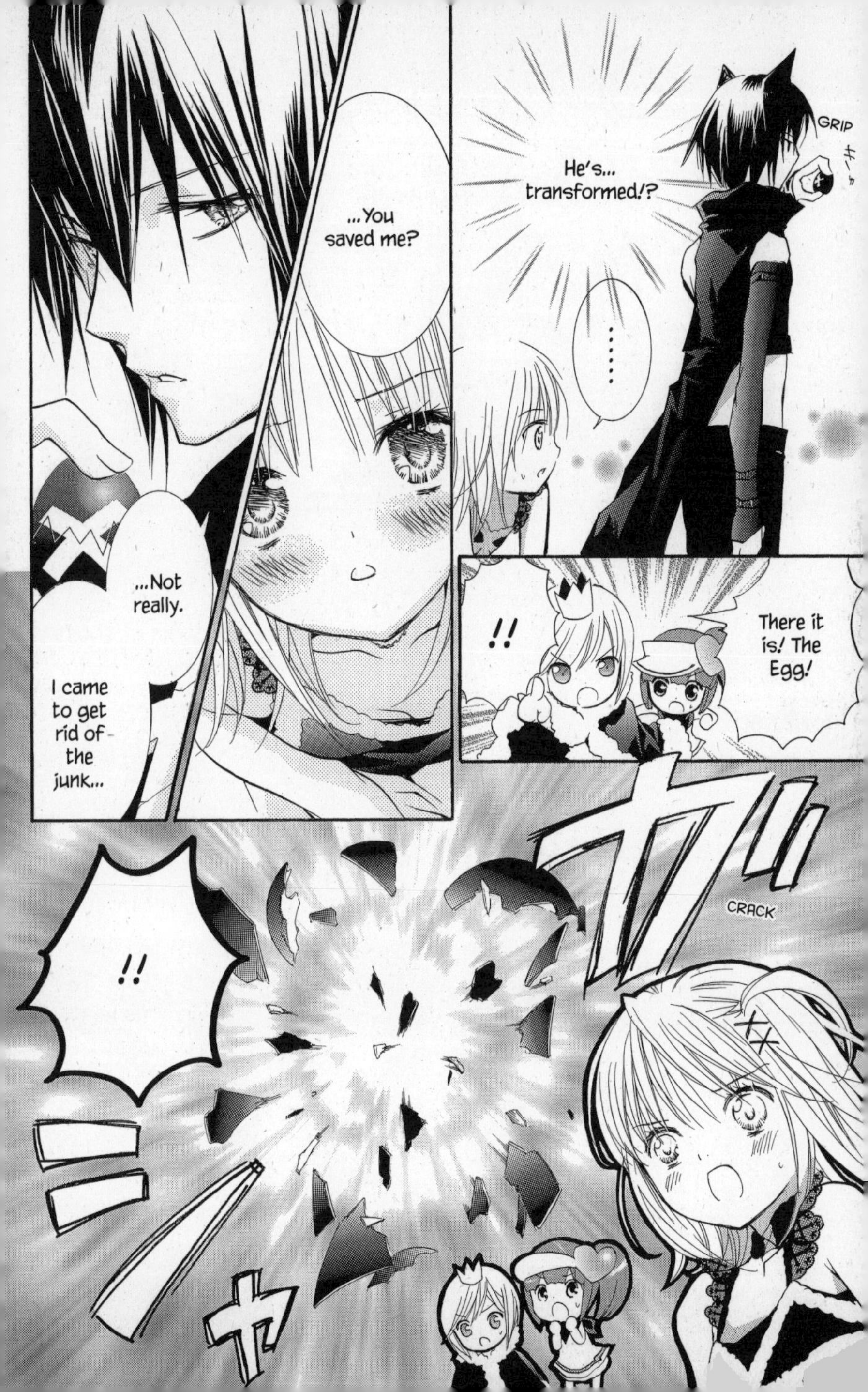
GRIP
He's... transformed!?
......
There it is! The Egg!
!!
...You saved me?
...Not really.
I came to get rid of the junk...
CRACK
!!

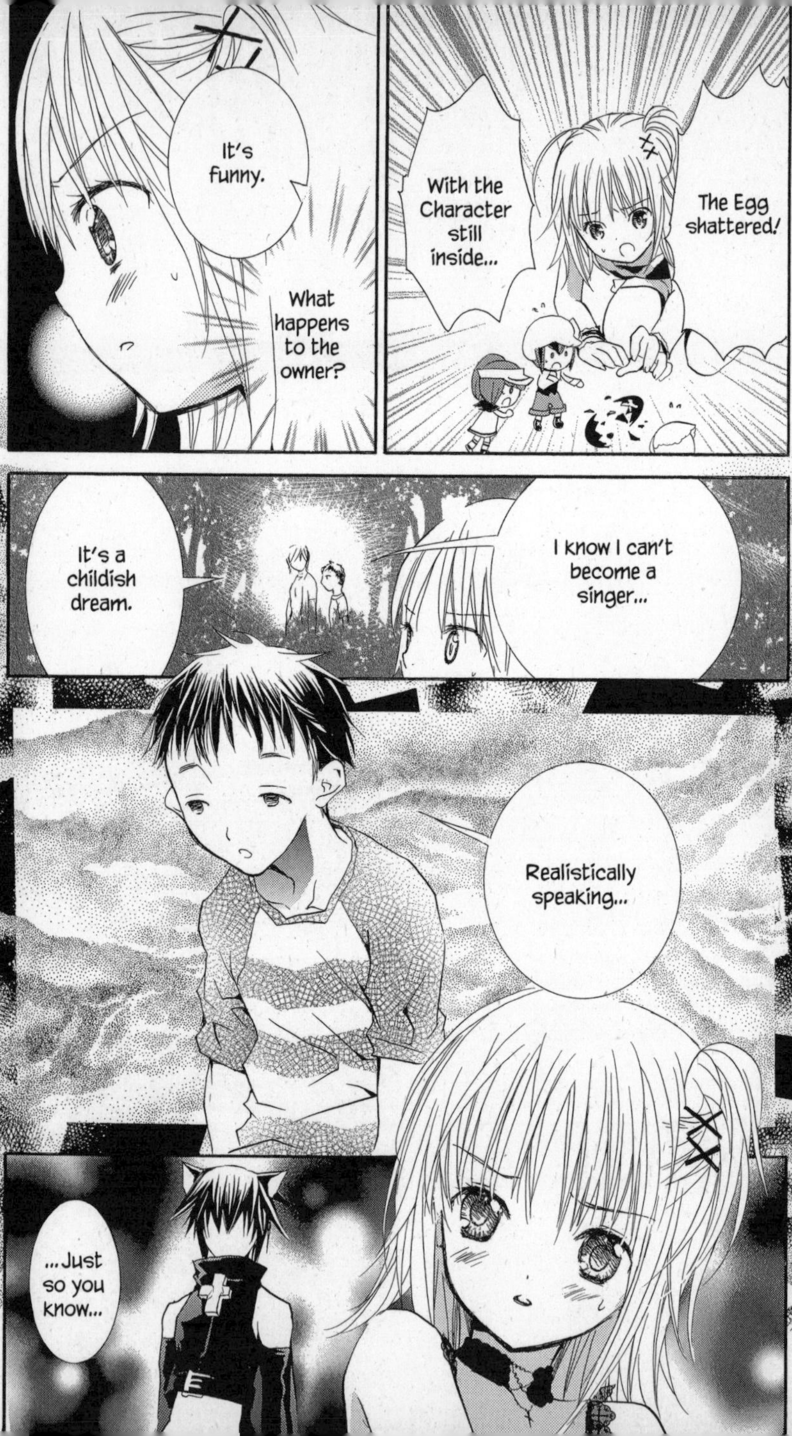
The Egg shattered!
With the Character still inside...
It's funny.
What happens to the owner?
I know I can't become a singer...
It's a childish dream.
Realistically speaking...
...Just so you know...

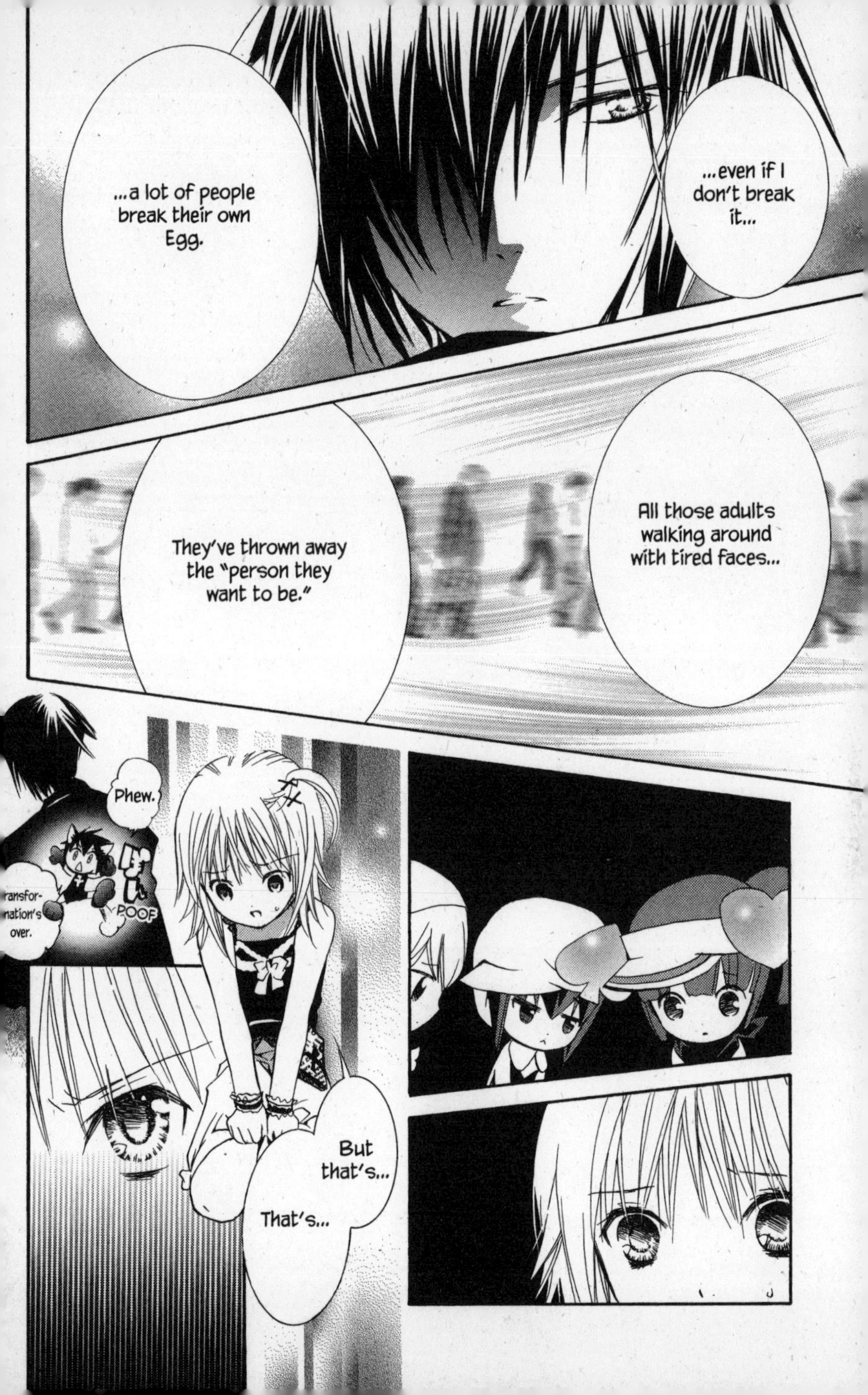
...even if I don't break it...
...a lot of people break their own Egg.
All those adults walking around with tired faces...
They've thrown away the "person they want to be."
Phew.
POOF
ransfor- nation's over.
But that's...
That's...

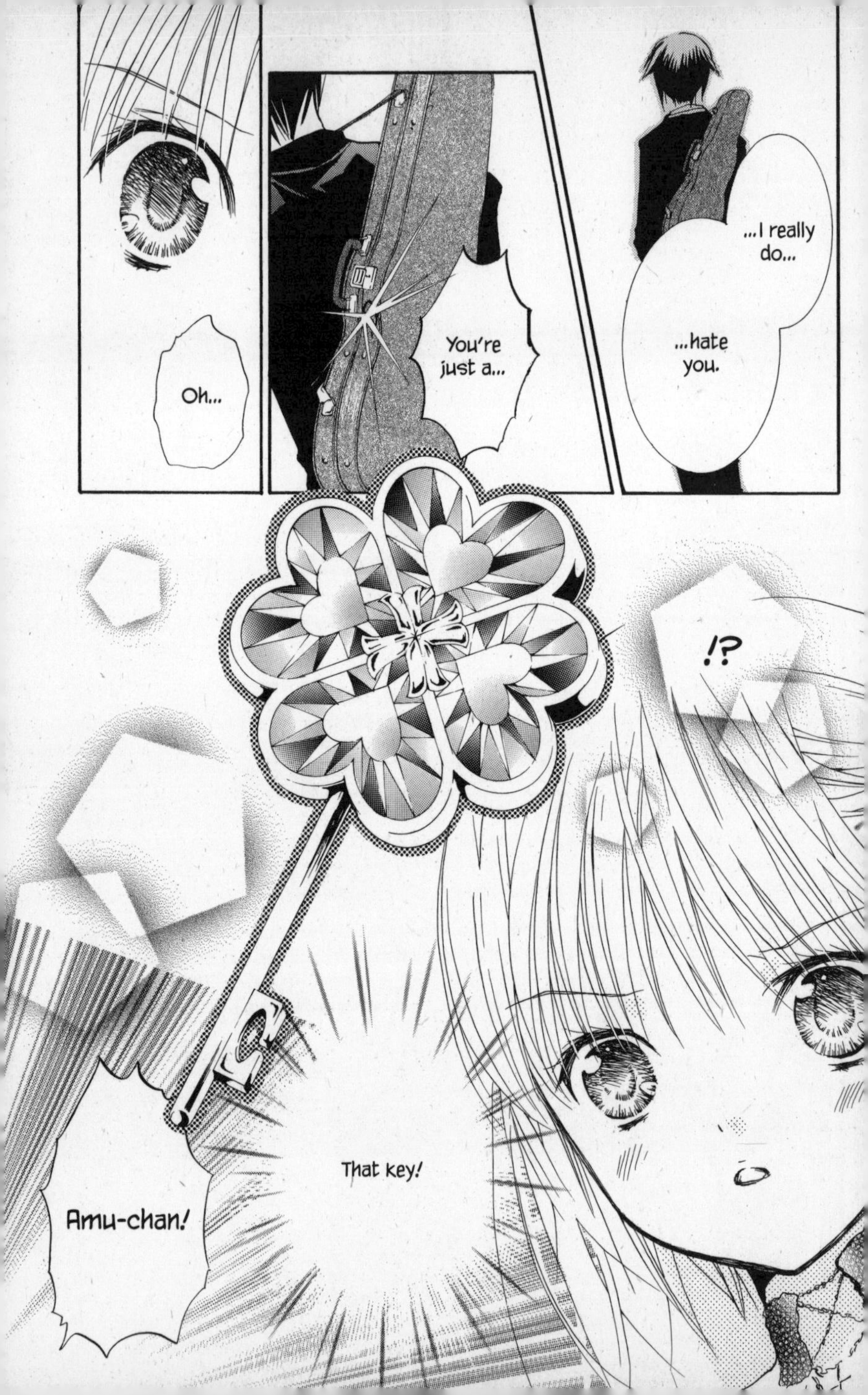
...I really do...
...hate you.
You're just a...
Oh...
!?
That key!
Amu-chan!

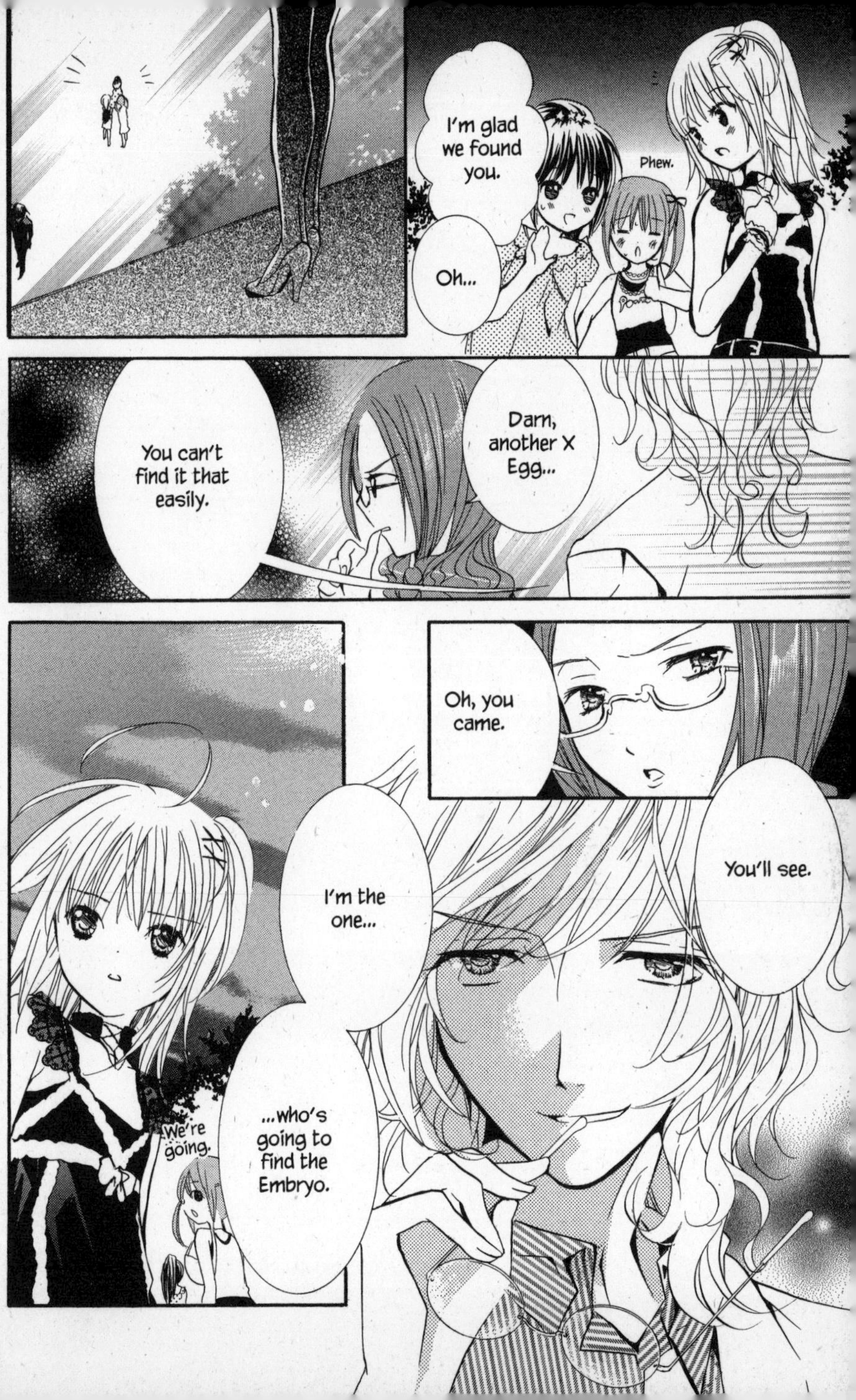
I'm glad we found you.
Phew.
Oh...
Darn, another X Egg...
You can't find it that easily.
Oh, you came.
You'll see.
I'm the one...
...who's going to find the Embryo.
We're going.

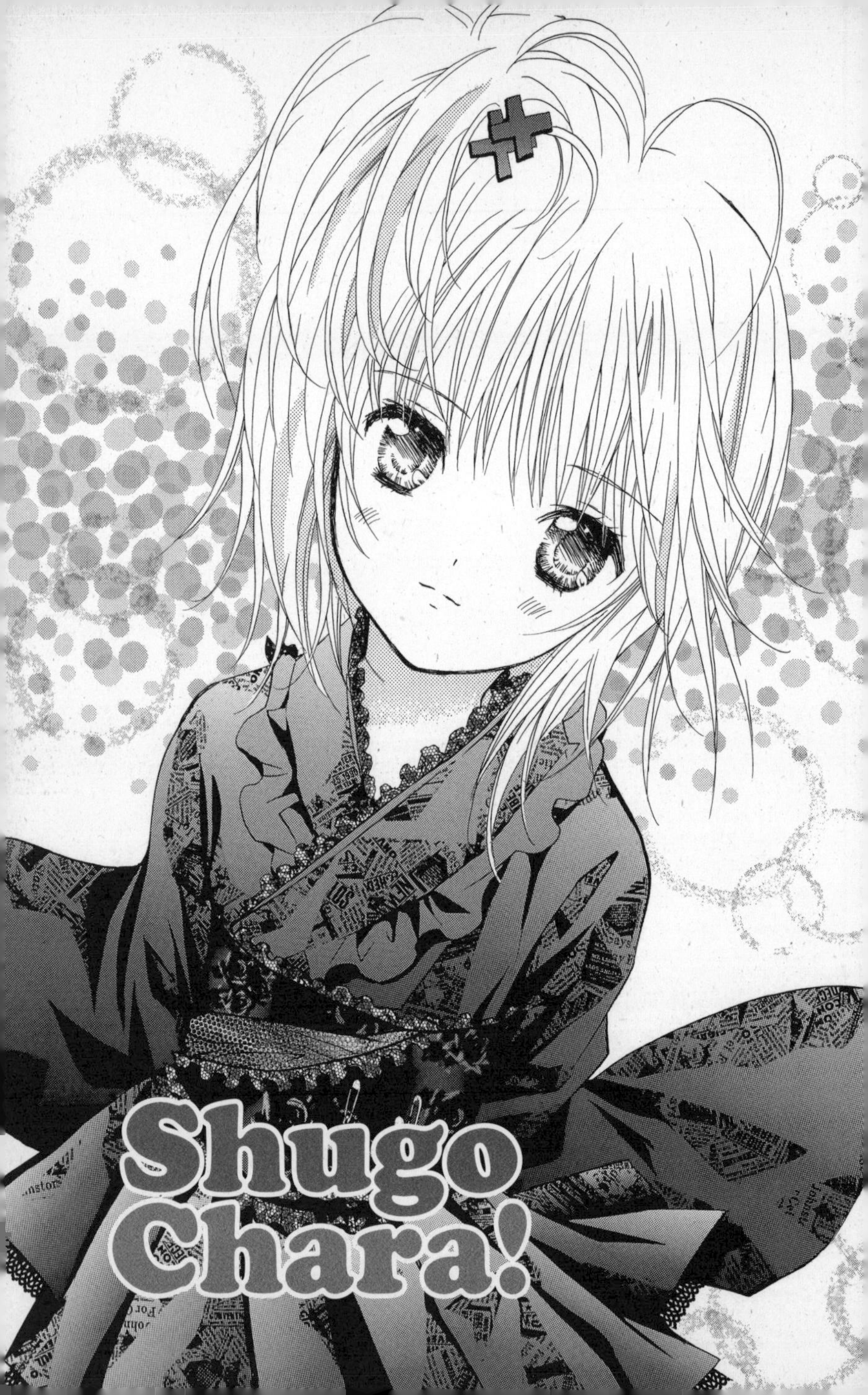
Shugo
Chara!

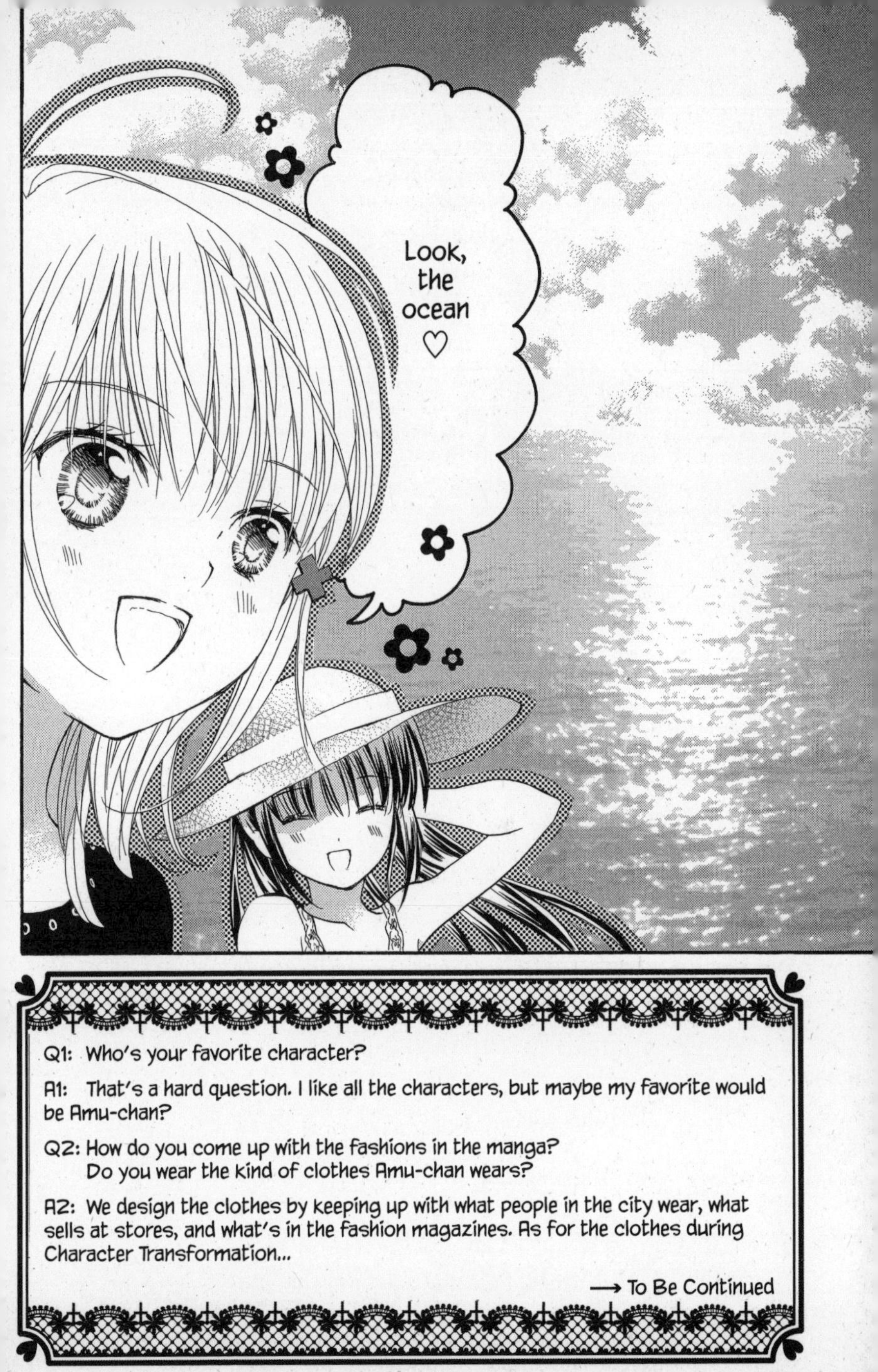
Look, the ocean ♡

Q1: Who's your favorite character?

A1: That's a hard question. I like all the characters, but maybe my favorite would be Amu-chan?

Q2: How do you come up with the fashions in the manga?
Do you wear the kind of clothes Amu-chan wears?

A2: We design the clothes by keeping up with what people in the city wear, what sells at stores, and what's in the fashion magazines. As for the clothes during Character Transformation...

→ To Be Continued

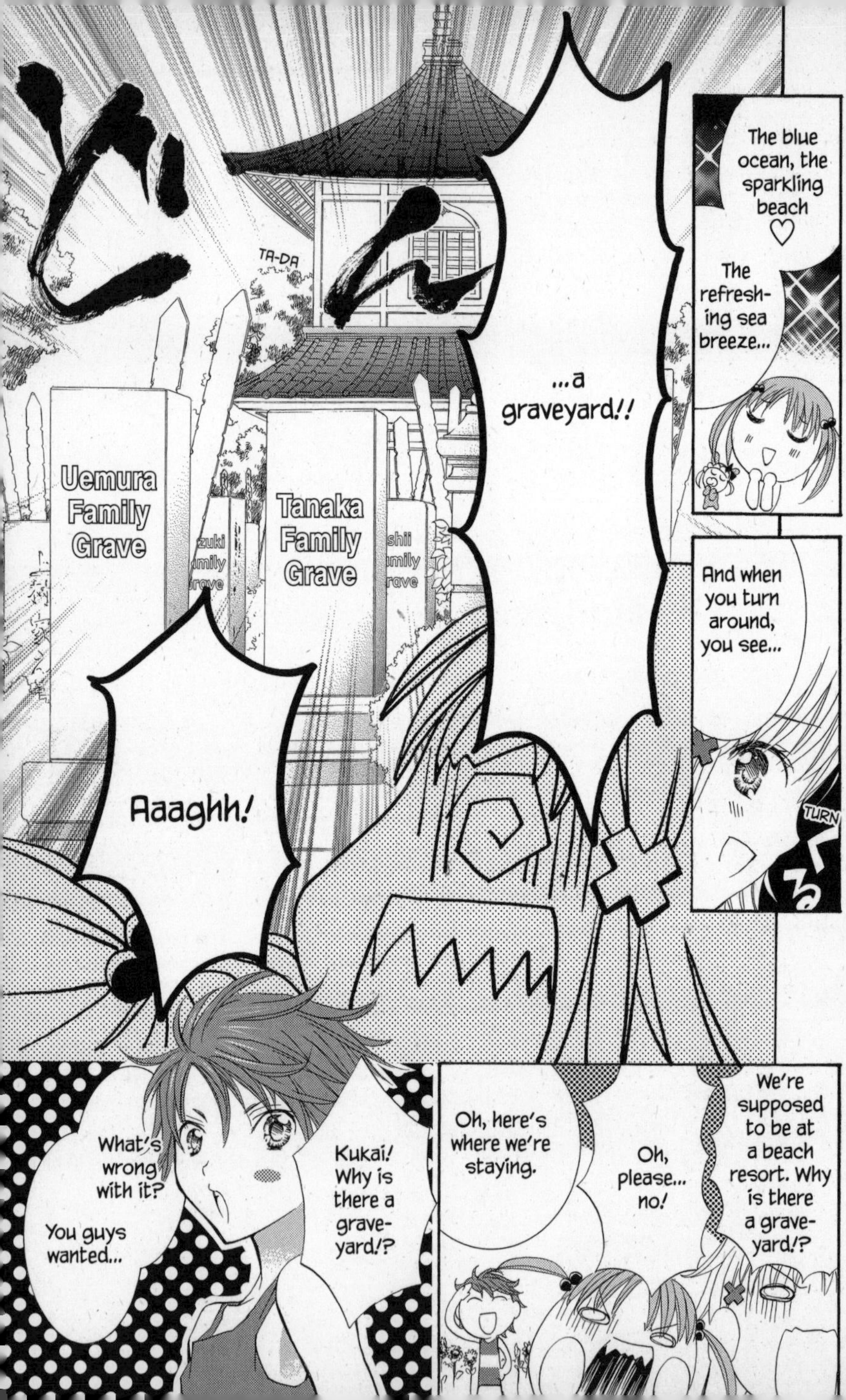
The blue ocean, the sparkling beach ♡
The refreshing sea breeze...
And when you turn around, you see...
TURN
...a graveyard!!
TA-DA
Tanaka Family Grave
Uemura Family Grave
Aaaghh!
We're supposed to be at a beach resort. Why is there a graveyard!?
Oh, please... no!
Oh, here's where we're staying.
Kukai! Why is there a graveyard!?
What's wrong with it?
You guys wanted...

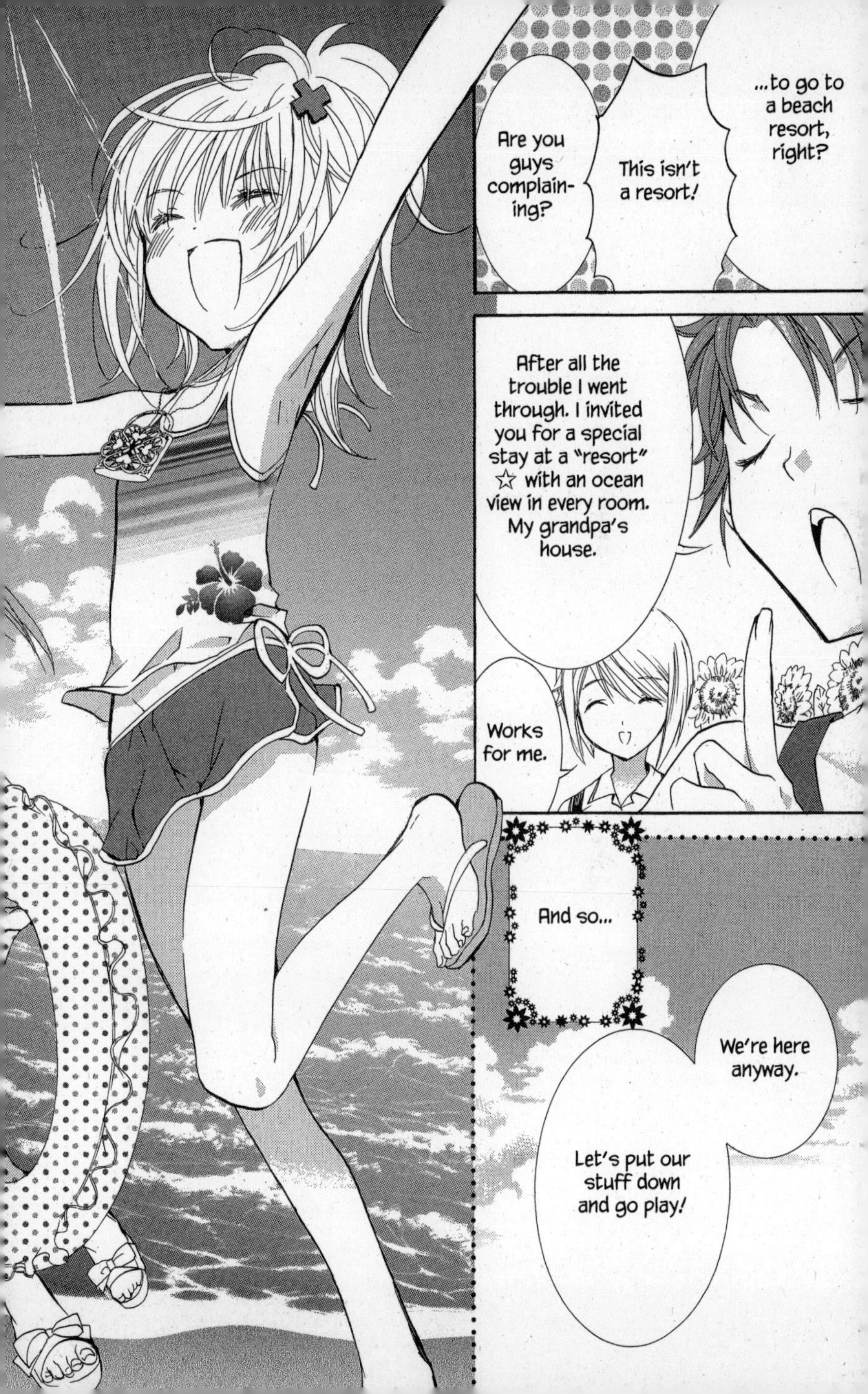
...to go to a beach resort, right?
This isn't a resort!
Are you guys complaining?
After all the trouble I went through. I invited you for a special stay at a "resort" ☆ with an ocean view in every room. My grandpa's house.
Works for me.
And so...
We're here anyway.
Let's put our stuff down and go play!

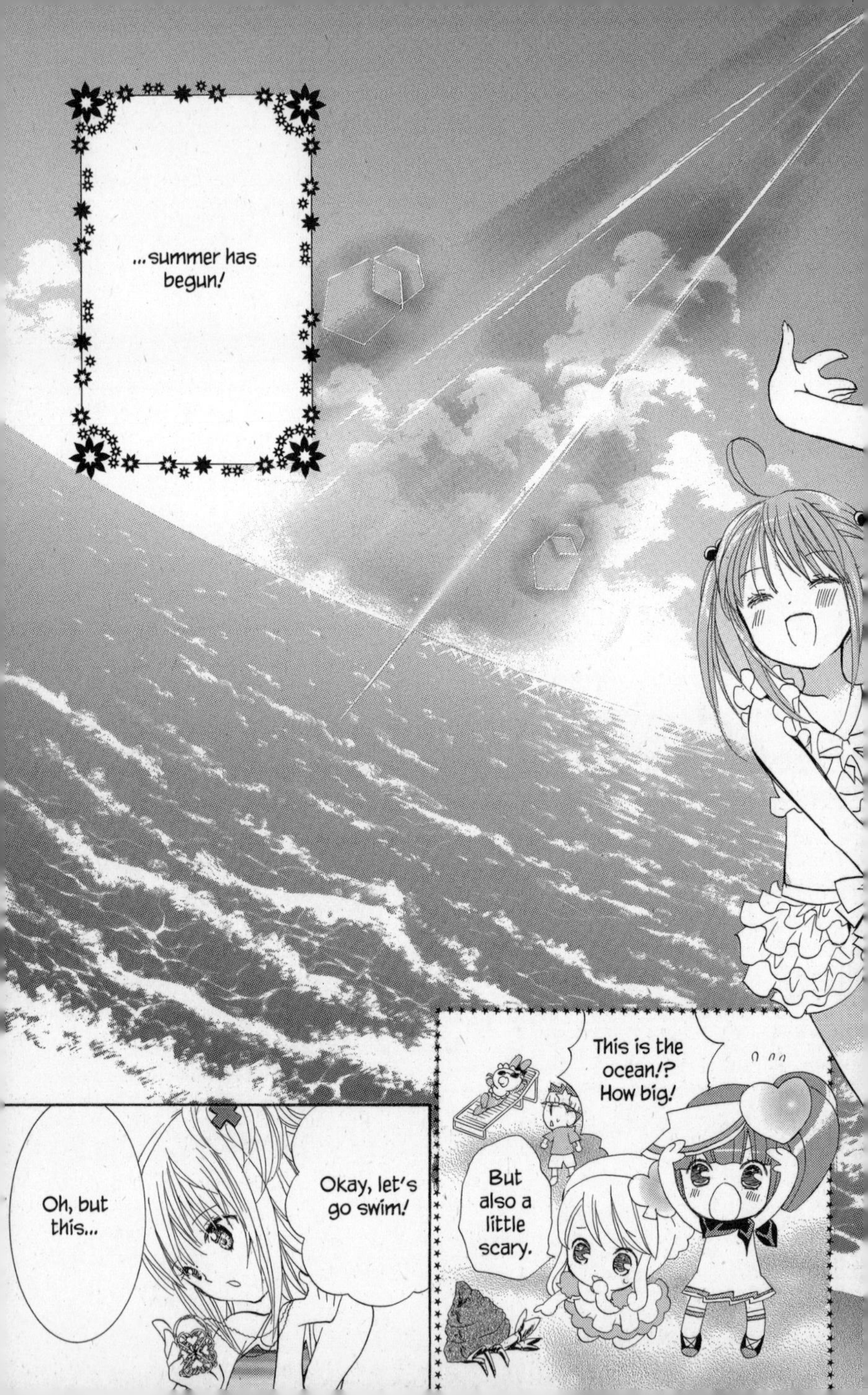
...summer has begun!
This is the ocean!? How big!
But also a little scary.
Okay, let's go swim!
Oh, but this...

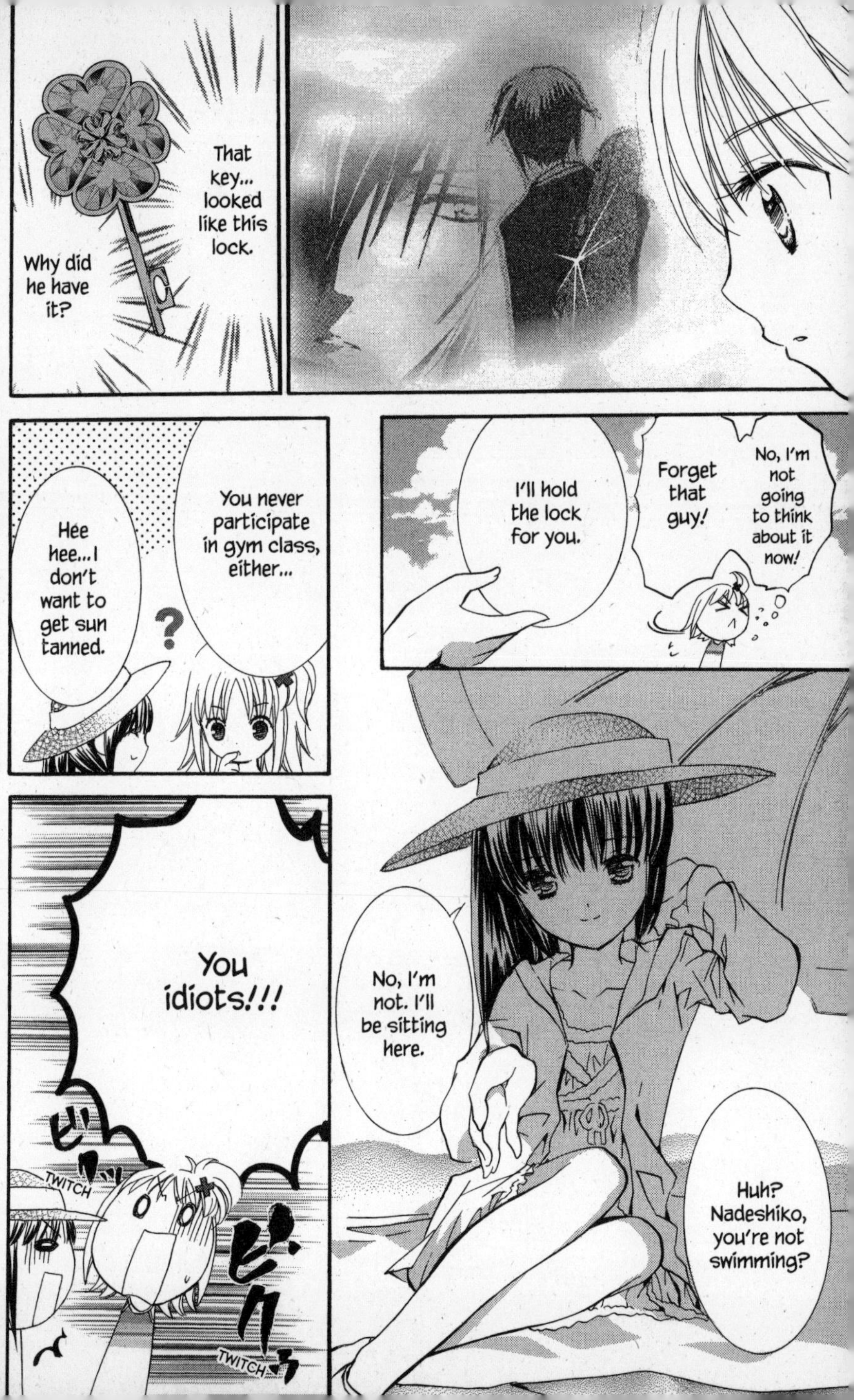
That key... looked like this lock.
Why did he have it?
No, I'm not going to think about it now!
Forget that guy!
I'll hold the lock for you.
Huh? Nadeshiko, you're not swimming?
No, I'm not. I'll be sitting here.
You never participate in gym class, either...
Hee hee...I don't want to get sun tanned.
You idiots!!!
TWITCH
TWITCH

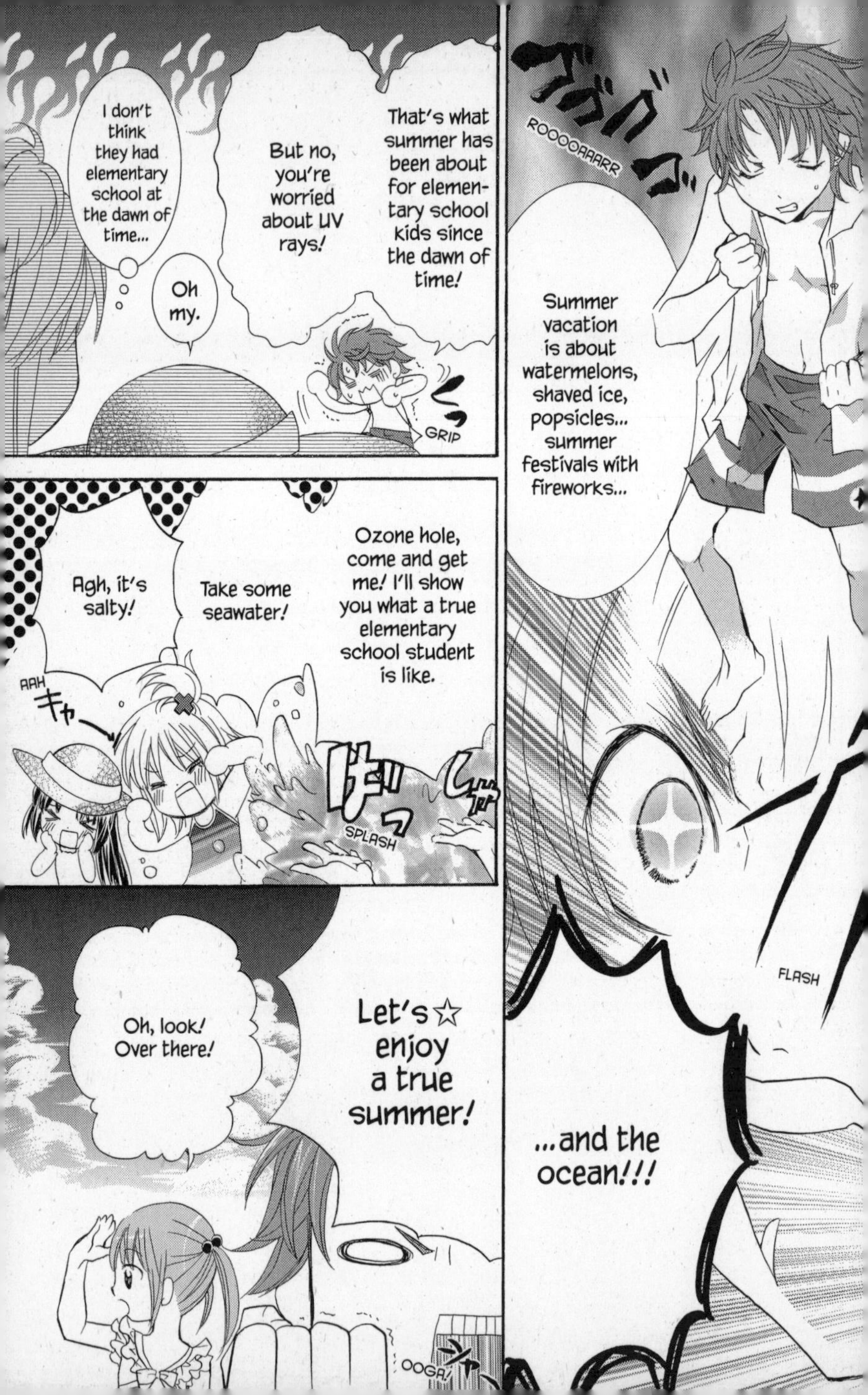

ROOOOARRRR
Summer vacation is about watermelons, shaved ice, popsicles... summer festivals with fireworks...
FLASH
...and the ocean!!!
That's what summer has been about for elementary school kids since the dawn of time!
But no, you're worried about UV rays!
GRIP
I don't think they had elementary school at the dawn of time...
Oh my.
Ozone hole, come and get me! I'll show you what a true elementary school student is like.
SPLASH
Take some seawater!
Agh, it's salty!
AAH
Let's☆ enjoy a true summer!
Oh, look! Over there!
OOGA!

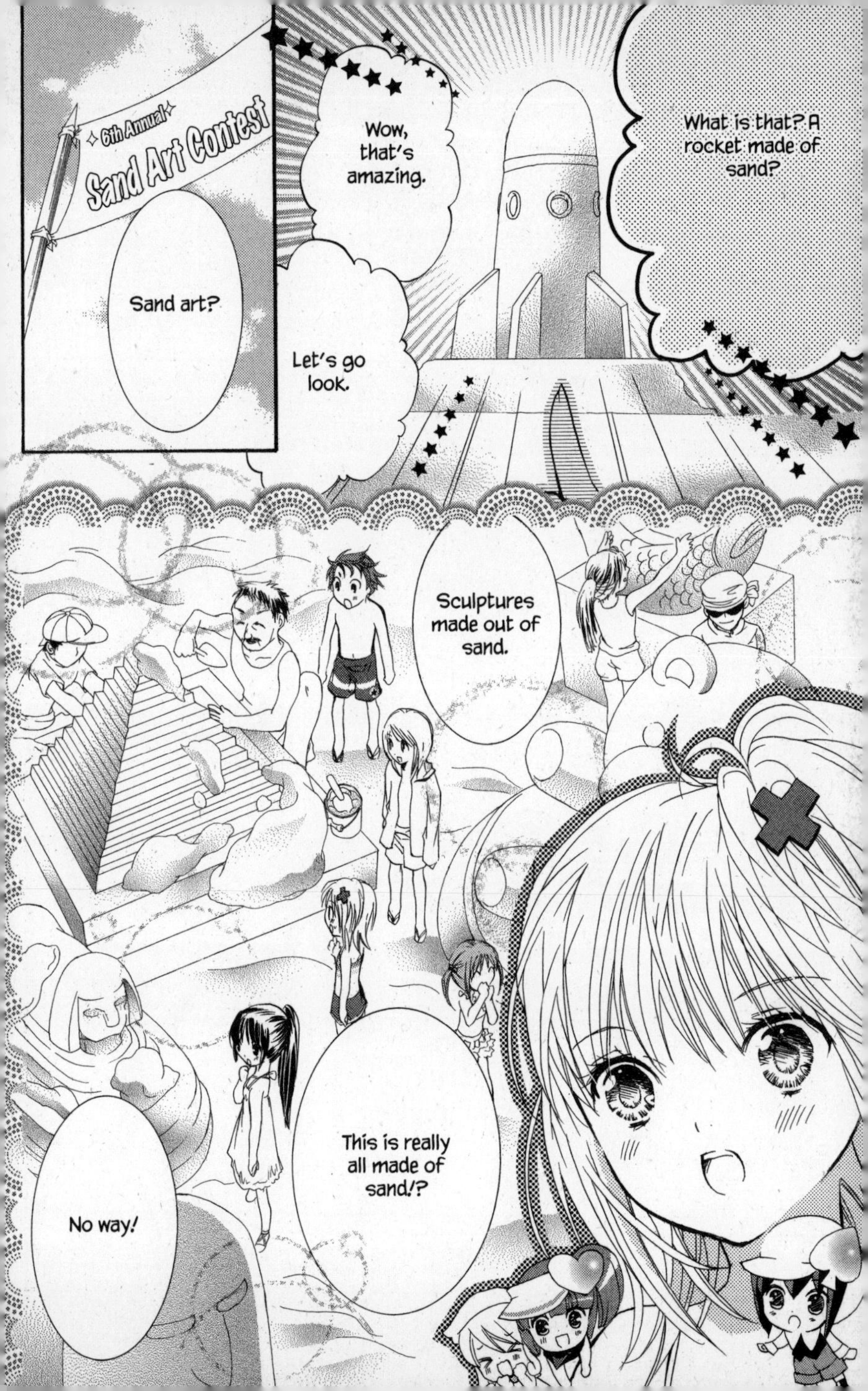
What is that? A rocket made of sand?
Wow, that's amazing.
Let's go look.
✧6th Annual✧
Sand Art Contest
Sand art?
Sculptures made out of sand.
This is really all made of sand!?
No way!

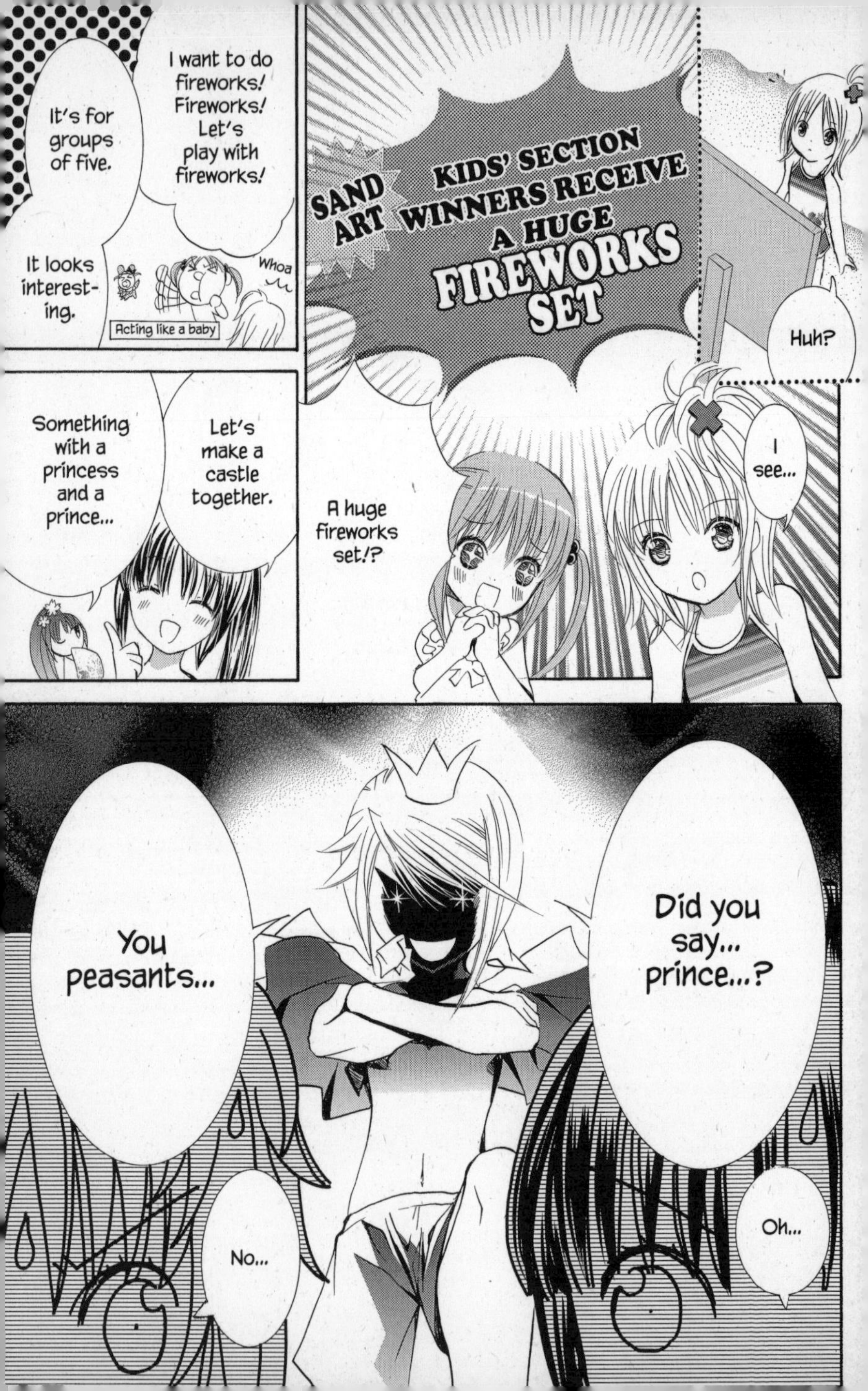

Huh?
SAND ART
KIDS' SECTION WINNERS RECEIVE A HUGE FIREWORKS SET
I want to do fireworks! Fireworks! Let's play with fireworks!
It's for groups of five.
Whoa
It looks interest-ing.
Acting like a baby
I see...
A huge fireworks set!?
Let's make a castle together.
Something with a princess and a prince...
Did you say... prince...?
You peasants...
Oh...
No...

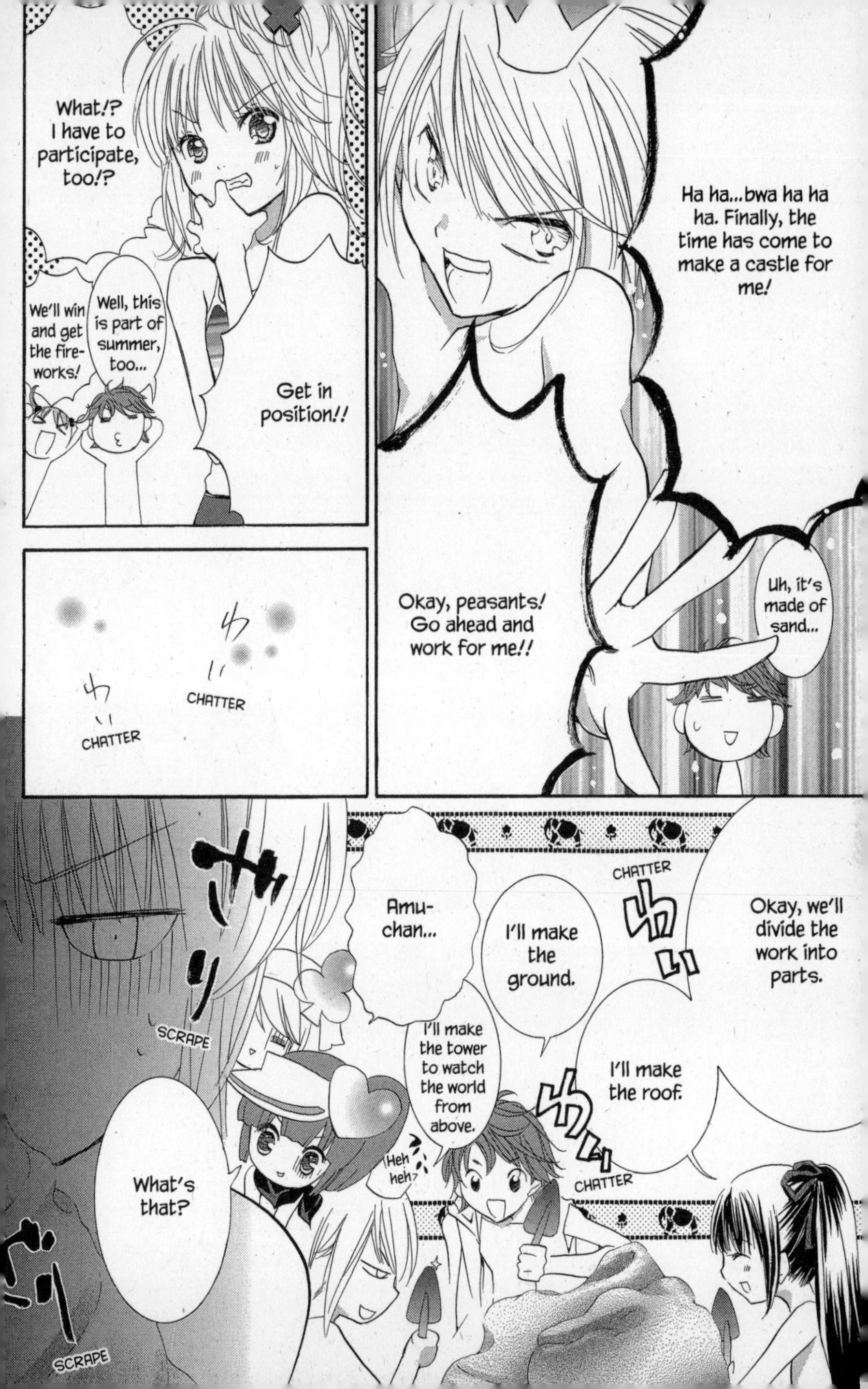
Ha ha...bwa ha ha ha. Finally, the time has come to make a castle for me!
Okay, peasants! Go ahead and work for me!!
Uh, it's made of sand...
What!? I have to participate, too!?
Get in position!!
Well, this is part of summer, too...
We'll win and get the fire-works!
CHATTER
CHATTER
Okay, we'll divide the work into parts.
CHATTER
I'll make the roof.
I'll make the ground.
Amu-chan...
I'll make the tower to watch the world from above.
Heh heh
CHATTER
What's that?
SCRAPE
SCRAPE

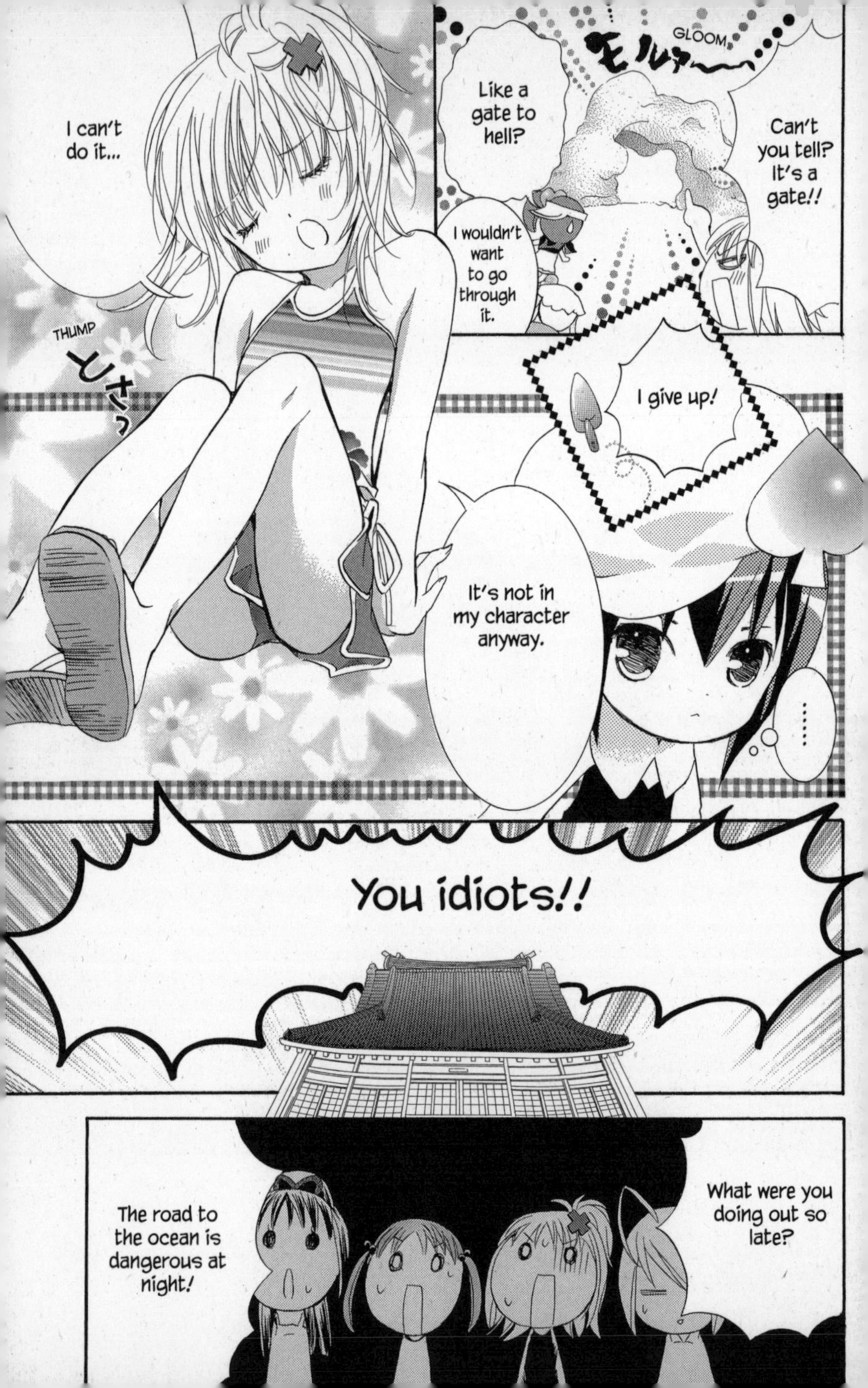
GLOOM
モルァ〜〜
Can't you tell? It's a gate!!
Like a gate to hell?
I wouldn't want to go through it.
I can't do it...
THUMP
とさっ
I give up!
It's not in my character anyway.
......
You idiots!!
What were you doing out so late?
The road to the ocean is dangerous at night!

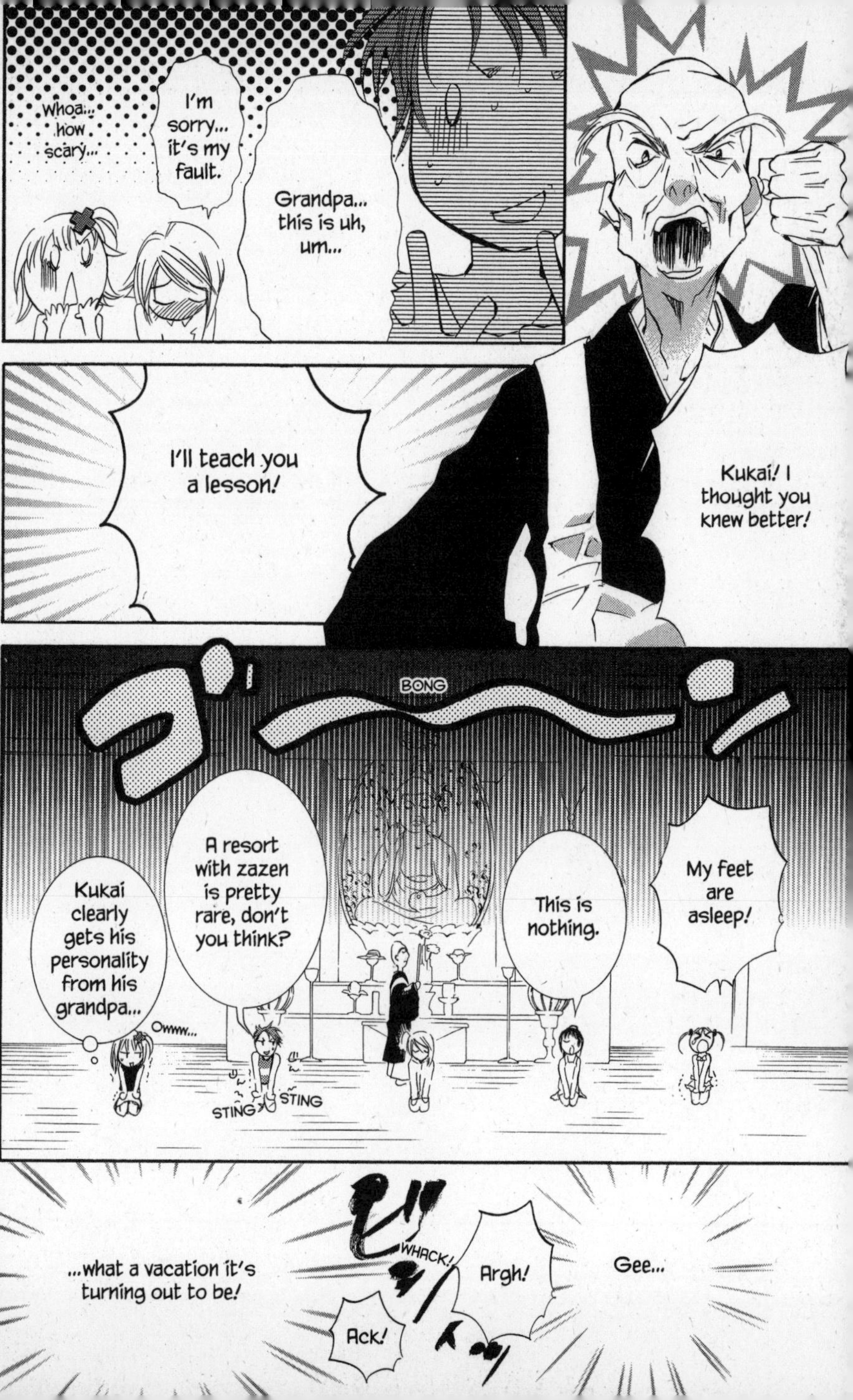

Grandpa... this is uh, um...
I'm sorry... it's my fault.
Whoa... how scary...
Kukai! I thought you knew better!
I'll teach you a lesson!
BONG
My feet are asleep!
This is nothing.
A resort with zazen is pretty rare, don't you think?
Kukai clearly gets his personality from his grandpa...
Owww...
STING
STING
Gee...
WHACK!
Argh!
Ack!
...what a vacation it's turning out to be!

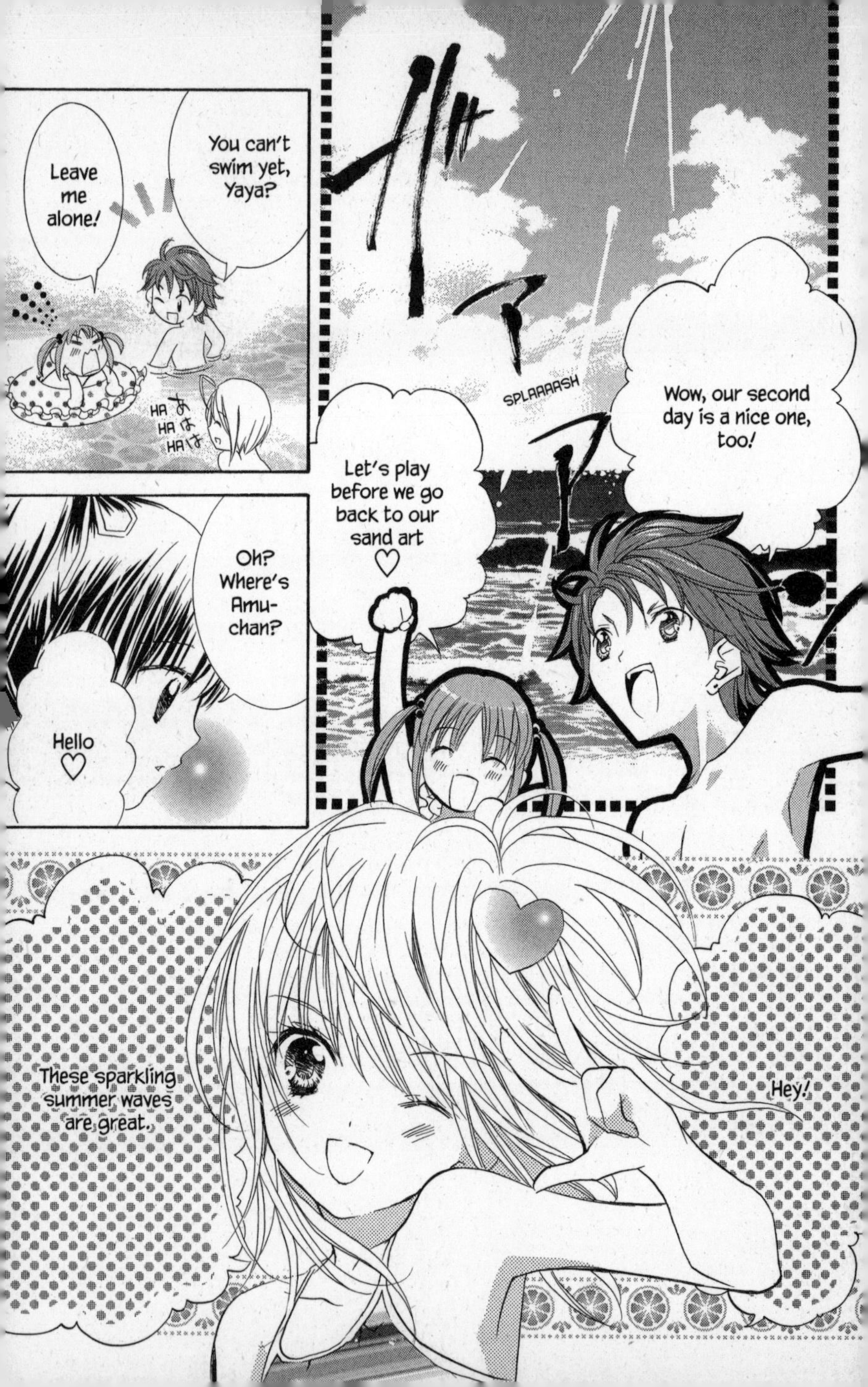
SPLAAAASH
Wow, our second day is a nice one, too!
Let's play before we go back to our sand art ♡
You can't swim yet, Yaya?
Leave me alone!
HA HA HA
Oh? Where's Amu-chan?
Hello ♡
Hey!
These sparkling summer waves are great.

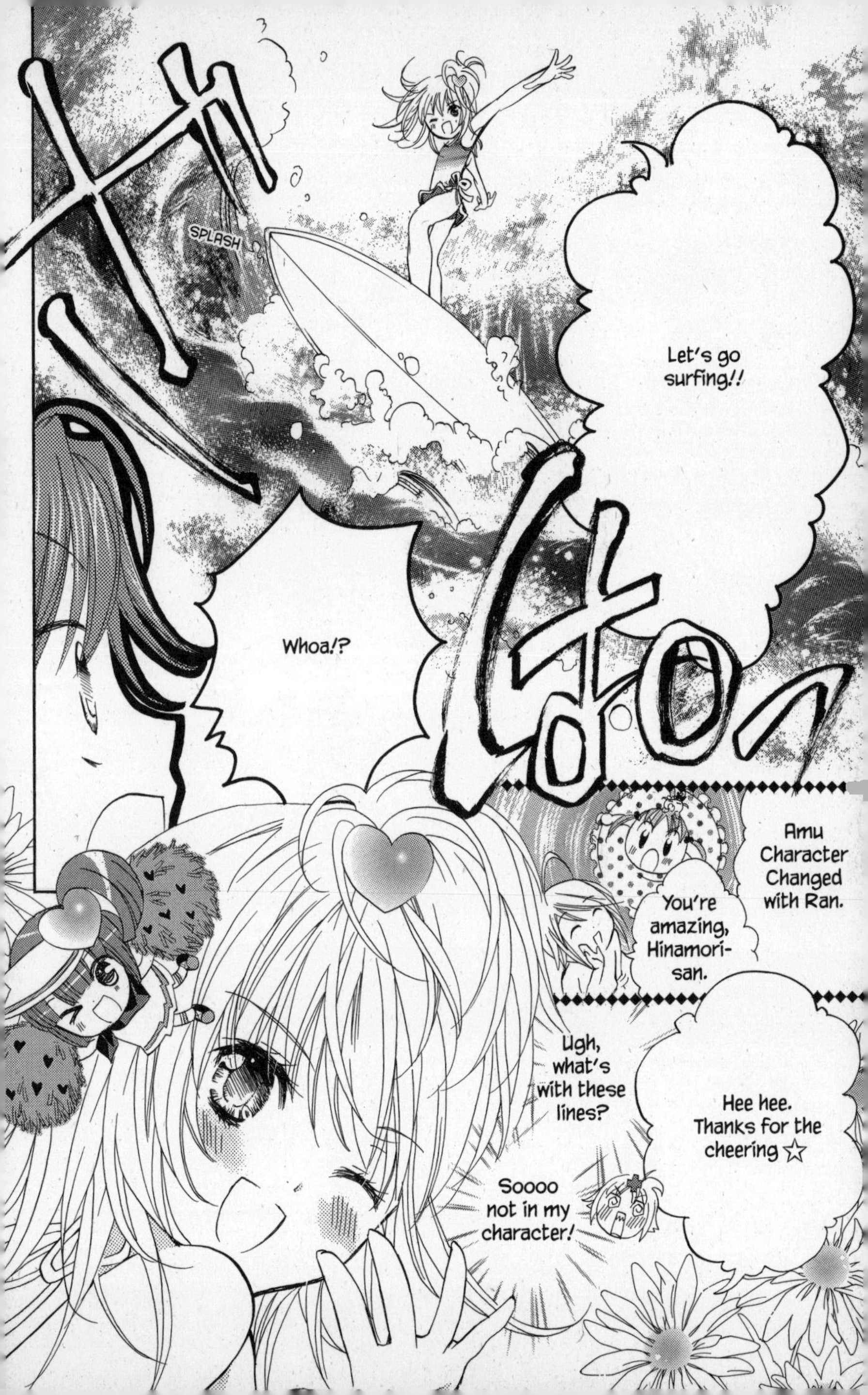
Let's go surfing!!
SPLASH
Whoa!?
Amu Character Changed with Ran.
You're amazing, Hinamori-san.
Hee hee. Thanks for the cheering ☆
Ugh, what's with these lines?
Soooo not in my character!

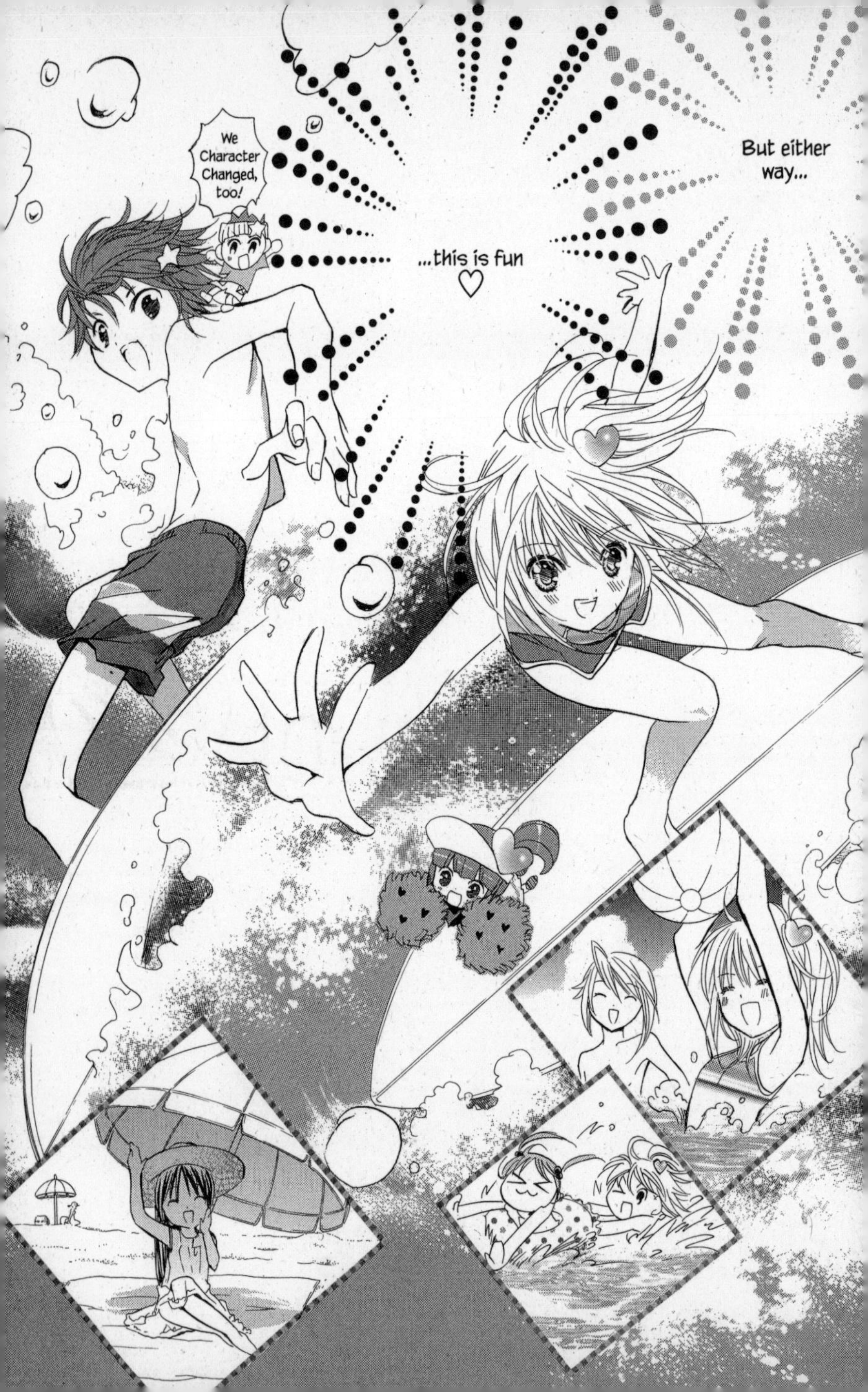
But either way...
...this is fun ♡
We Character Changed, too!

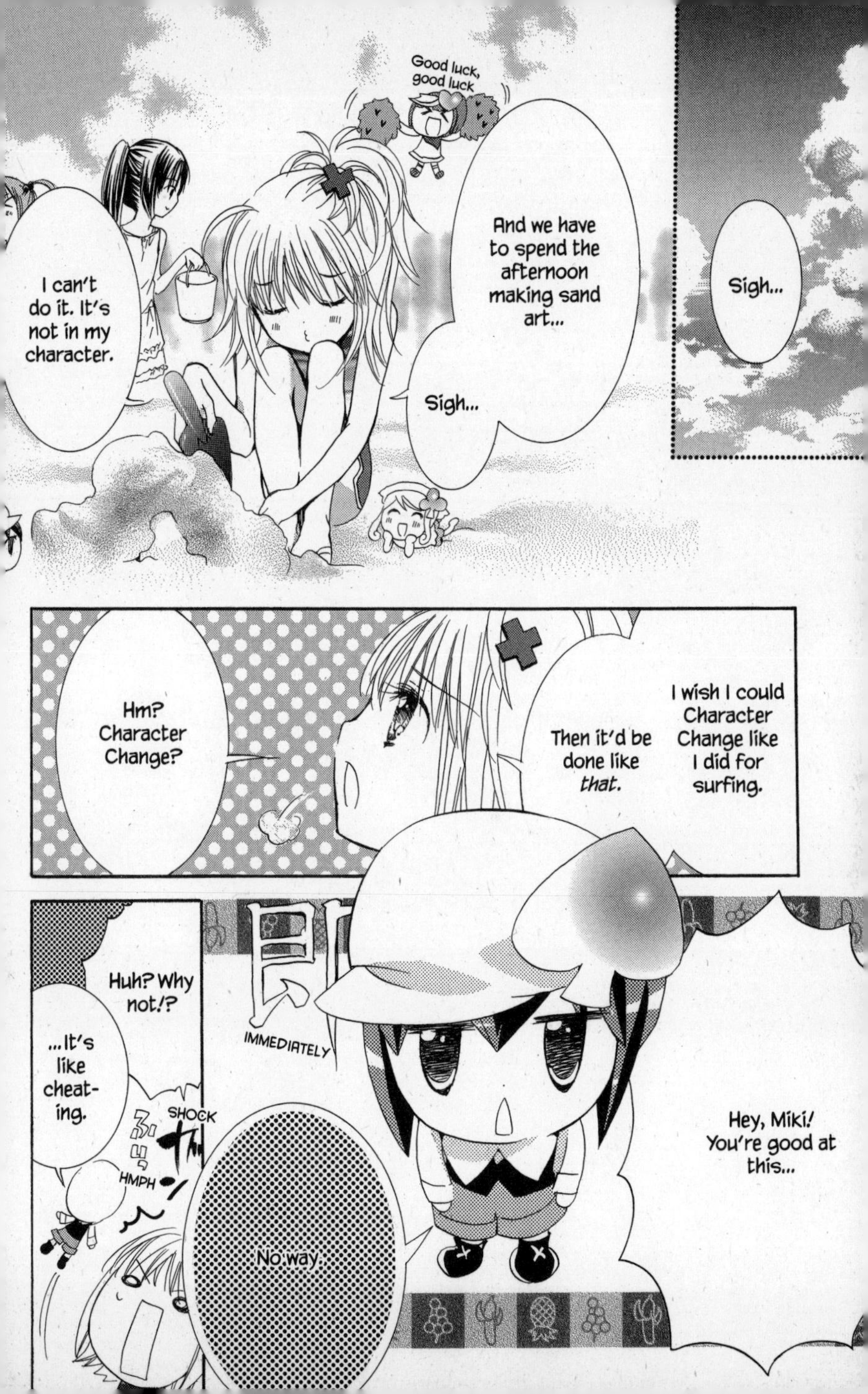
Sigh...
Good luck, good luck
And we have to spend the afternoon making sand art...
Sigh...
I can't do it. It's not in my character.
I wish I could Character Change like I did for surfing.
Then it'd be done like *that*.
Hm? Character Change?
Hey, Miki! You're good at this...
IMMEDIATELY
No way.
Huh? Why not!?
...It's like cheating.
SHOCK
HMPH

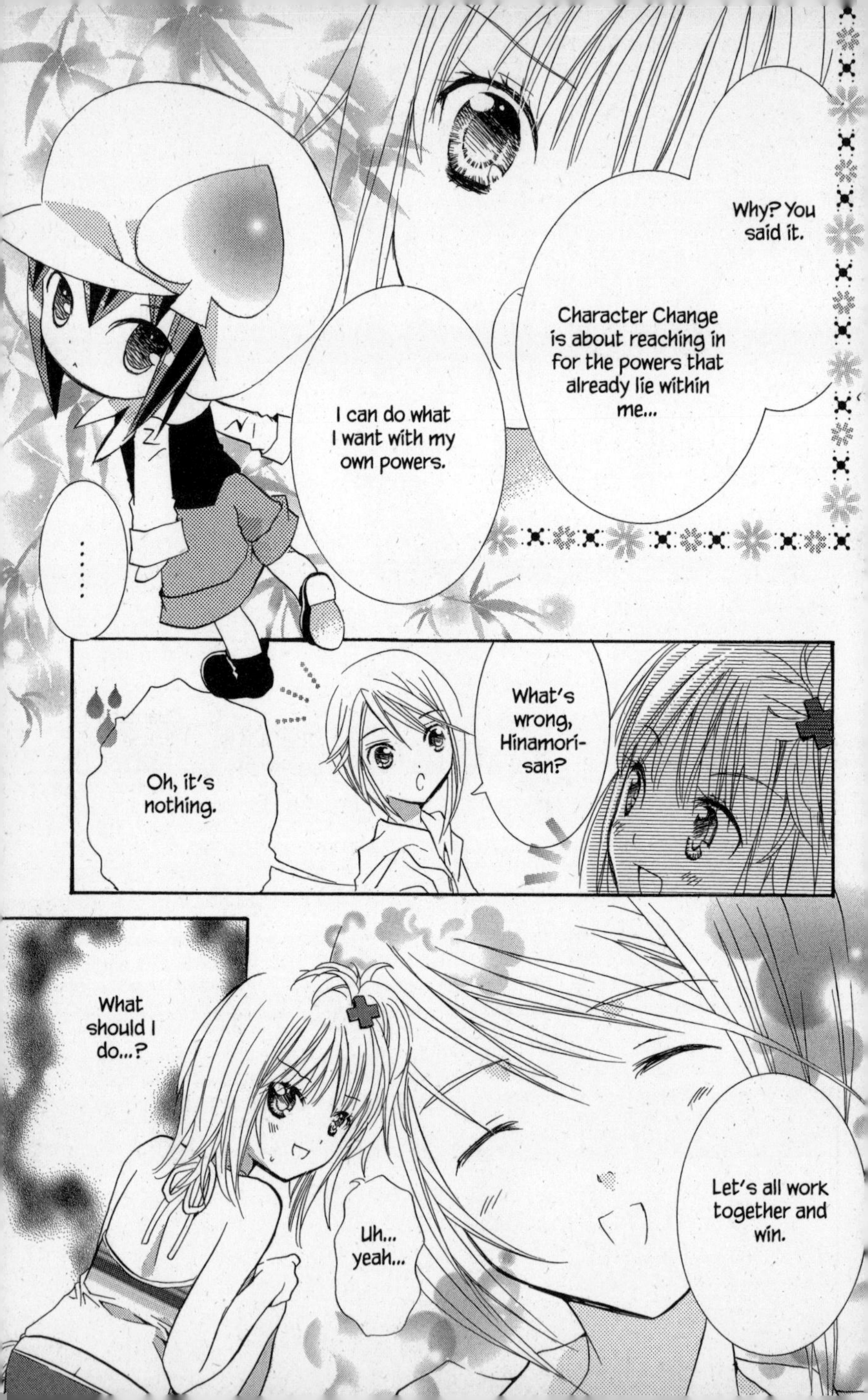
Why? You said it.
Character Change is about reaching in for the powers that already lie within me...
I can do what I want with my own powers.
......
What's wrong, Hinamori-san?
Oh, it's nothing.
Let's all work together and win.
Uh... yeah...
What should I do...?

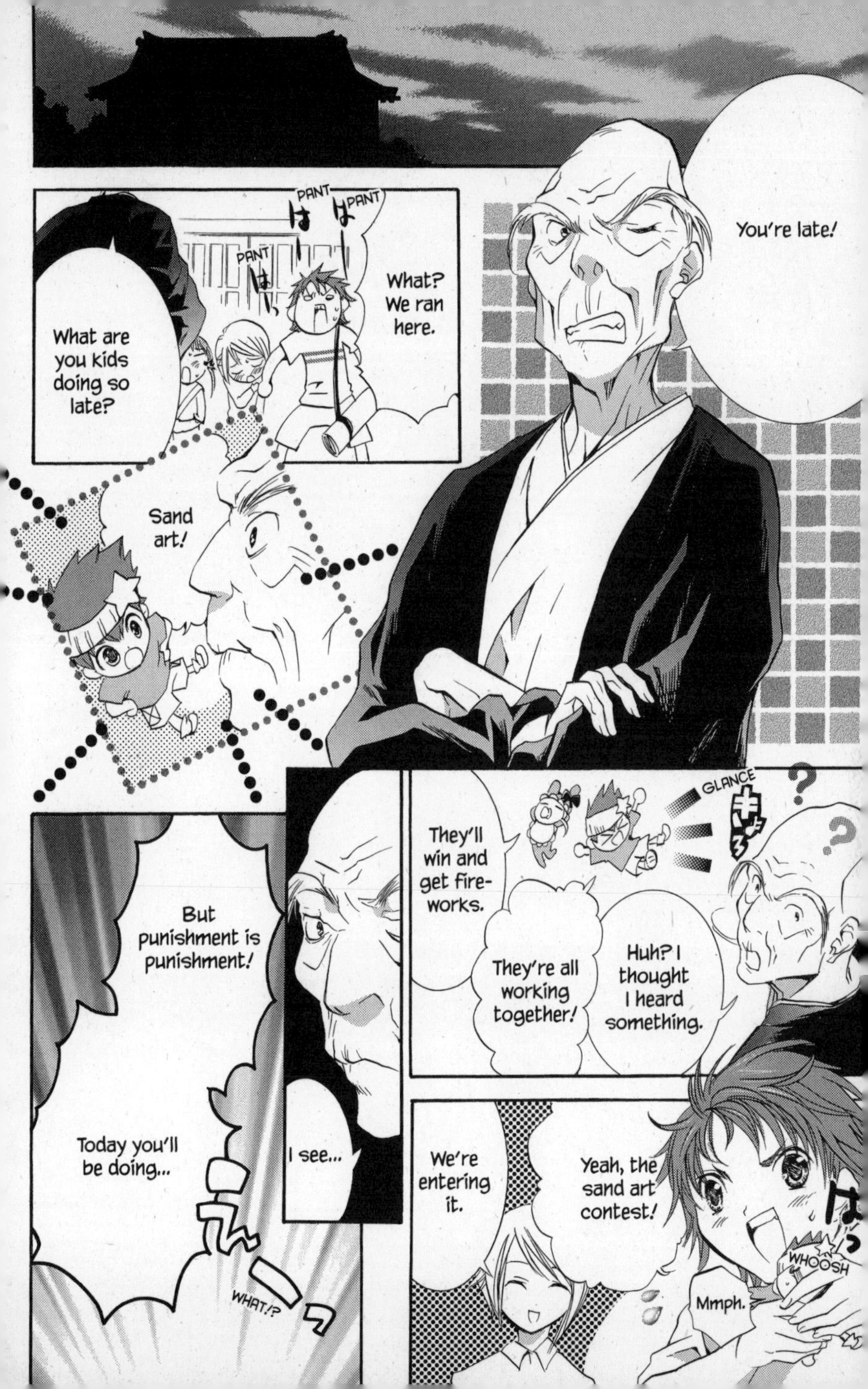
You're late!
PANT
PANT
What? We ran here.
PANT
What are you kids doing so late?
Sand art!
GLANCE
Huh? I thought I heard something.
They'll win and get fire-works.
They're all working together!
Yeah, the sand art contest!
We're entering it.
WHOOSH
Mmph.
I see...
But punishment is punishment!
Today you'll be doing...
WHAT!?

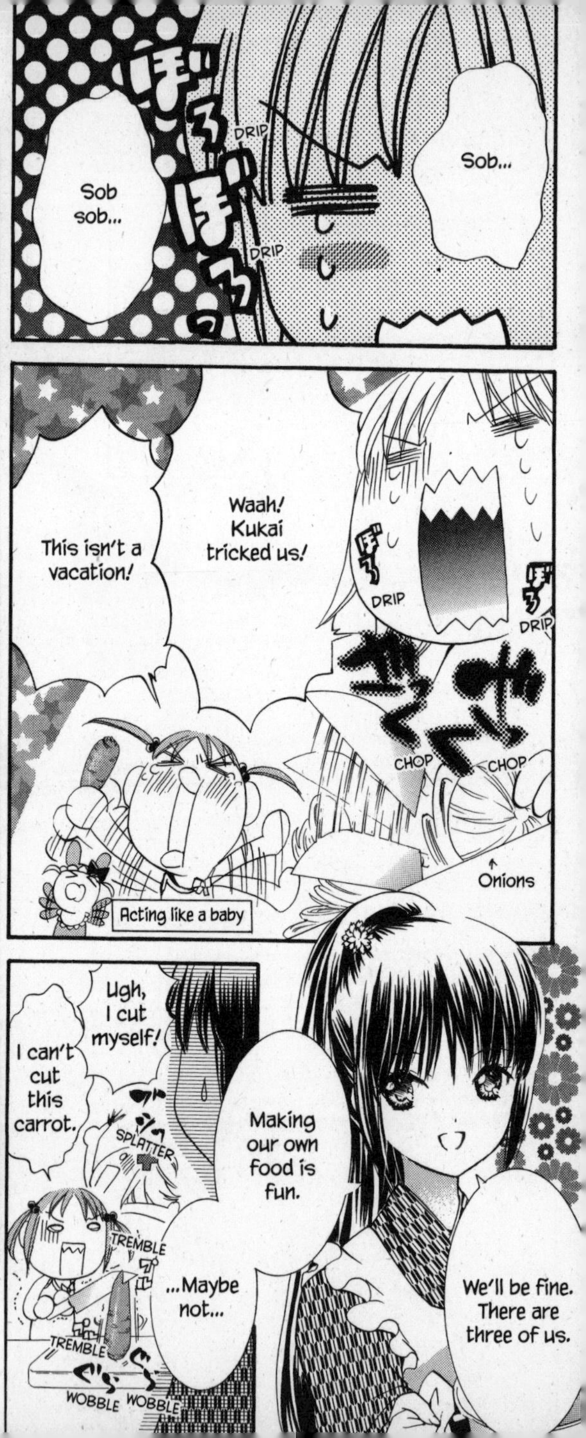
Sob...
DRIP
DRIP
Sob sob...
Waah! Kukai tricked us!
This isn't a vacation!
DRIP
DRIP
CHOP
CHOP
Onions
Acting like a baby
We'll be fine. There are three of us.
Making our own food is fun.
...Maybe not...
Ugh, I cut myself!
I can't cut this carrot.
SPLATTER
TREMBLE
TREMBLE
WOBBLE
WOBBLE

character profile

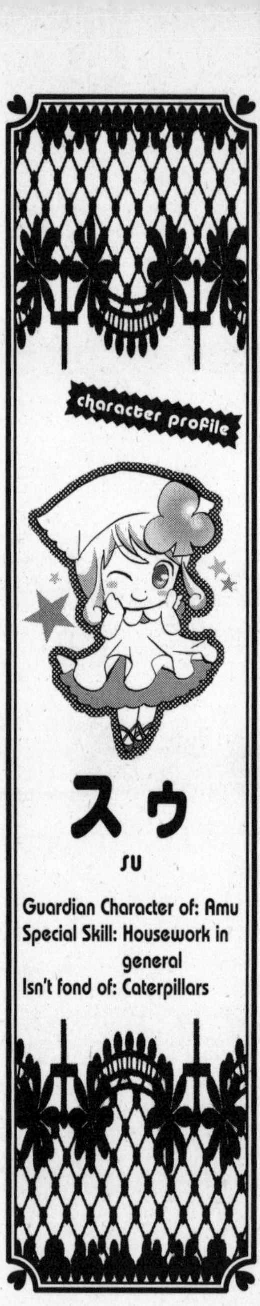

スゥ

SU

Guardian Character of: Amu
Special Skill: Housework in general
Isn't fond of: Caterpillars

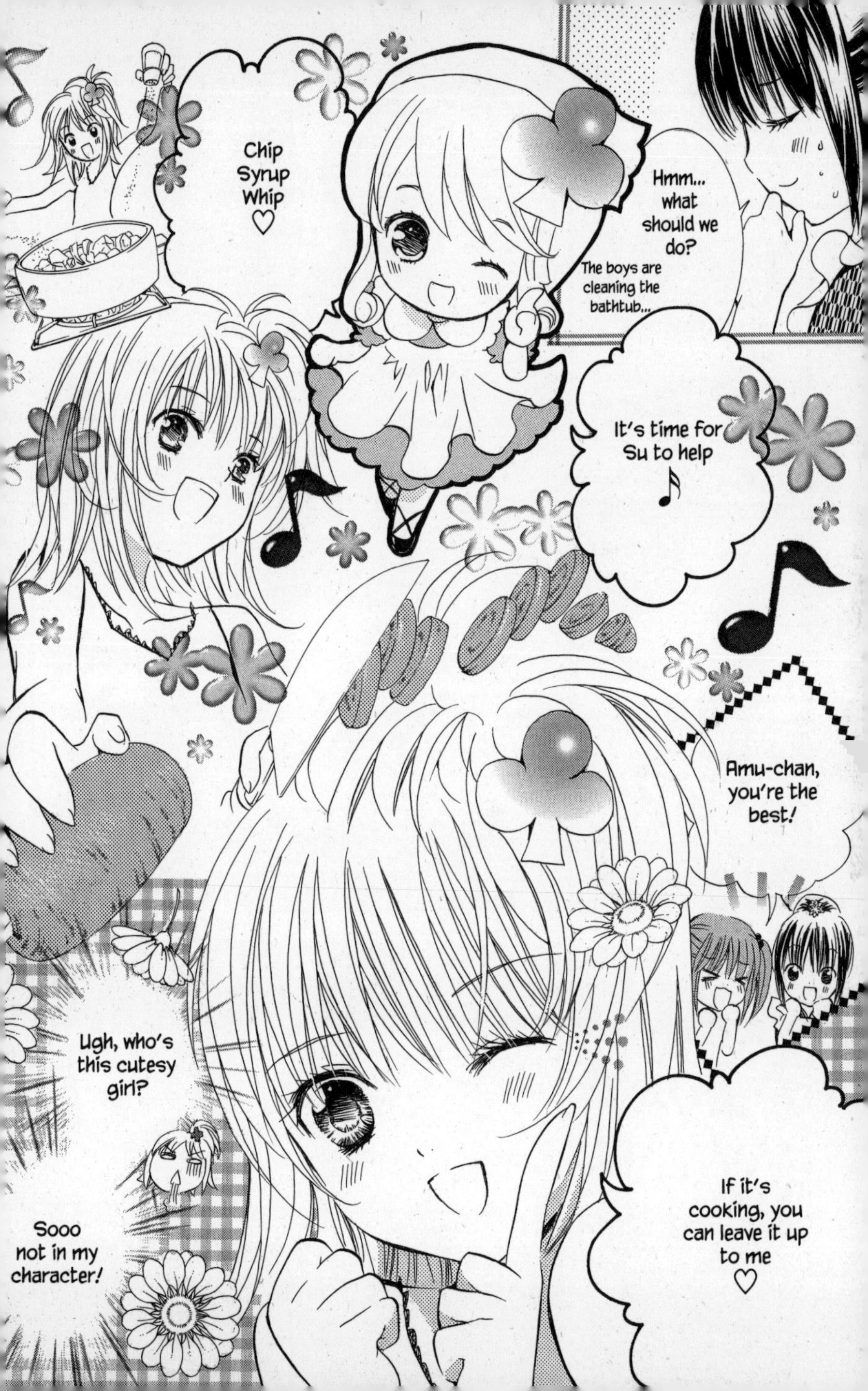
Hmm... what should we do?
The boys are cleaning the bathtub...
Chip Syrup Whip ♡
It's time for Su to help ♪
Amu-chan, you're the best!
If it's cooking, you can leave it up to me ♡
Ugh, who's this cutesy girl?
Sooo not in my character!

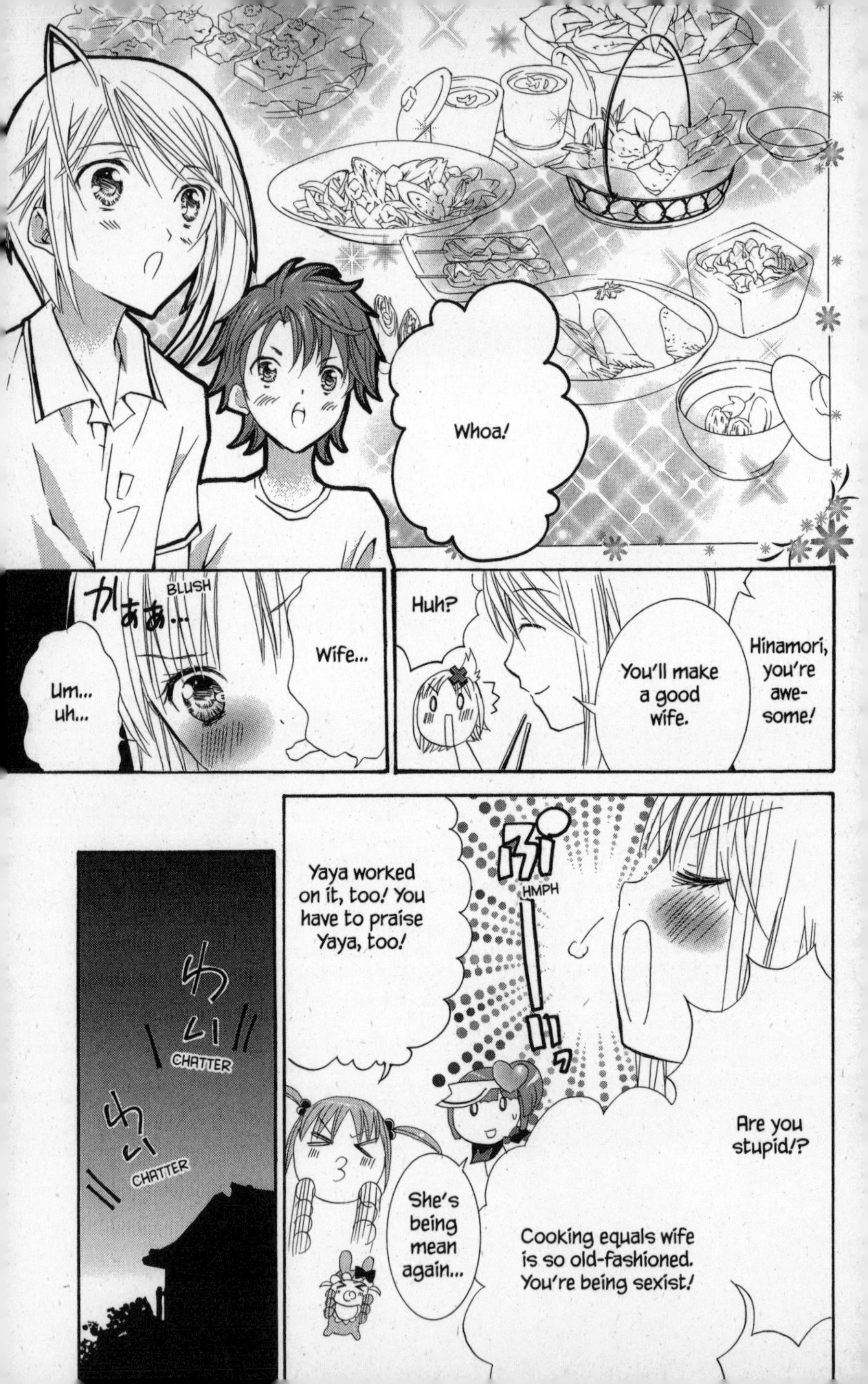
Whoa!
Hinamori, you're awesome!
You'll make a good wife.
Huh?
Wife...
BLUSH
Um... uh...
Are you stupid!?
Cooking equals wife is so old-fashioned. You're being sexist!
HMPH
Yaya worked on it, too! You have to praise Yaya, too!
She's being mean again...
わい
CHATTER
わい
CHATTER

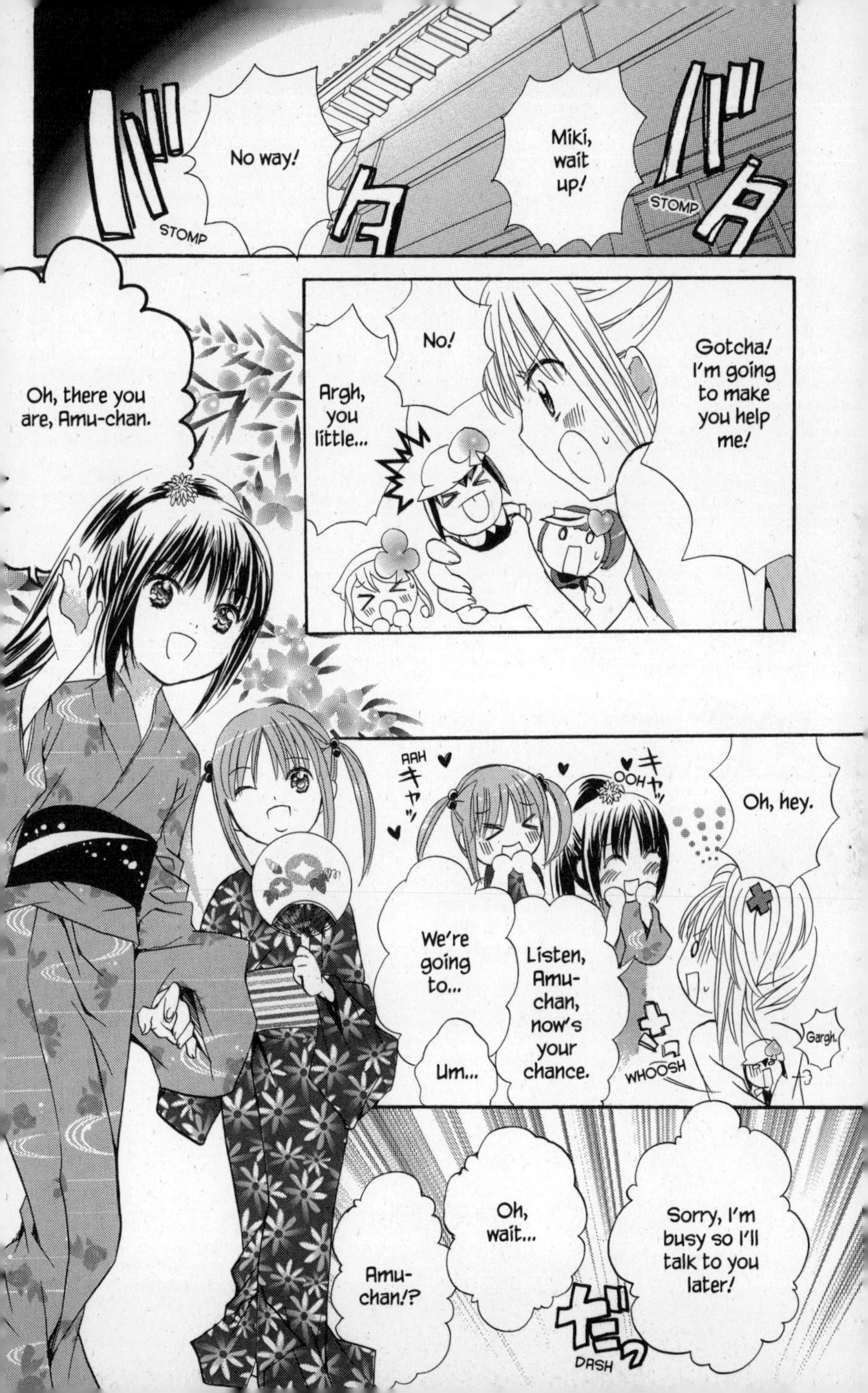
STOMP
Miki, wait up!
No way!
STOMP
Gotcha! I'm going to make you help me!
No!
Argh, you little...
Oh, hey.
OOH
AAH
Listen, Amu-chan, now's your chance.
We're going to...
Um...
WHOOSH
Gargh.
Oh, there you are, Amu-chan.
Sorry, I'm busy so I'll talk to you later!
DASH
Oh, wait...
Amu-chan!?

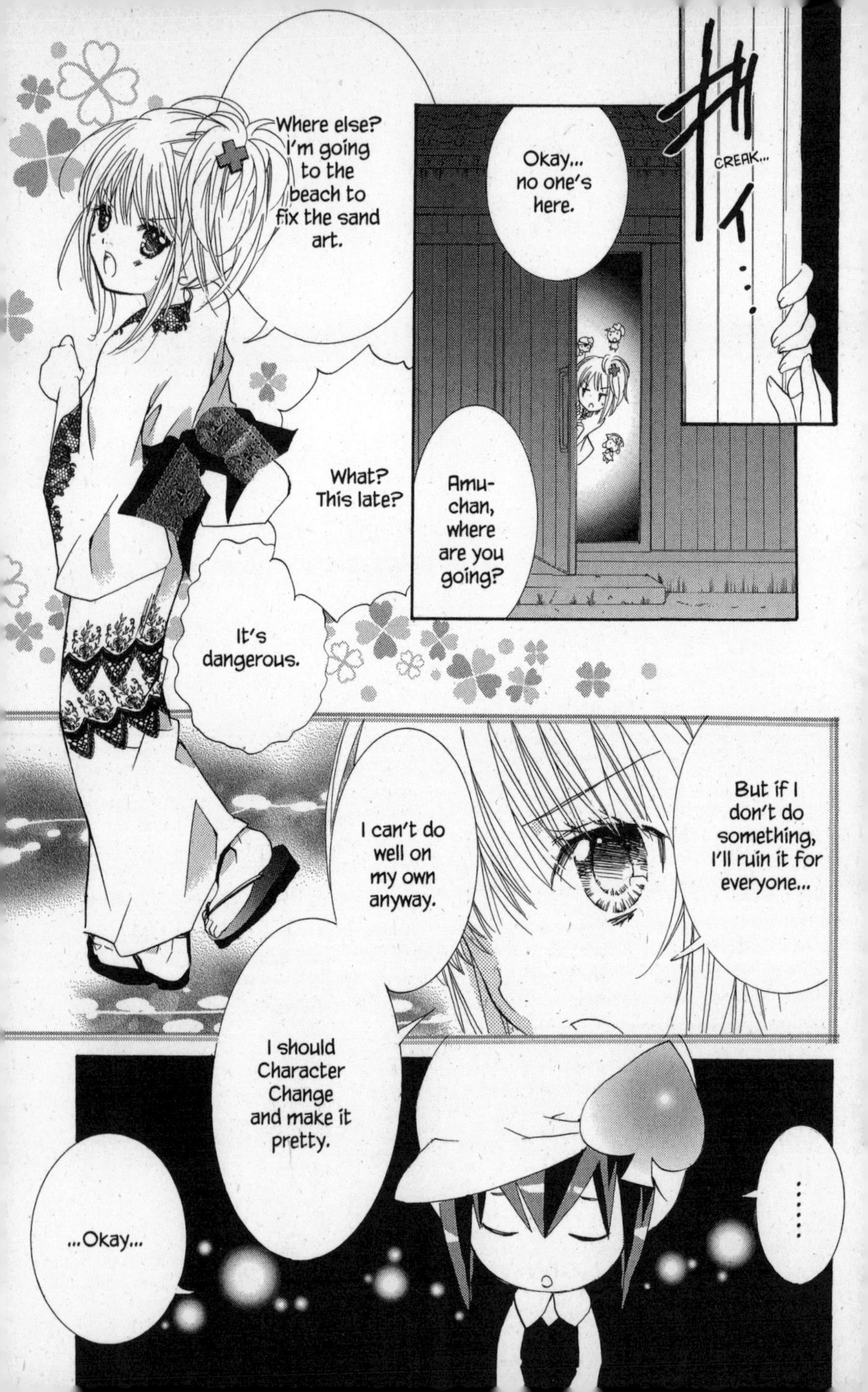
CREAK...
...
Okay... no one's here.
Amu-chan, where are you going?
Where else? I'm going to the beach to fix the sand art.
What? This late?
It's dangerous.
But if I don't do something, I'll ruin it for everyone...
I can't do well on my own anyway.
I should Character Change and make it pretty.
......
...Okay...

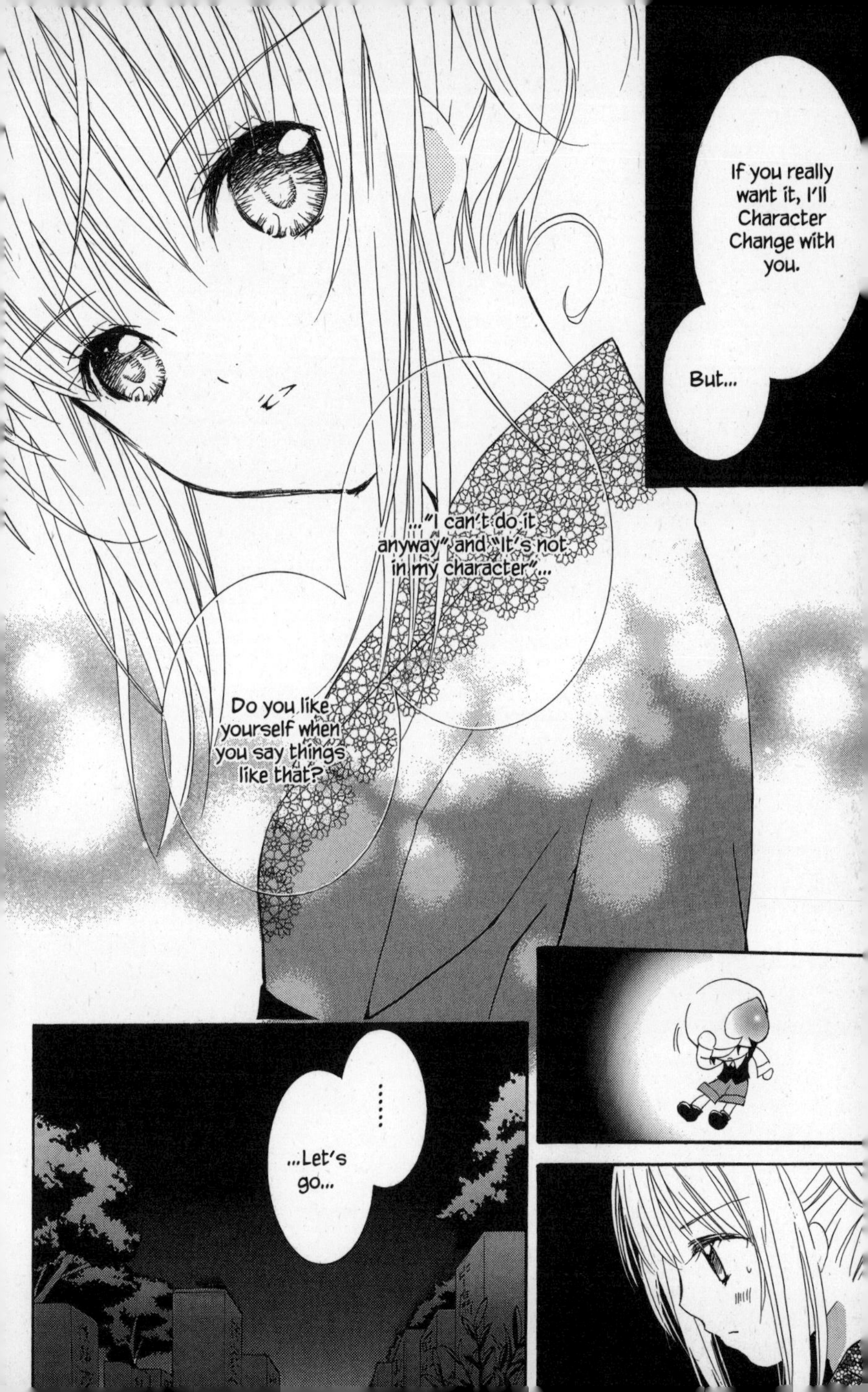
If you really want it, I'll Character Change with you.
But...
..."I can't do it anyway" and "It's not in my character"...
Do you like yourself when you say things like that?
......
...Let's go...

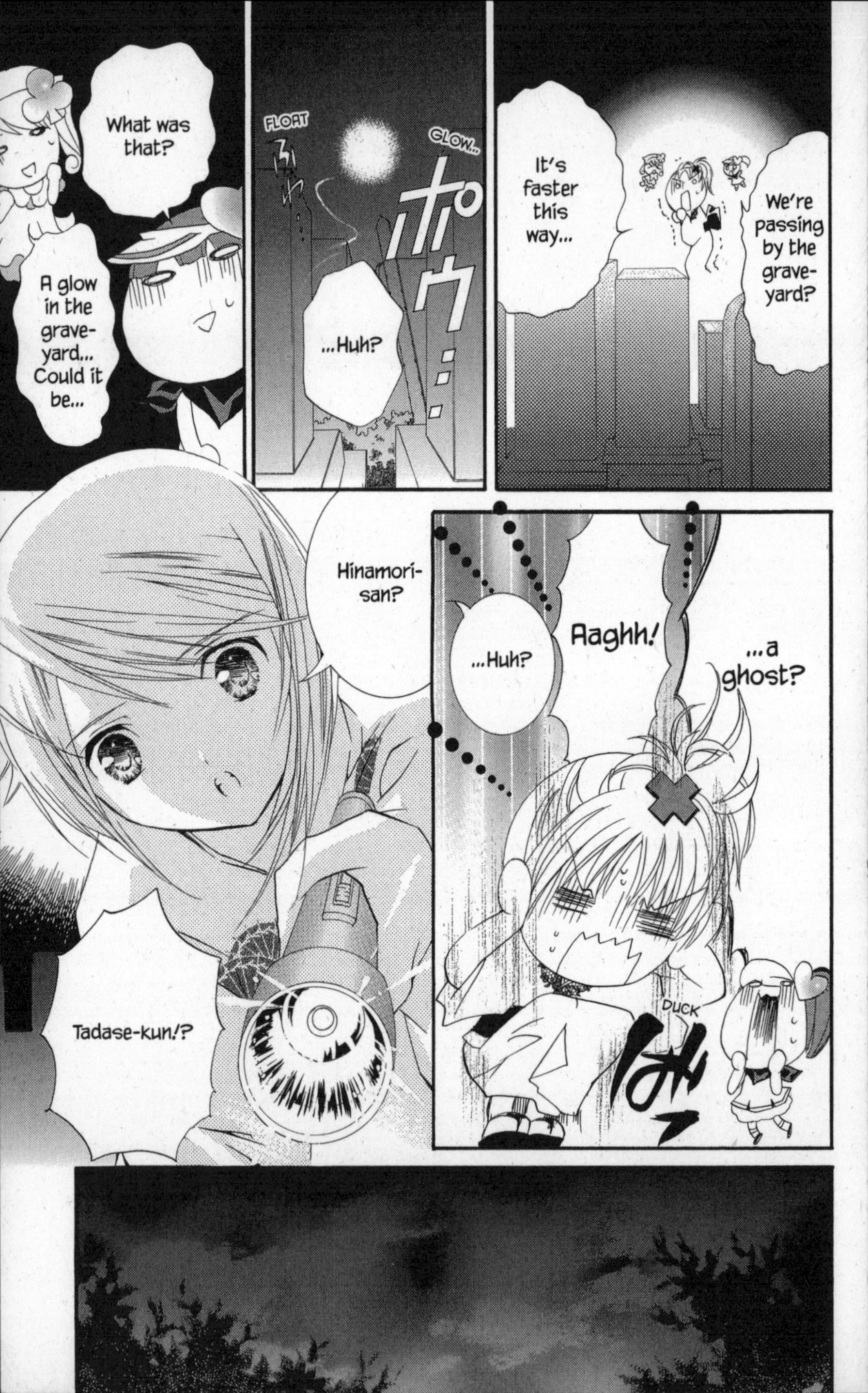
We're passing by the graveyard?
It's faster this way...
GLOW...
FLOAT
...Huh?
What was that?
A glow in the graveyard... Could it be...
...a ghost?
Aaghh!
...Huh?
DUCK
Hinamori-san?
Tadase-kun!?

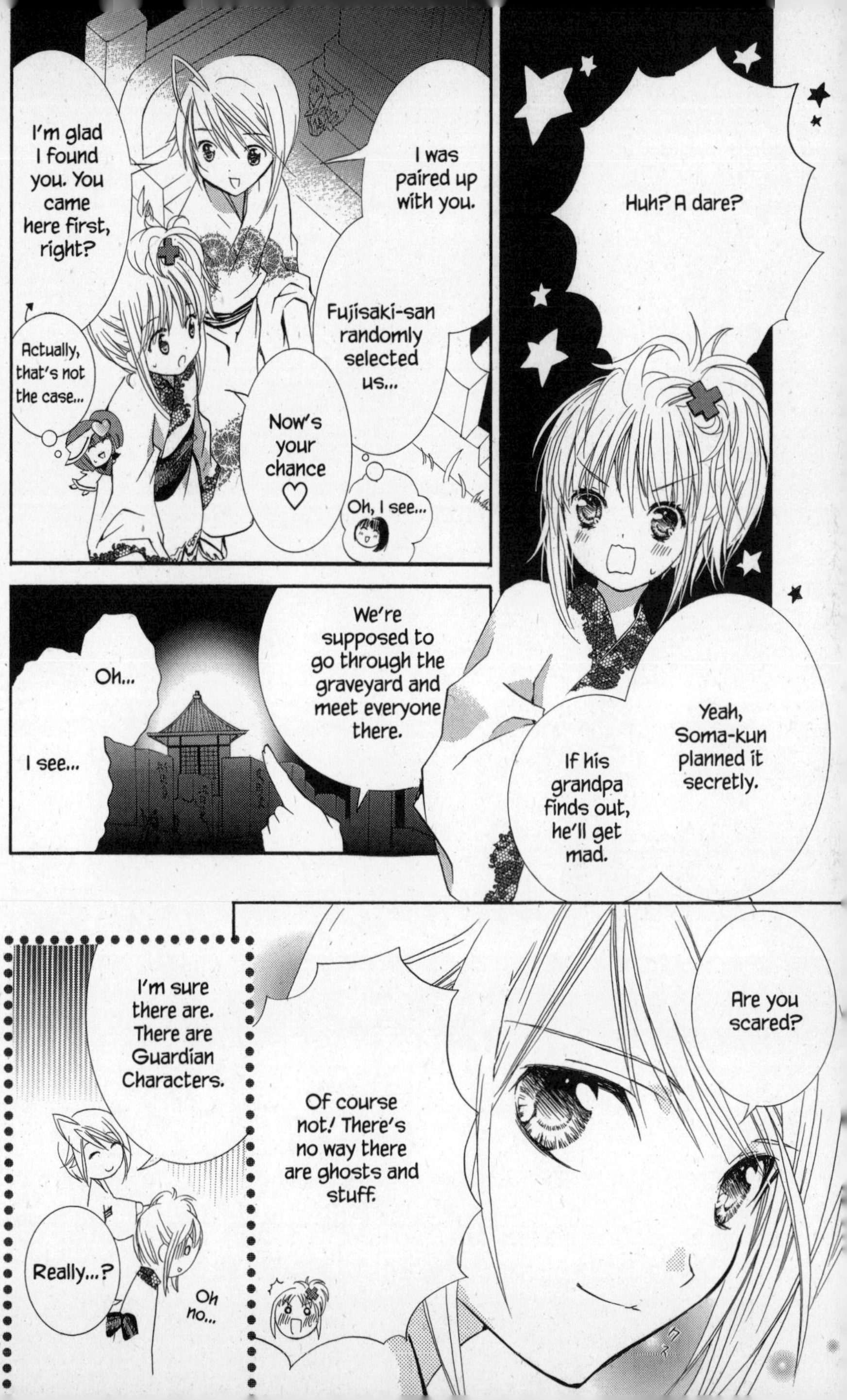

Huh? A dare?
Yeah, Soma-kun planned it secretly.
If his grandpa finds out, he'll get mad.
I was paired up with you.
I'm glad I found you. You came here first, right?
Fujisaki-san randomly selected us...
Now's your chance ♡
Oh, I see...
Actually, that's not the case...
We're supposed to go through the graveyard and meet everyone there.
Oh...
I see...
Are you scared?
Of course not! There's no way there are ghosts and stuff.
I'm sure there are. There are Guardian Characters.
Really...?
Oh no...

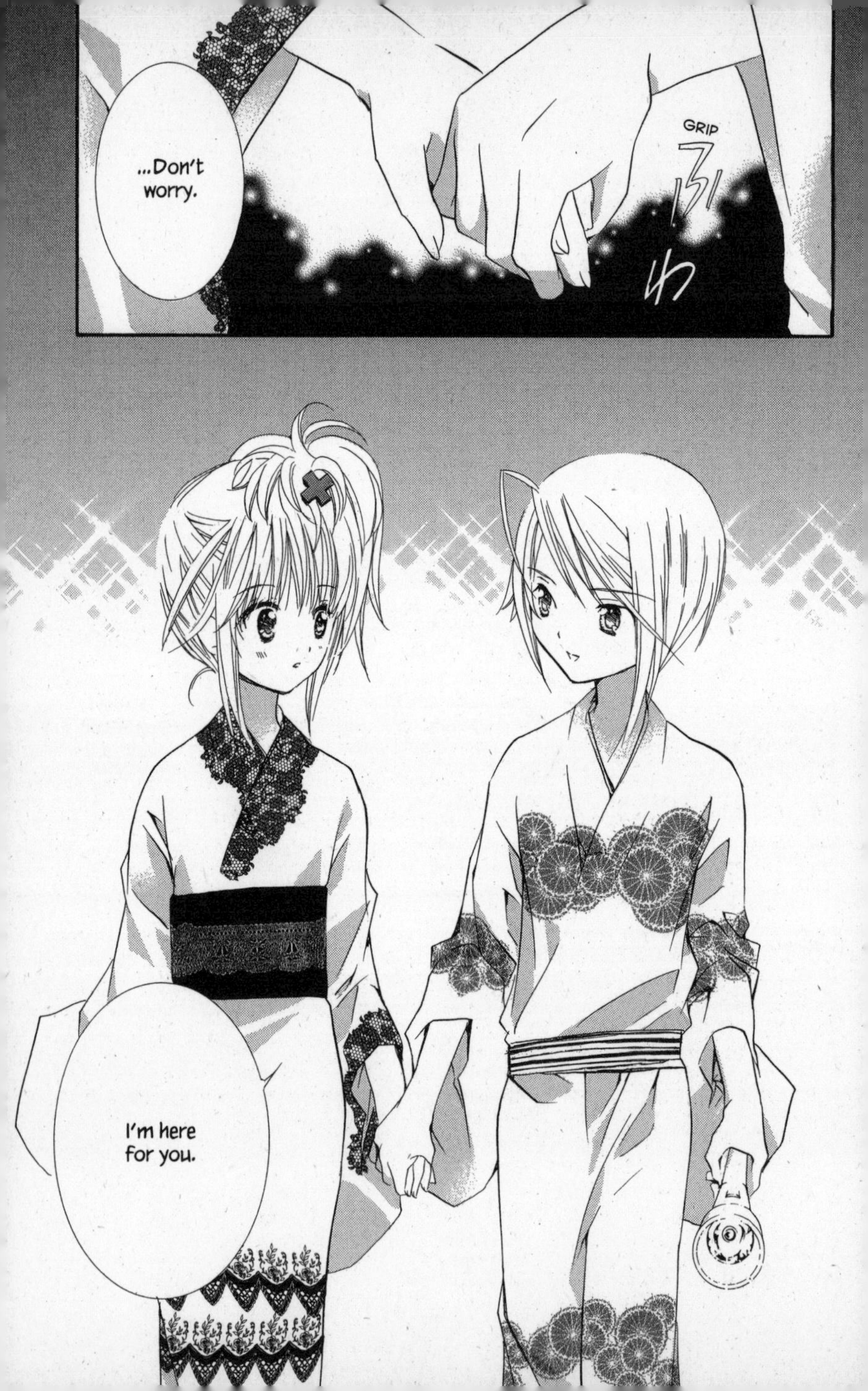
...Don't worry.
GRIP
ぎゅ
I'm here for you.

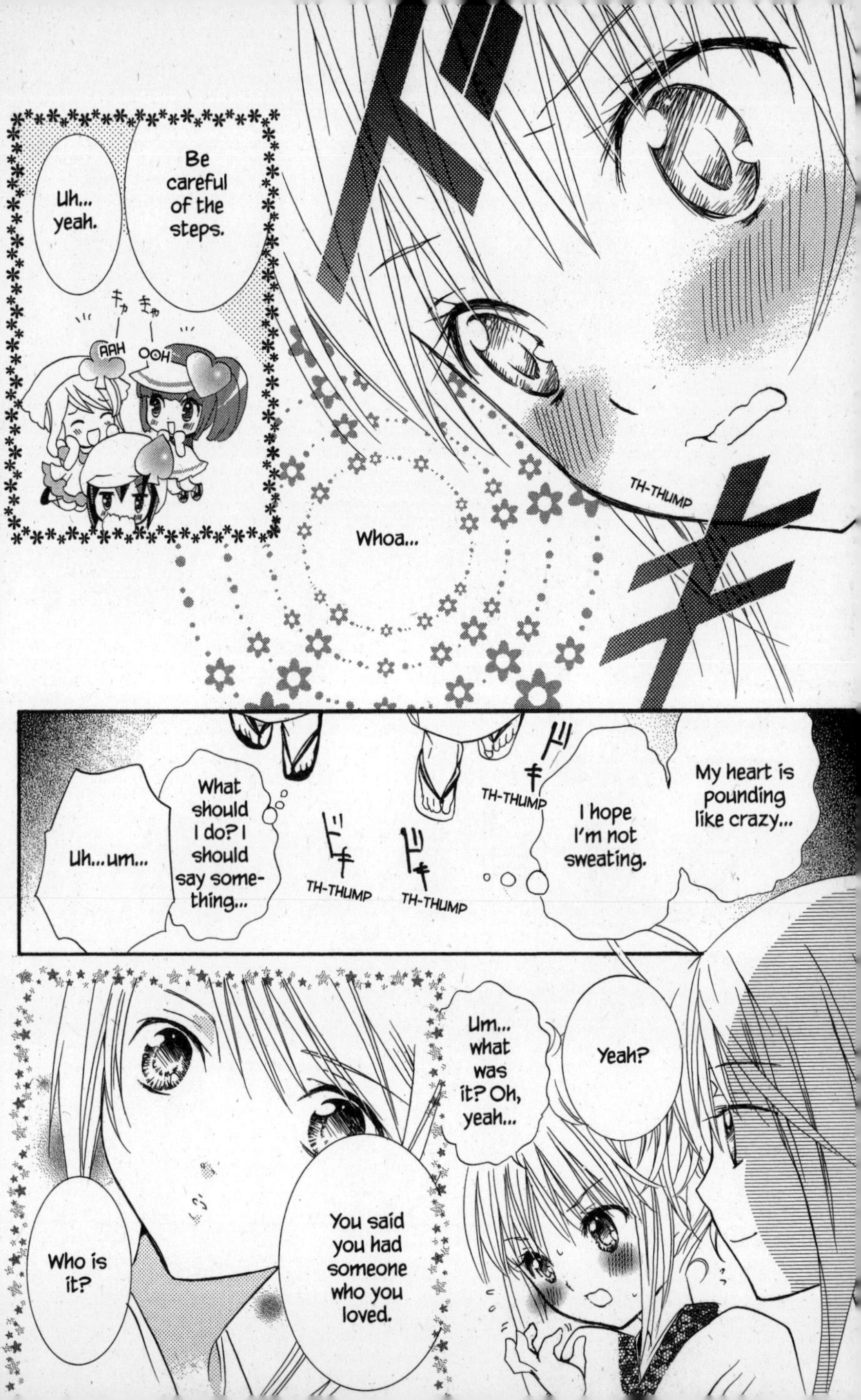
TH-THUMP
Whoa...
Be careful of the steps.
Uh... yeah.
AAH
OOH
My heart is pounding like crazy...
I hope I'm not sweating.
TH-THUMP
TH-THUMP
TH-THUMP
What should I do? I should say something...
Uh...um...
Yeah?
Um... what was it? Oh, yeah...
You said you had someone who you loved.
Who is it?

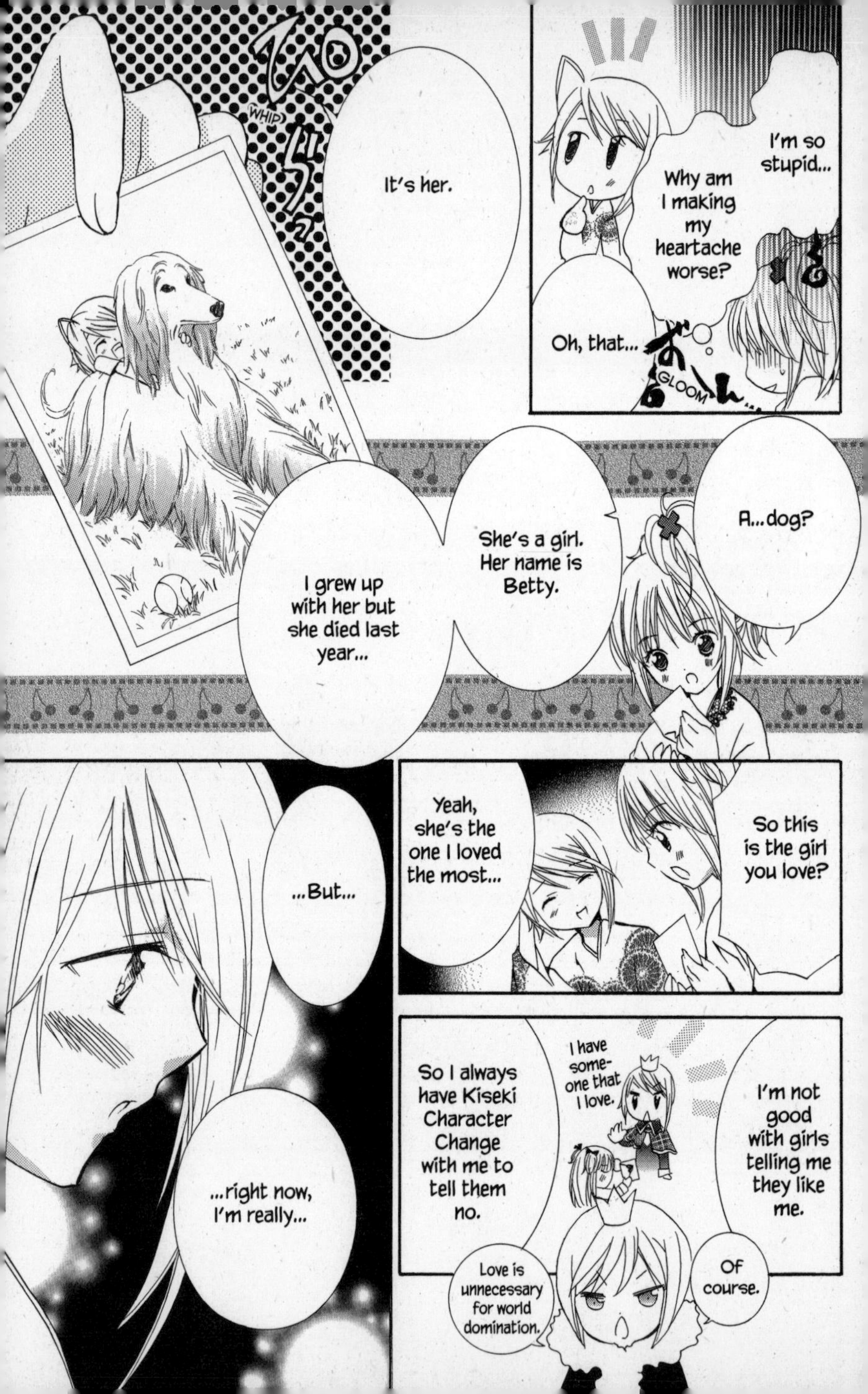
I'm so stupid...
Why am I making my heartache worse?
Oh, that...
GLOOM
WHIP
It's her.
A...dog?
She's a girl. Her name is Betty.
I grew up with her but she died last year...
So this is the girl you love?
Yeah, she's the one I loved the most...
I'm not good with girls telling me they like me.
I have someone that I love.
So I always have Kiseki Character Change with me to tell them no.
Of course.
Love is unnecessary for world domination.
...But...
...right now, I'm really...

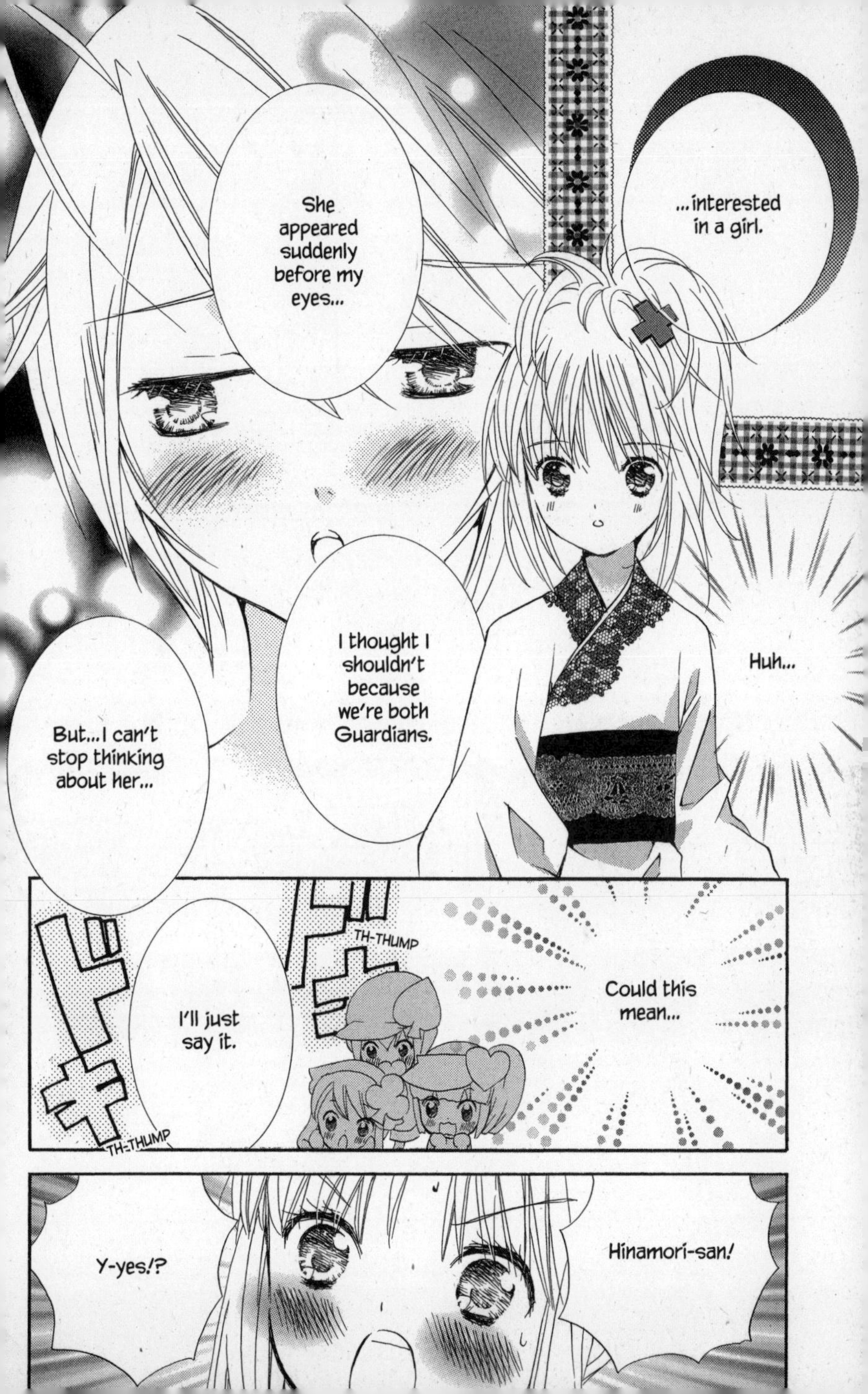
...interested in a girl.
She appeared suddenly before my eyes...
Huh...
I thought I shouldn't because we're both Guardians.
But...I can't stop thinking about her...
Could this mean...
TH-THUMP
I'll just say it.
TH-THUMP
Hinamori-san!
Y-yes!?

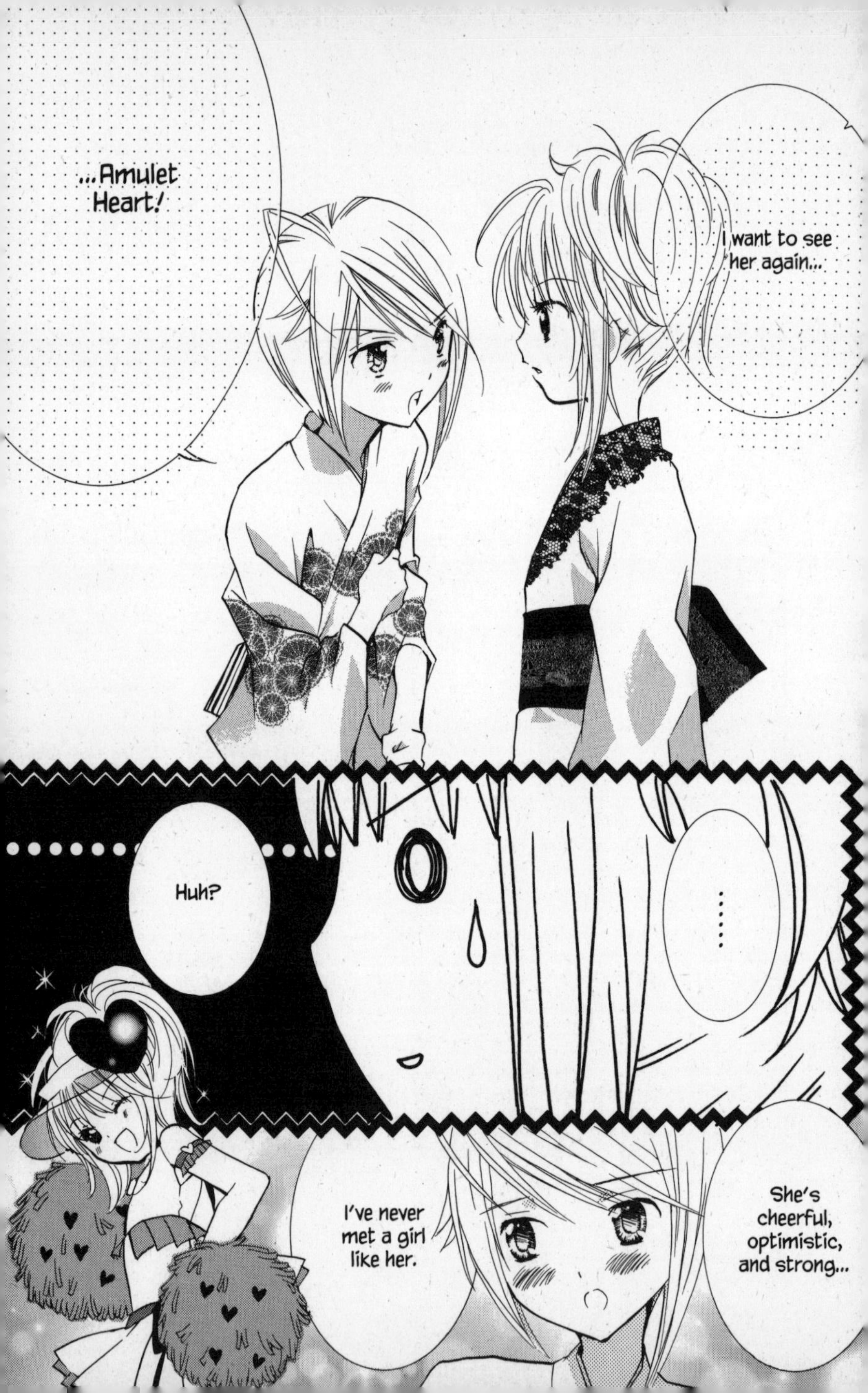
I want to see her again...
...Amulet Heart!
......
Huh?
She's cheerful, optimistic, and strong...
I've never met a girl like her.

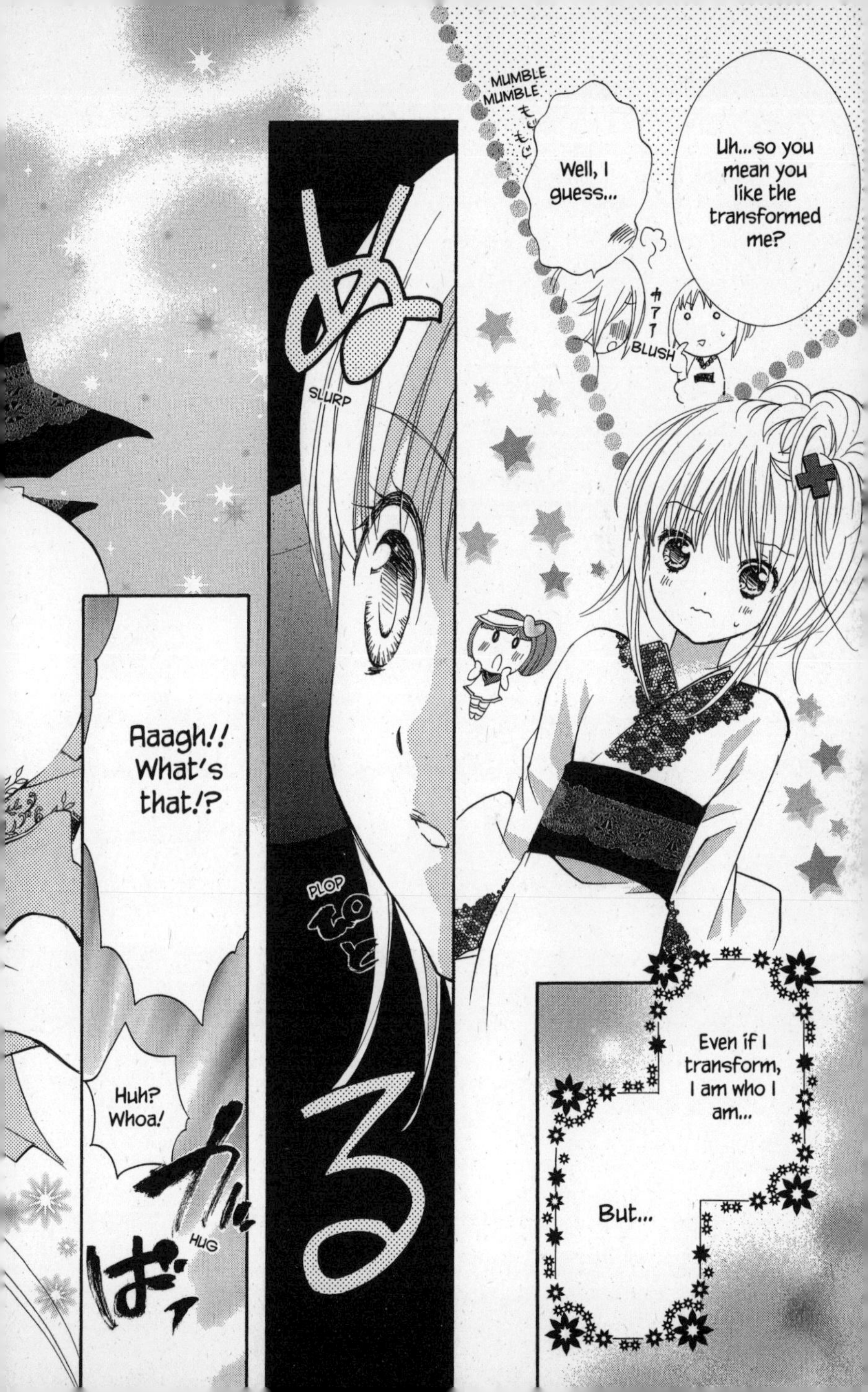
Uh...so you mean you like the transformed me?
MUMBLE MUMBLE
Well, I guess...
BLUSH
Even if I transform, I am who I am...
But...
SLURP
PLOP
Aaagh!! What's that!?
Huh? Whoa!
HUG

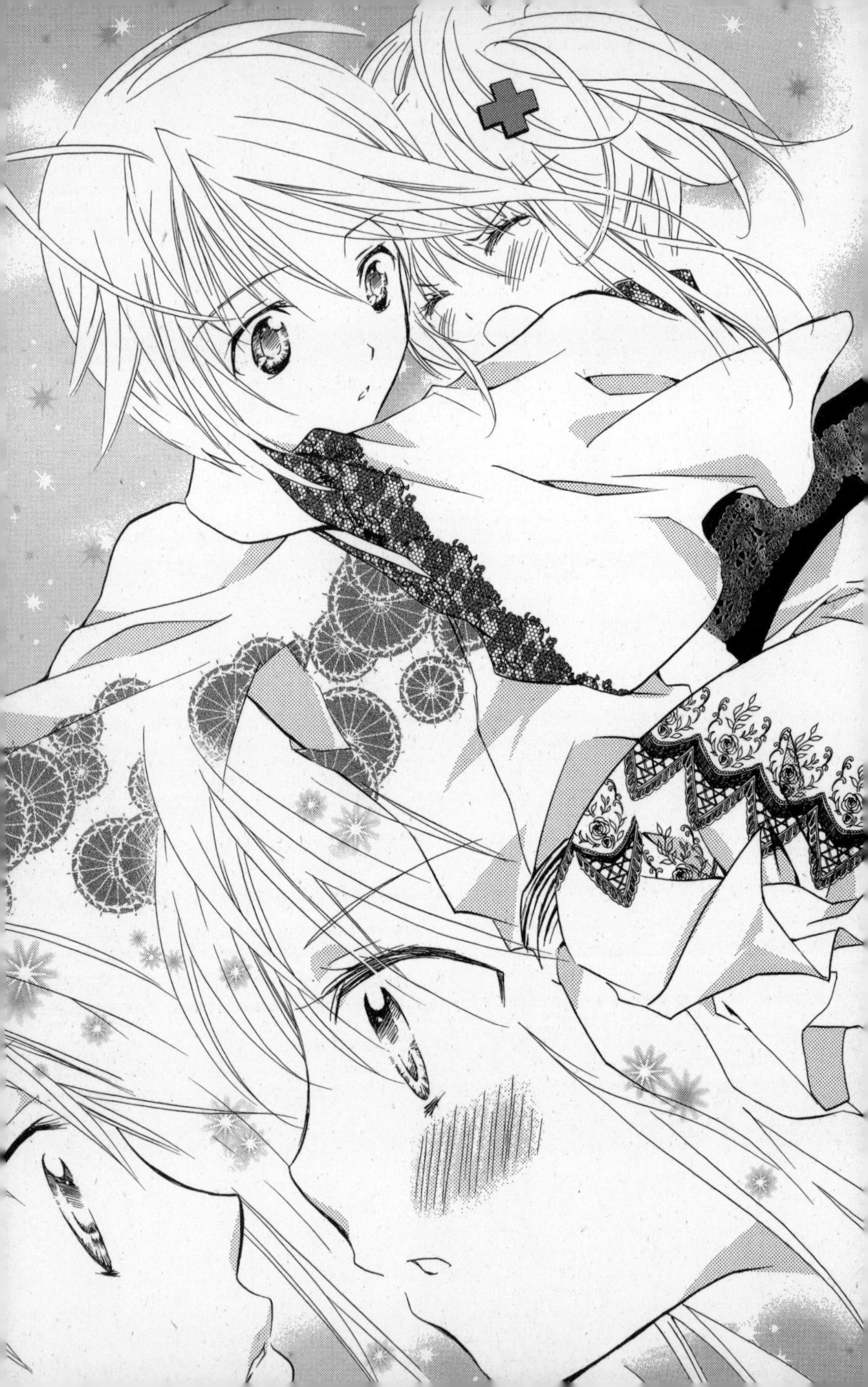

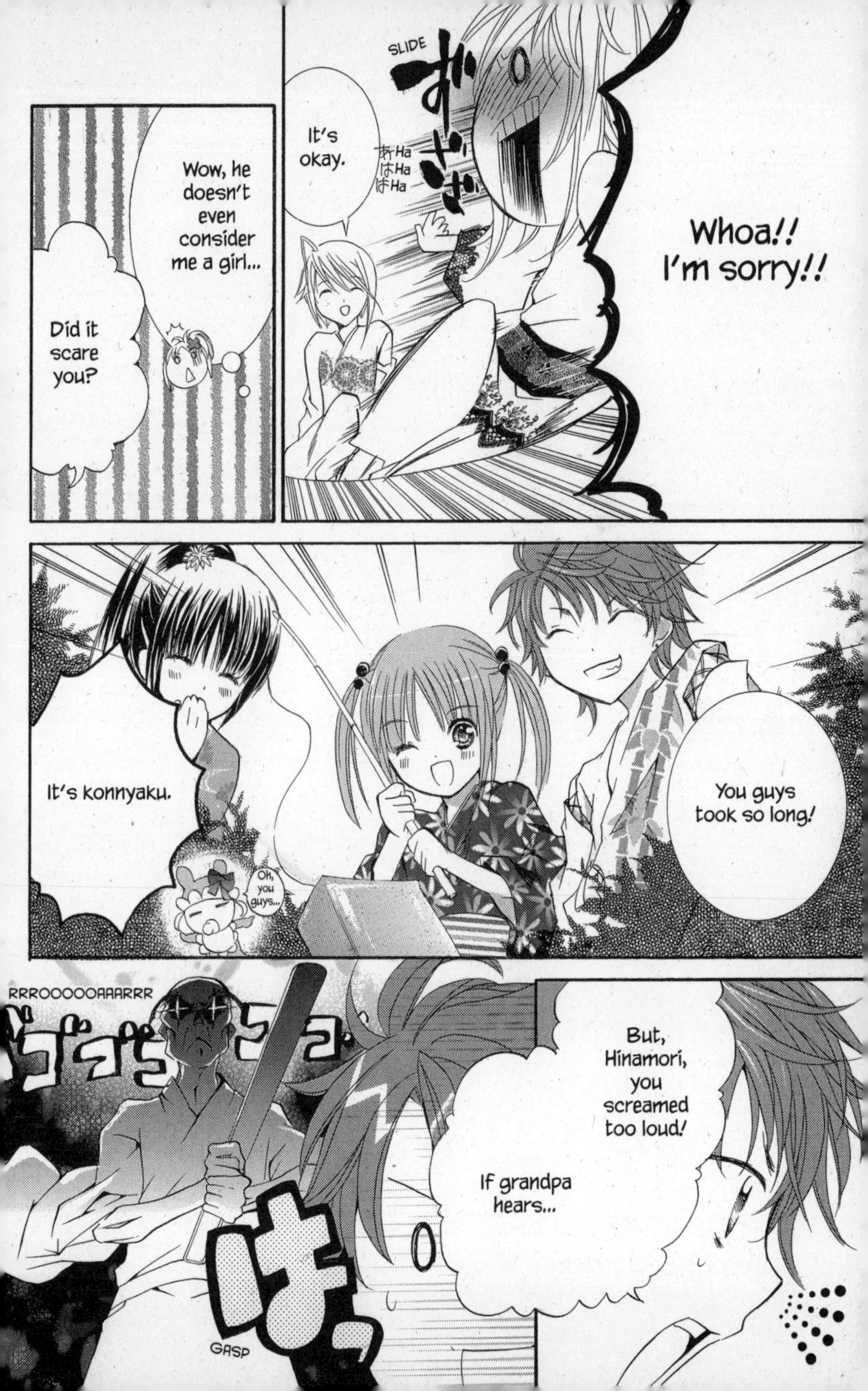
SLIDE
It's okay.
Ha Ha Ha
Whoa!! I'm sorry!!
Wow, he doesn't even consider me a girl...
Did it scare you?
You guys took so long!
Oh, you guys...
It's konnyaku.
But, Hinamori, you screamed too loud!
If grandpa hears...
GASP
RRROOOOOAAARRR

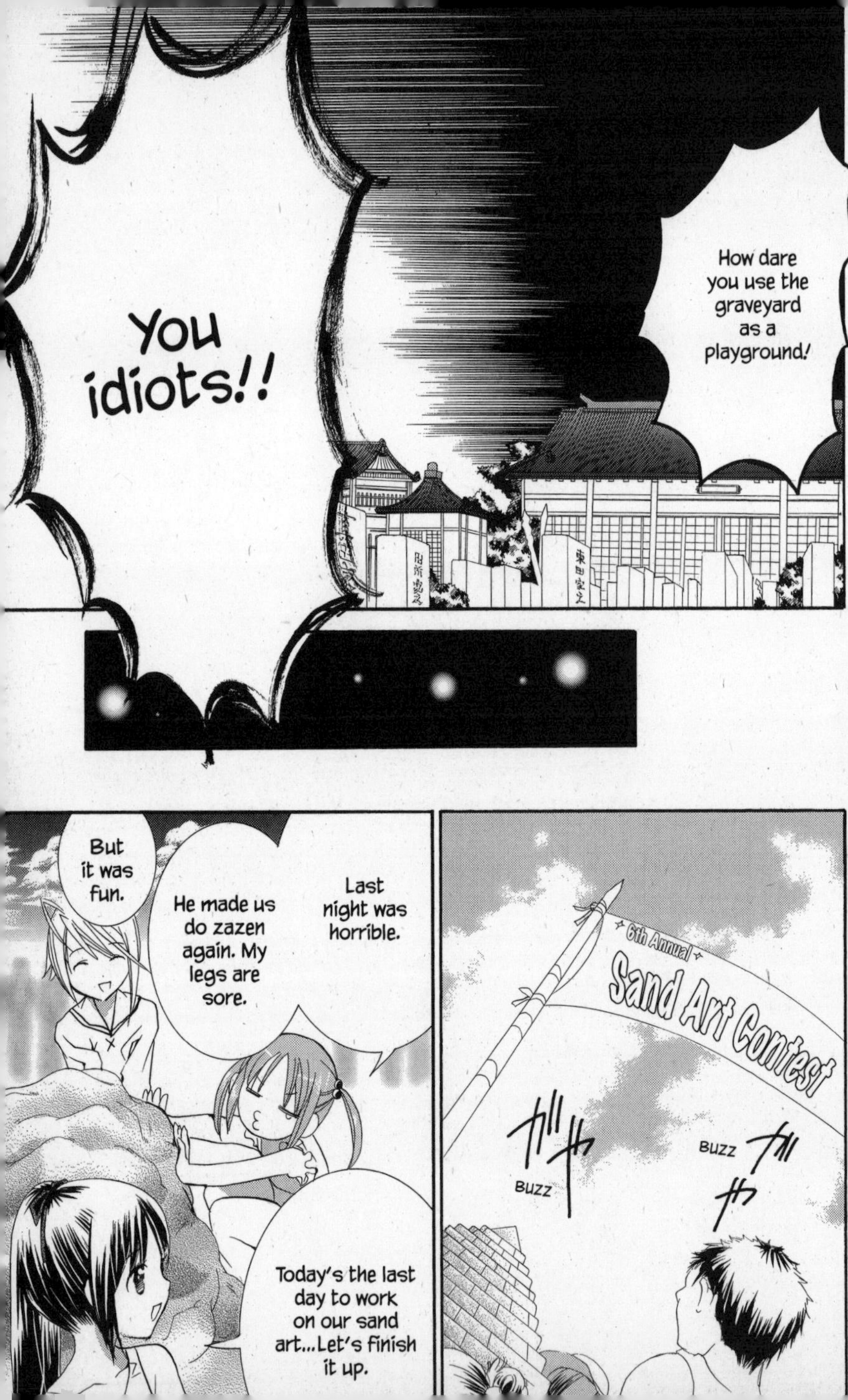
How dare you use the graveyard as a playground!
You idiots!!
6th Annual
Sand Art Contest
BUZZ
BUZZ
Last night was horrible.
He made us do zazen again. My legs are sore.
But it was fun.
Today's the last day to work on our sand art...Let's finish it up.

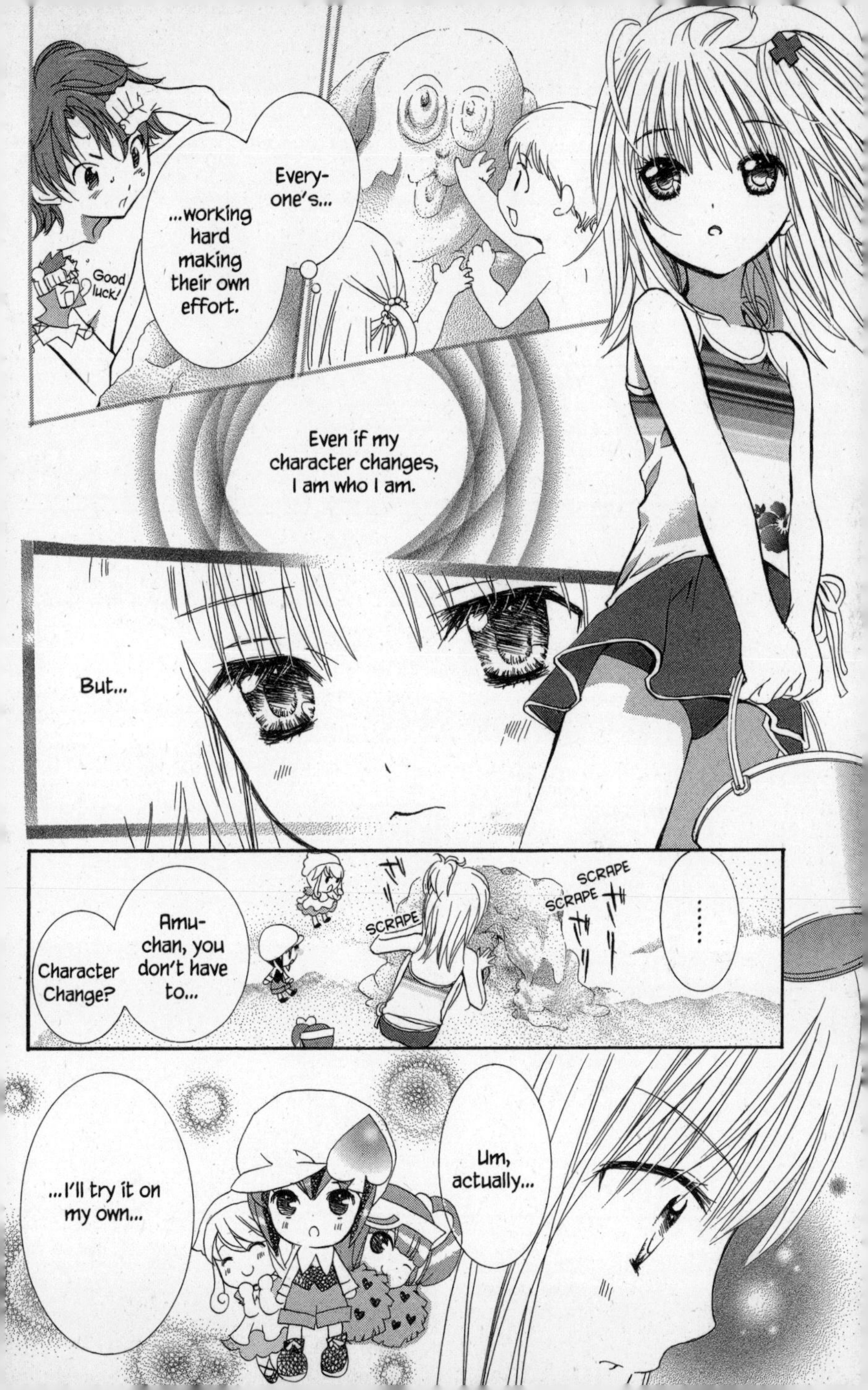
Every-one's...
...working hard making their own effort.
Good luck!
Even if my character changes, I am who I am.
But...
......
SCRAPE
SCRAPE
SCRAPE
Amu-chan, you don't have to...
Character Change?
Um, actually...
...I'll try it on my own...

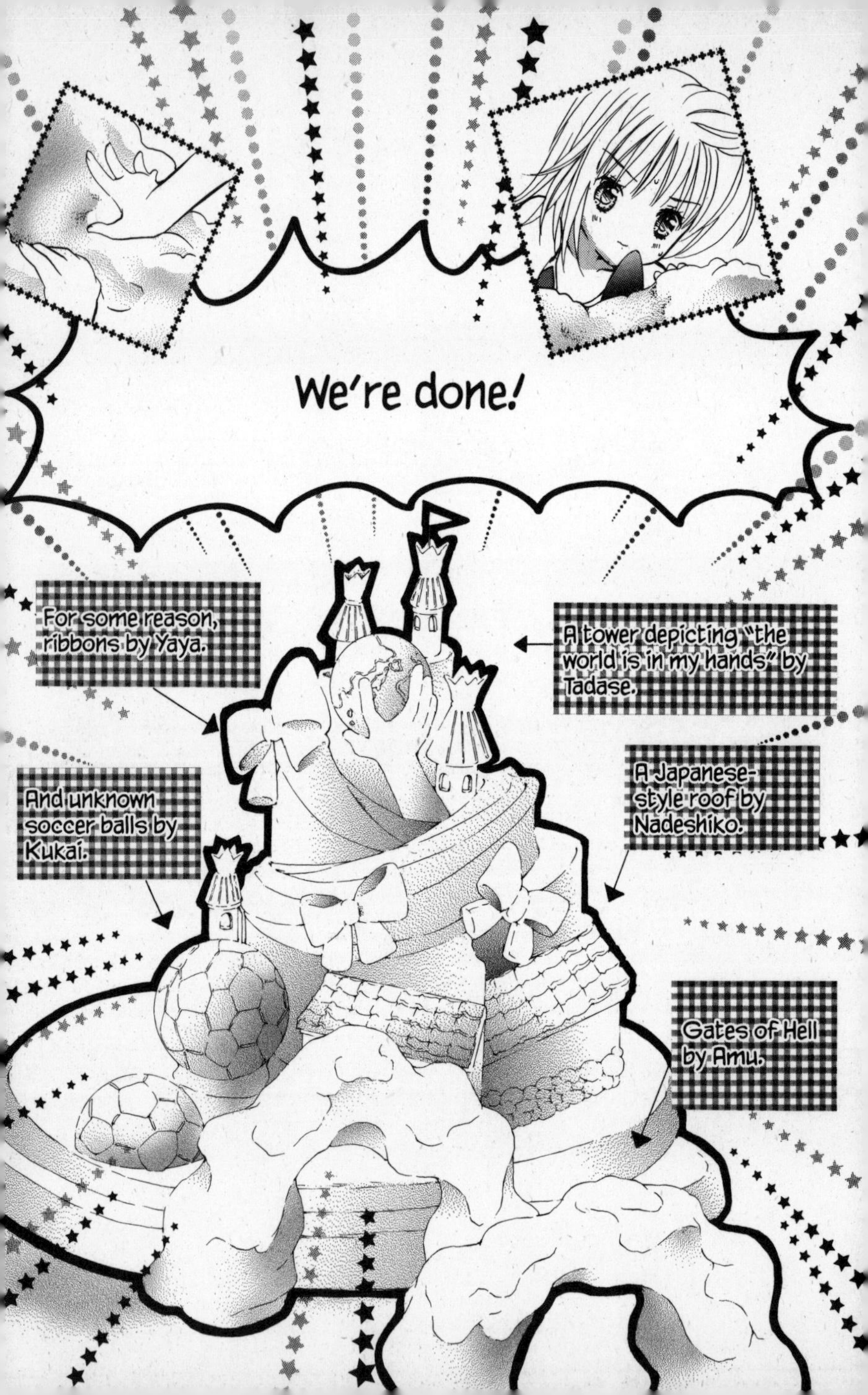
We're done!
A tower depicting "the world is in my hands" by Tadase.
For some reason, ribbons by Yaya.
A Japanese-style roof by Nadeshiko.
And unknown soccer balls by Kukai.
Gates of Hell by Amu.

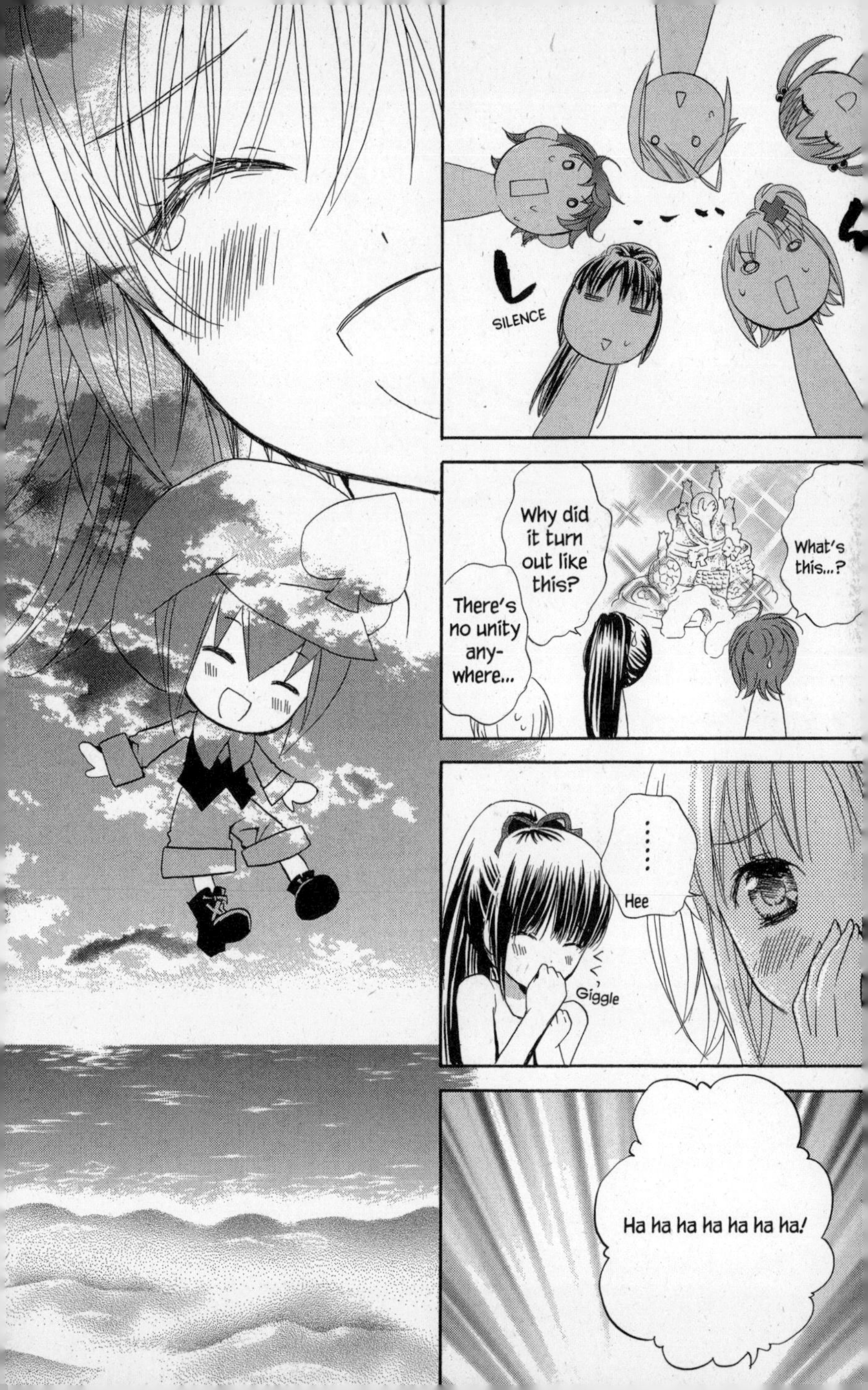
SILENCE
What's this...?
Why did it turn out like this?
There's no unity anywhere...
......
Hee
Giggle
Ha ha ha ha ha ha ha!

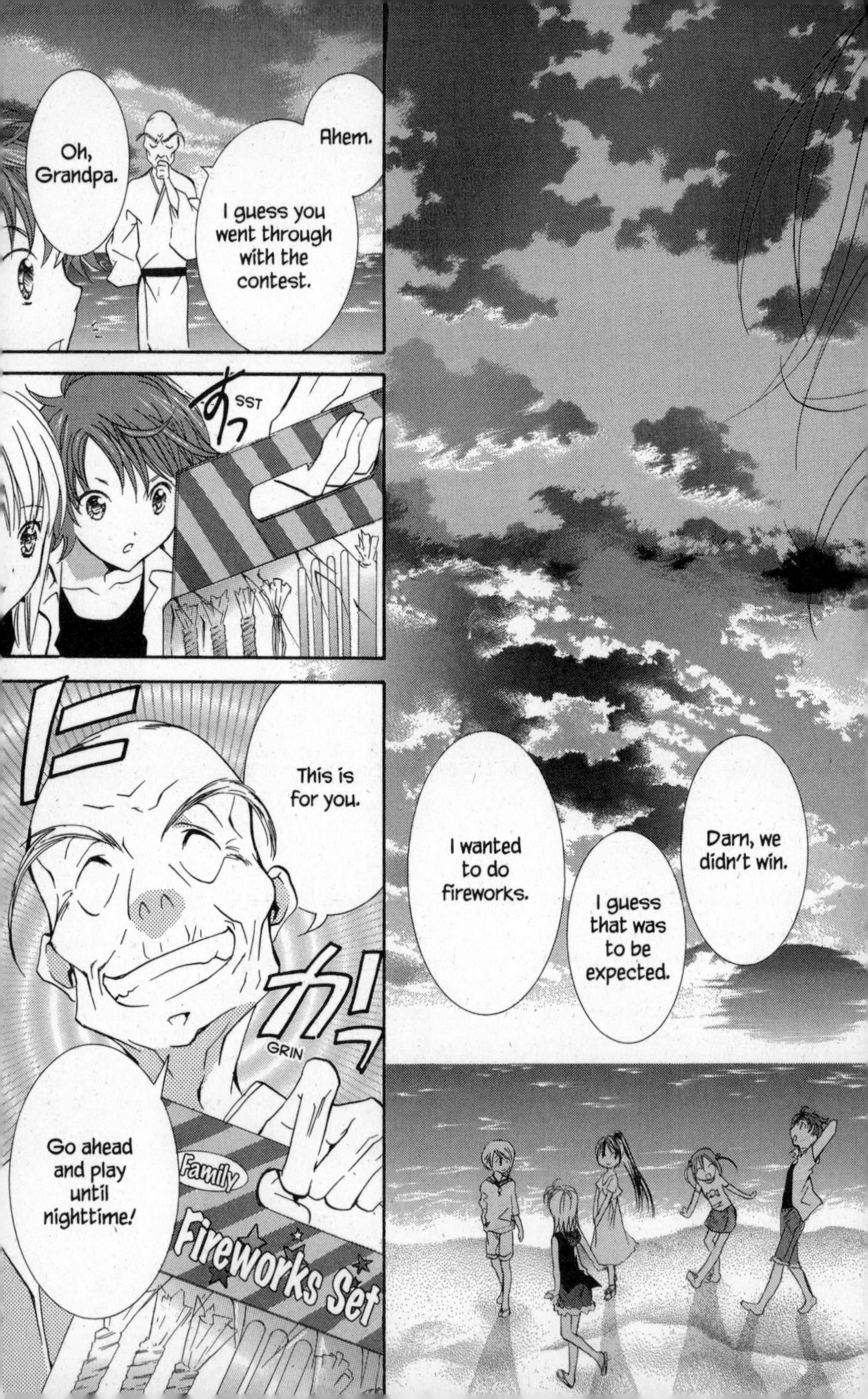
Darn, we didn't win.
I guess that was to be expected.
I wanted to do fireworks.
Ahem.
I guess you went through with the contest.
Oh, Grandpa.
SST
This is for you.
GRIN
Go ahead and play until nighttime!
Family
Fireworks Set

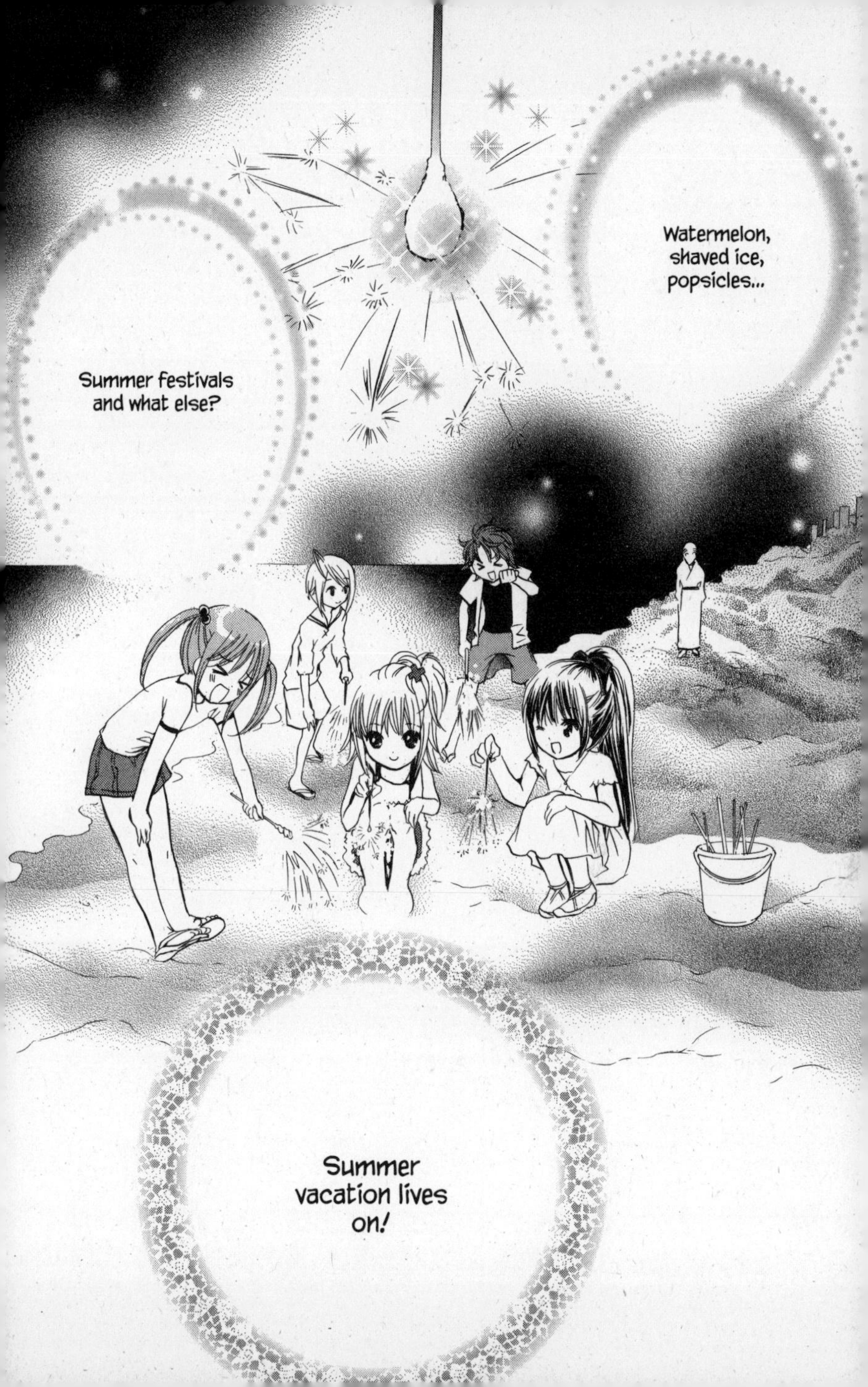
Watermelon, shaved ice, popsicles...
Summer festivals and what else?
Summer vacation lives on!

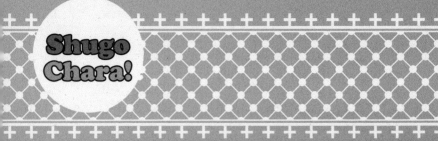

Shugo Chara!

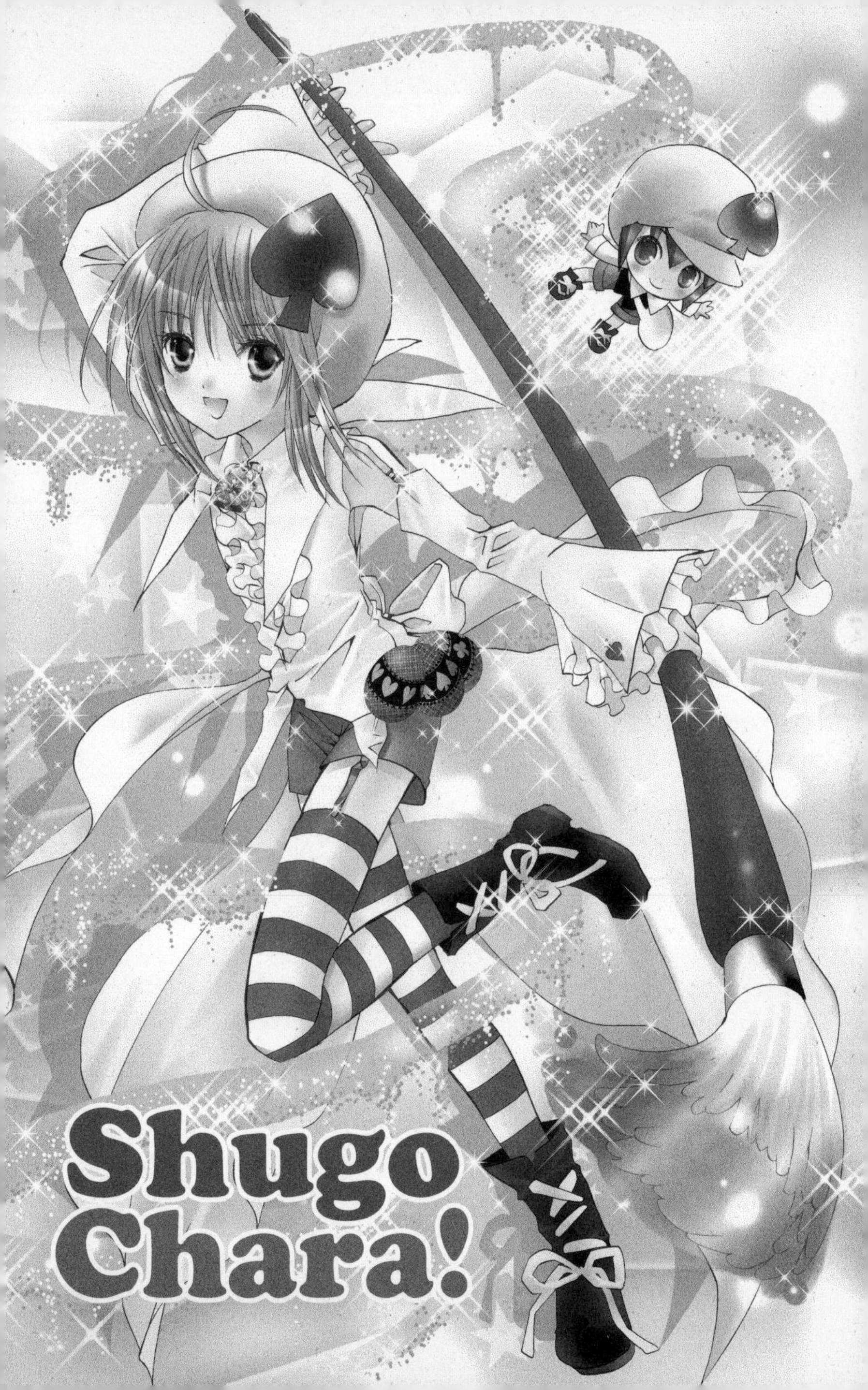
Shugo
Chara!

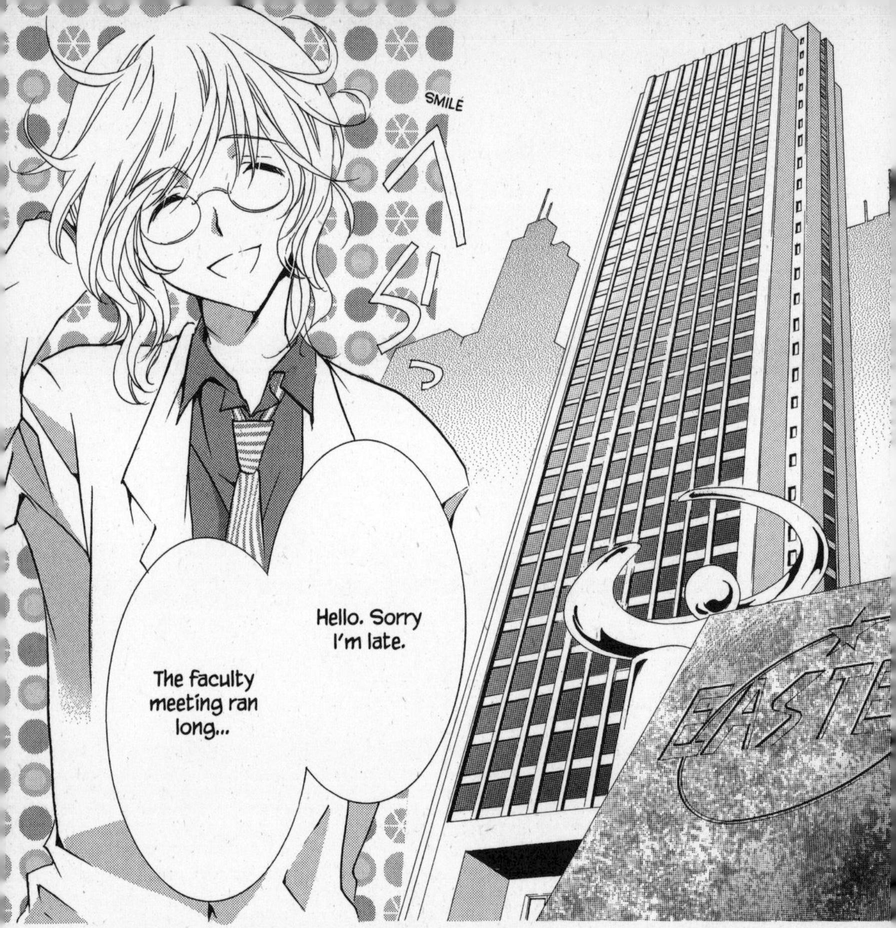
SMILE
Hello. Sorry I'm late.
The faculty meeting ran long...

Continued

The costumes for Character Transformation were decided on by first picking a theme. I thought it should be cheerleader-like.

We don't wear clothes like Amu-chan, but we like to see and draw them! When we see girls wearing them, we gawk.

Q3: Do you like Tadase or Ikuto?

A3: I like them both. I can't decide!

Thank you for all the letters! Sorry we can't answer all of the questions. We'll answer more questions in volume 3. We'll see you then!

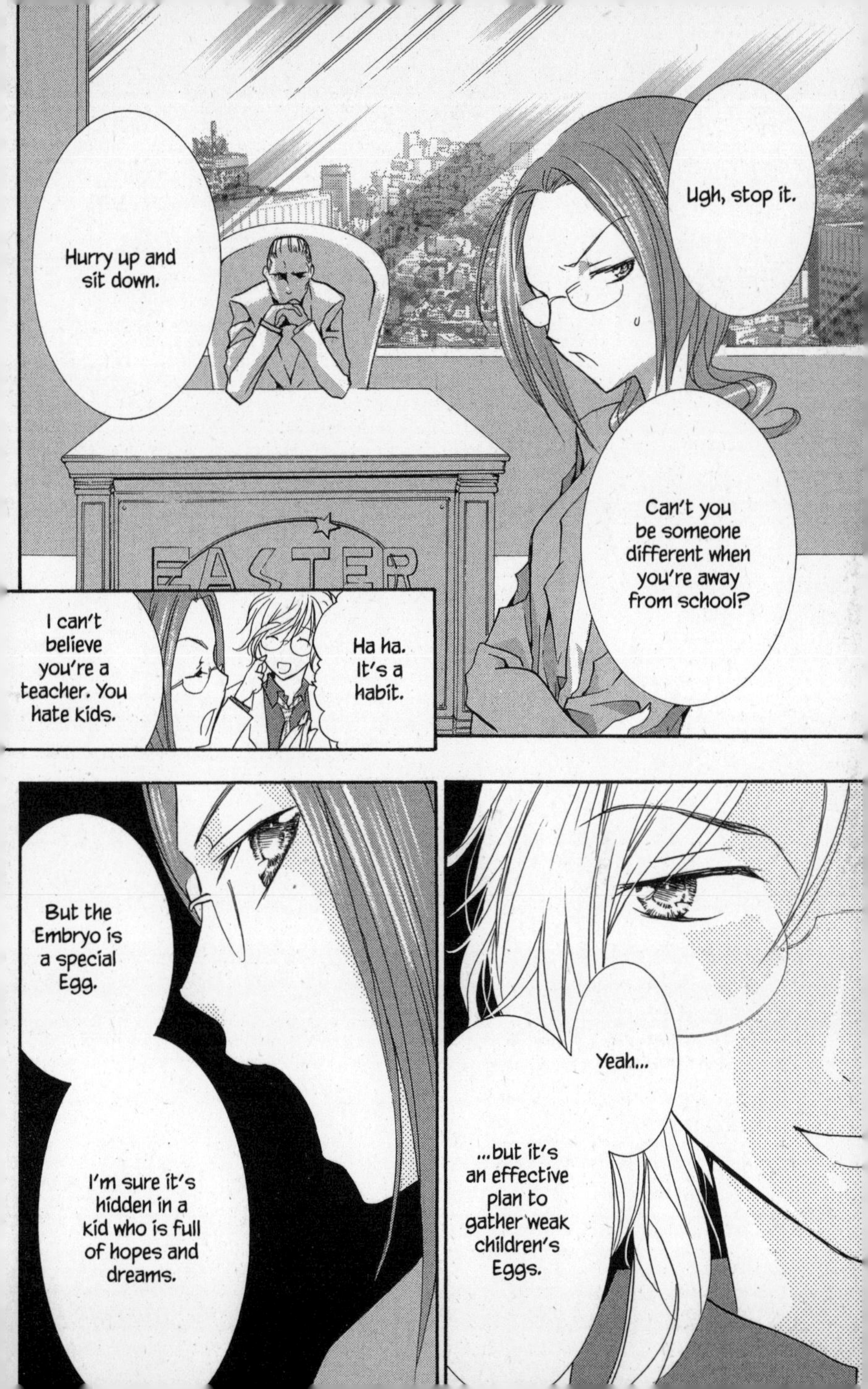
Ugh, stop it.
Hurry up and sit down.
EASTER
Can't you be someone different when you're away from school?
Ha ha. It's a habit.
I can't believe you're a teacher. You hate kids.
Yeah...
...but it's an effective plan to gather weak children's Eggs.
But the Embryo is a special Egg.
I'm sure it's hidden in a kid who is full of hopes and dreams.

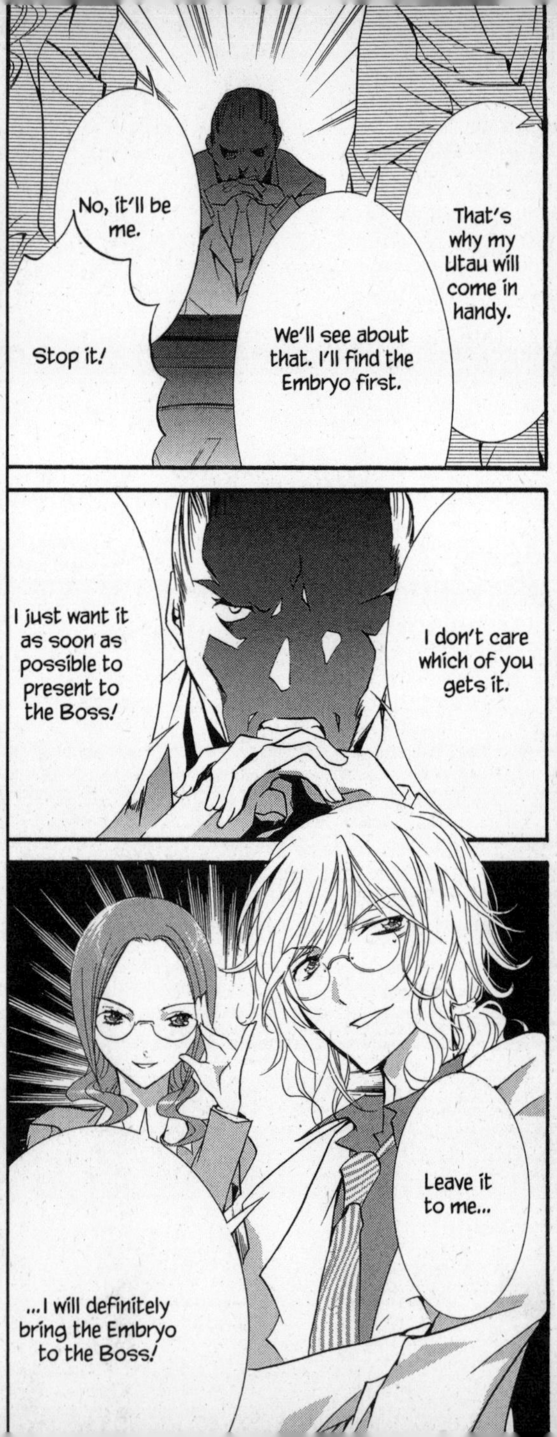
That's why my Utau will come in handy.
We'll see about that. I'll find the Embryo first.
No, it'll be me.
Stop it!
I don't care which of you gets it.
I just want it as soon as possible to present to the Boss!
Leave it to me...
...I will definitely bring the Embryo to the Boss!

character profile

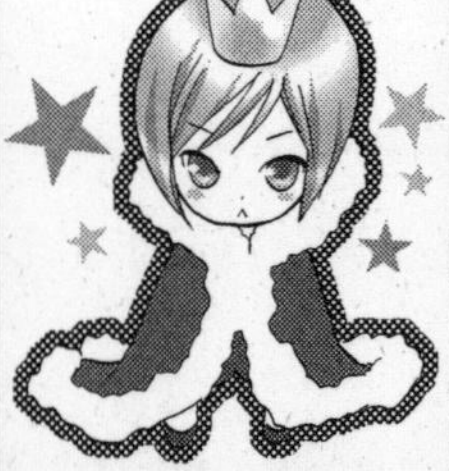

キセキ

KISEKI

Guardian Character of: Tadase

Special Skill: Giving orders

Does not like to: Obey

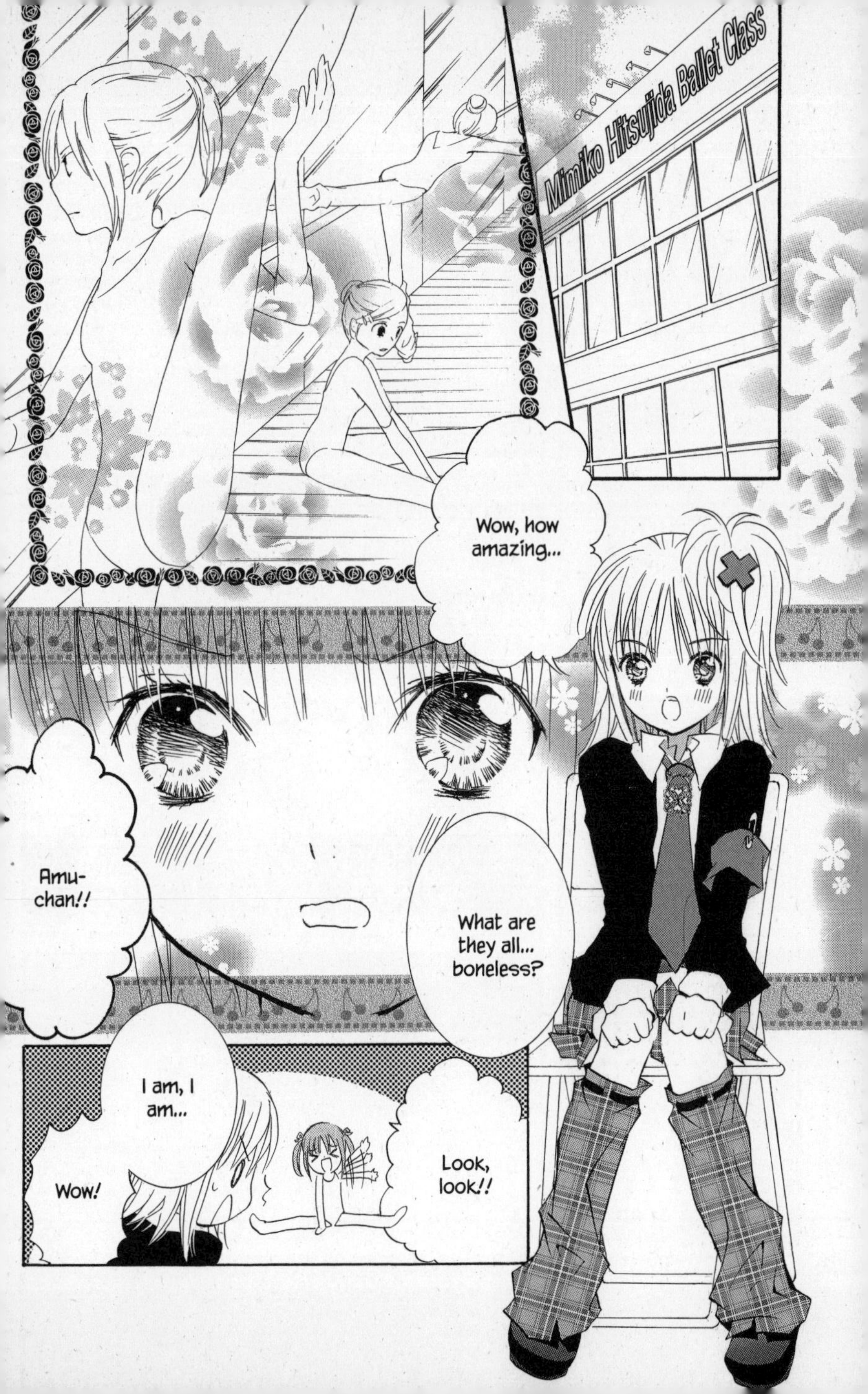
Mimiko Hitsujida Ballet Class
Wow, how amazing...
What are they all... boneless?
Amu-chan!!
Look, look!!
I am, I am...
Wow!

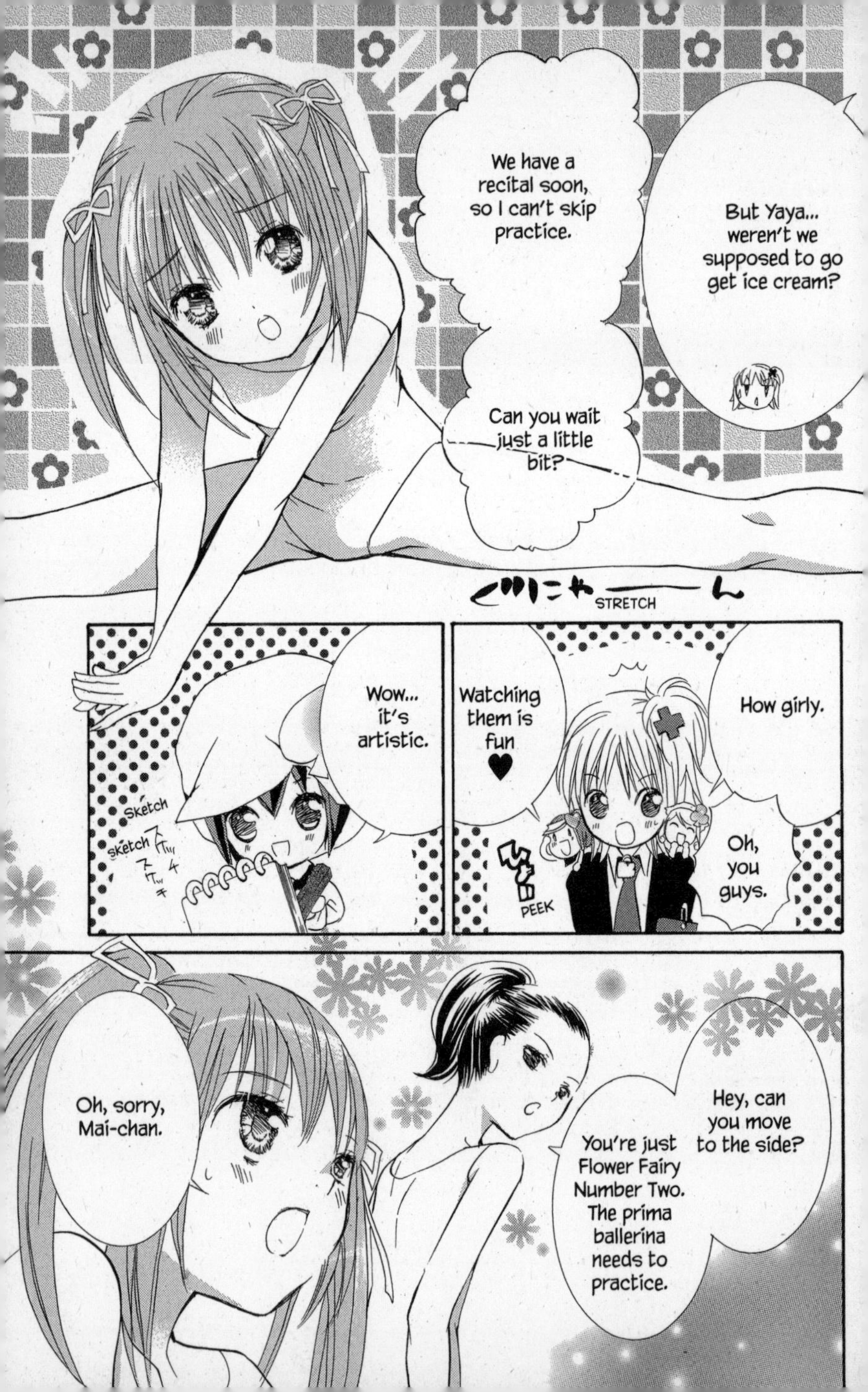
But Yaya... weren't we supposed to go get ice cream?
We have a recital soon, so I can't skip practice.
Can you wait just a little bit?
STRETCH
How girly.
Oh, you guys.
Watching them is fun ♥
PEEK
Wow... it's artistic.
Sketch
sketch
Hey, can you move to the side?
You're just Flower Fairy Number Two. The prima ballerina needs to practice.
Oh, sorry, Mai-chan.

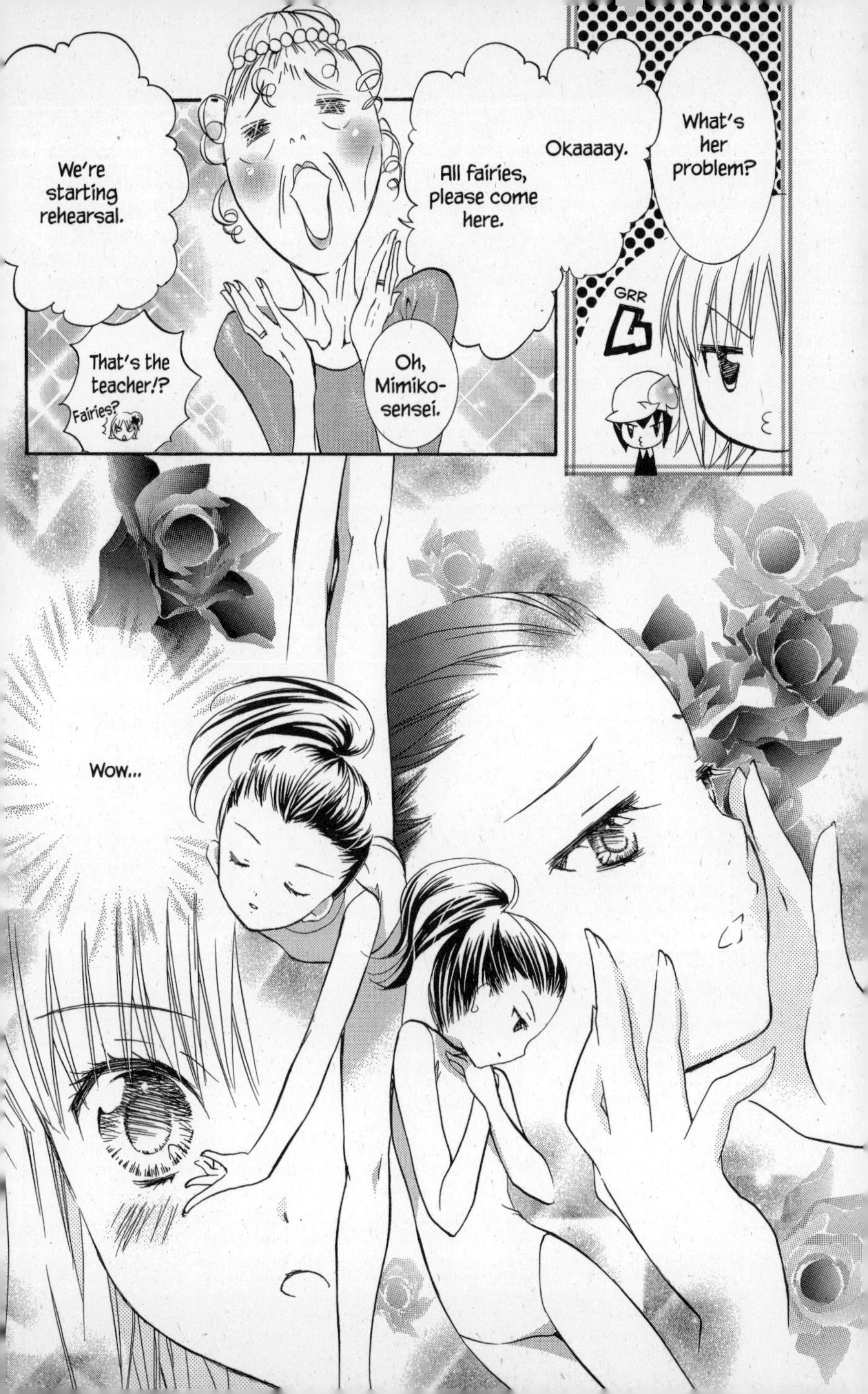
What's her problem?
GRR
Okaaaay.
All fairies, please come here.
We're starting rehearsal.
Oh, Mimiko-sensei.
That's the teacher!?
Fairies?
Wow...

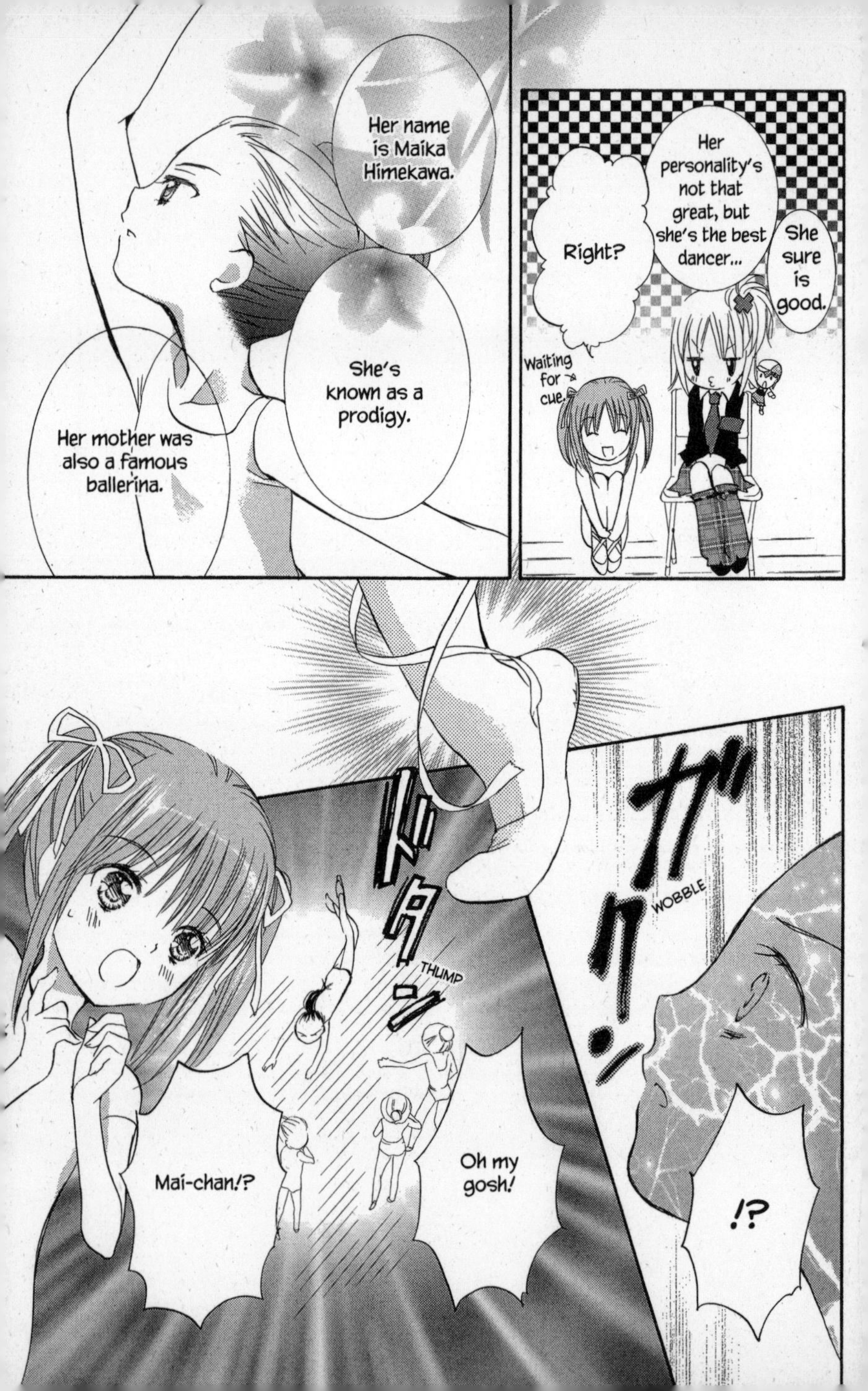
She sure is good.
Her personality's not that great, but she's the best dancer...
Right?
Waiting for cue.
Her name is Maika Himekawa.
She's known as a prodigy.
Her mother was also a famous ballerina.
WOBBLE
!?
THUMP
Oh my gosh!
Mai-chan!?

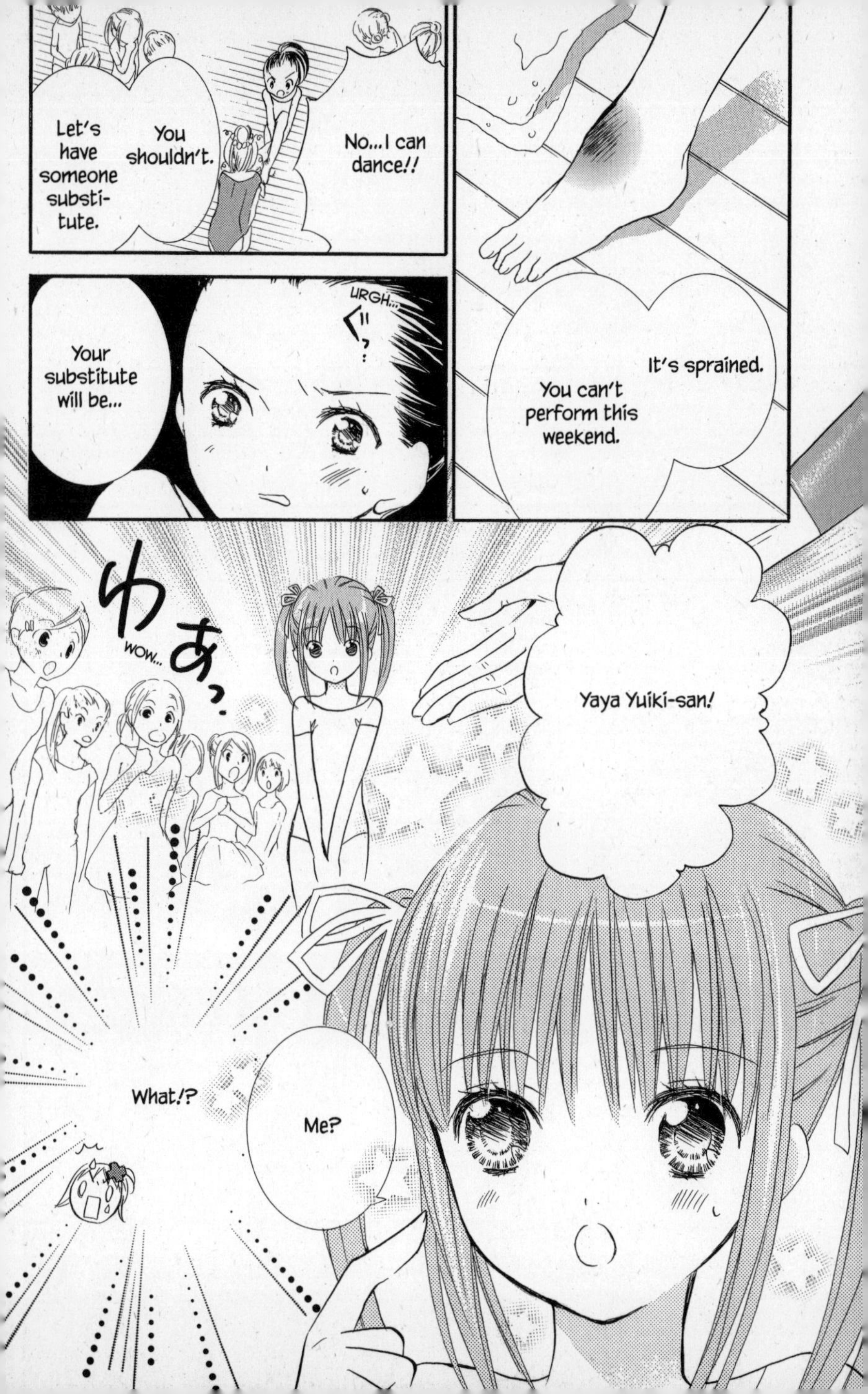
It's sprained.
You can't perform this weekend.
No...I can dance!!
You shouldn't.
Let's have someone substi-tute.
URGH...
Your substitute will be...
Yaya Yuiki-san!
ゆあっ
WOW...
Me?
What!?

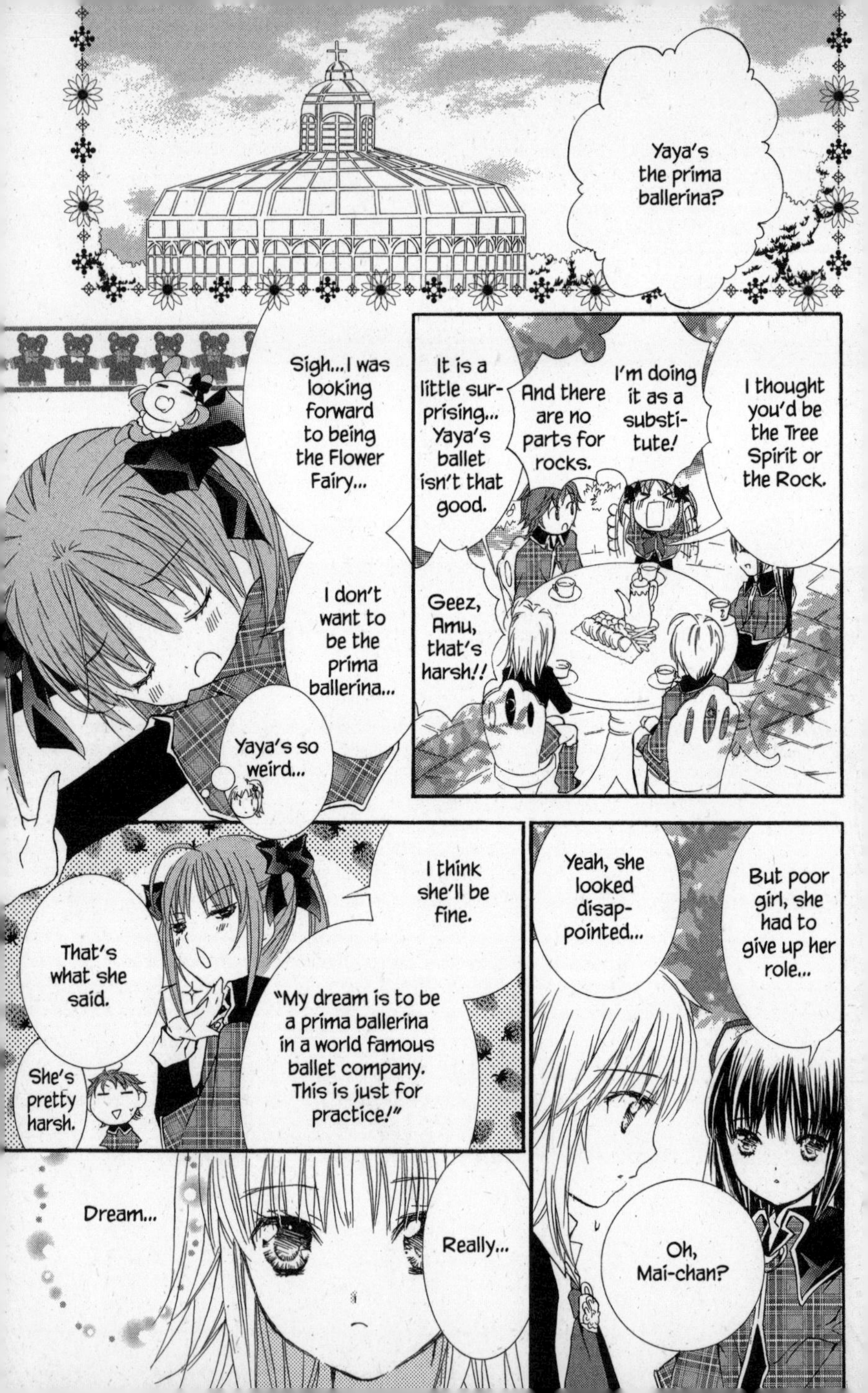
Yaya's the prima ballerina?
I thought you'd be the Tree Spirit or the Rock.
I'm doing it as a substitute!
And there are no parts for rocks.
It is a little surprising... Yaya's ballet isn't that good.
Geez, Amu, that's harsh!!
Sigh...I was looking forward to being the Flower Fairy...
I don't want to be the prima ballerina...
Yaya's so weird...
But poor girl, she had to give up her role...
Yeah, she looked disappointed...
I think she'll be fine.
"My dream is to be a prima ballerina in a world famous ballet company. This is just for practice!"
That's what she said.
She's pretty harsh.
Oh, Mai-chan?
Really...
Dream...

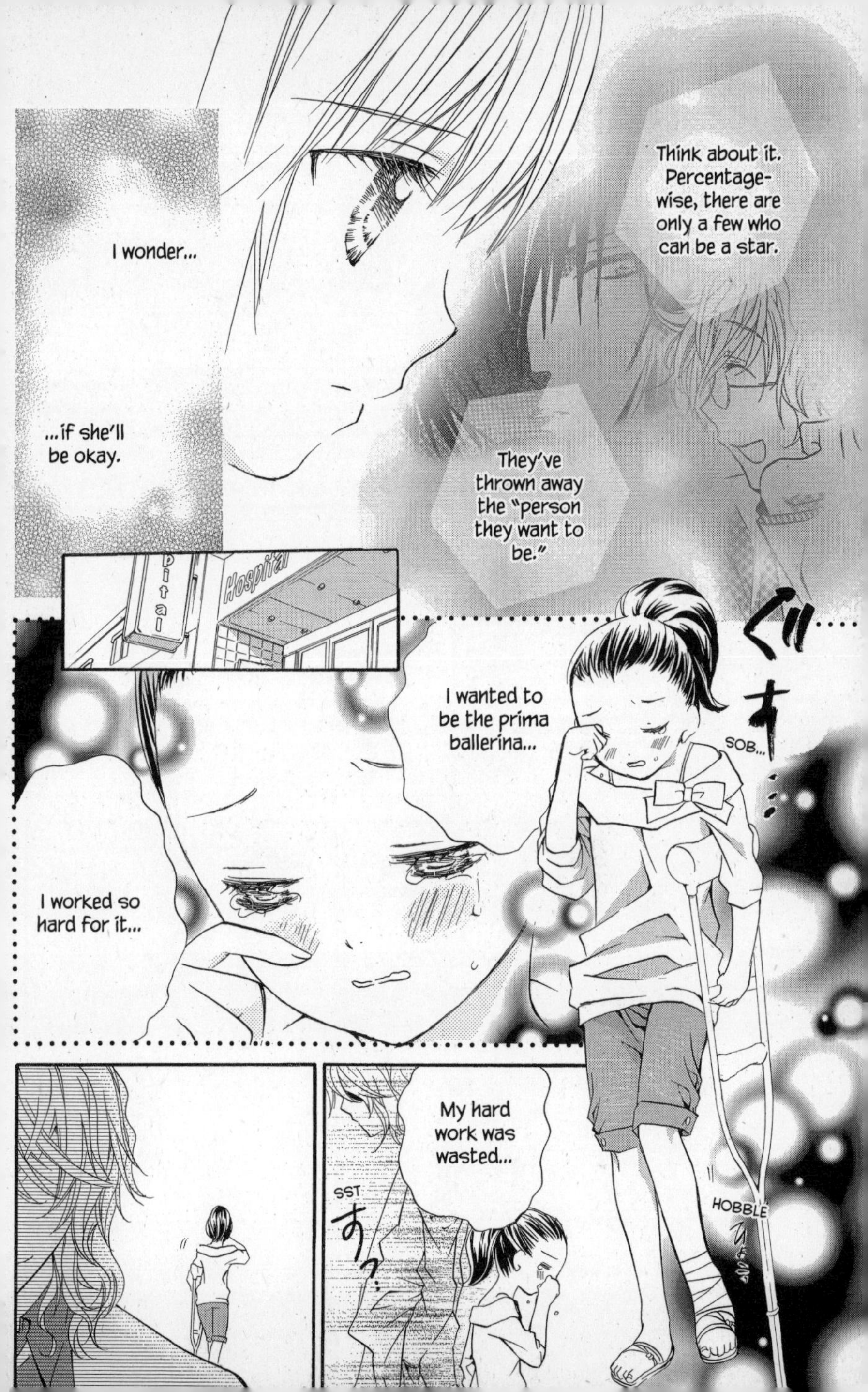
Think about it. Percentage-wise, there are only a few who can be a star.
They've thrown away the "person they want to be."
I wonder...
...if she'll be okay.
Hospital
SOB...
I wanted to be the prima ballerina...
I worked so hard for it...
HOBBLE
My hard work was wasted...
SST

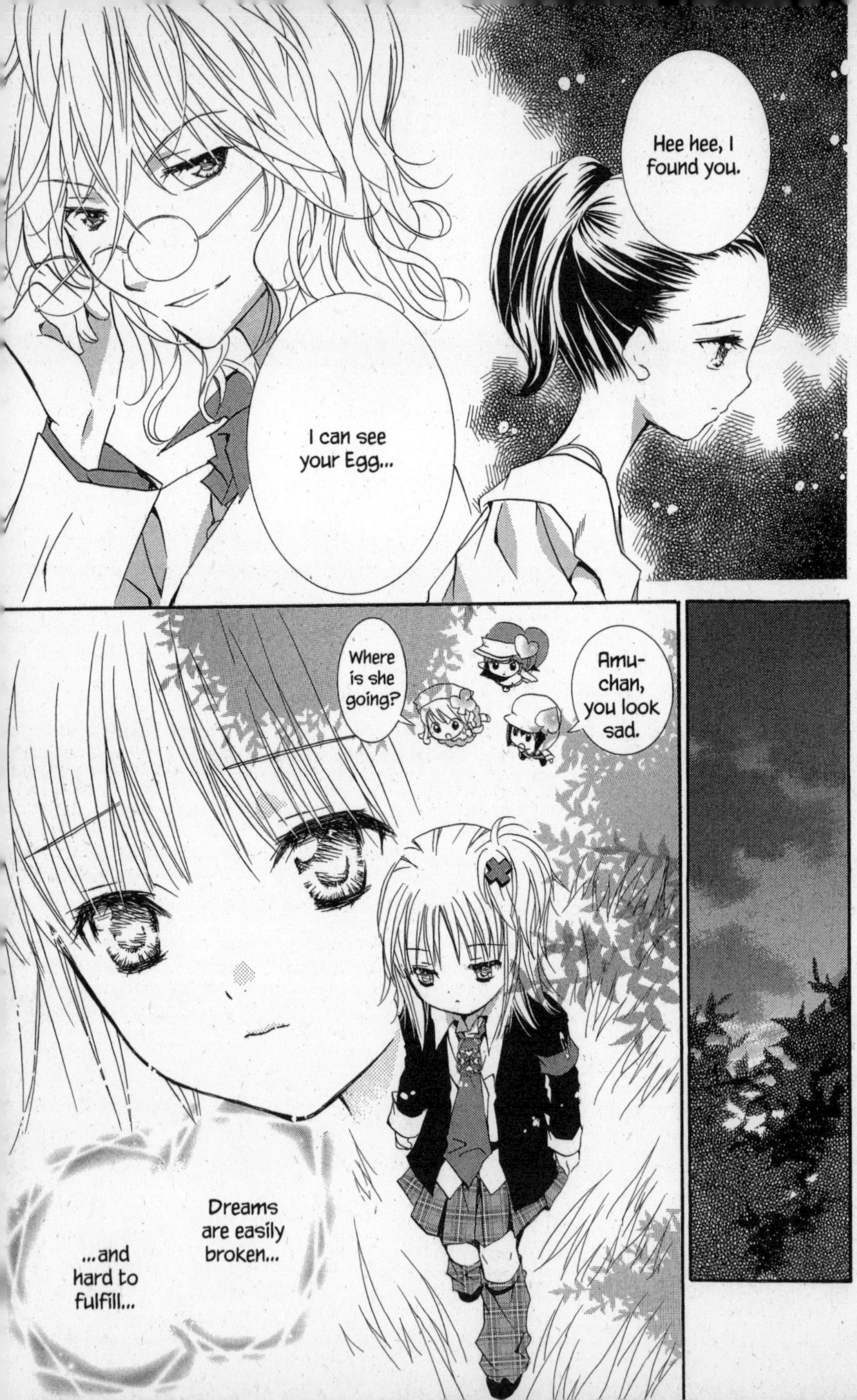
Hee hee, I found you.
I can see your Egg...
Amu-chan, you look sad.
Where is she going?
Dreams are easily broken...
...and hard to fulfill...

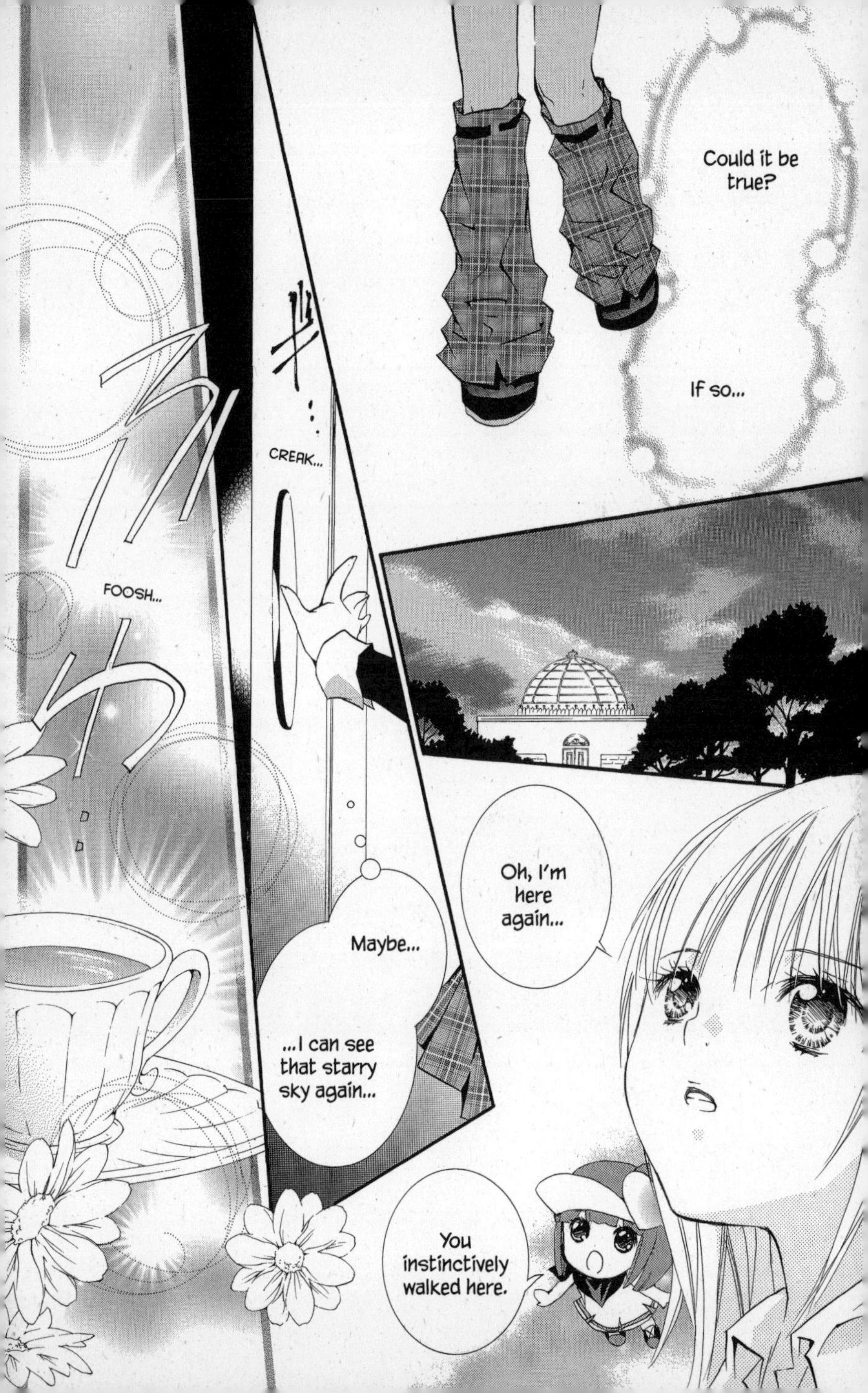
Could it be true?
If so...
Oh, I'm here again...
You instinctively walked here.
CREAK...
Maybe...
...I can see that starry sky again...
FOOSH...

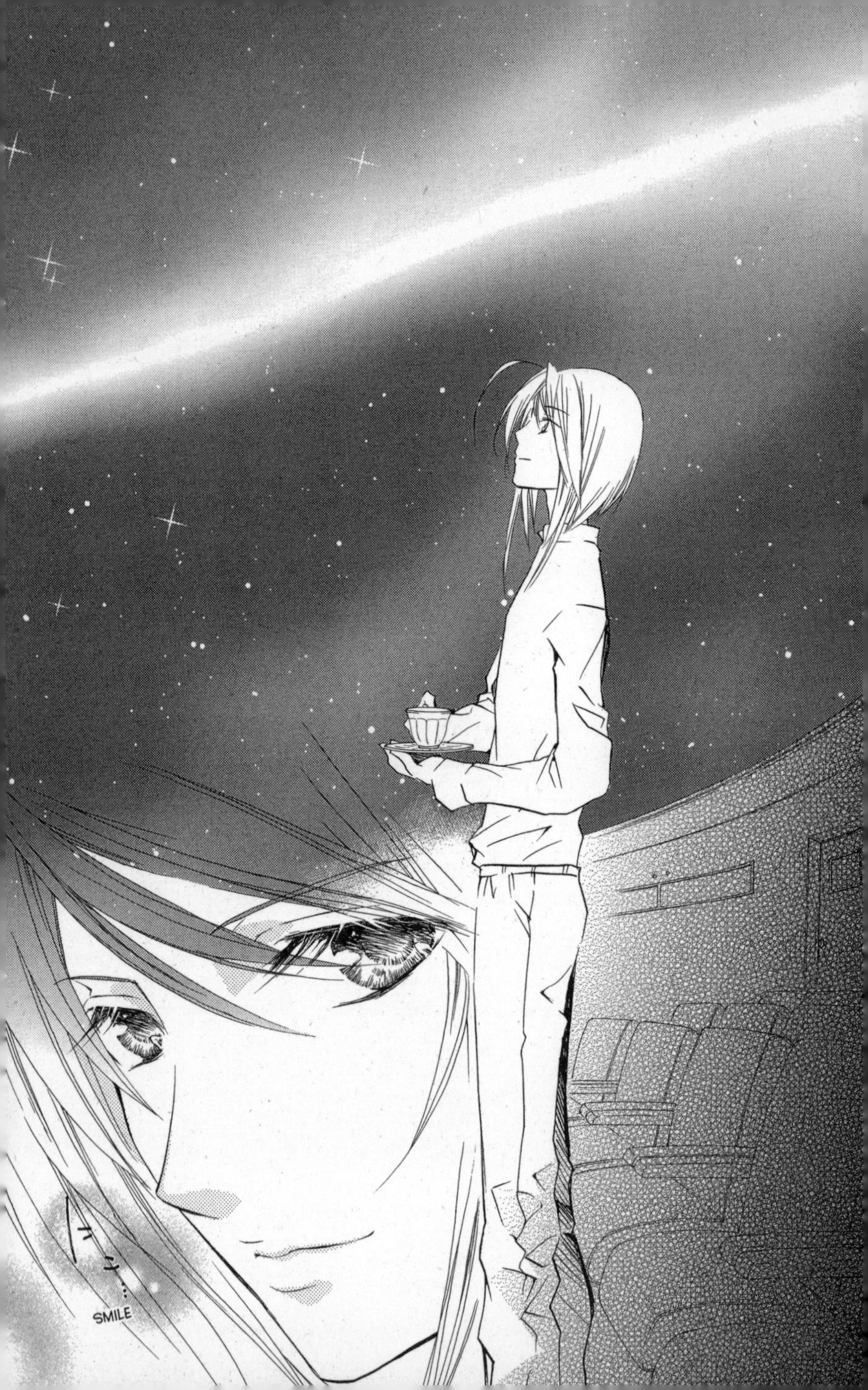
SMILE

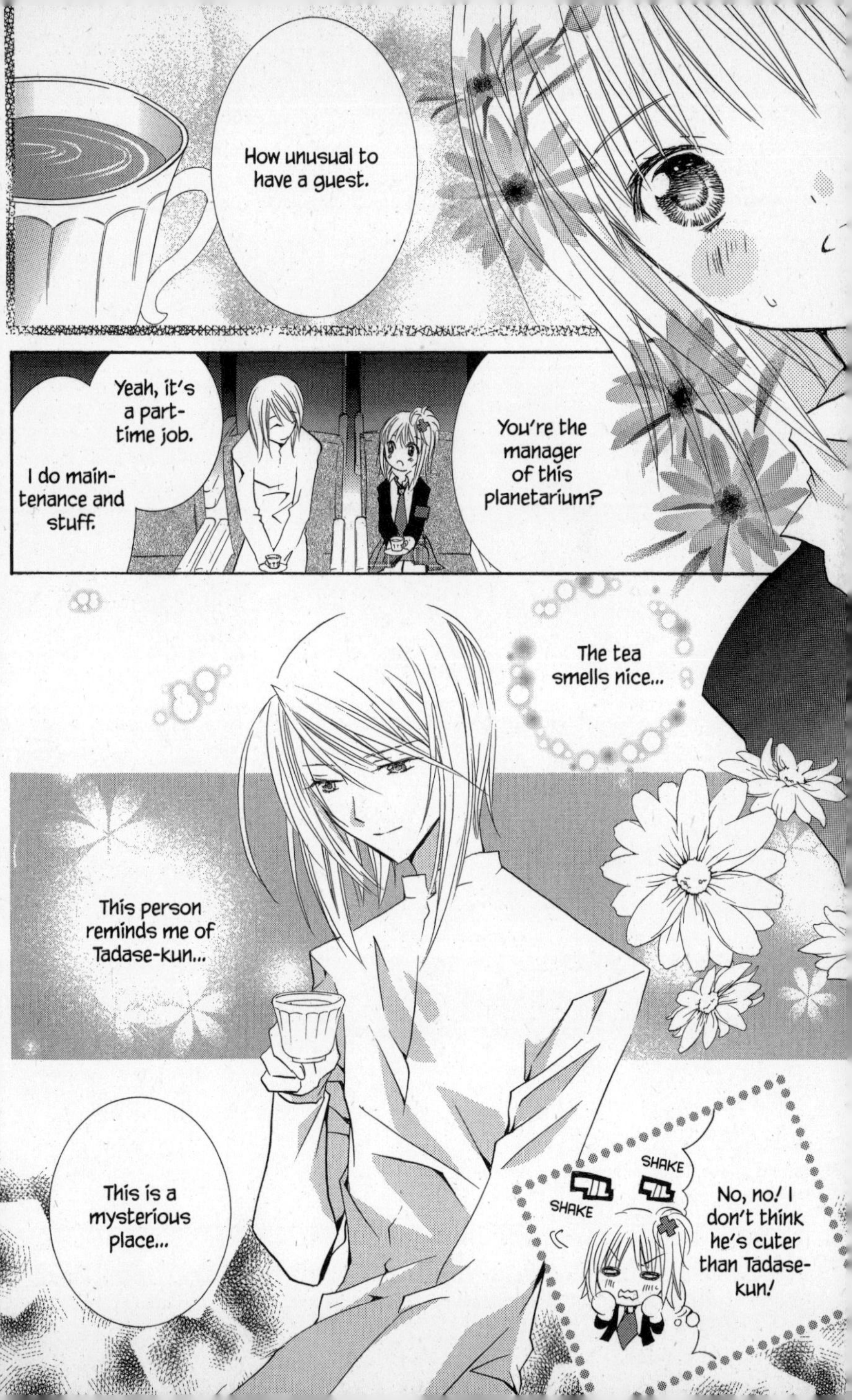
How unusual to have a guest.
You're the manager of this planetarium?
Yeah, it's a part-time job.
I do main-tenance and stuff.
The tea smells nice...
This person reminds me of Tadase-kun...
SHAKE
SHAKE
No, no! I don't think he's cuter than Tadase-kun!
This is a mysterious place...

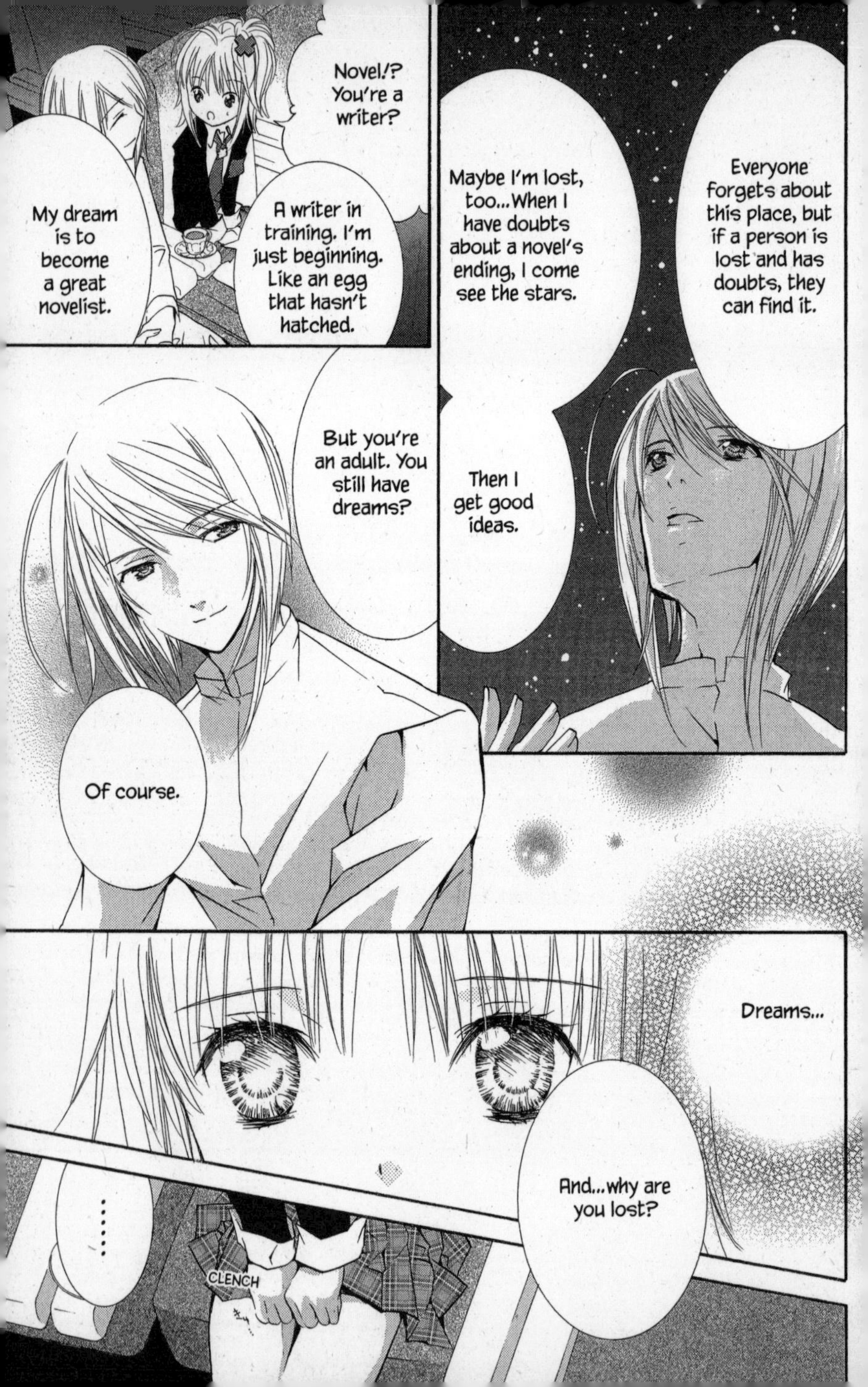
Everyone forgets about this place, but if a person is lost and has doubts, they can find it.
Maybe I'm lost, too...When I have doubts about a novel's ending, I come see the stars.
Then I get good ideas.
Novel!? You're a writer?
A writer in training. I'm just beginning. Like an egg that hasn't hatched.
My dream is to become a great novelist.
But you're an adult. You still have dreams?
Of course.
Dreams...
And...why are you lost?
......
CLENCH

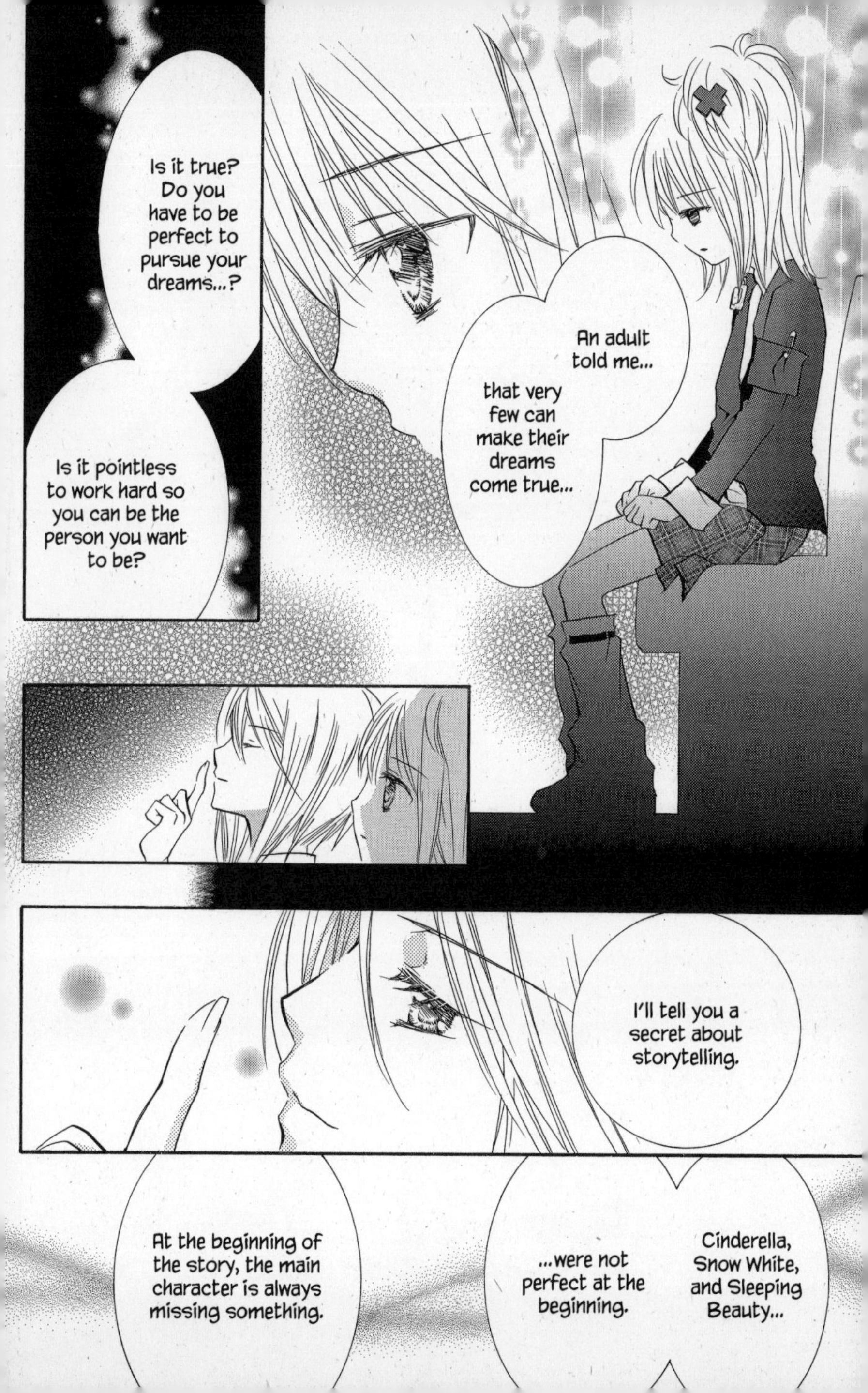
An adult told me...
that very few can make their dreams come true...
Is it true? Do you have to be perfect to pursue your dreams...?
Is it pointless to work hard so you can be the person you want to be?
I'll tell you a secret about storytelling.
Cinderella, Snow White, and Sleeping Beauty...
...were not perfect at the beginning.
At the beginning of the story, the main character is always missing something.

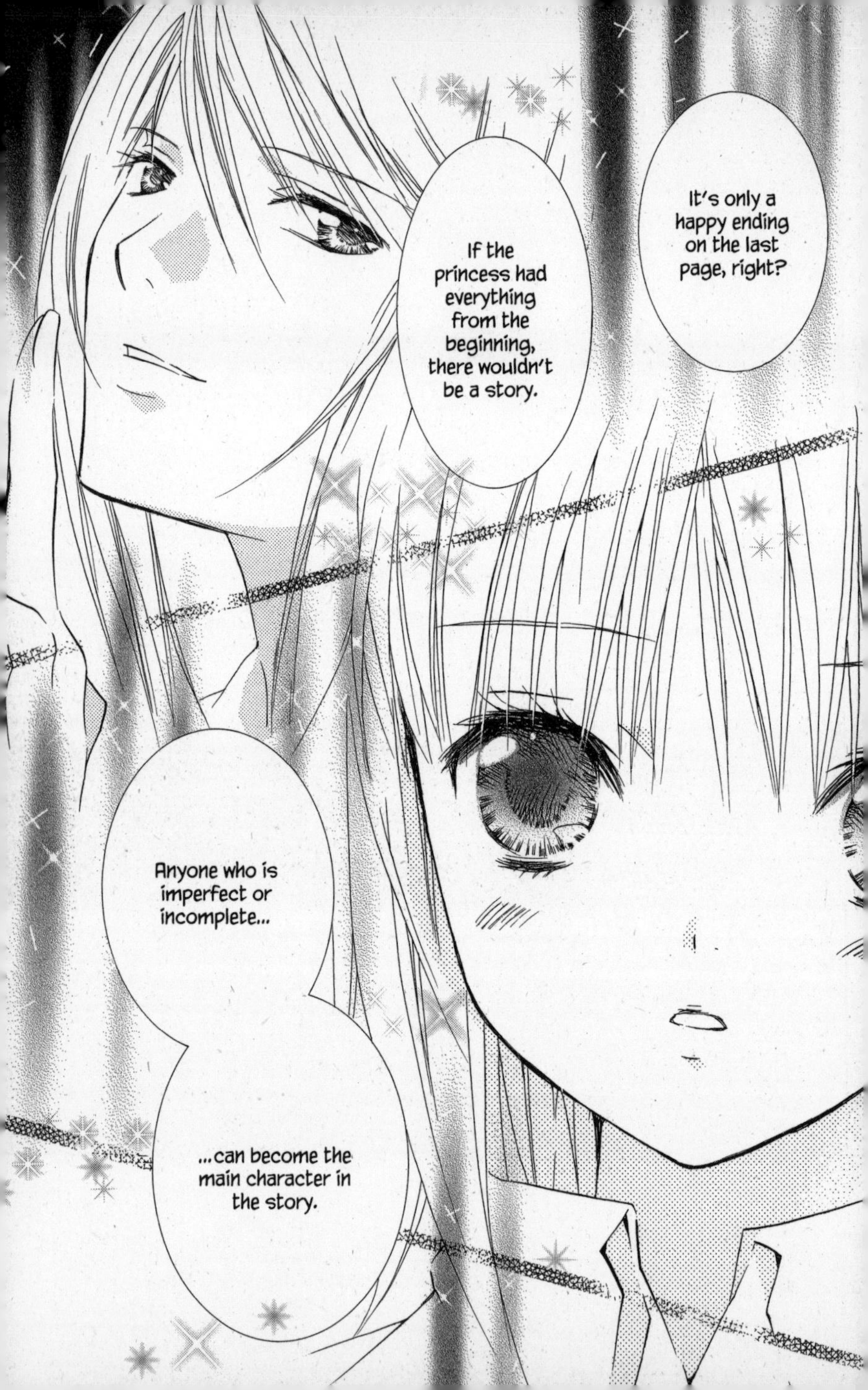
It's only a happy ending on the last page, right?
If the princess had everything from the beginning, there wouldn't be a story.
Anyone who is imperfect or incomplete...
...can become the main character in the story.

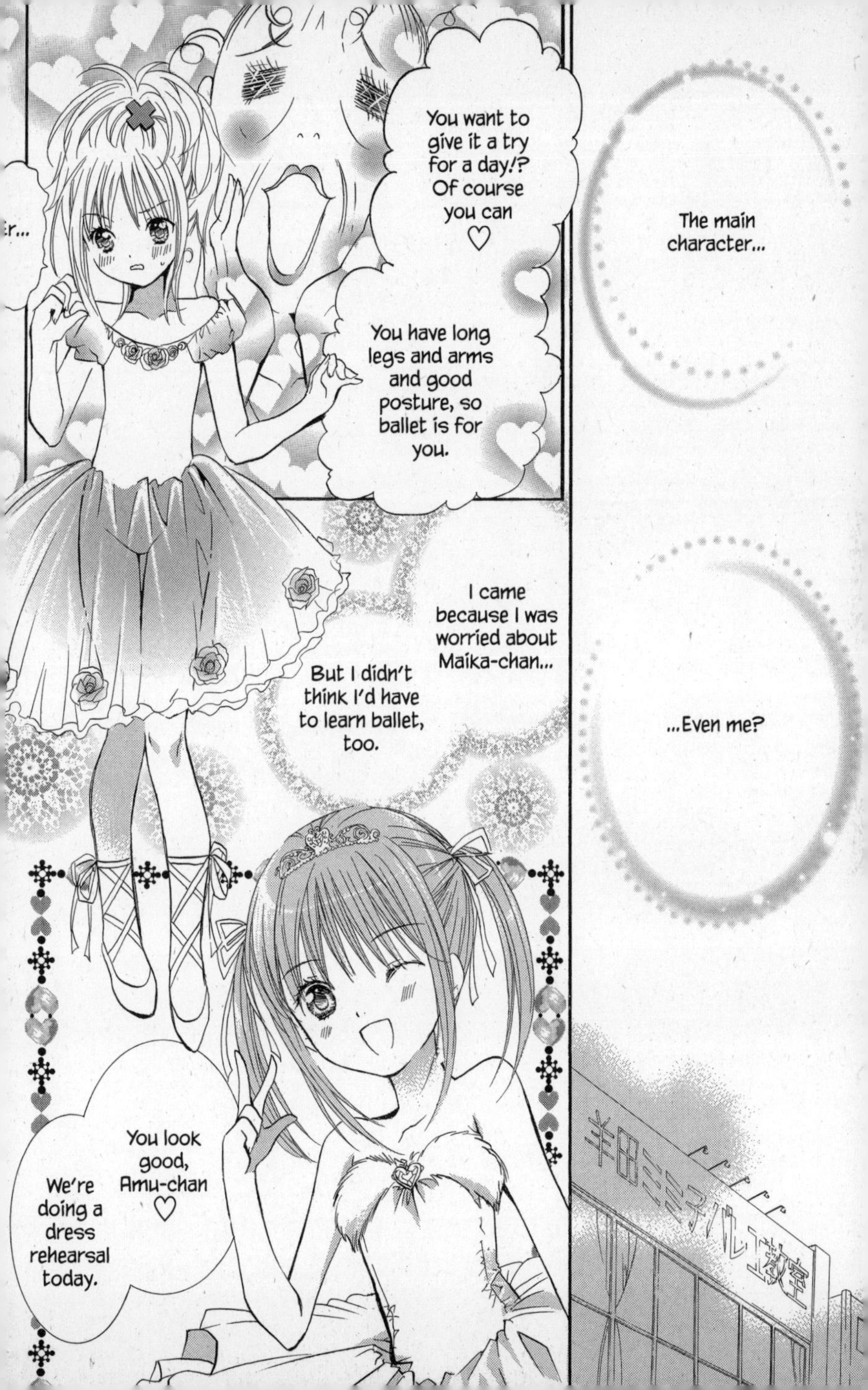

The main character...
...Even me?
You want to give it a try for a day!? Of course you can ♡
You have long legs and arms and good posture, so ballet is for you.
I came because I was worried about Maika-chan...
But I didn't think I'd have to learn ballet, too.
You look good, Amu-chan ♡
We're doing a dress rehearsal today.

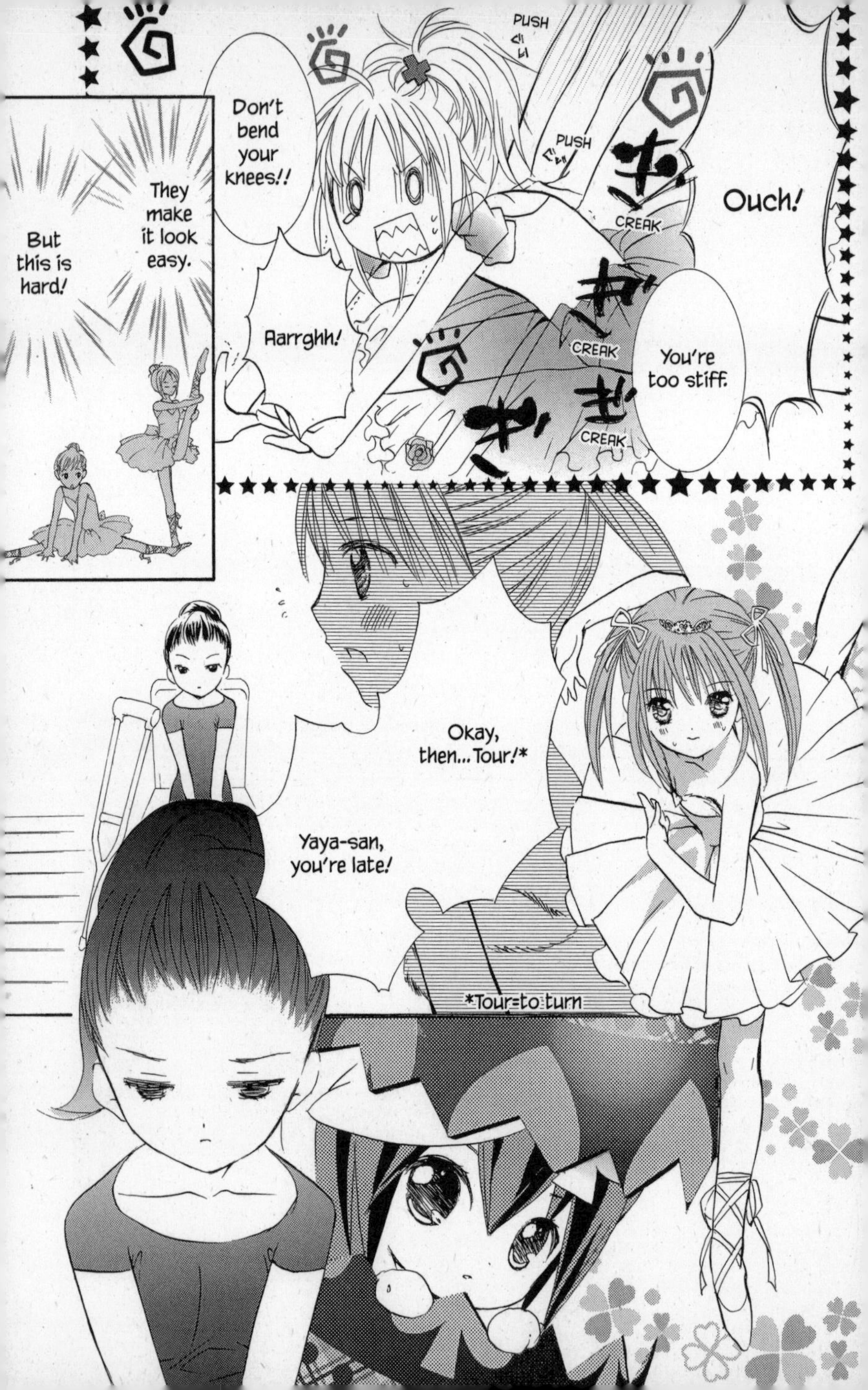
PUSH
Ouch!
PUSH
CREAK
CREAK
CREAK
You're too stiff.
Don't bend your knees!!
Aarrghh!
They make it look easy.
But this is hard!
Okay, then... Tour!*
Yaya-san, you're late!
*Tour=to turn

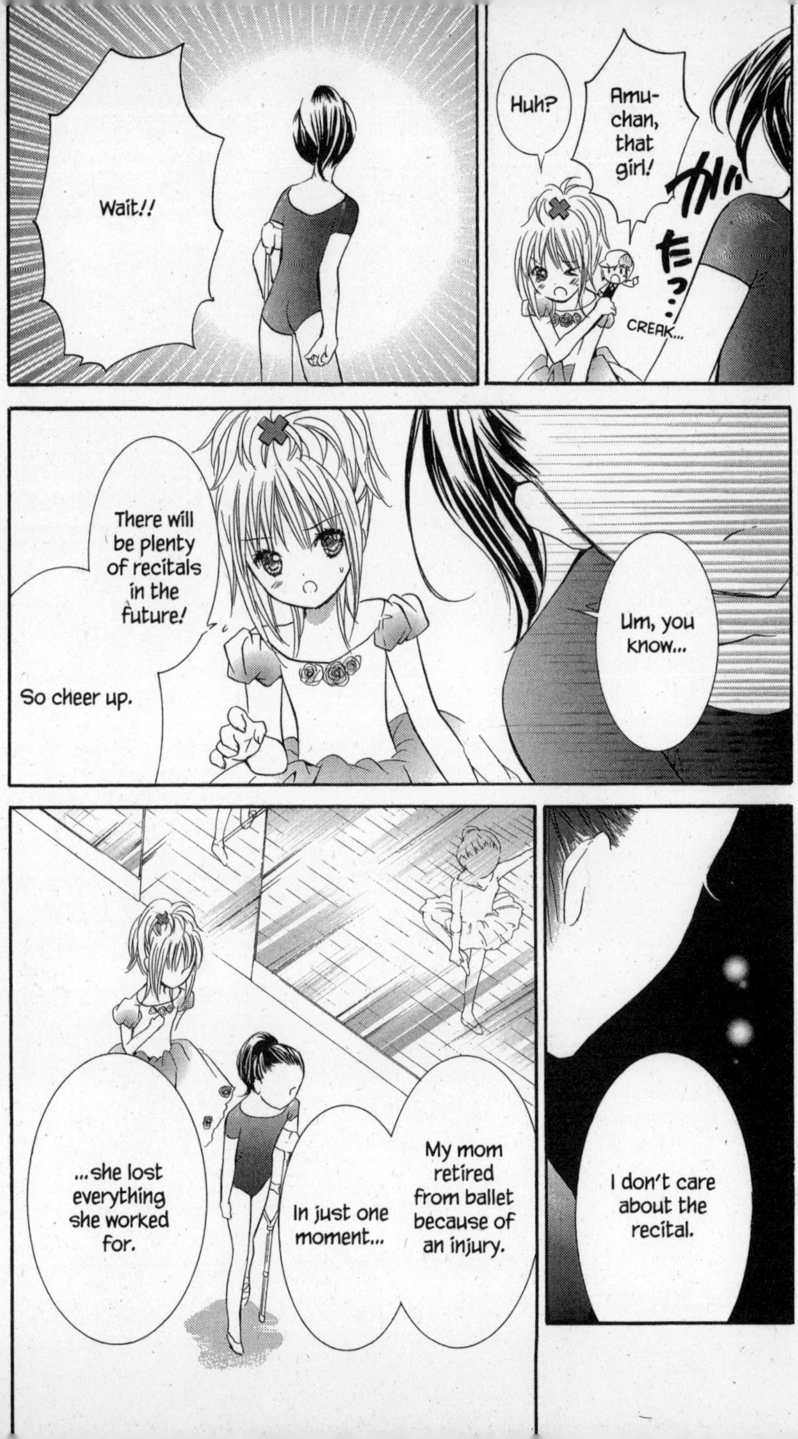
Amu-chan, that girl!
Huh?
CREAK...
Wait!!
Um, you know...
There will be plenty of recitals in the future!
So cheer up.
I don't care about the recital.
My mom retired from ballet because of an injury.
In just one moment...
...she lost everything she worked for.

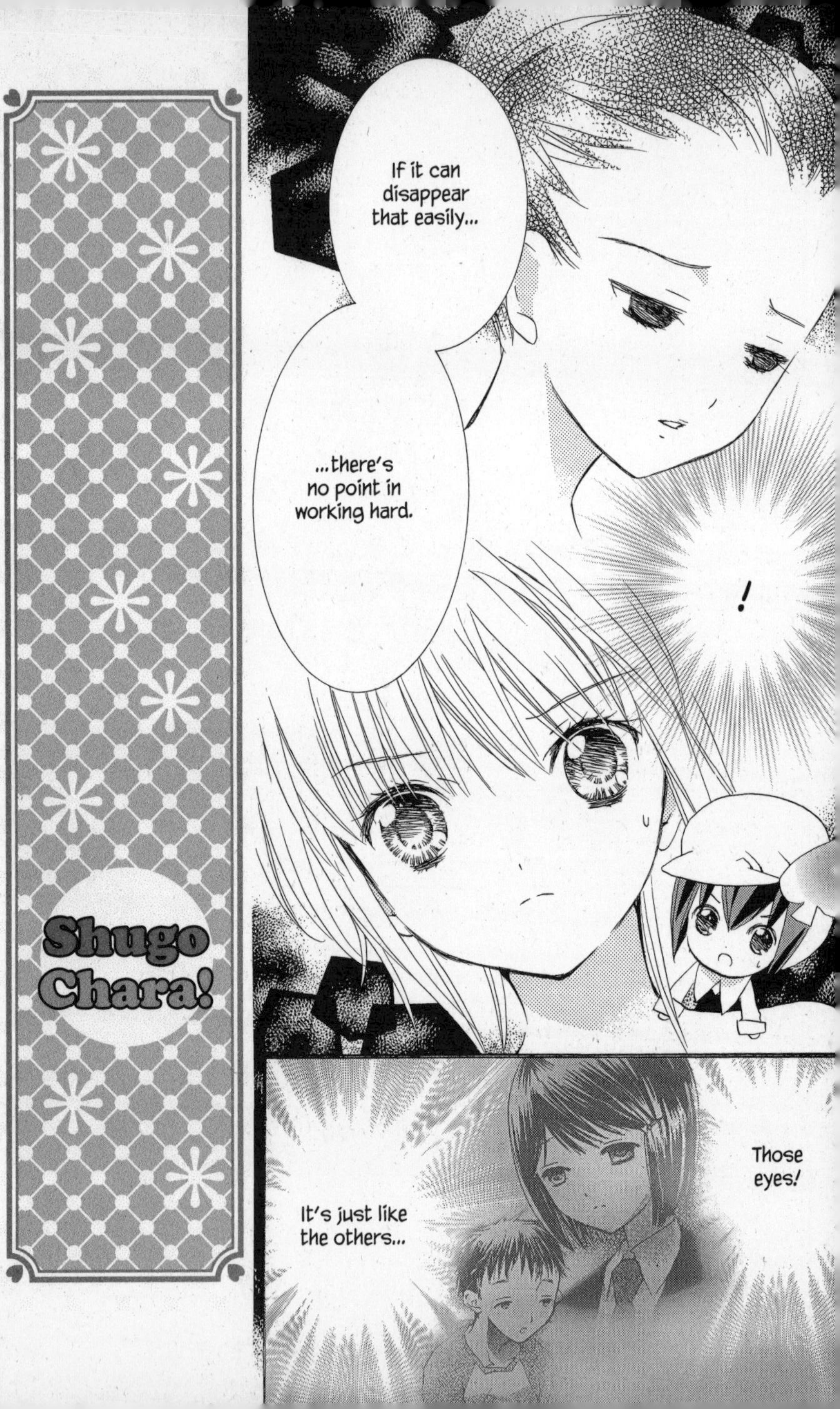
If it can disappear that easily...
...there's no point in working hard.
!
Those eyes!
It's just like the others...

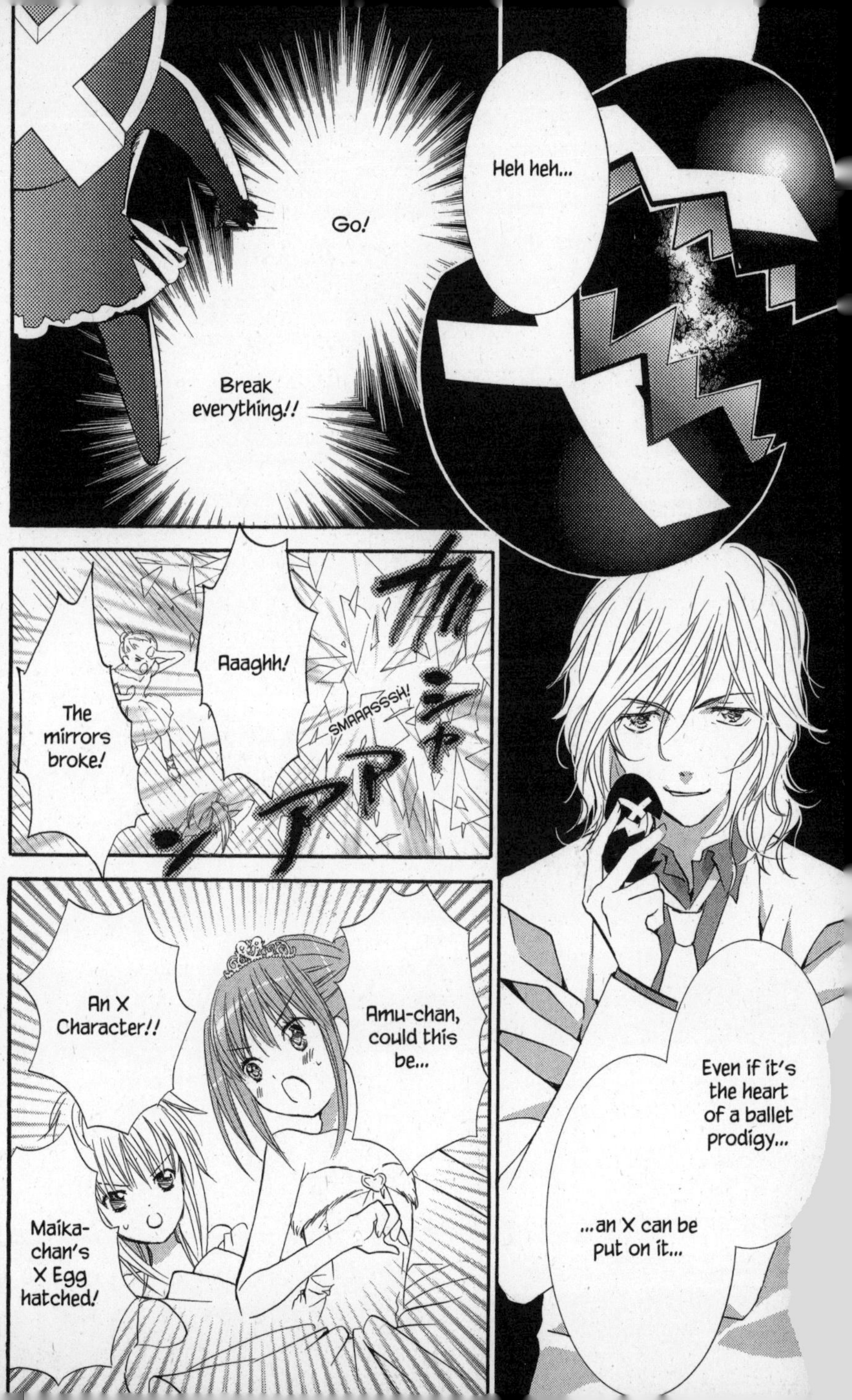
Heh heh...
Go!
Break everything!!
Even if it's the heart of a ballet prodigy...
...an X can be put on it...
Aaaghh!
The mirrors broke!
SMAAASSSH!
Amu-chan, could this be...
An X Character!!
Maika-chan's X Egg hatched!

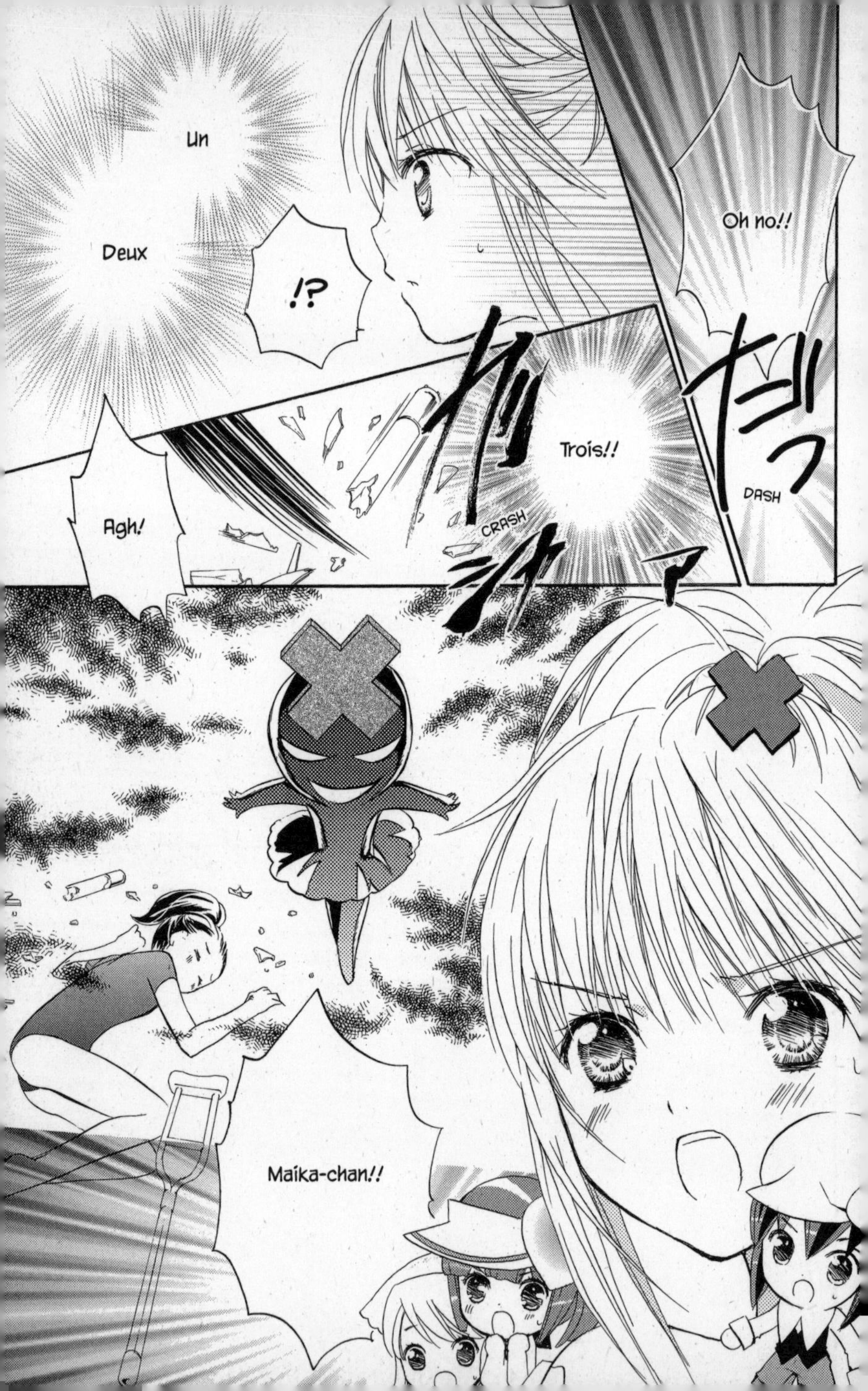
Oh no!!
DASH
Un
Deux
!?
Trois!!
CRASH
Agh!
Maika-chan!!

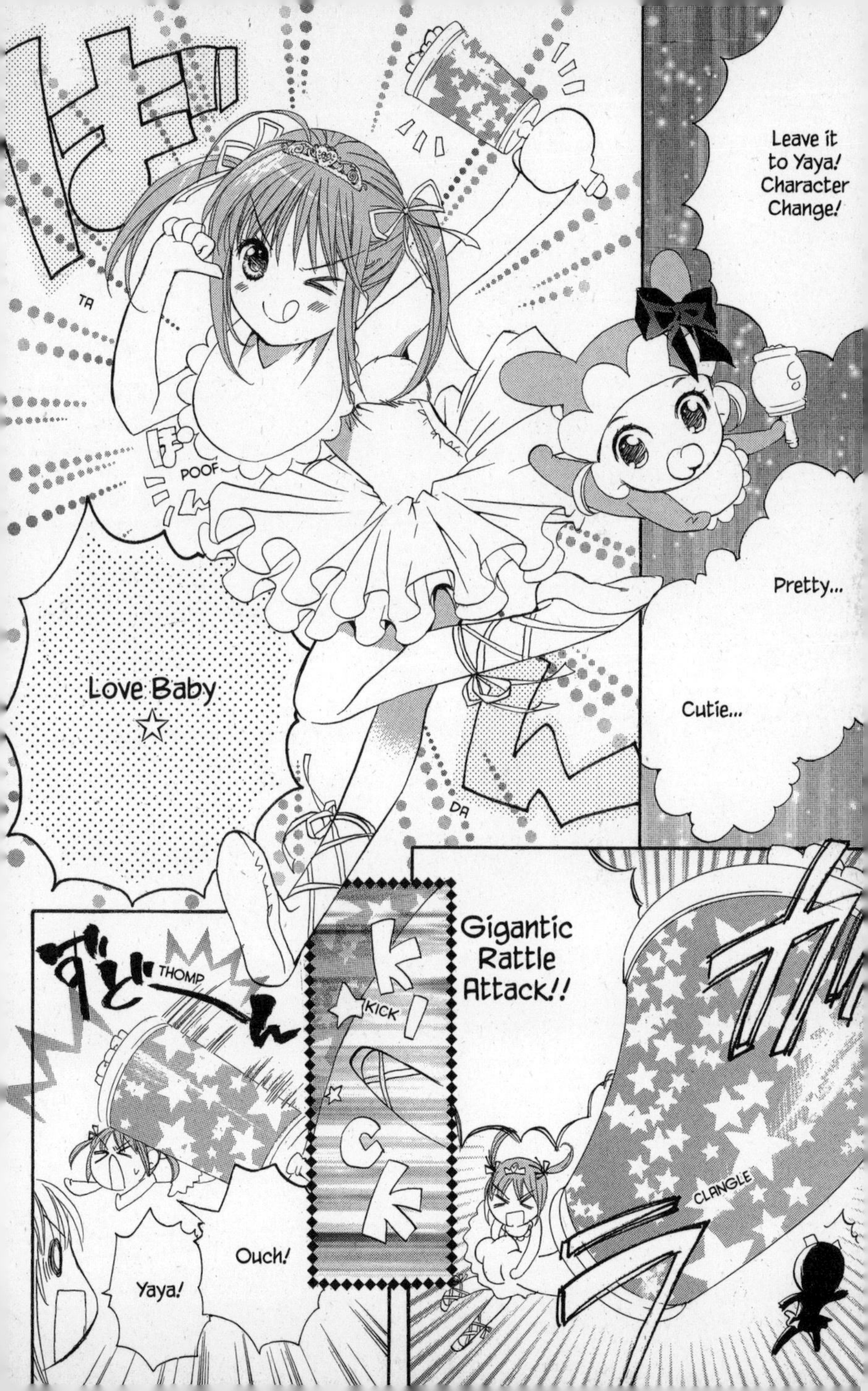
Leave it to Yaya! Character Change!
Pretty...
Cutie...
TA
POOF
Love Baby ☆
DA
Gigantic Rattle Attack!!
CLANGLE
KICK
THOMP
Ouch!
Yaya!

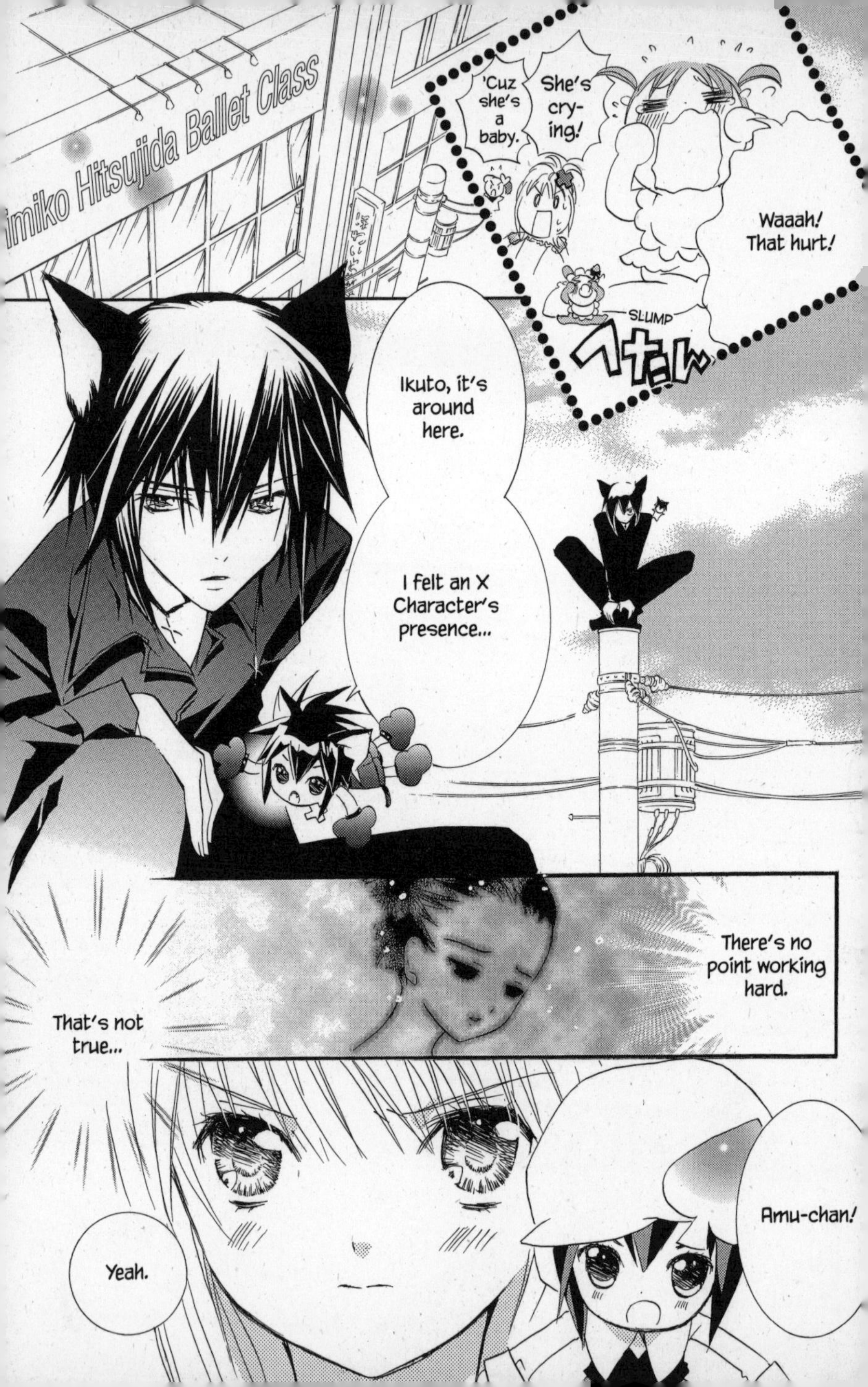
Waaah! That hurt!
She's crying!
'Cuz she's a baby.
SLUMP
imiko Hitsujida Ballet Class
Ikuto, it's around here.
I felt an X Character's presence...
There's no point working hard.
That's not true...
Amu-chan!
Yeah.

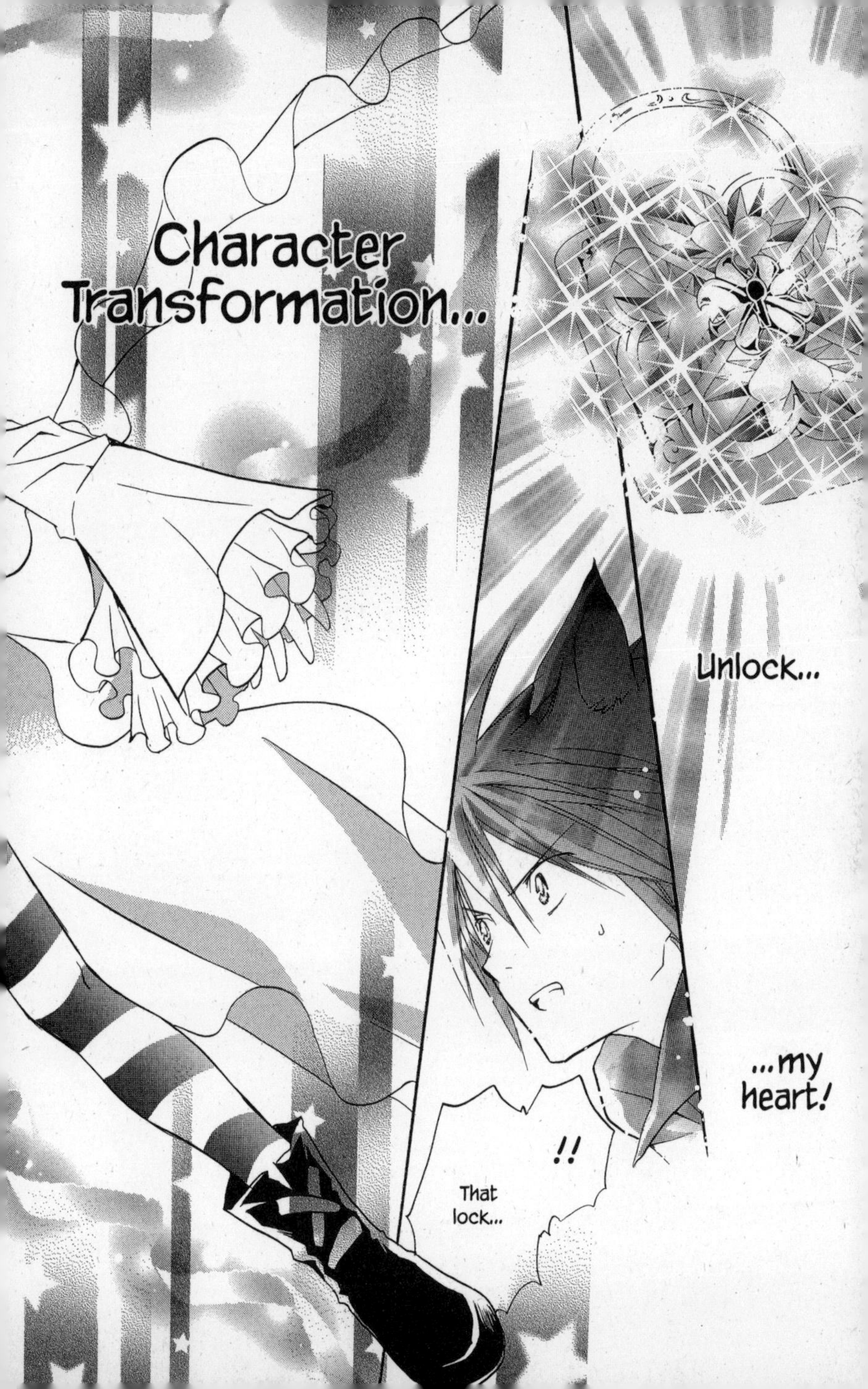
Unlock...
...my heart!
!!
That lock...
Character Transformation...

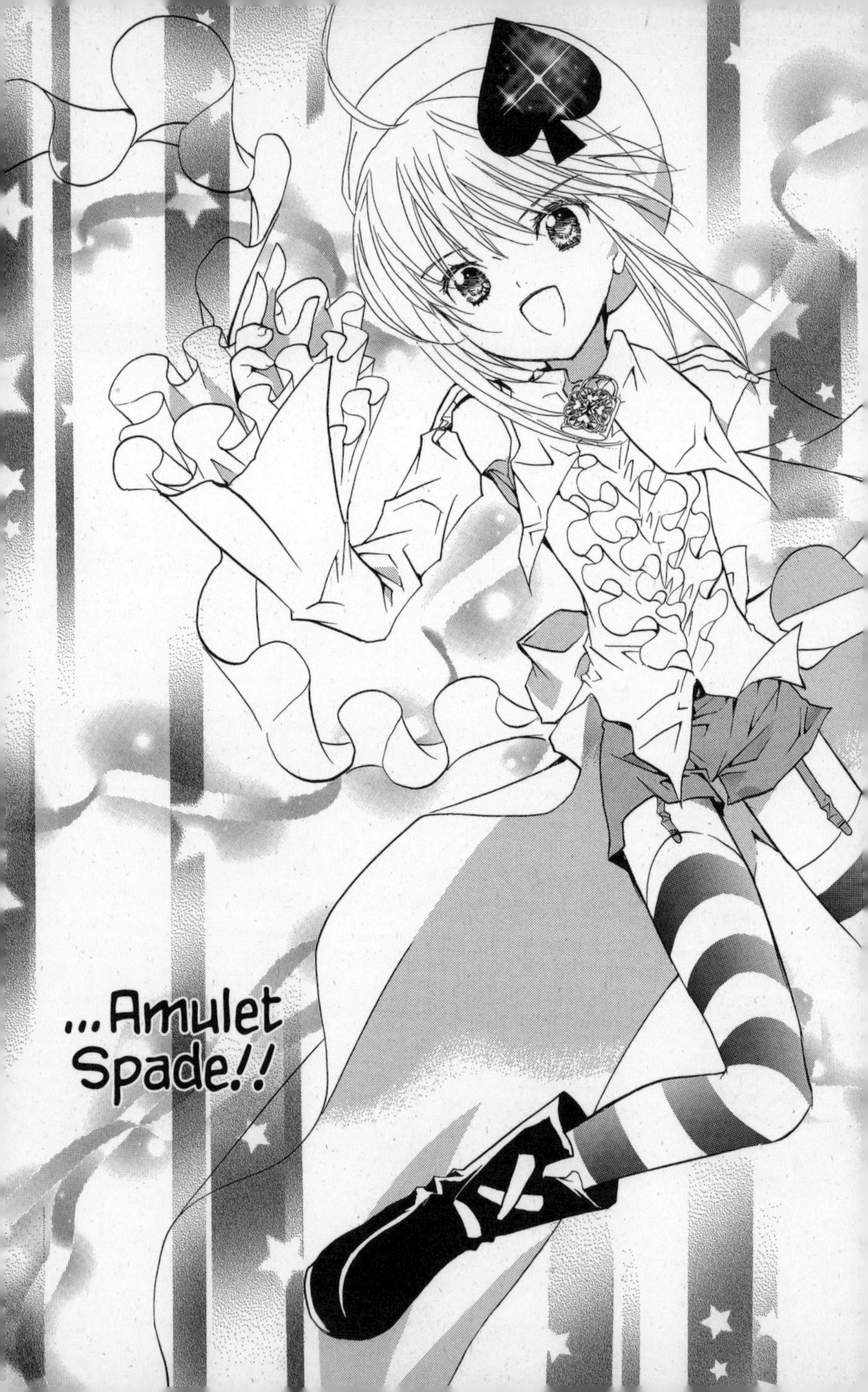
...Amulet
Spade!!

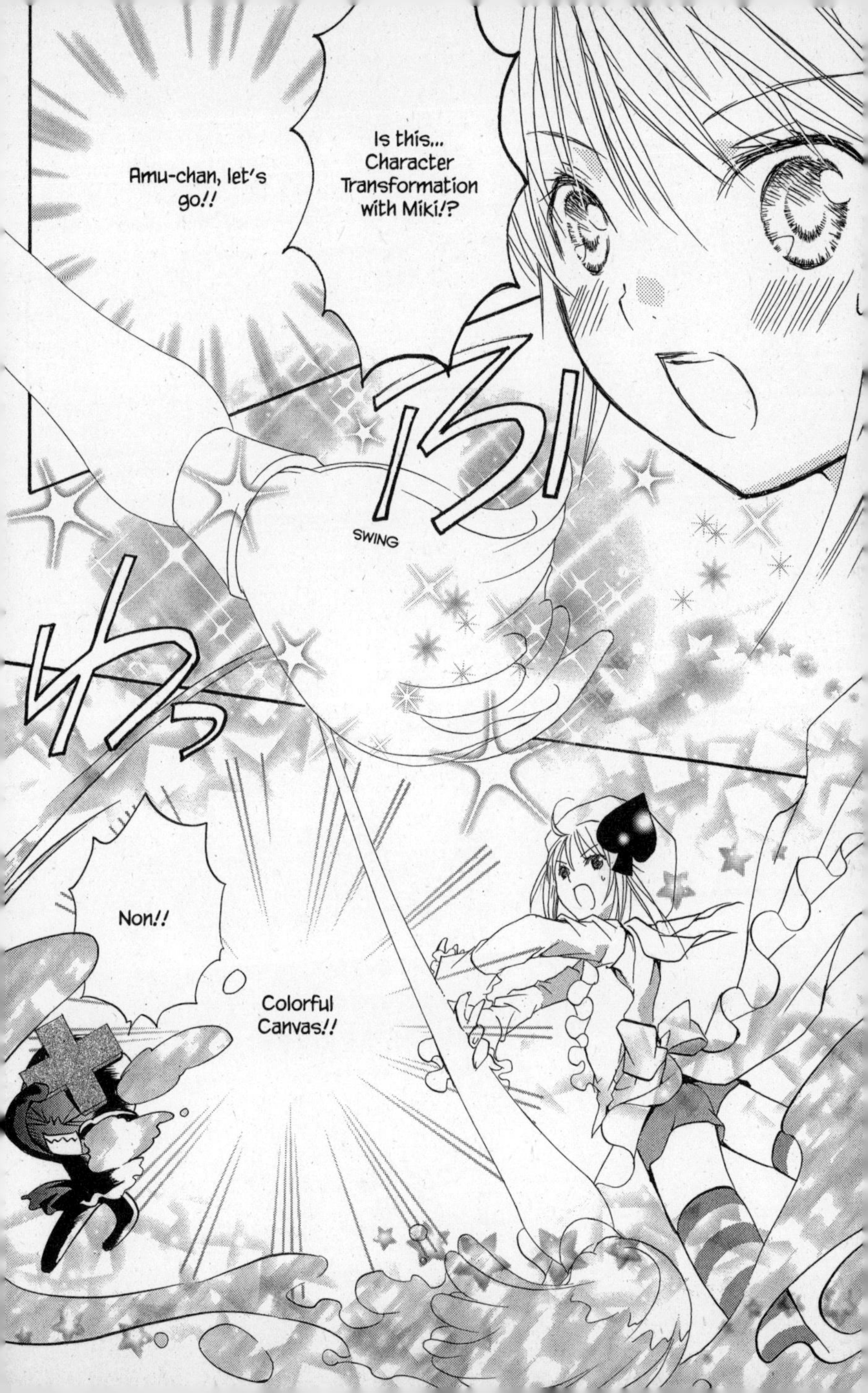

Is this... Character Transformation with Miki!?
Amu-chan, let's go!!
SWING
Non!!
Colorful Canvas!!

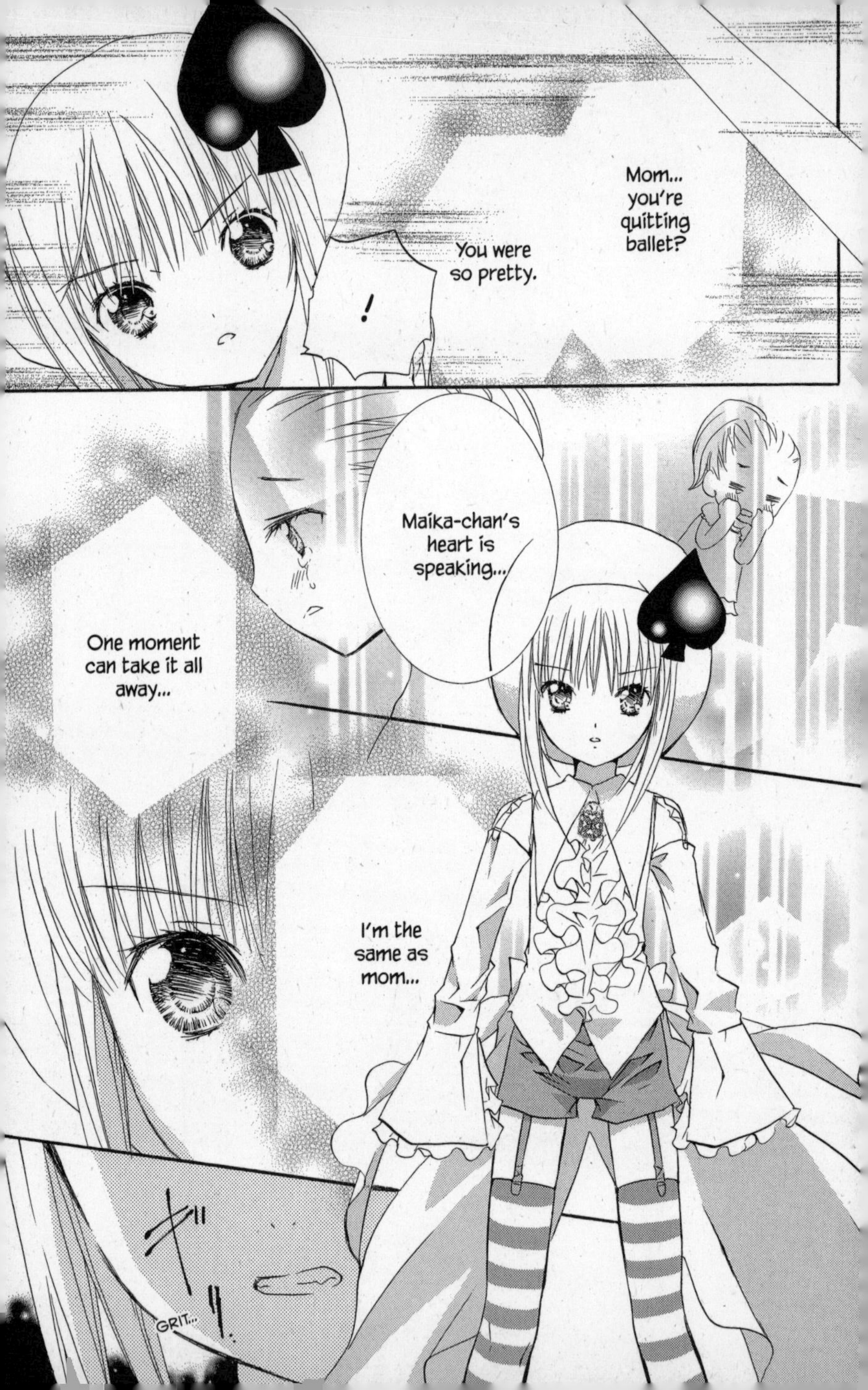
Mom... you're quitting ballet?
You were so pretty.
!
Maika-chan's heart is speaking...
One moment can take it all away...
I'm the same as mom...
GRIT...

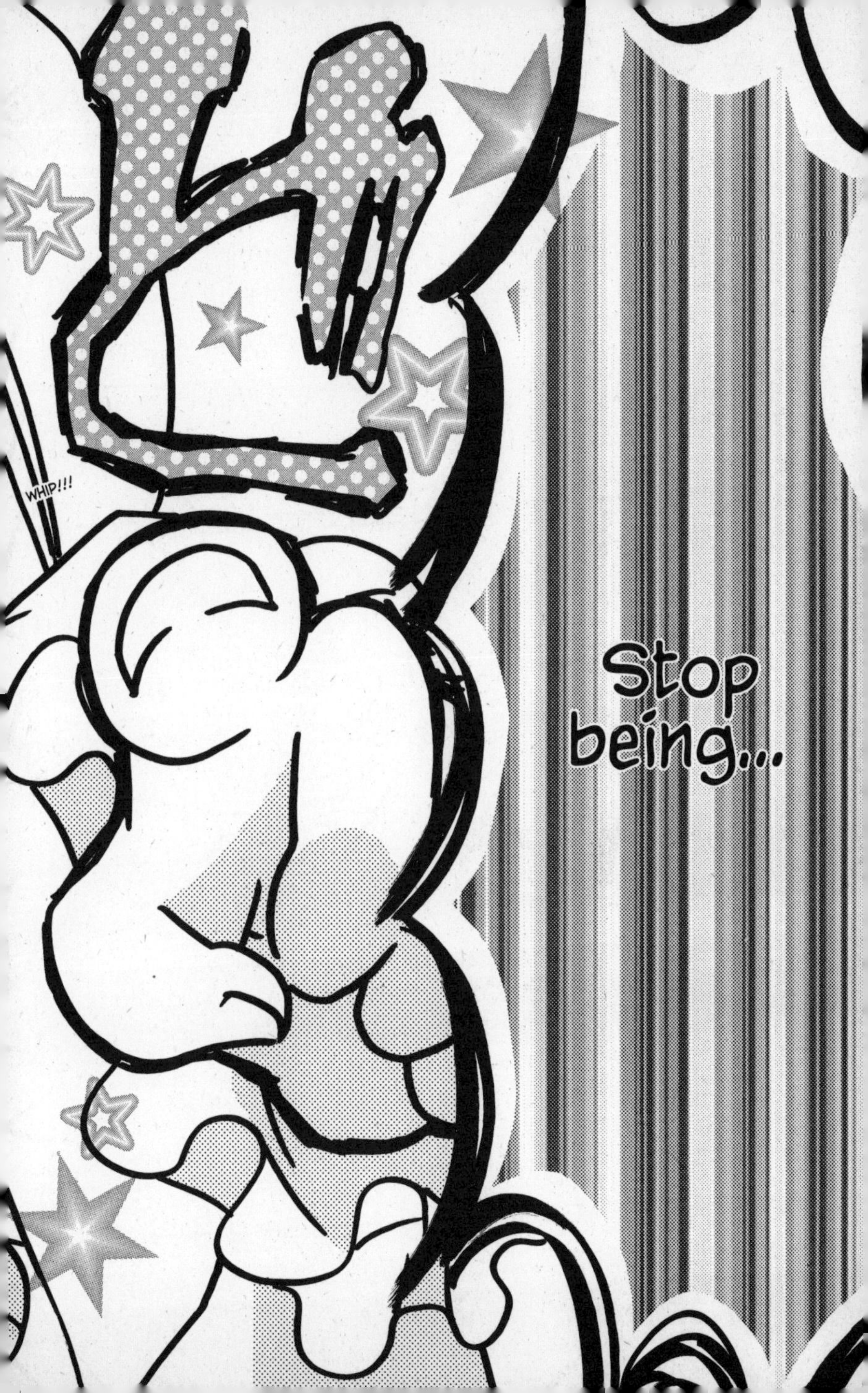
Stop being...
WHIP!!!

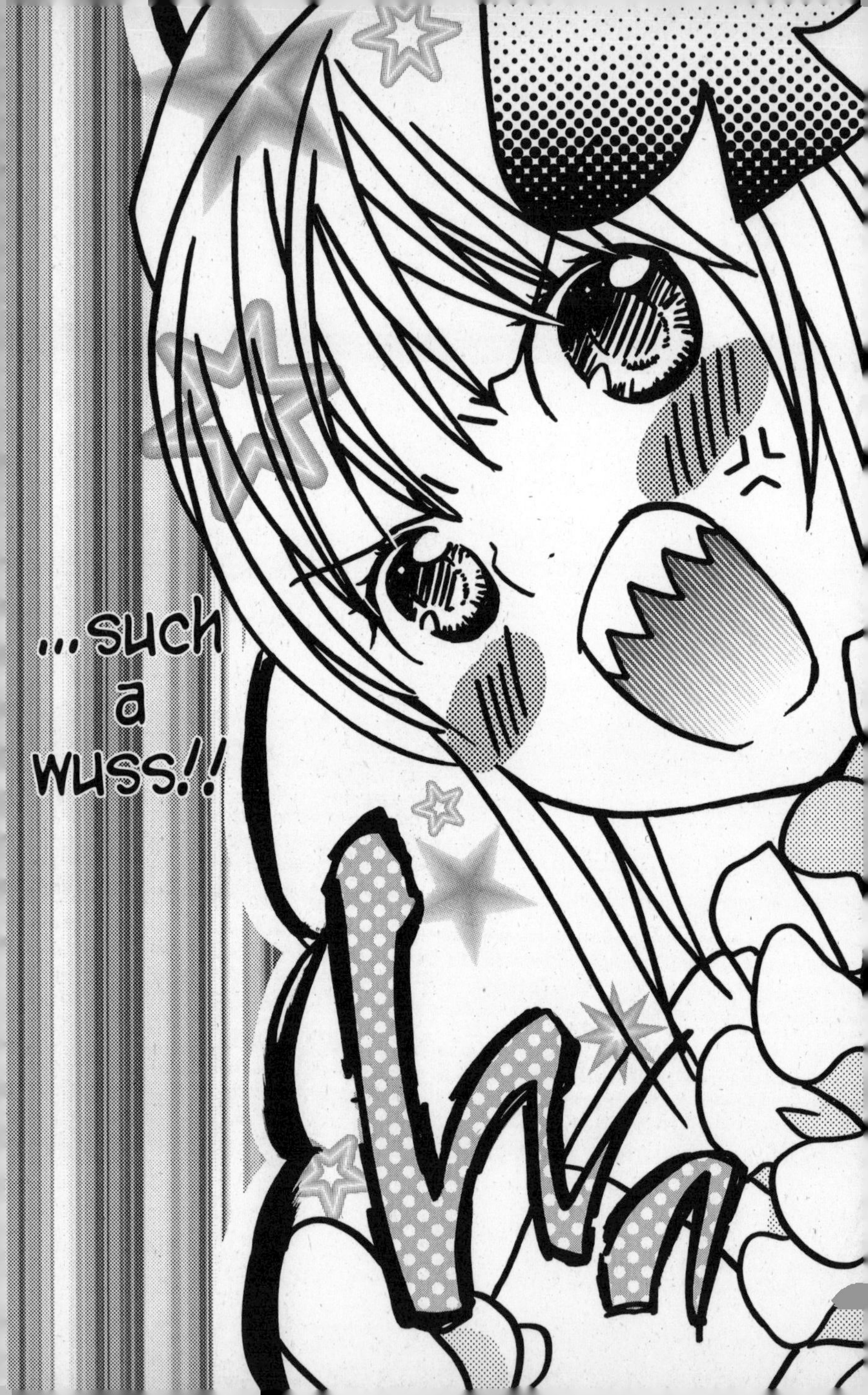
...such a wuss!!

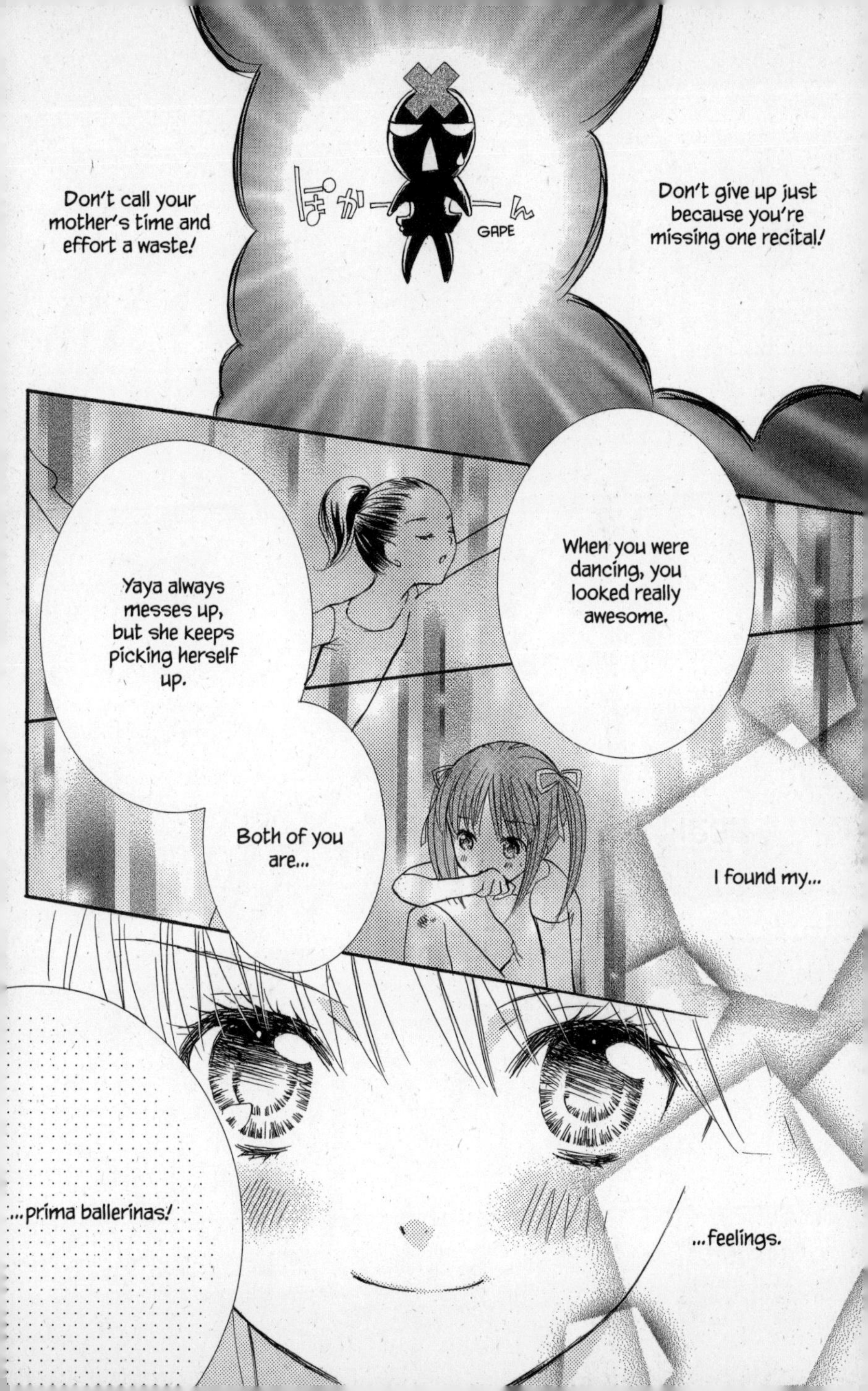
Don't give up just because you're missing one recital!
Don't call your mother's time and effort a waste!
ぽかーん
GAPE
When you were dancing, you looked really awesome.
Yaya always messes up, but she keeps picking herself up.
Both of you are...
...prima ballerinas!
I found my...
...feelings.

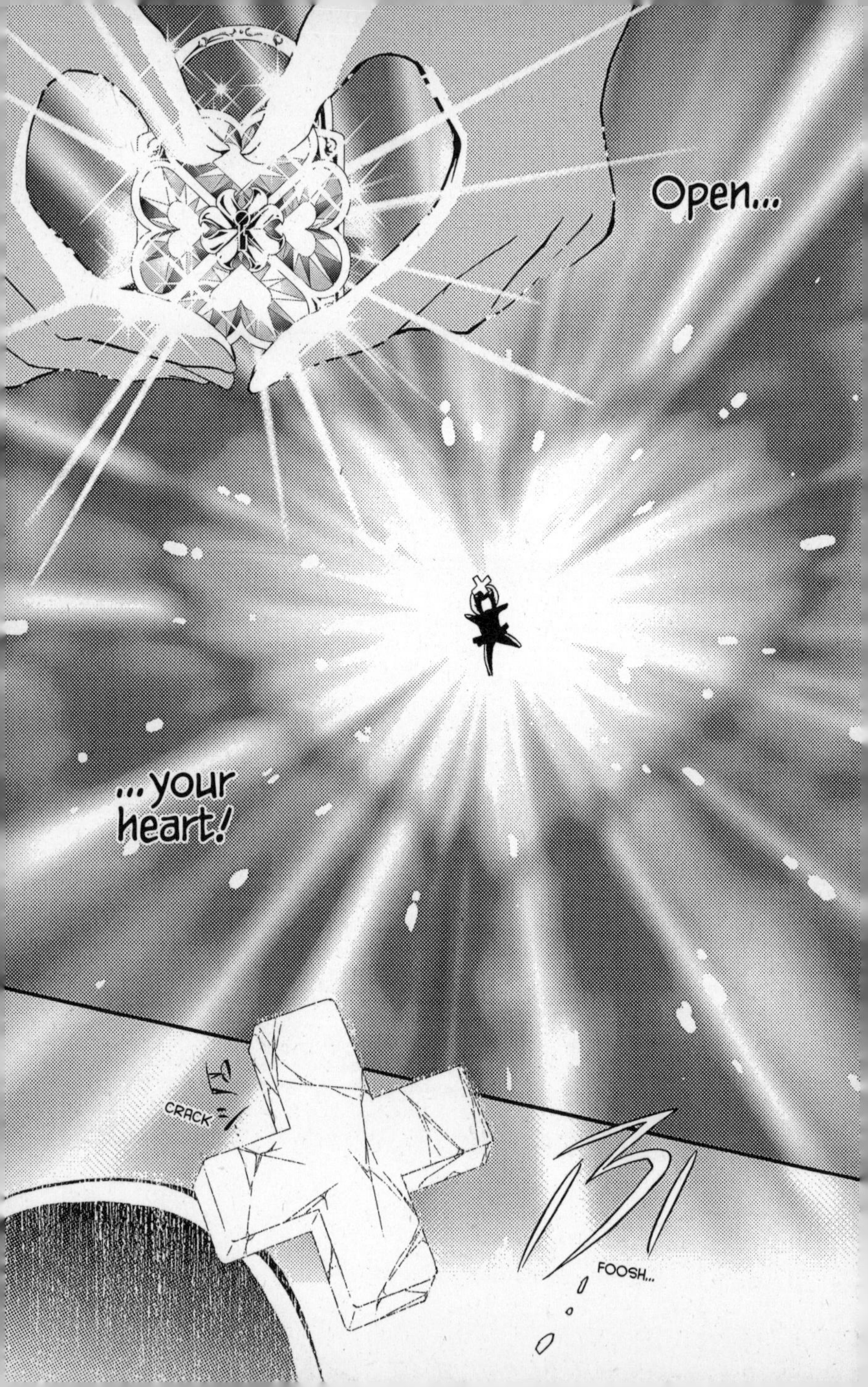
Open...
...your heart!
CRACK
FOOSH...

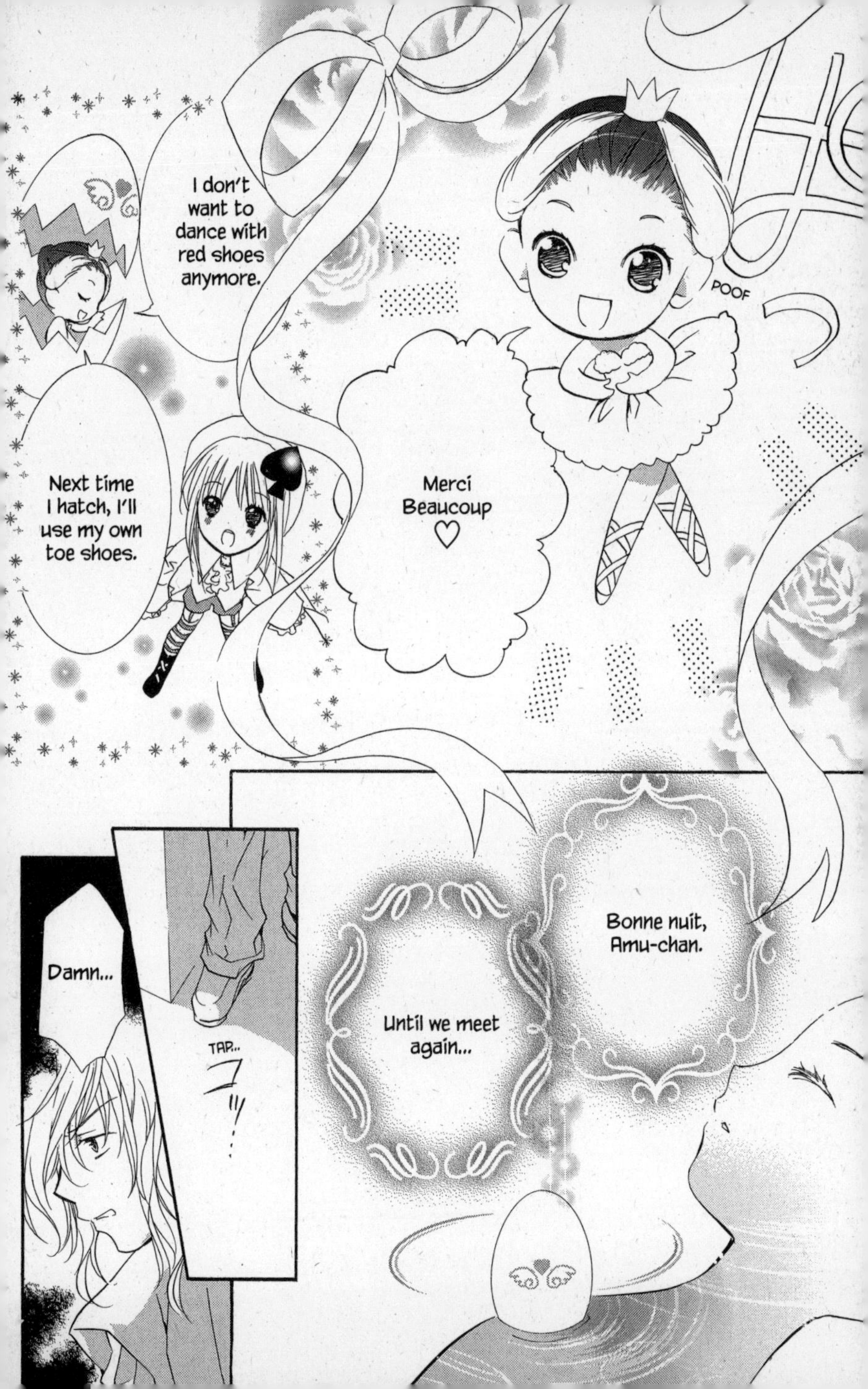
POOF
Merci Beaucoup ♡
I don't want to dance with red shoes anymore.
Next time I hatch, I'll use my own toe shoes.
Bonne nuit, Amu-chan.
Until we meet again...
TAP...
Damn...

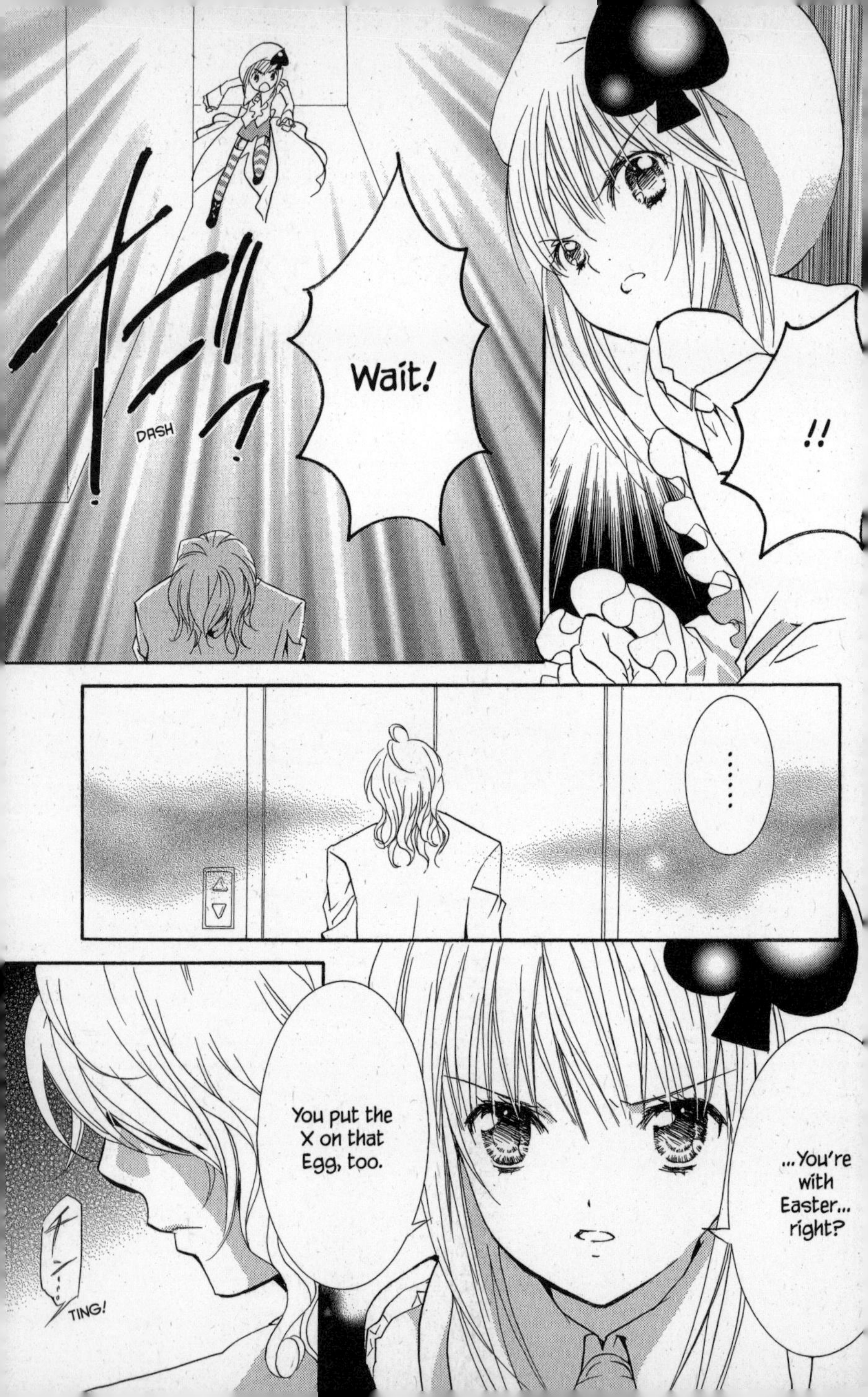
!!
Wait!
DASH
......
...You're with Easter... right?
You put the X on that Egg, too.
TING!

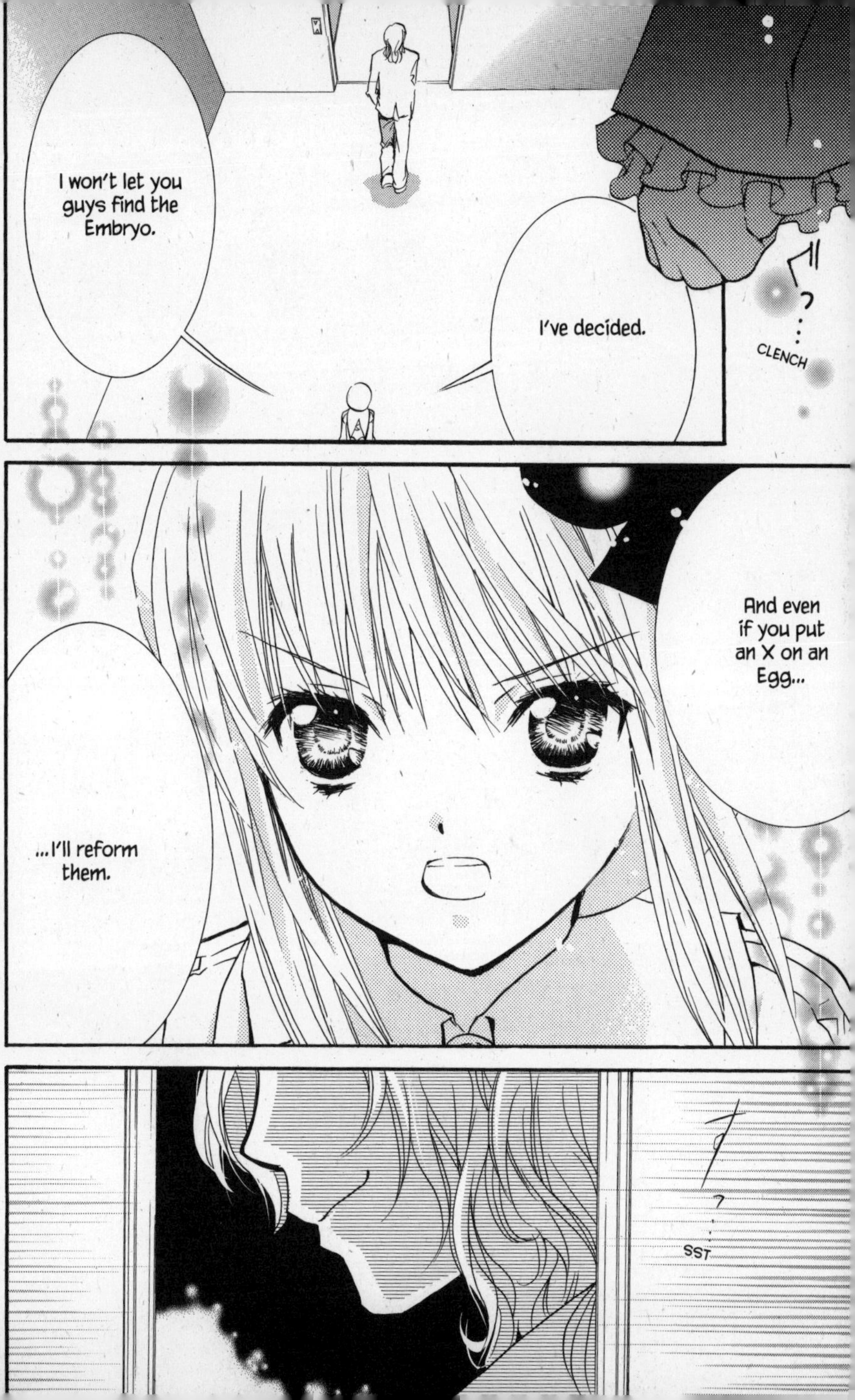
CLENCH
I've decided.
I won't let you guys find the Embryo.
And even if you put an X on an Egg...
...I'll reform them.
SST

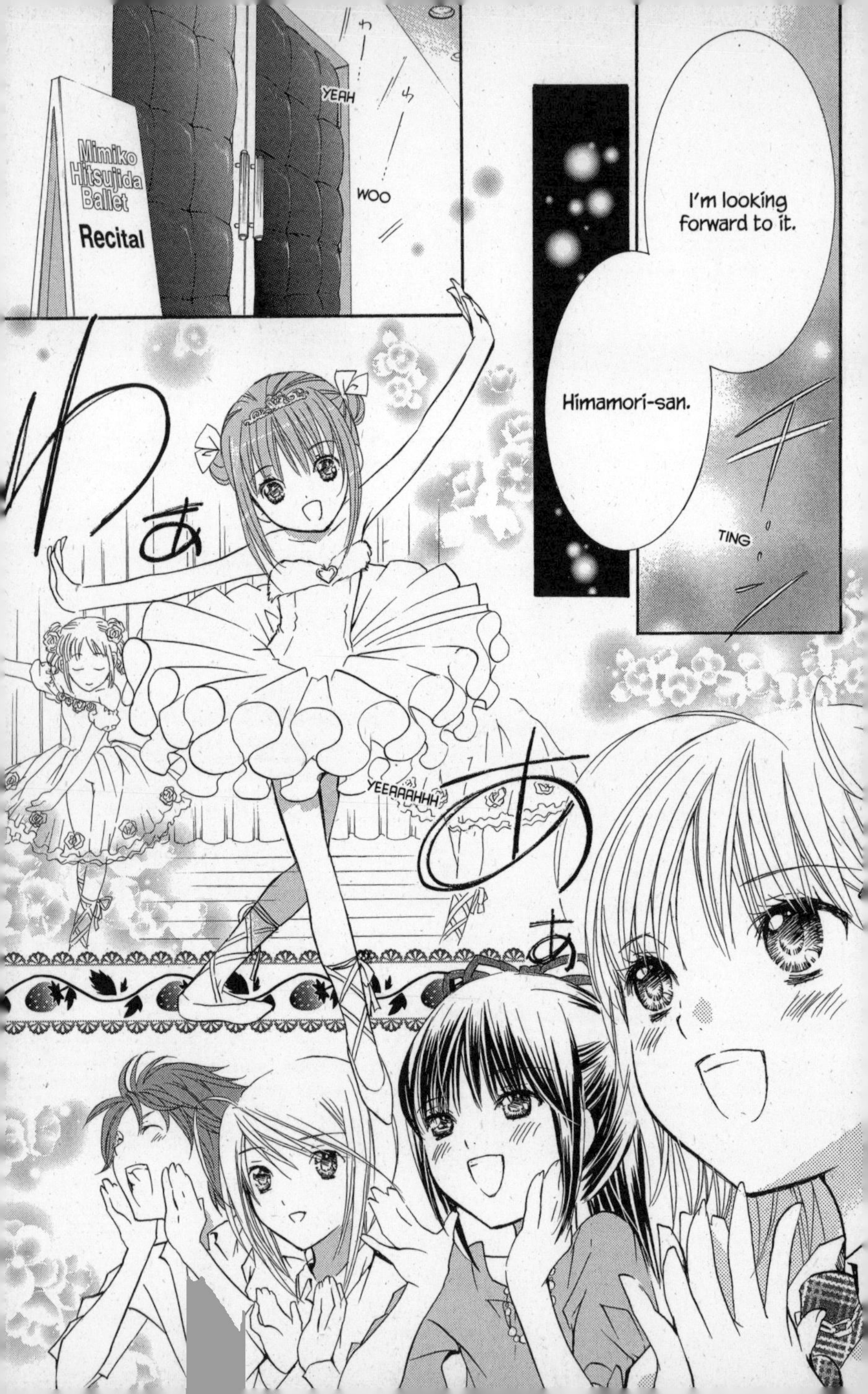

I'm looking forward to it.
Himamori-san.
TING
Mimiko Hitsujida Ballet
Recital
YEAH
WOO
YEEAAAHHH

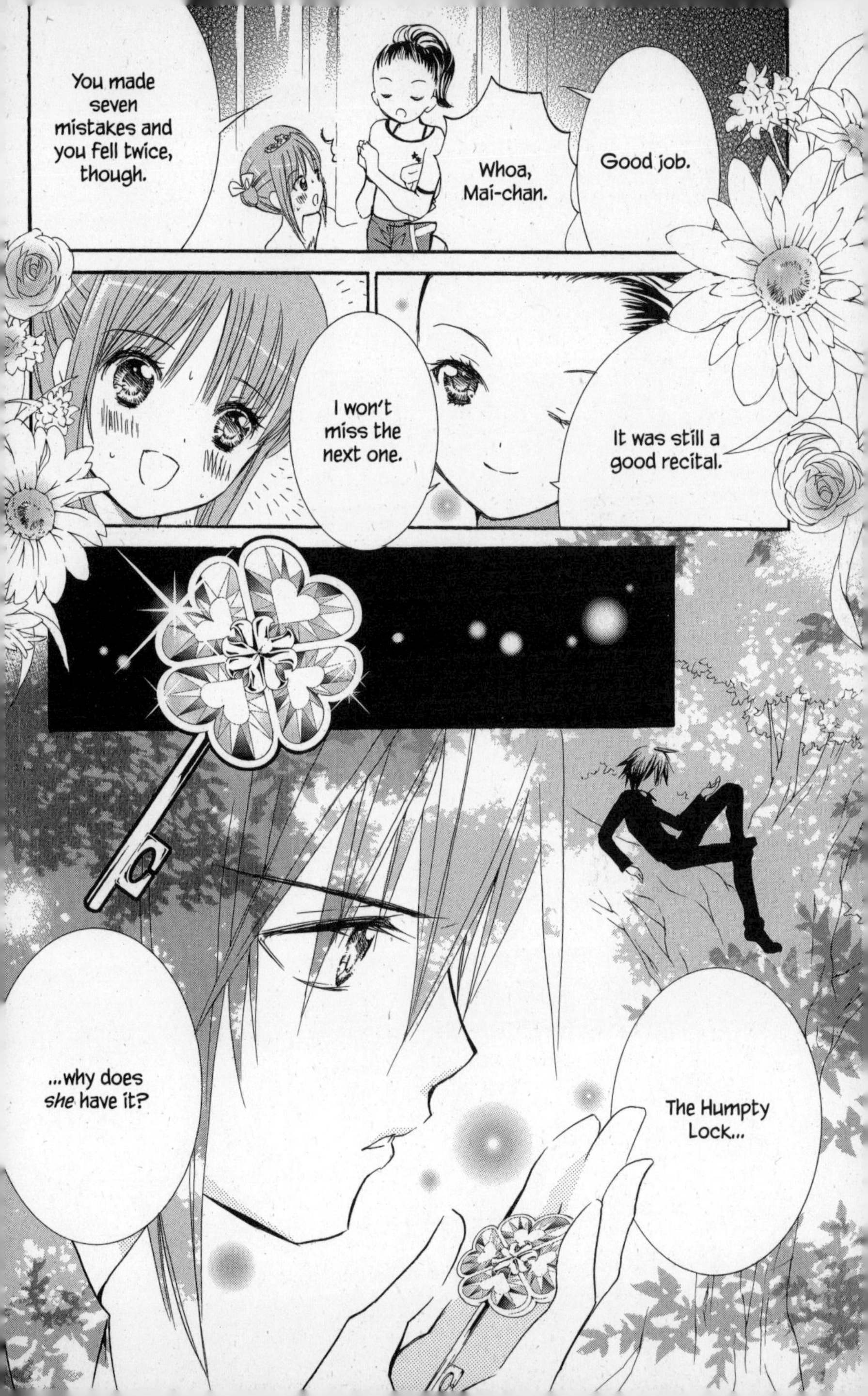
Good job.
Whoa, Mai-chan.
You made seven mistakes and you fell twice, though.
It was still a good recital.
I won't miss the next one.
The Humpty Lock...
...why does *she* have it?

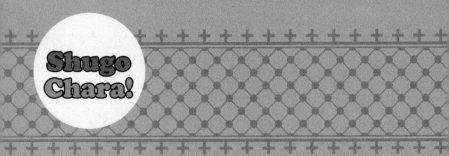

Shugo Chara!

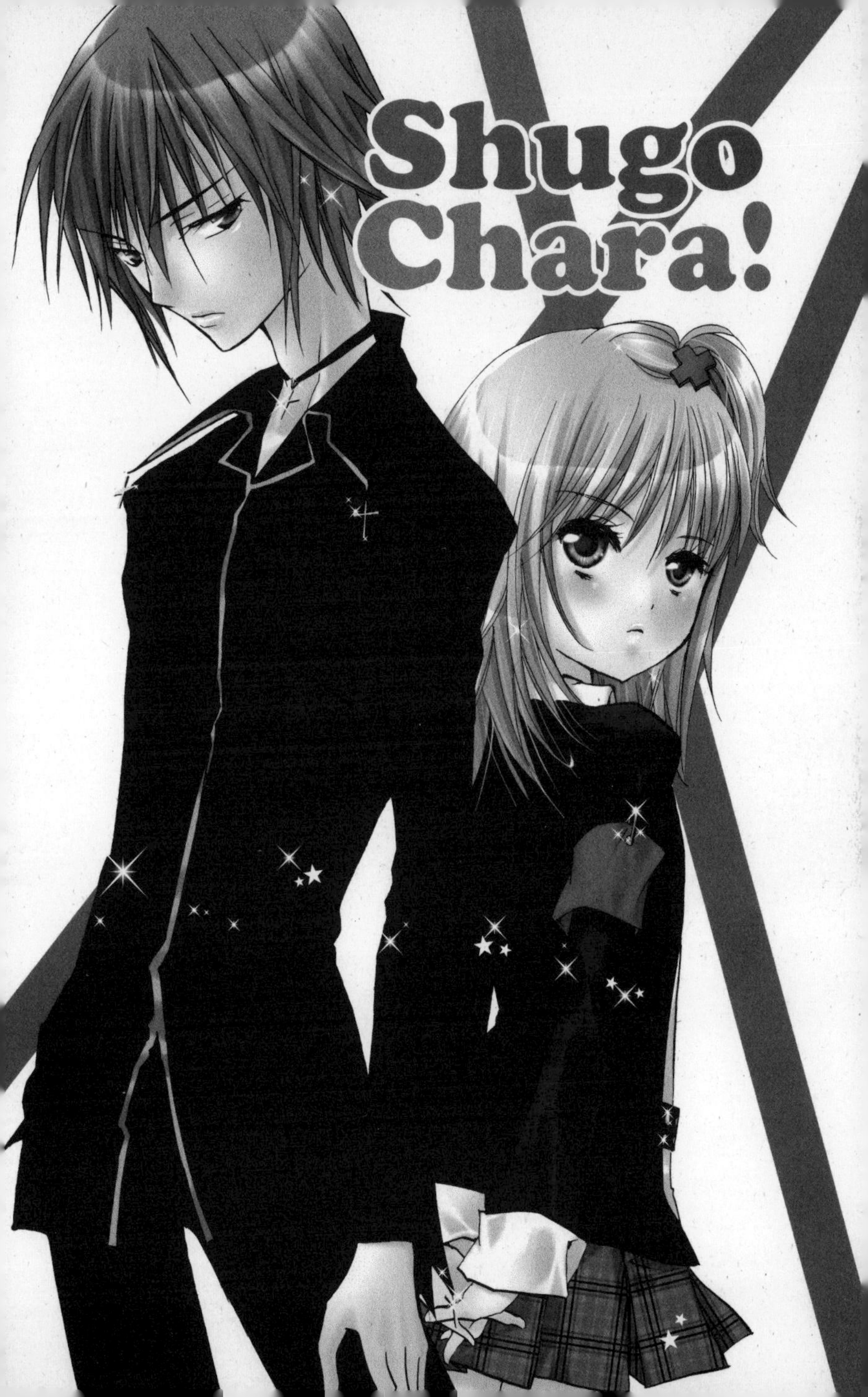
Shugo Chara!

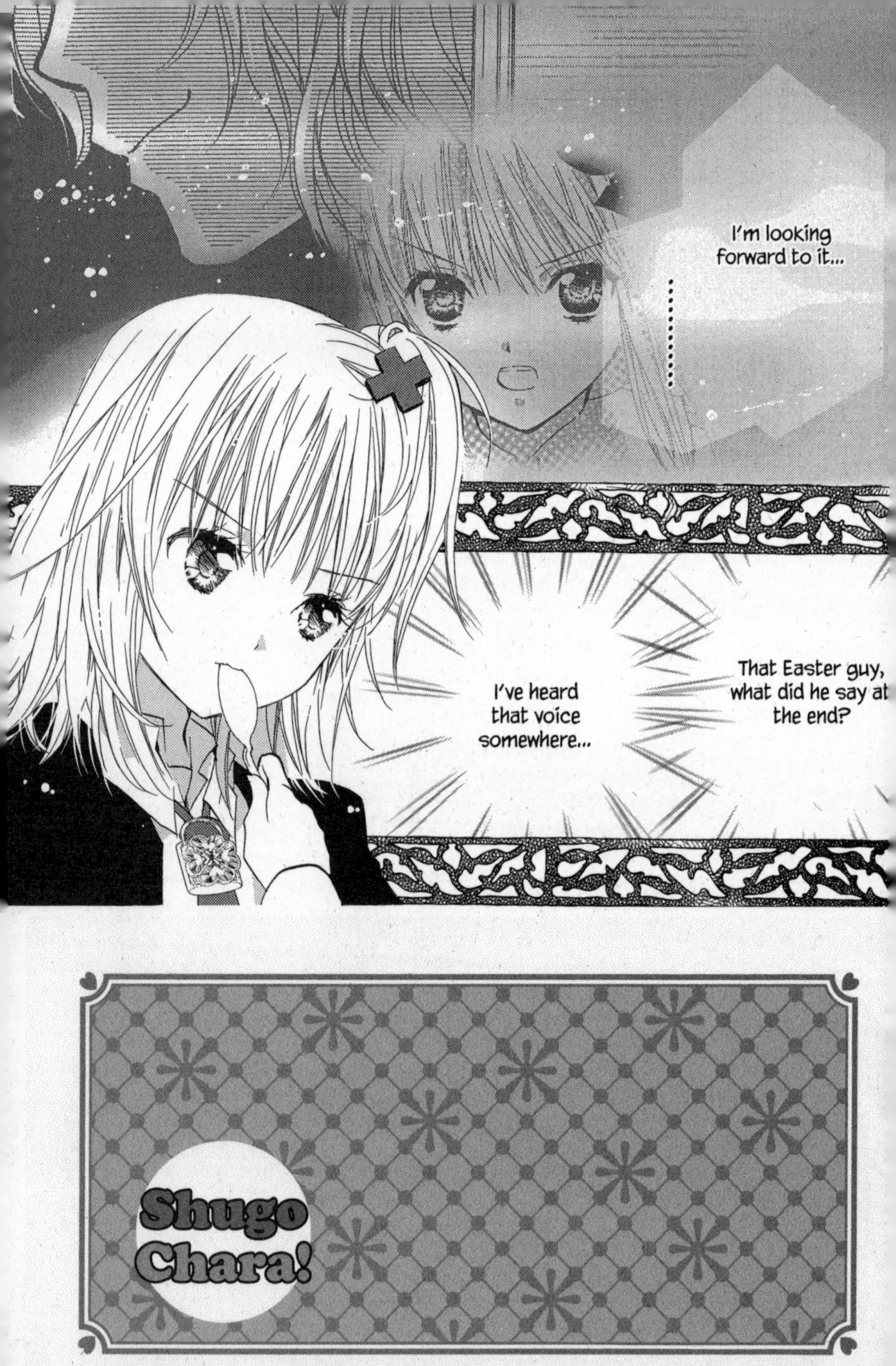
I'm looking forward to it...
......
That Easter guy, what did he say at the end?
I've heard that voice somewhere...

Shugo Chara!

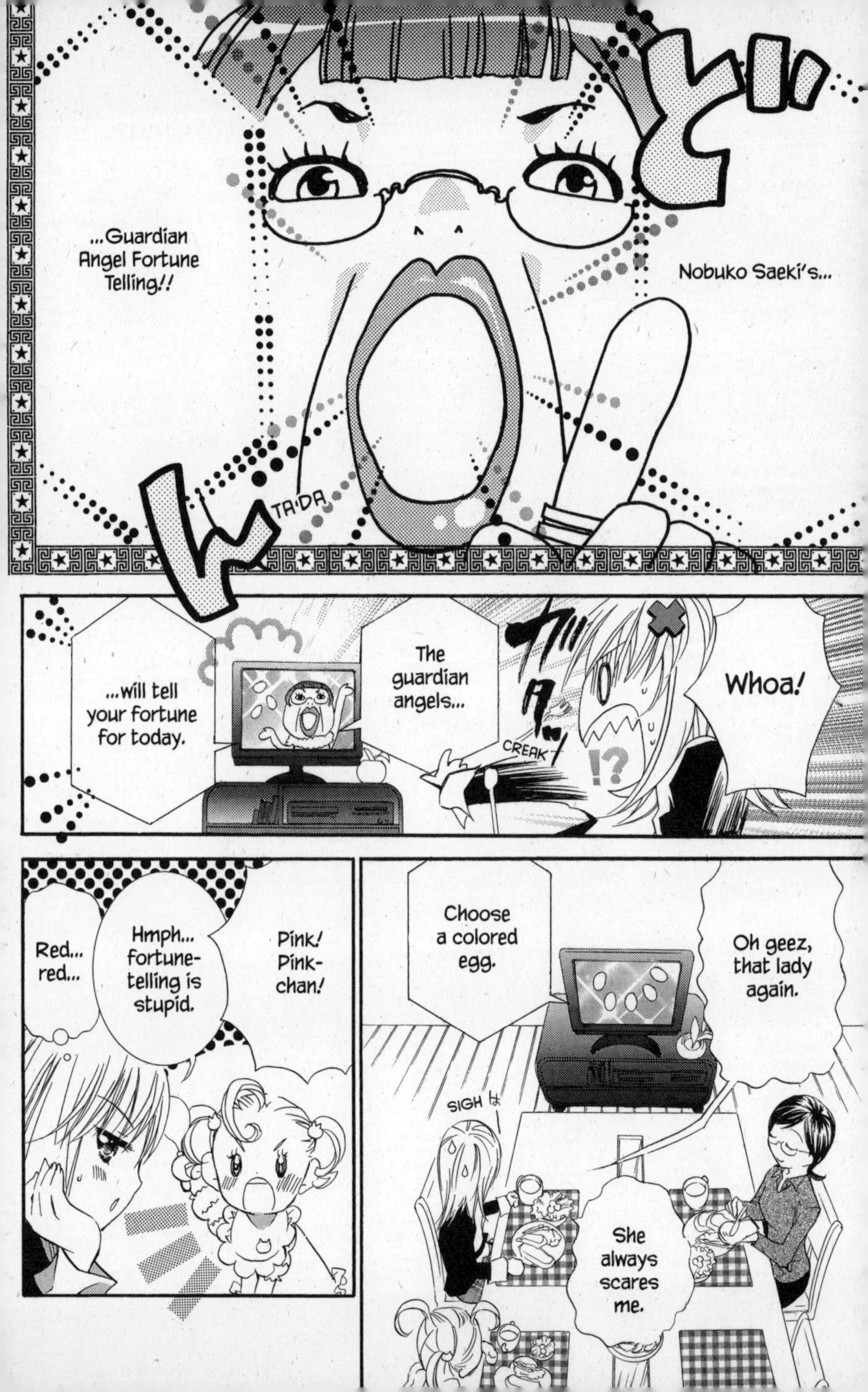
Nobuko Saeki's...
...Guardian Angel Fortune Telling!!
TA'DA
Whoa!
CREAK
!?
The guardian angels...
...will tell your fortune for today.
Oh geez, that lady again.
Choose a colored egg.
SIGH は
She always scares me.
Pink! Pink-chan!
Hmph... fortune-telling is stupid.
Red... red...

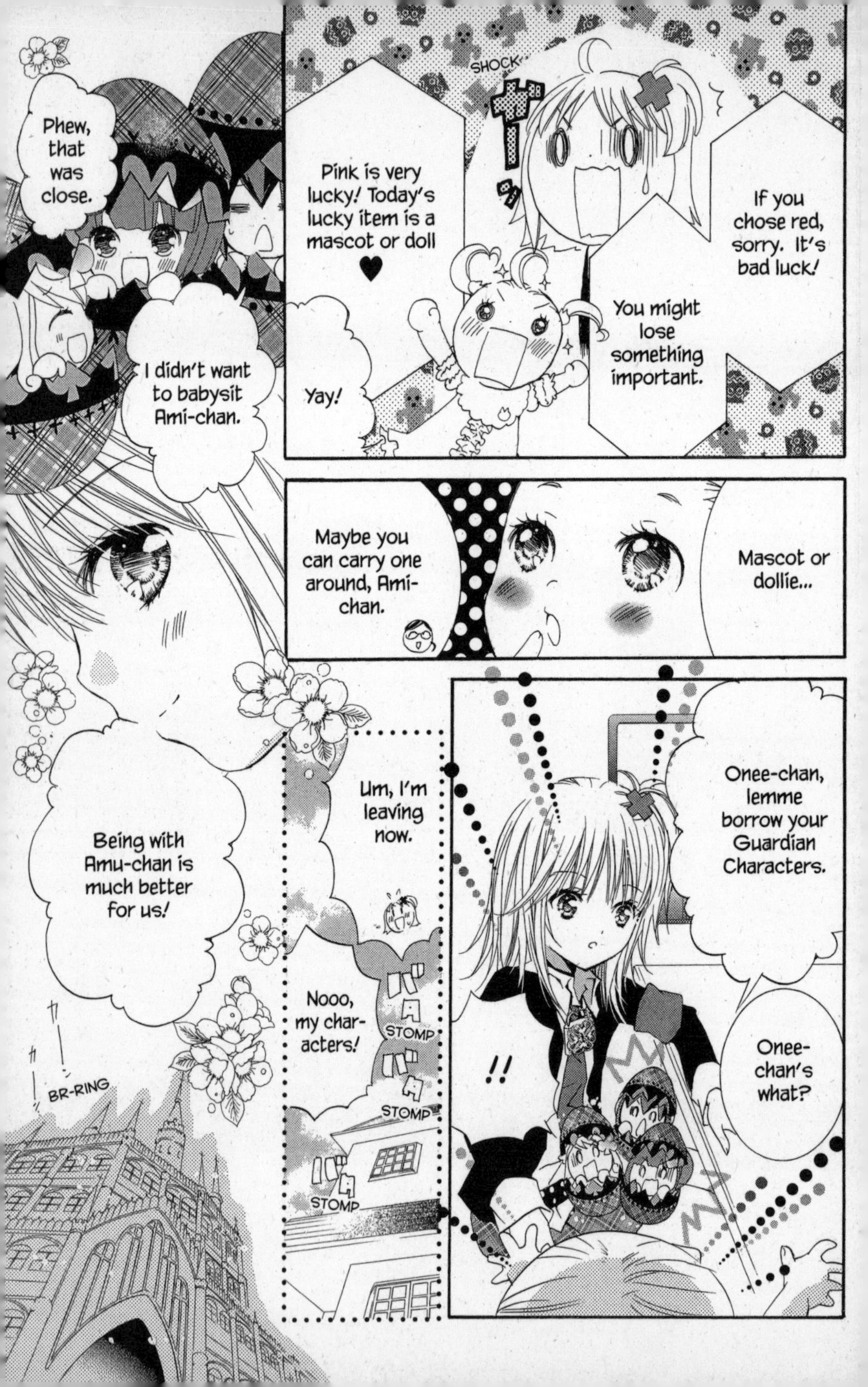

If you chose red, sorry. It's bad luck!
You might lose something important.
SHOCK
Pink is very lucky! Today's lucky item is a mascot or doll ♥
Yay!
Mascot or dollie...
Maybe you can carry one around, Ami-chan.
Onee-chan, lemme borrow your Guardian Characters.
Onee-chan's what?
!!
Um, I'm leaving now.
Nooo, my characters!
STOMP
STOMP
STOMP
Phew, that was close.
I didn't want to babysit Ami-chan.
Being with Amu-chan is much better for us!
BR-RING

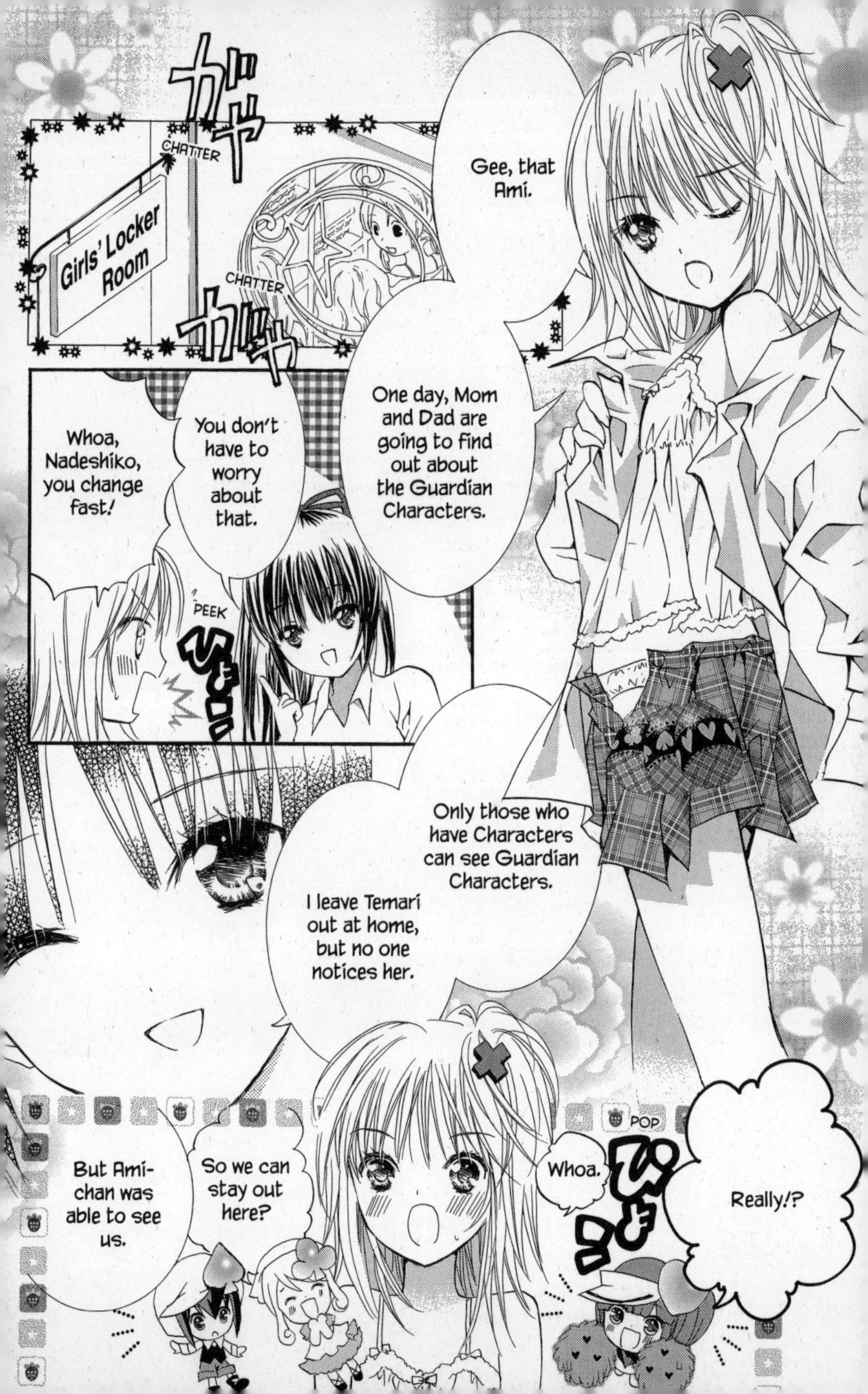
Gee, that Ami.
One day, Mom and Dad are going to find out about the Guardian Characters.
CHATTER
CHATTER
Girls' Locker Room
You don't have to worry about that.
Whoa, Nadeshiko, you change fast!
PEEK
Only those who have Characters can see Guardian Characters.
I leave Temari out at home, but no one notices her.
Really!?
POP
Whoa.
So we can stay out here?
But Ami-chan was able to see us.

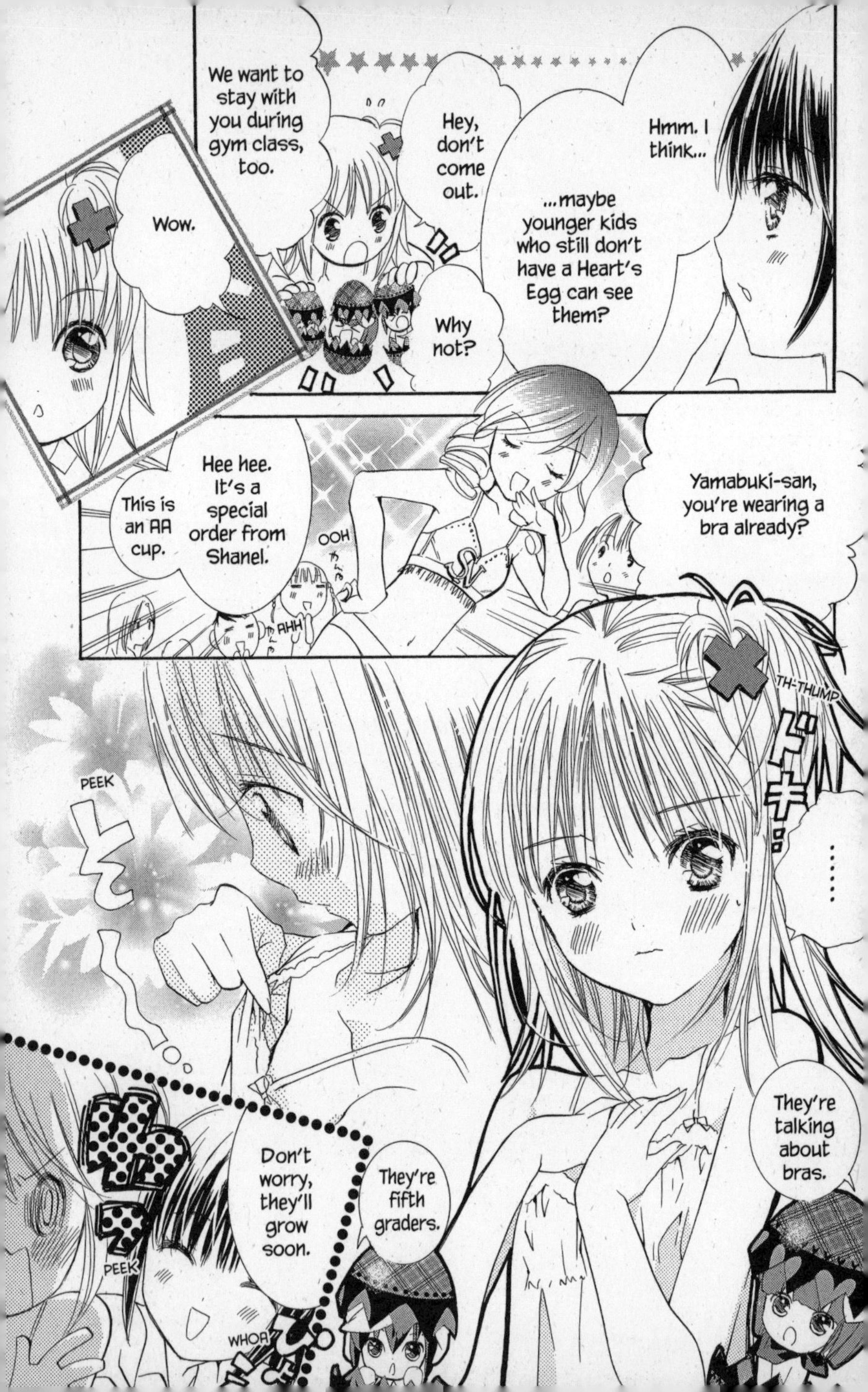
Hmm. I think...
...maybe younger kids who still don't have a Heart's Egg can see them?
Hey, don't come out.
Why not?
We want to stay with you during gym class, too.
Wow.
Yamabuki-san, you're wearing a bra already?
Hee hee. It's a special order from Shanel.
This is an AA cup.
OOH
AHH
TH-THUMP
......
PEEK
They're talking about bras.
They're fifth graders.
Don't worry, they'll grow soon.
PEEK
WHOA

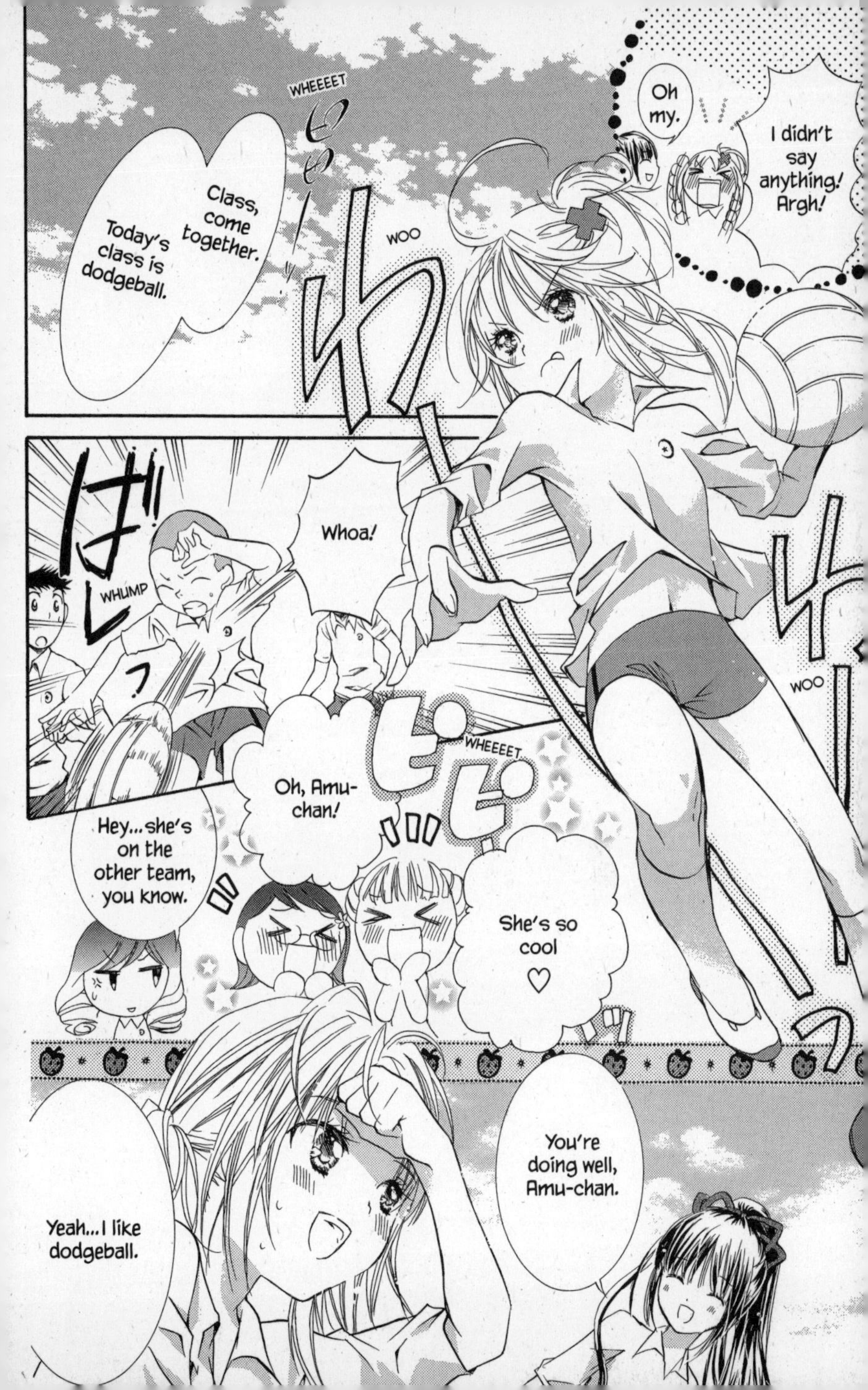

I didn't say anything! Argh!
Oh my.
WOO
WOO
WHEEEET
Class, come together. Today's class is dodgeball.
Whoa!
WHUMP
WHEEEET
Oh, Amu-chan!
She's so cool ♡
Hey...she's on the other team, you know.
You're doing well, Amu-chan.
Yeah...I like dodgeball.

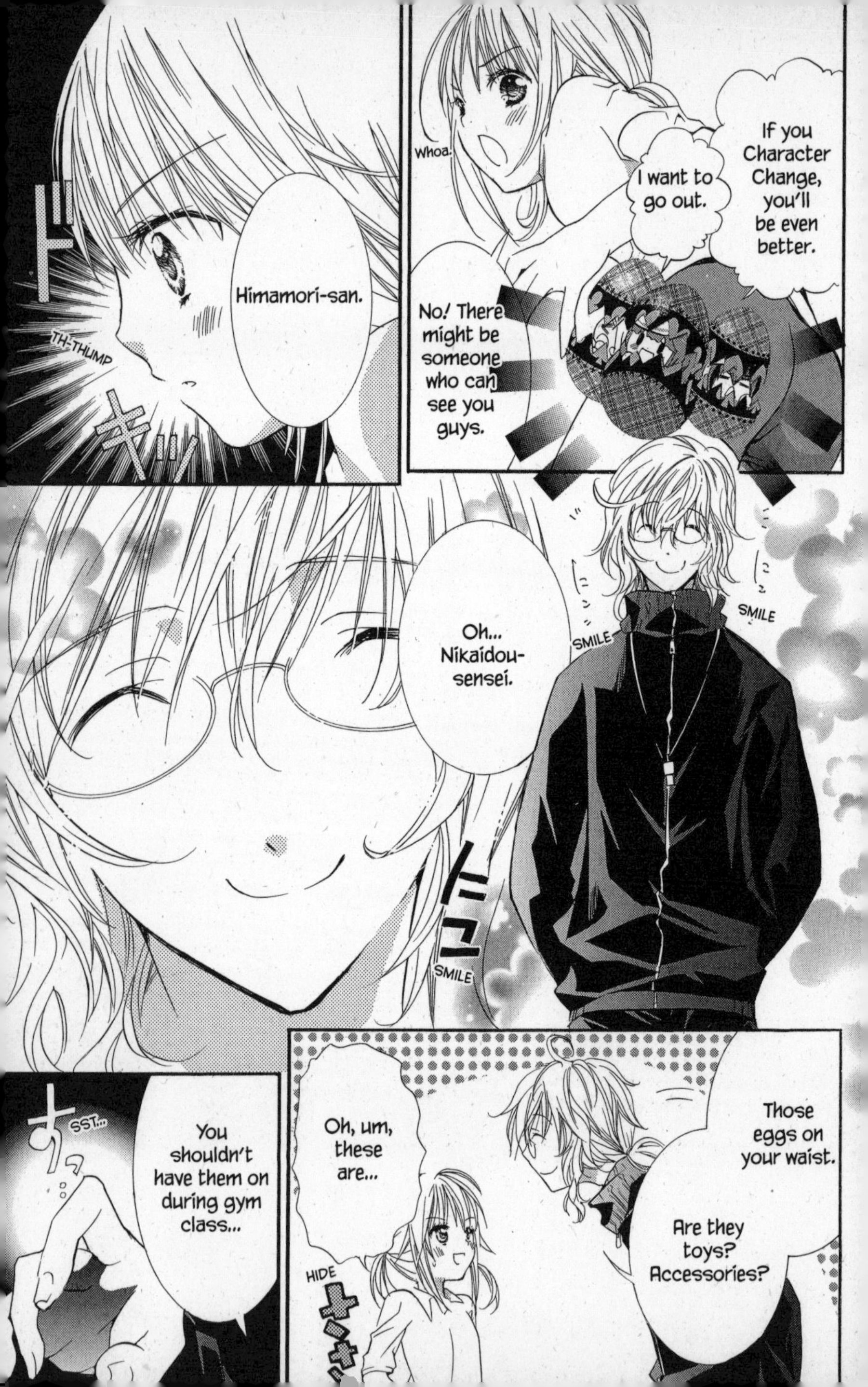
If you Character Change, you'll be even better.
I want to go out.
Whoa.
No! There might be someone who can see you guys.
TH-THUMP
Himamori-san.
SMILE
SMILE
Oh... Nikaidou-sensei.
SMILE
Those eggs on your waist.
Are they toys? Accessories?
Oh, um, these are...
HIDE
SST...
You shouldn't have them on during gym class...

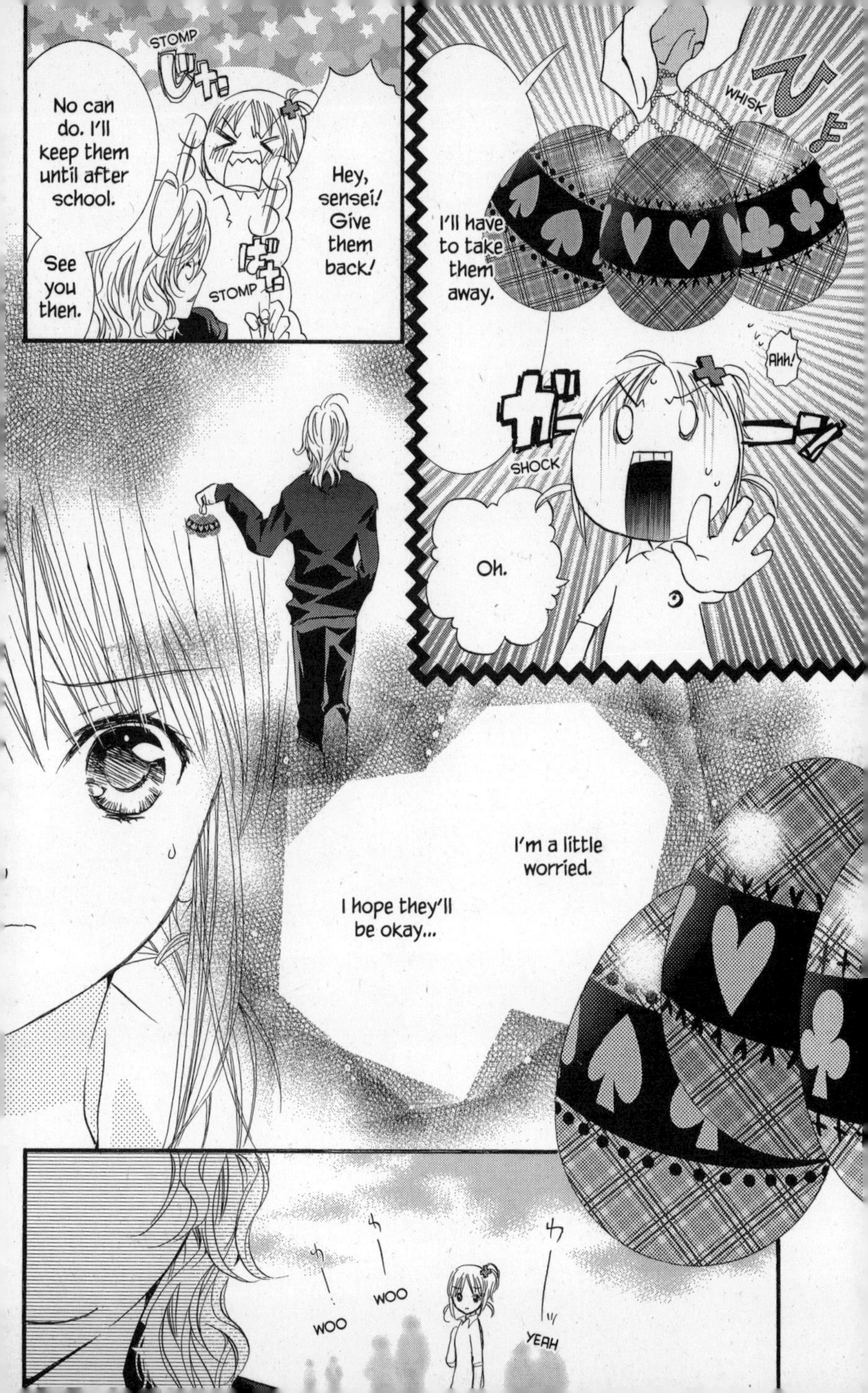
WHISK
I'll have to take them away.
Ahh!
SHOCK
Oh.
STOMP
Hey, sensei! Give them back!
STOMP
No can do. I'll keep them until after school.
See you then.
I'm a little worried.
I hope they'll be okay...
YEAH
WOO
WOO

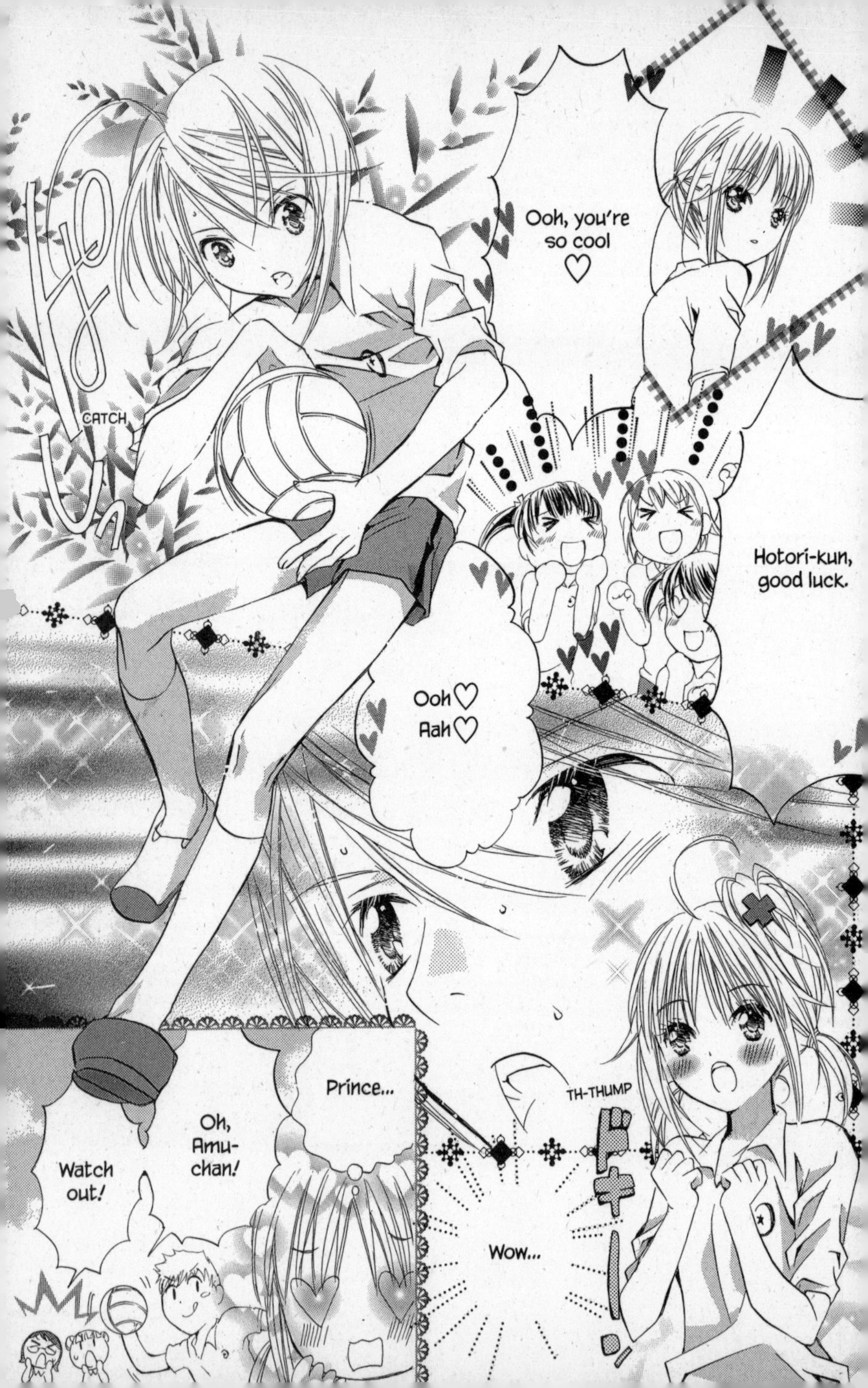

Ooh, you're so cool ♡
Hotori-kun, good luck.
CATCH
Ooh♡ Aah♡
TH-THUMP
Wow...
Prince...
Oh, Amu-chan!
Watch out!

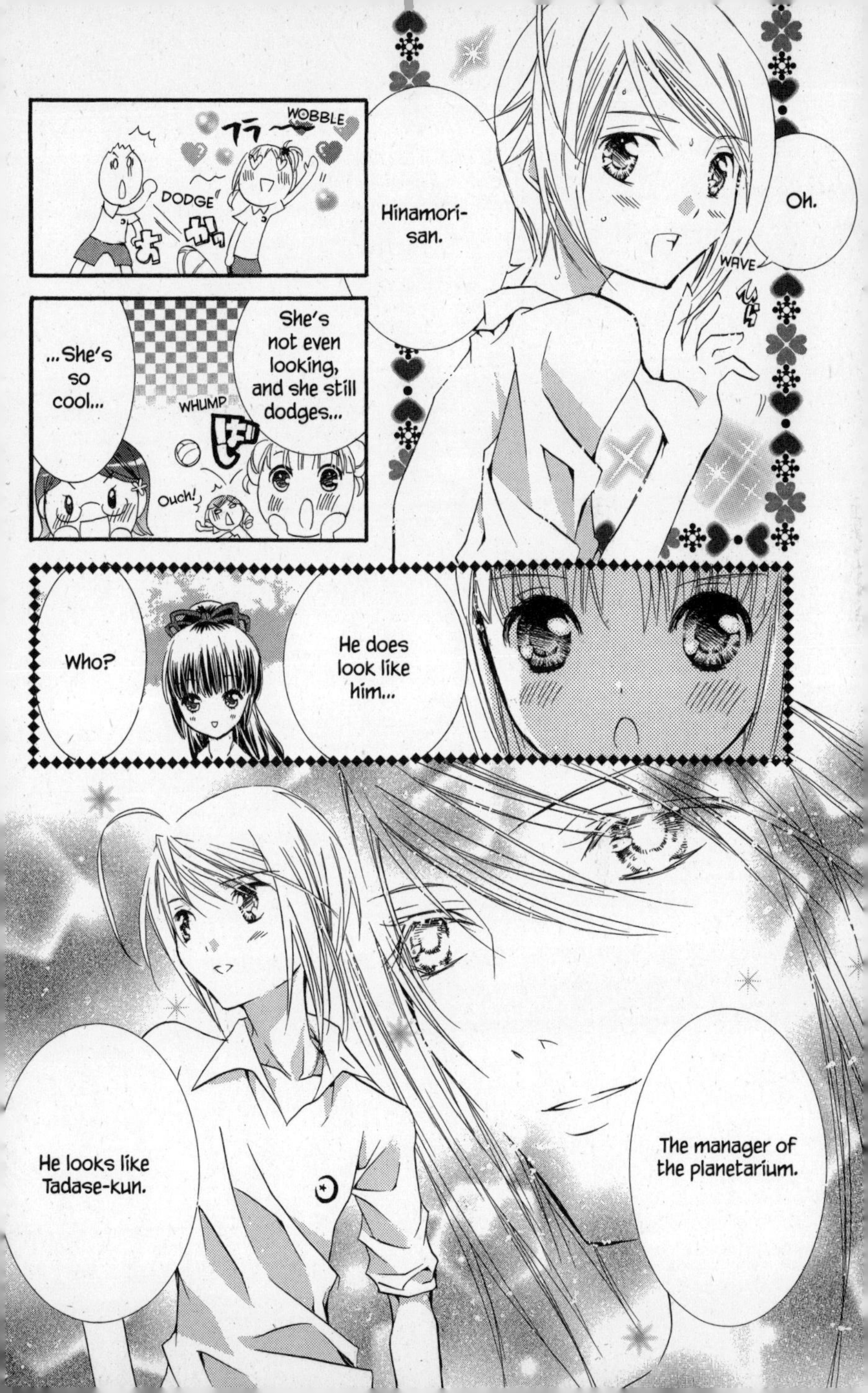

Oh.
WAVE
Hinamori-san.
WOBBLE
DODGE
She's not even looking, and she still dodges...
WHUMP
...She's so cool...
Ouch!
He does look like him...
Who?
The manager of the planetarium.
He looks like Tadase-kun.

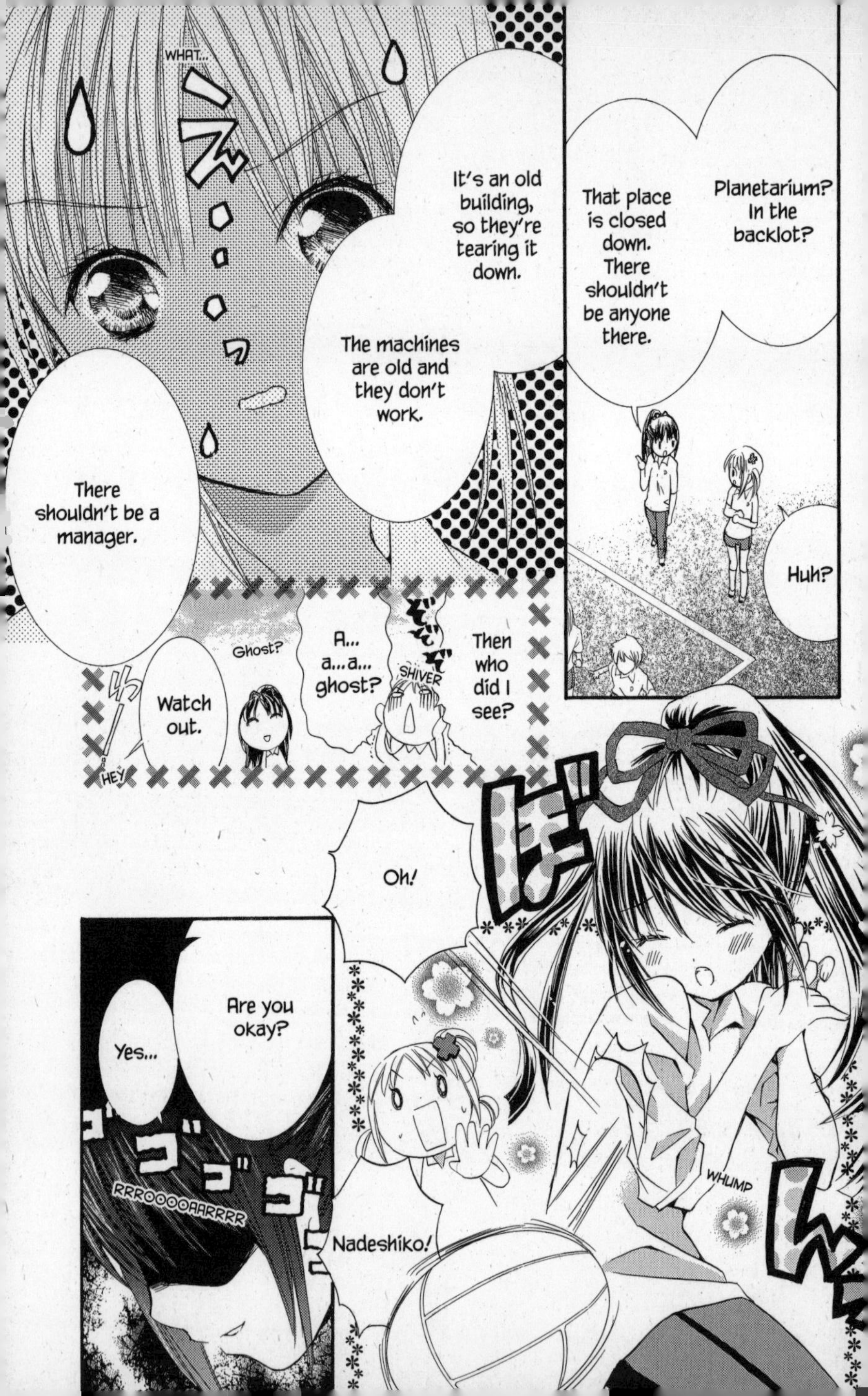
Planetarium? In the backlot?
That place is closed down. There shouldn't be anyone there.
Huh?
It's an old building, so they're tearing it down.
The machines are old and they don't work.
WHAT...
There shouldn't be a manager.
Then who did I see?
A... a...a... ghost?
SHIVER
Ghost?
Watch out.
HEY
Oh!
WHUMP
Nadeshiko!
Are you okay?
Yes...
RRROOOOAARRRR

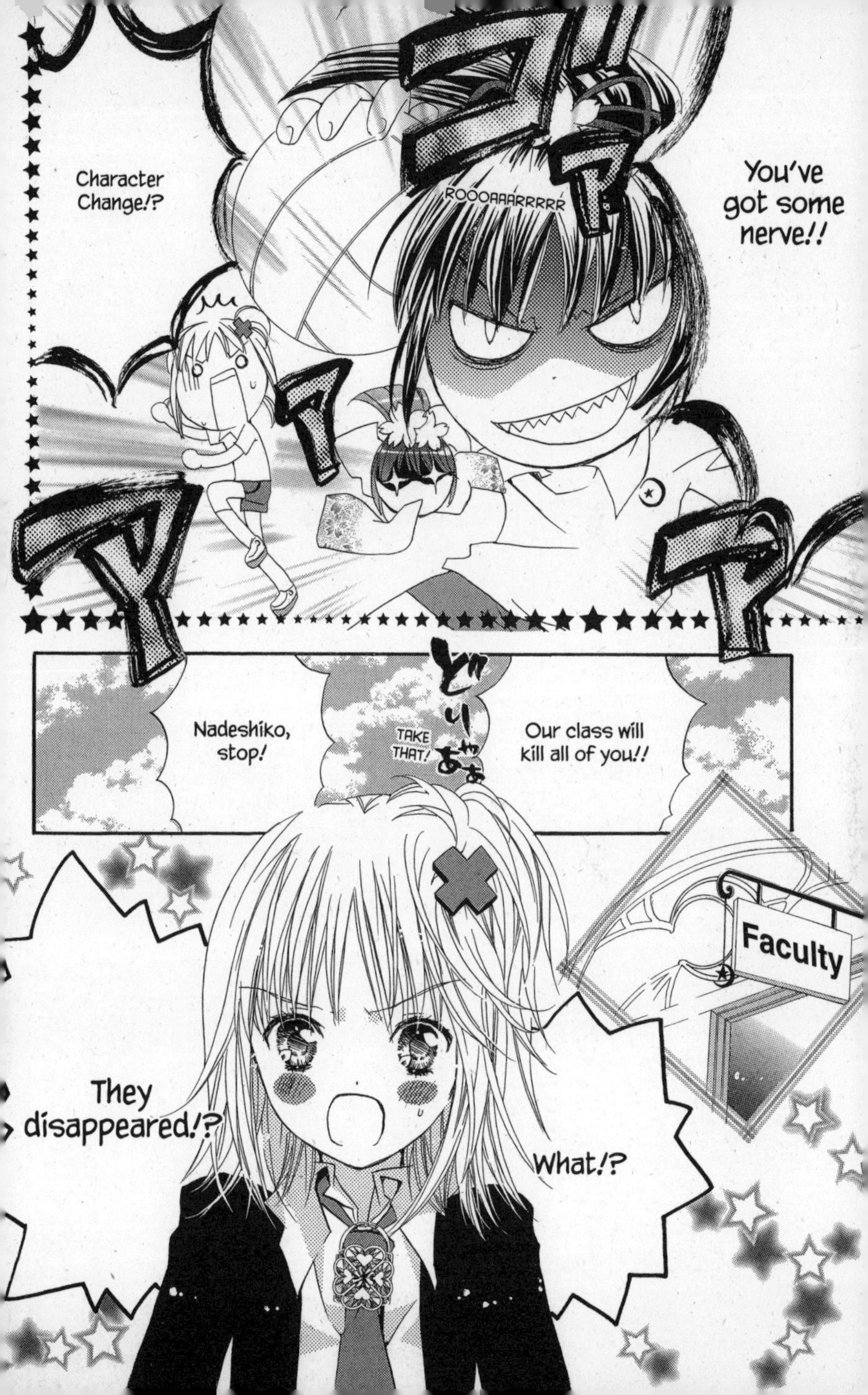
You've got some nerve!!
ROOOAAARRRRR
Character Change!?
Our class will kill all of you!!
TAKE THAT!
Nadeshiko, stop!
Faculty
What!?
They disappeared!?

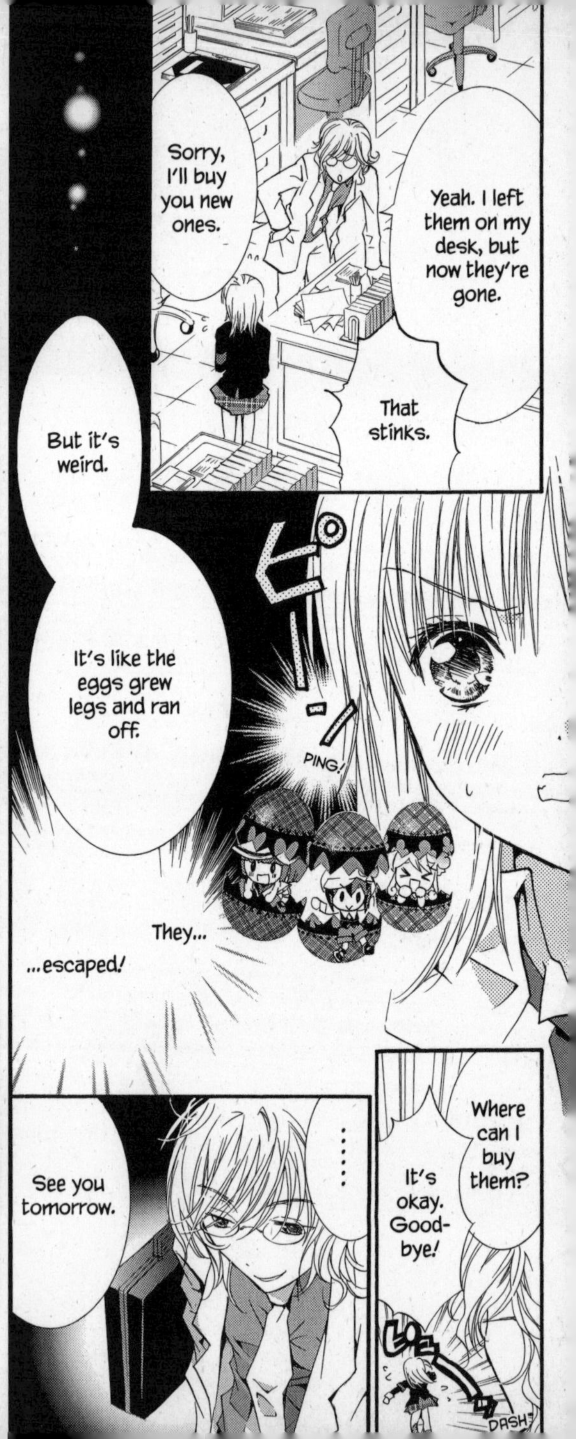
Yeah. I left them on my desk, but now they're gone.
That stinks.
Sorry, I'll buy you new ones.
But it's weird.
It's like the eggs grew legs and ran off.
PING!
They...
...escaped!
Where can I buy them?
It's okay. Good-bye!
DASH
......
See you tomorrow.

character profile

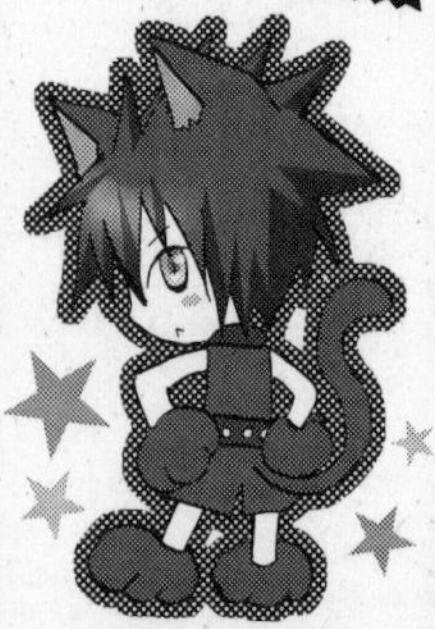

ヨル

YORU

Guardian Character of: Ikuto
Special Skill: Going out
Hates: Dogs

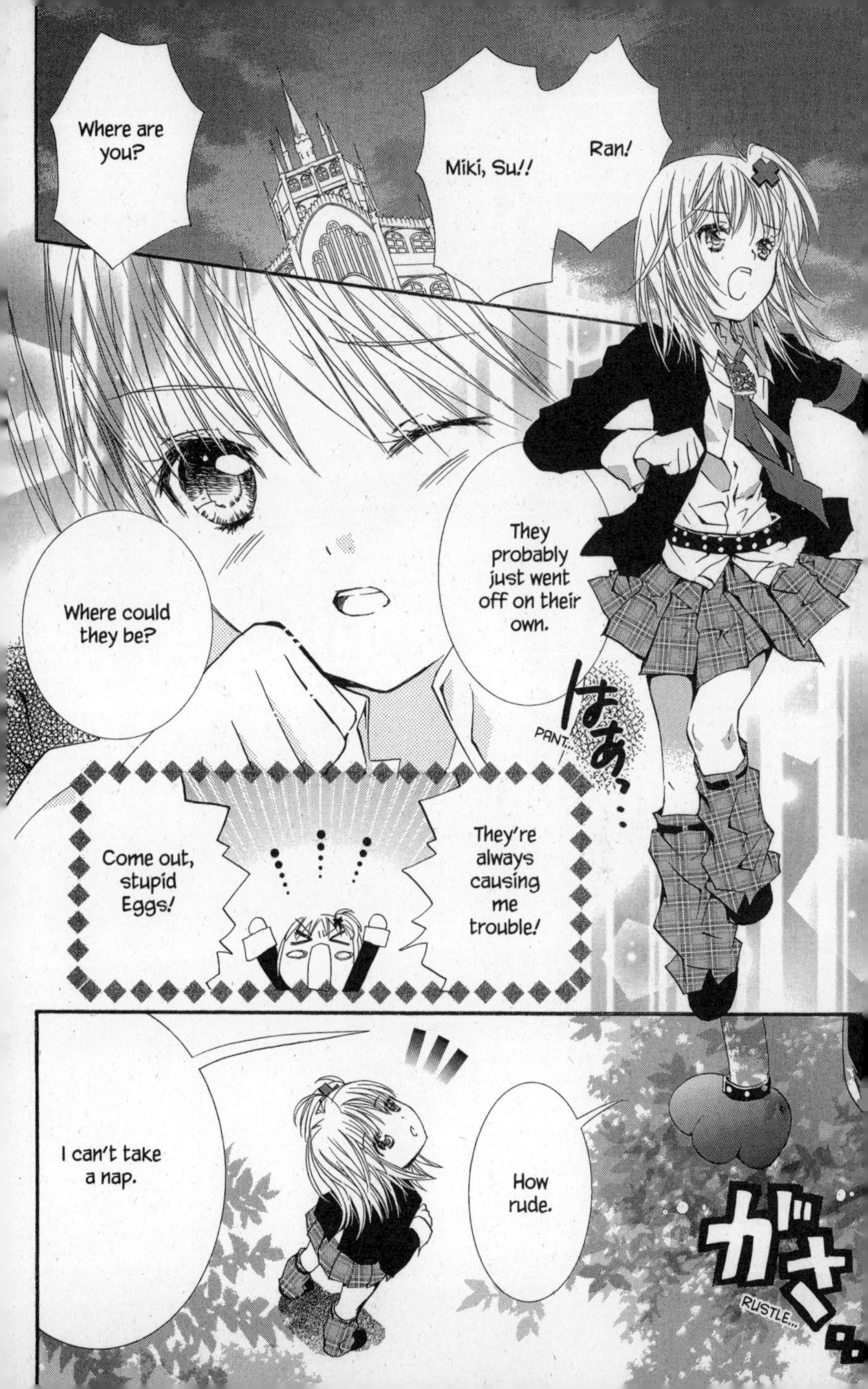
Ran!
Miki, Su!!
Where are you?
They probably just went off on their own.
はぁ
PANT...
Where could they be?
They're always causing me trouble!
Come out, stupid Eggs!
ガさ
RUSTLE...
How rude.
I can't take a nap.

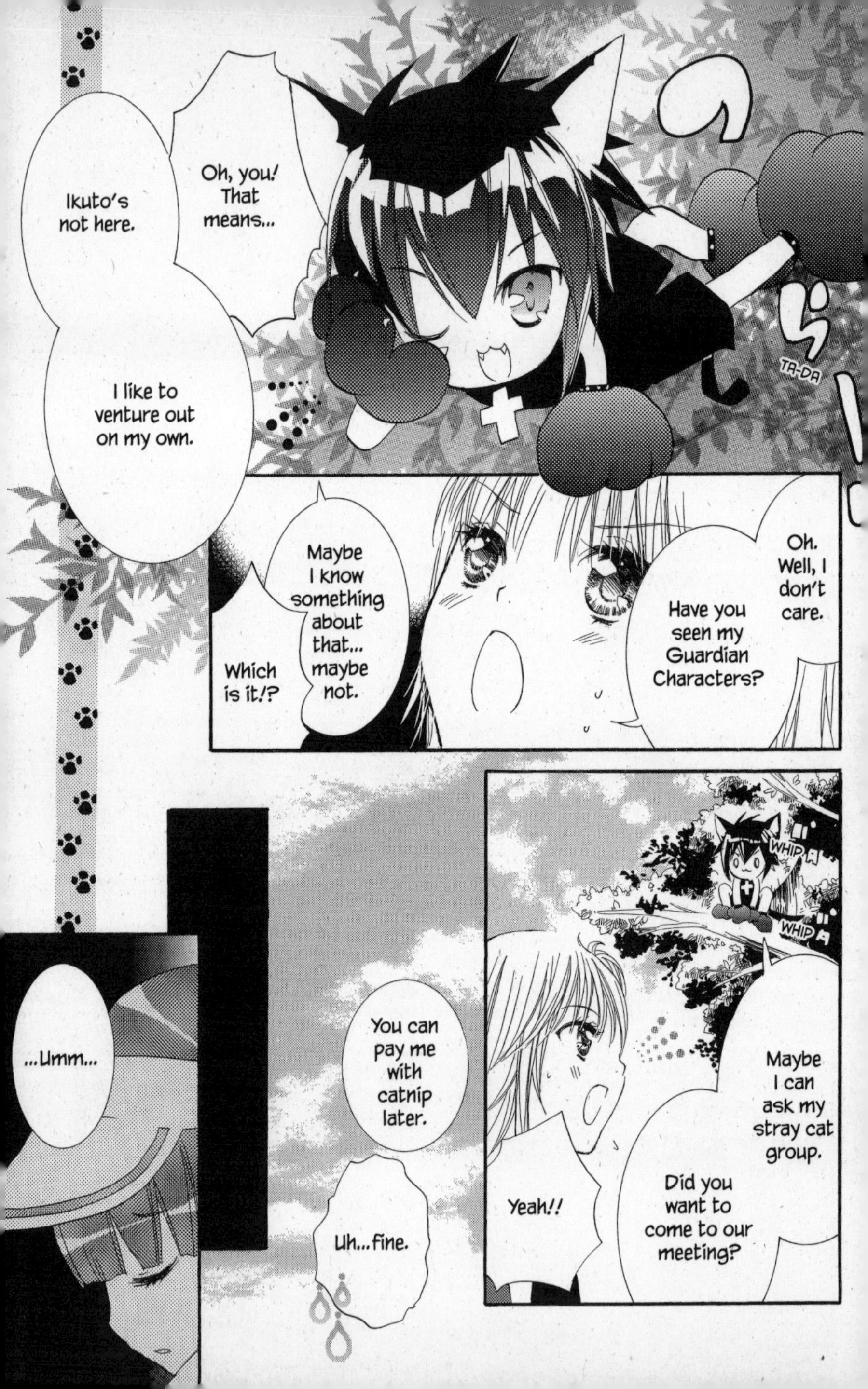
TA-DA
Oh, you! That means...
Ikuto's not here.
I like to venture out on my own.
Oh. Well, I don't care.
Have you seen my Guardian Characters?
Maybe I know something about that... maybe not.
Which is it!?
WHIP
WHIP
Maybe I can ask my stray cat group.
Did you want to come to our meeting?
Yeah!!
You can pay me with catnip later.
Uh...fine.
...Umm...

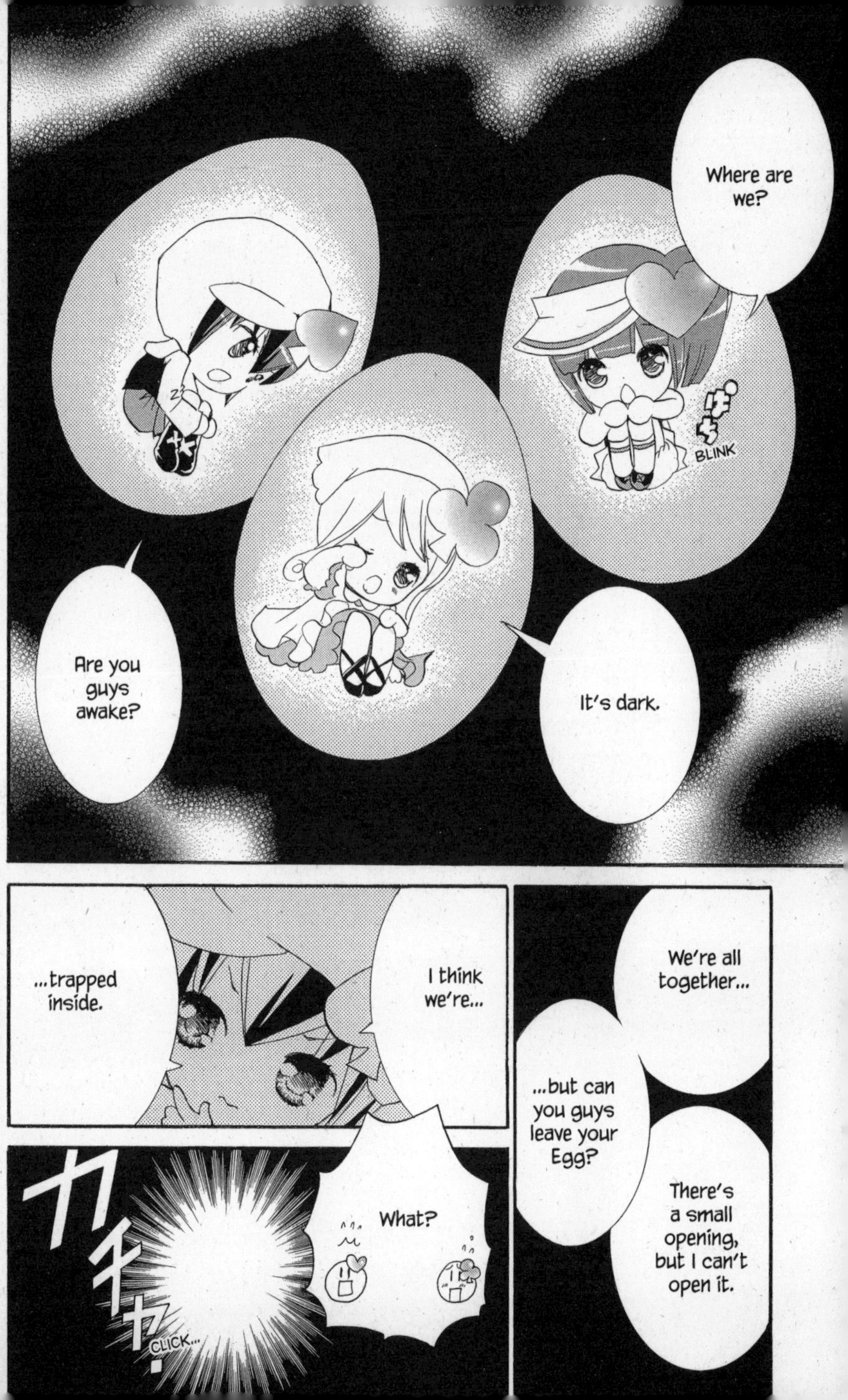
Where are we?
BLINK
It's dark.
Are you guys awake?
We're all together...
...but can you guys leave your Egg?
There's a small opening, but I can't open it.
I think we're...
...trapped inside.
What?
CLICK...

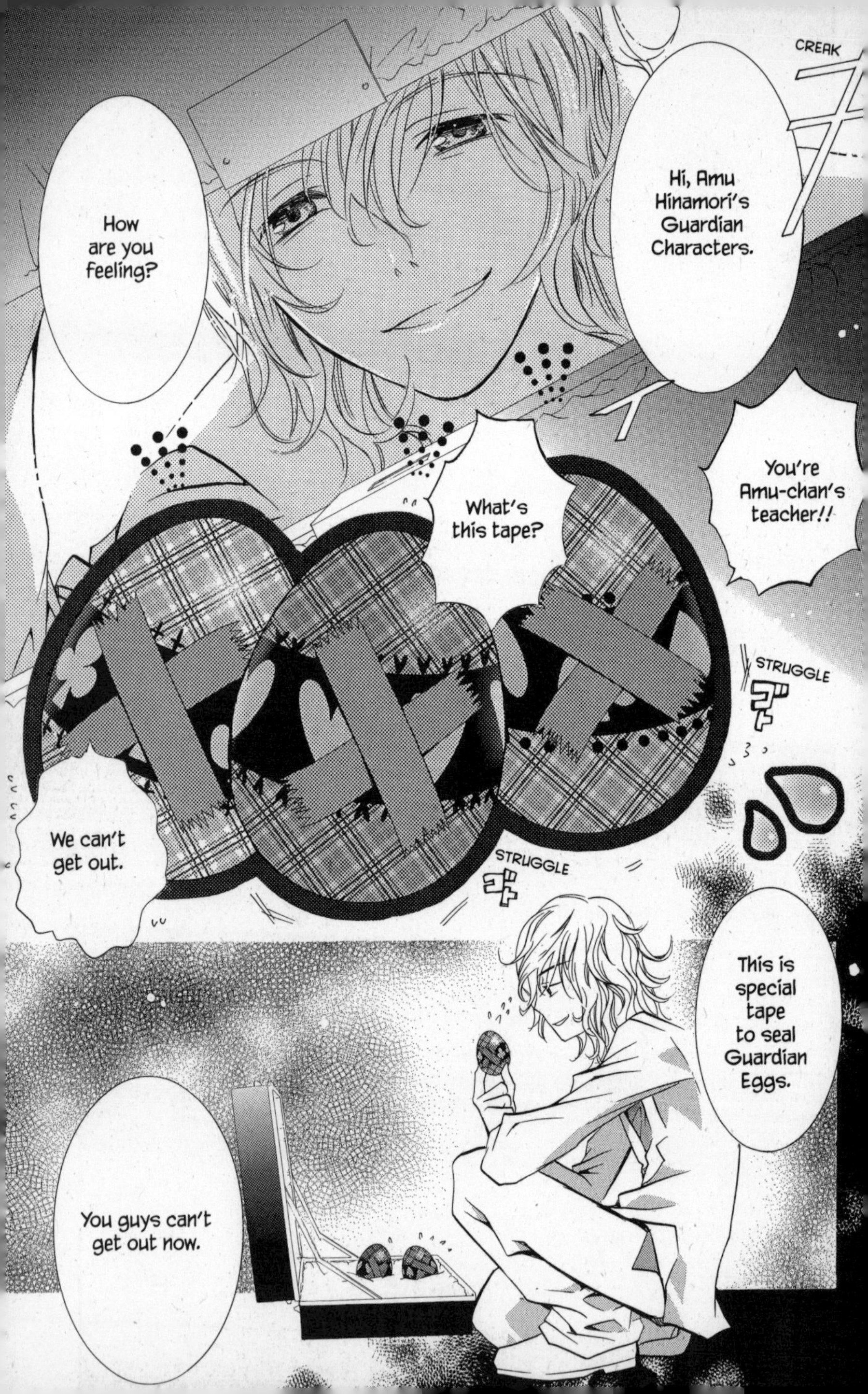
CREAK
Hi, Amu Hinamori's Guardian Characters.
How are you feeling?
You're Amu-chan's teacher!!
What's this tape?
STRUGGLE
STRUGGLE
We can't get out.
This is special tape to seal Guardian Eggs.
You guys can't get out now.

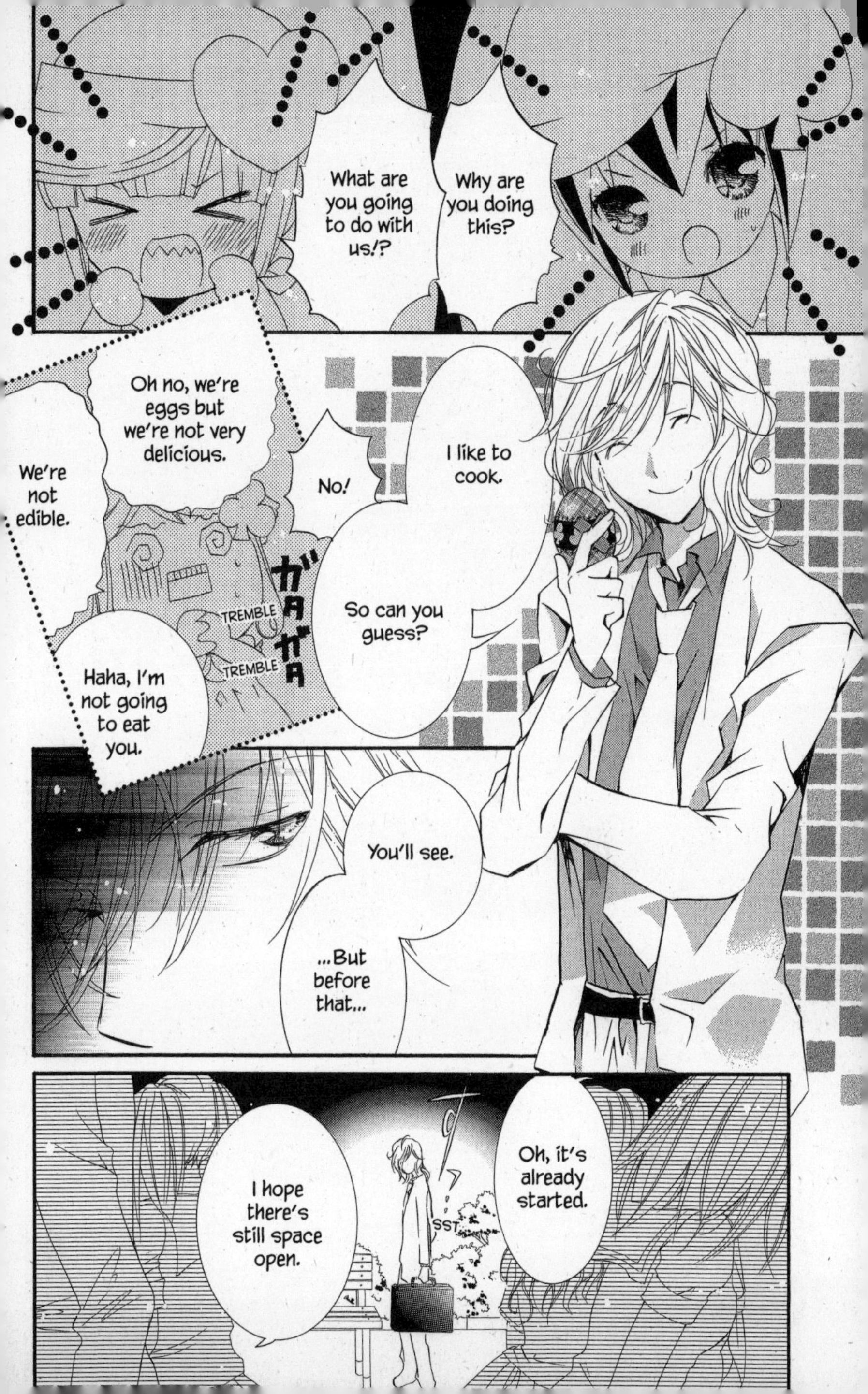
Why are you doing this?
What are you going to do with us!?
I like to cook.
So can you guess?
No!
Oh no, we're eggs but we're not very delicious.
We're not edible.
TREMBLE
TREMBLE
Haha, I'm not going to eat you.
You'll see.
...But before that...
Oh, it's already started.
SST
I hope there's still space open.

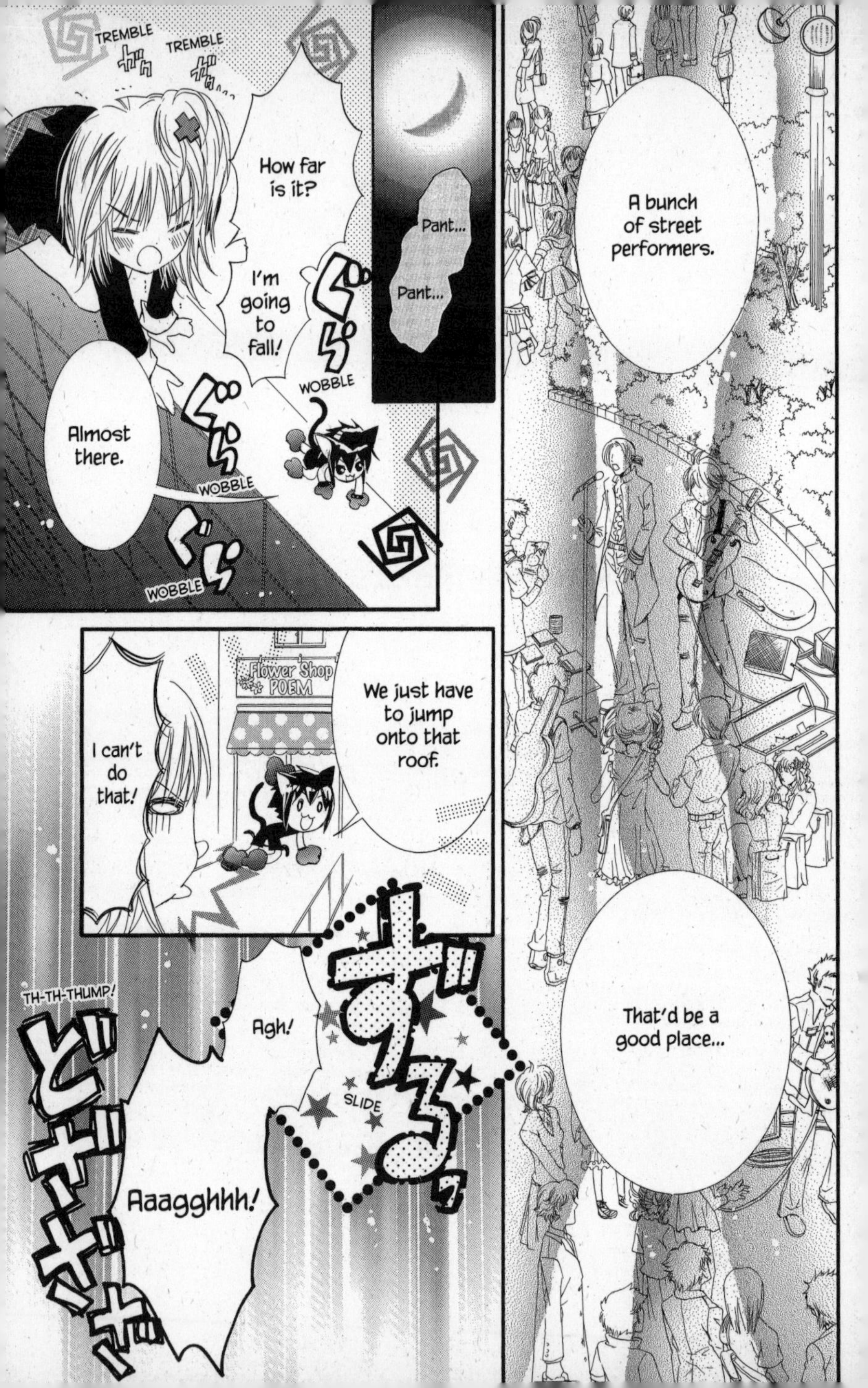
A bunch of street performers.
That'd be a good place...
Pant...
Pant...
TREMBLE
TREMBLE
How far is it?
I'm going to fall!
WOBBLE
Almost there.
WOBBLE
WOBBLE
Flower Shop POEM
We just have to jump onto that roof.
I can't do that!
SLIDE
Agh!
TH-TH-THUMP!
Aaagghhh!

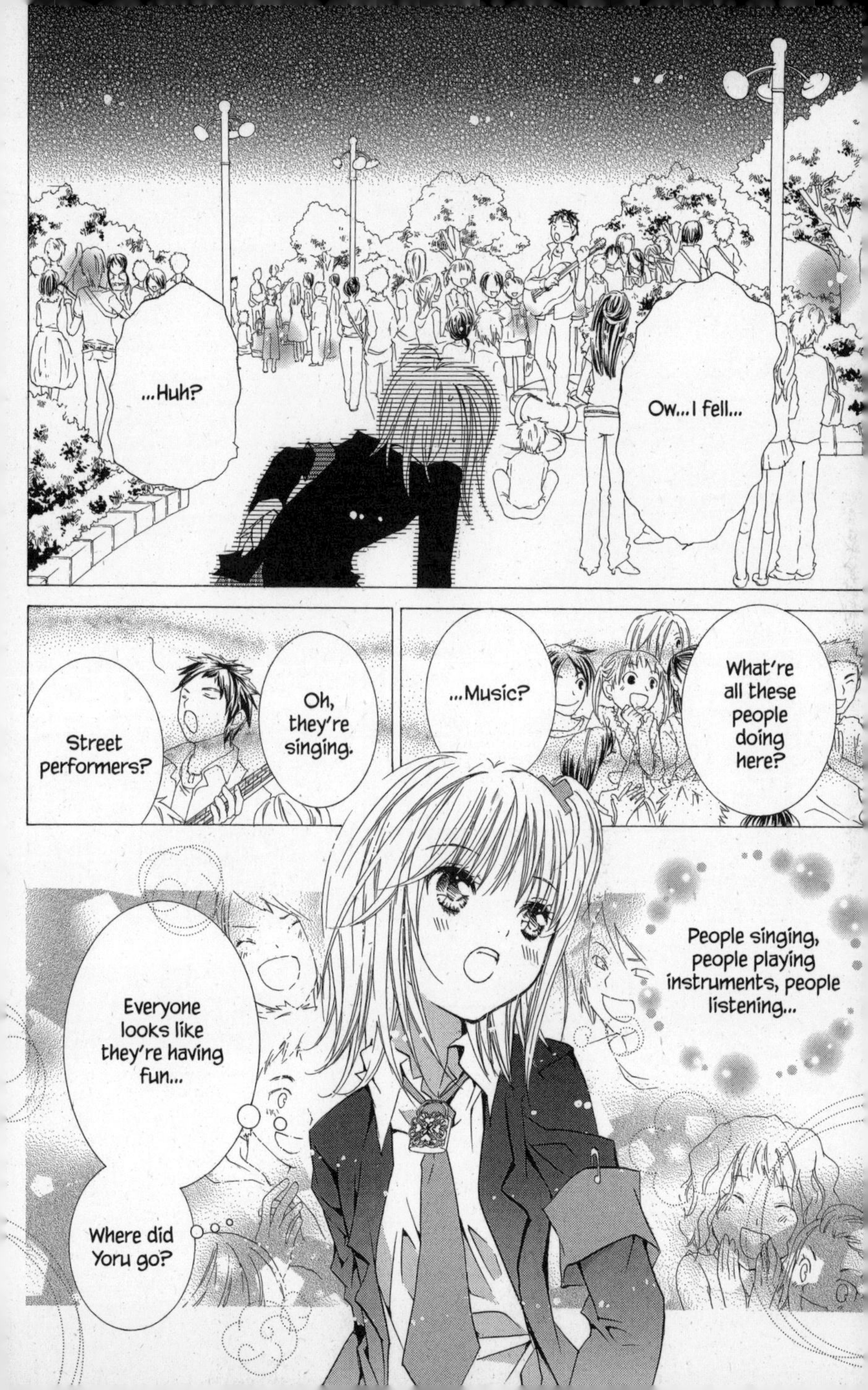
Ow...I fell...
...Huh?
What're all these people doing here?
...Music?
Oh, they're singing.
Street performers?
People singing, people playing instruments, people listening...
Everyone looks like they're having fun...
Where did Yoru go?

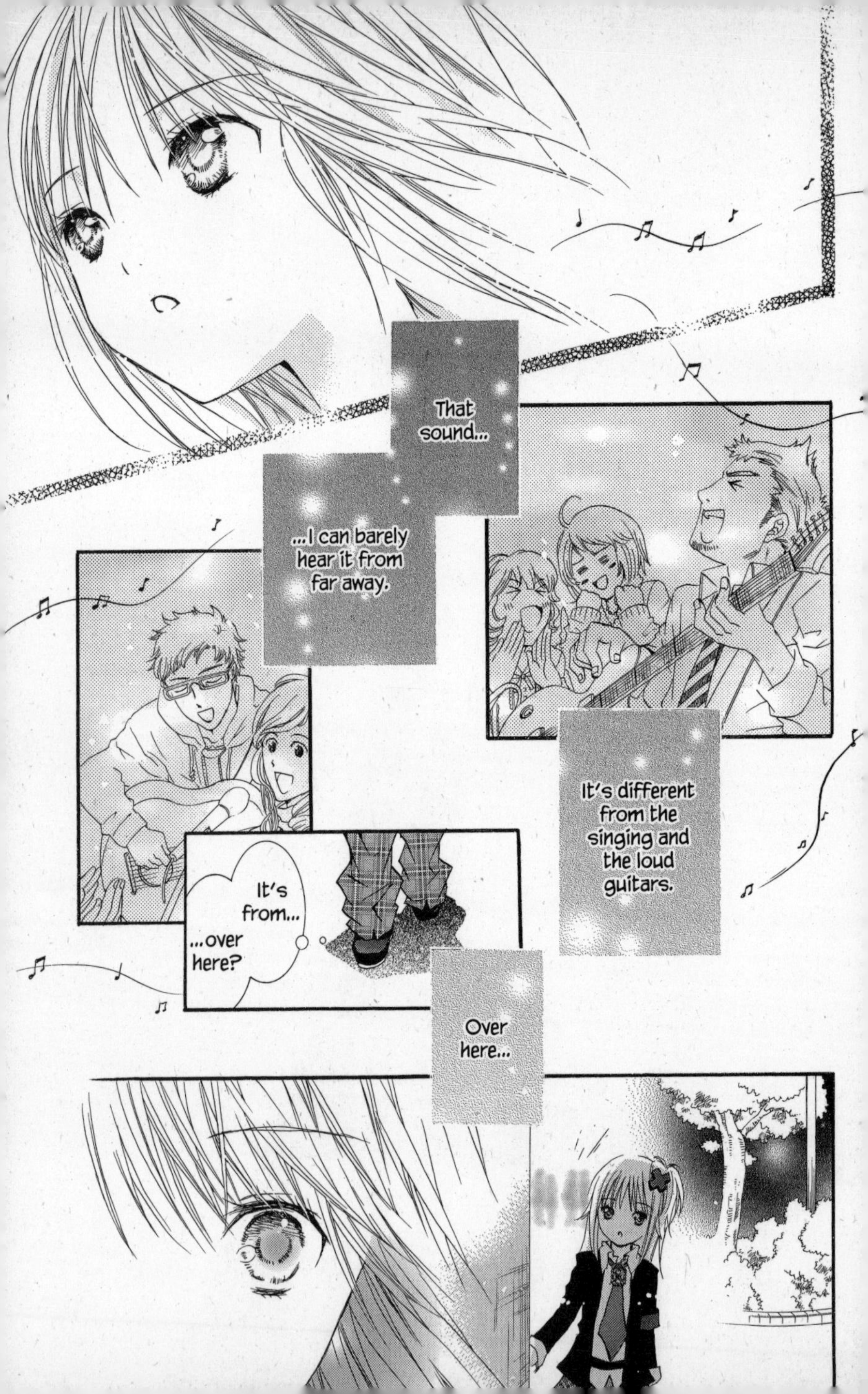
That sound...
...I can barely hear it from far away.
It's different from the singing and the loud guitars.
It's from... ...over here?
Over here...

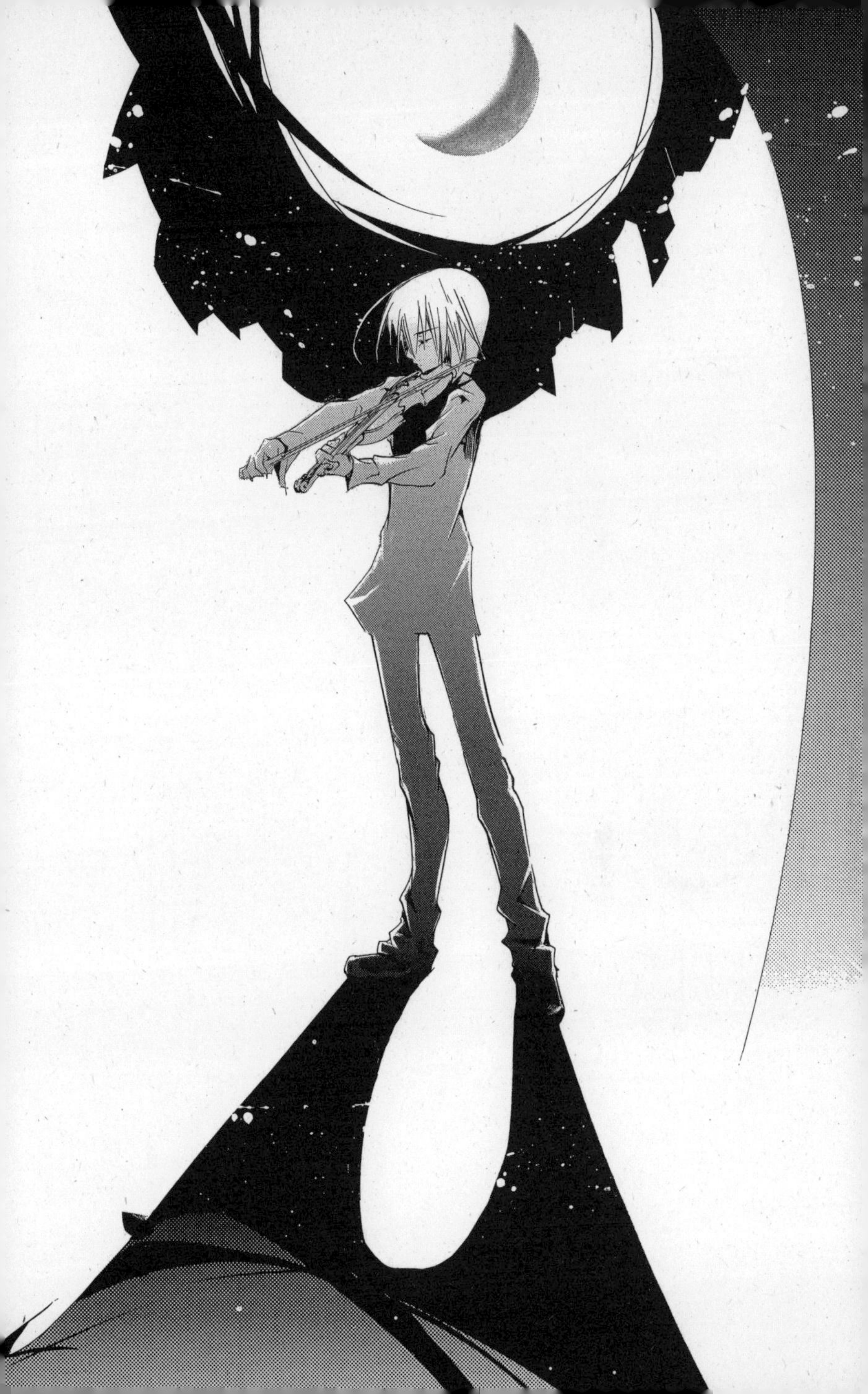

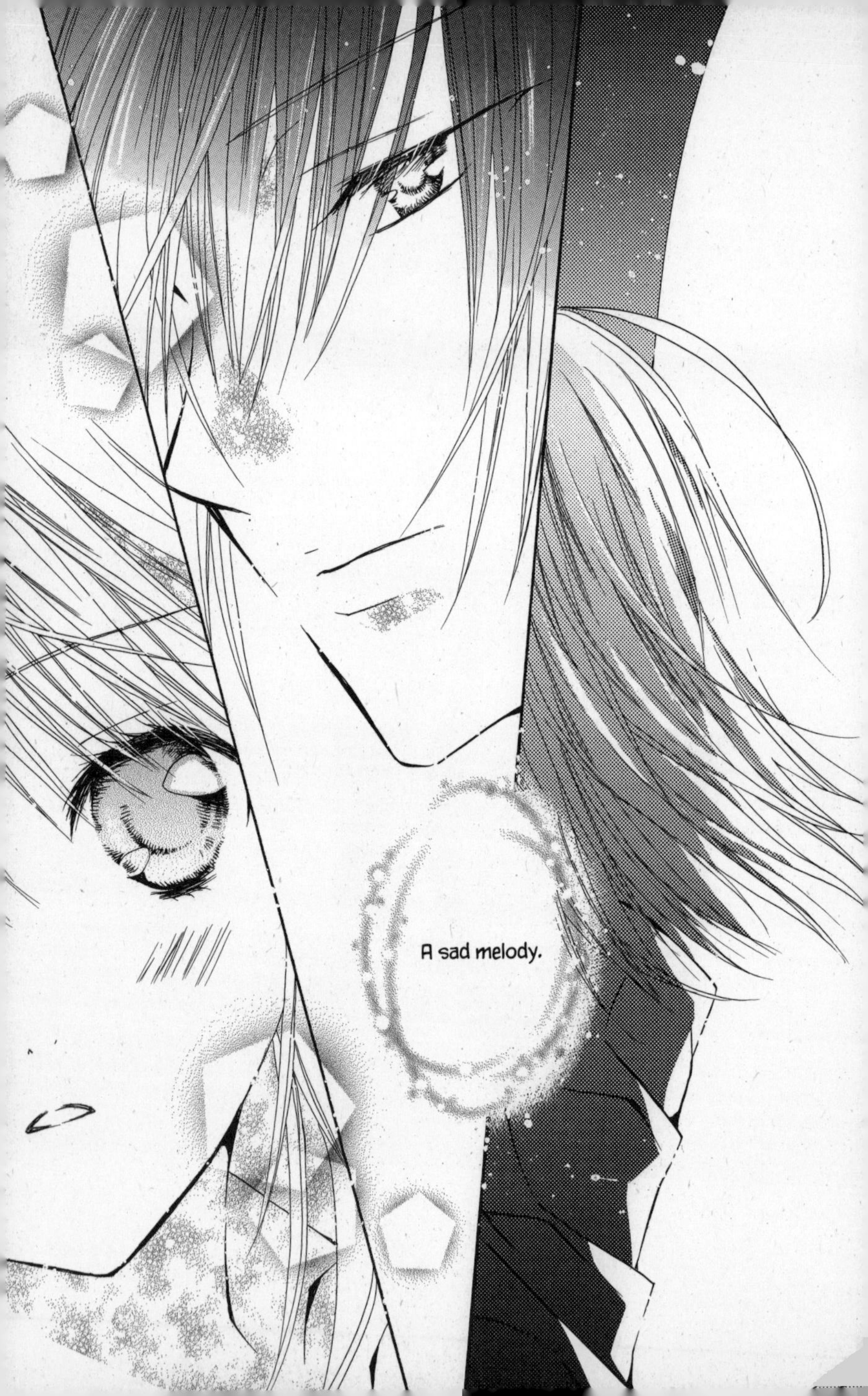
A sad melody.

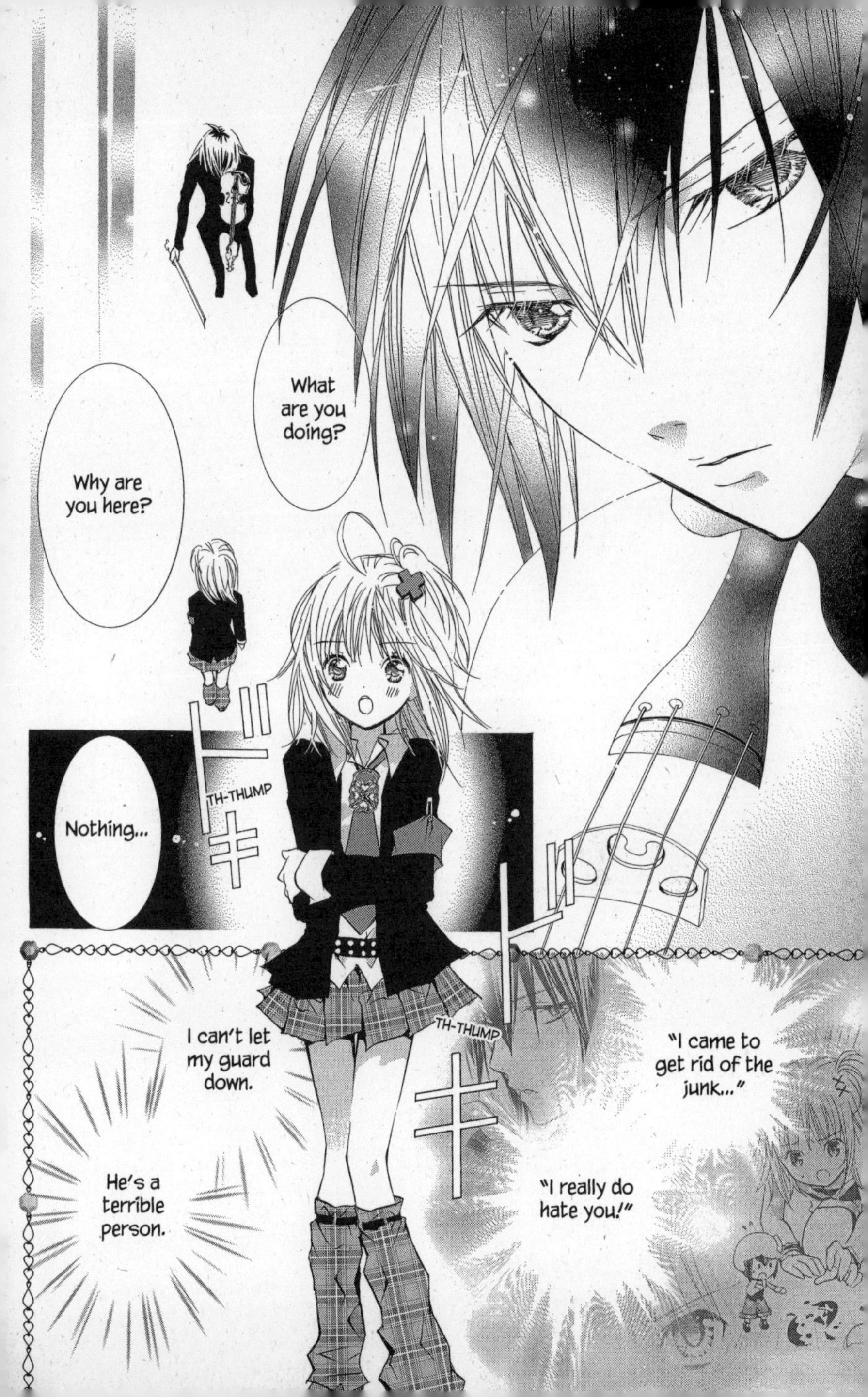
What are you doing?
Why are you here?
TH-THUMP
Nothing...
TH-THUMP
"I came to get rid of the junk..."
"I really do hate you!"
I can't let my guard down.
He's a terrible person.

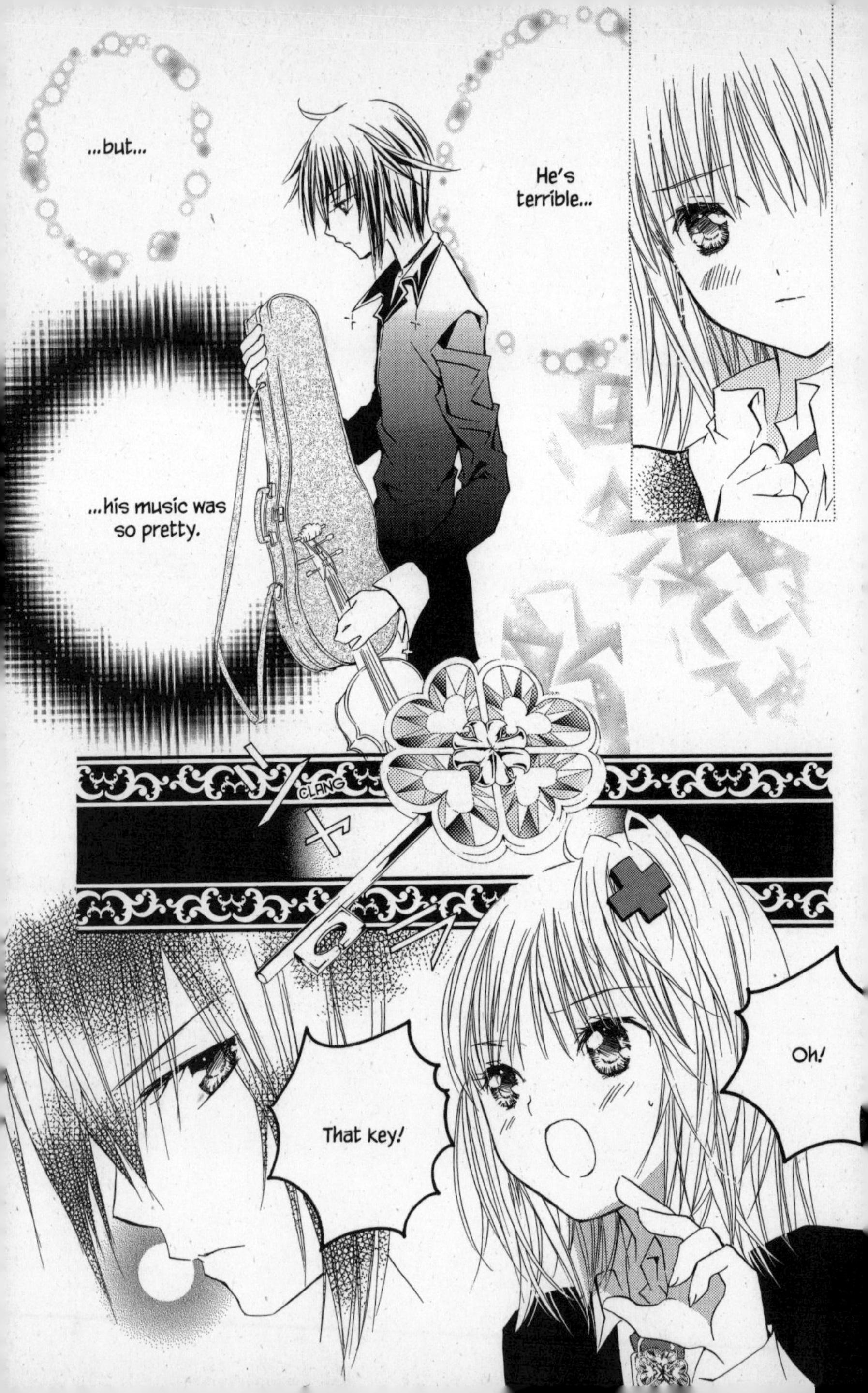
He's terrible...
...but...
...his music was so pretty.
CLANG
Oh!
That key!

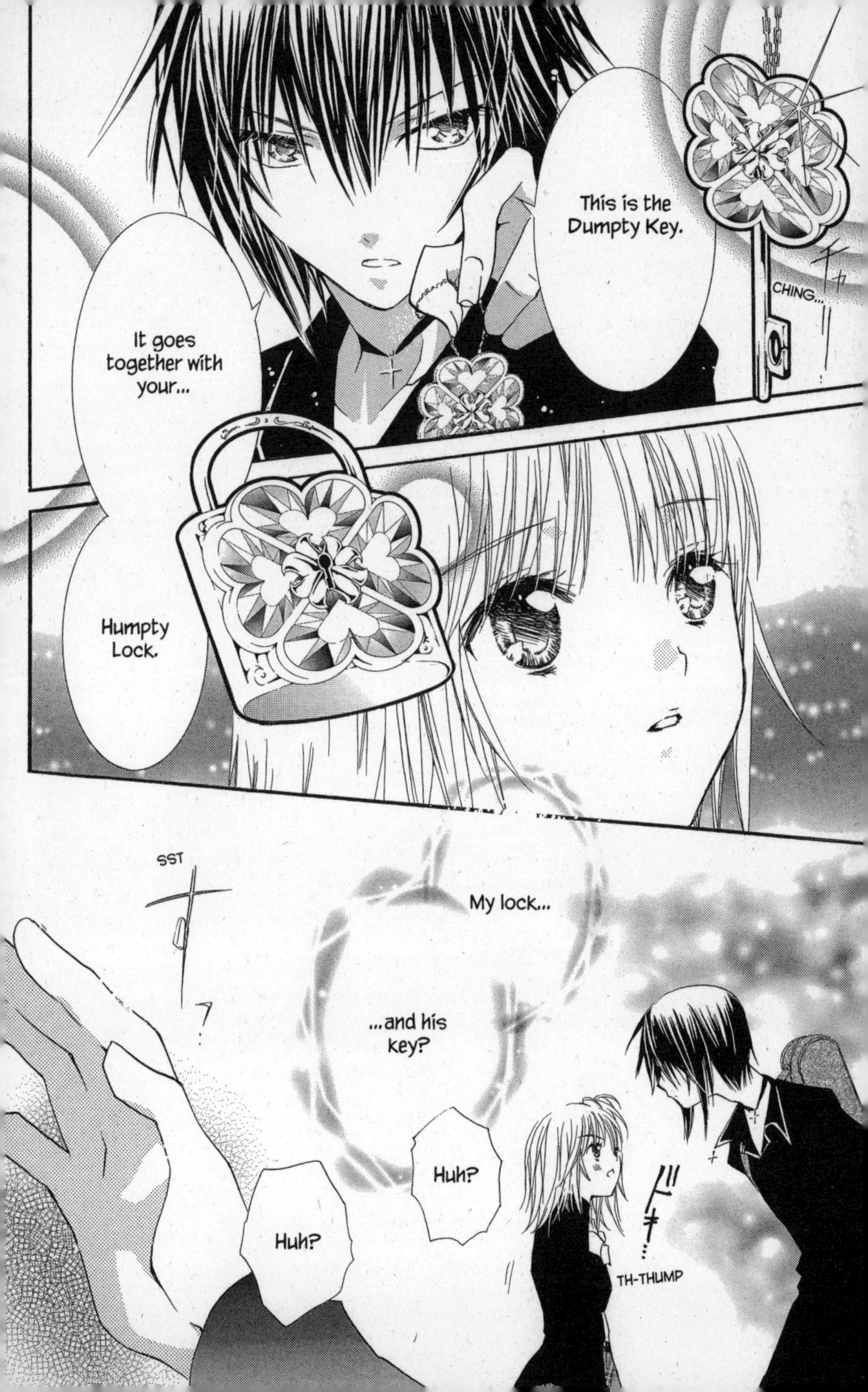
This is the Dumpty Key.
CHING...
It goes together with your...
Humpty Lock.
My lock...
SST
...and his key?
TH-THUMP
Huh?
Huh?

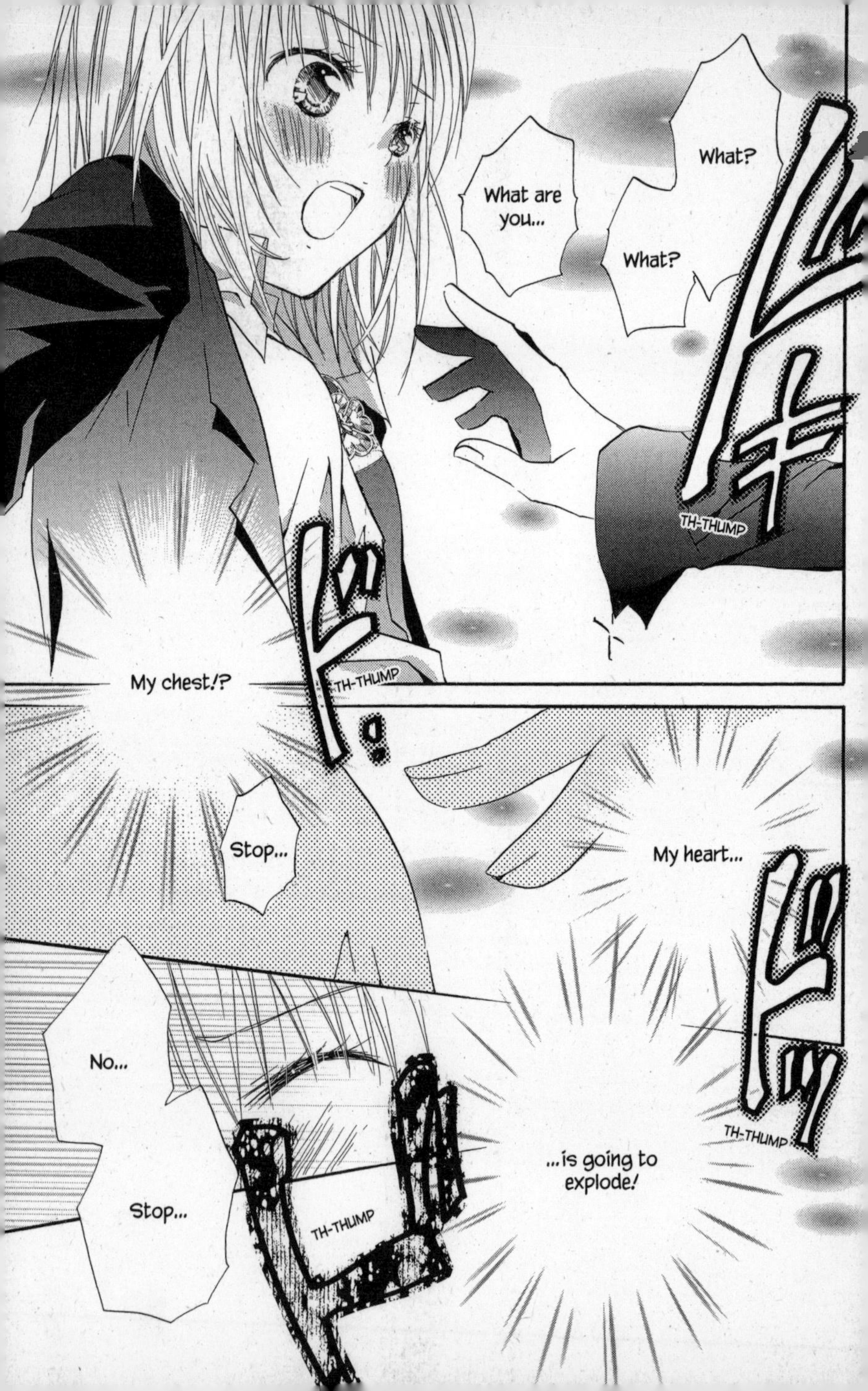
What?
What?
What are you...
TH-THUMP
TH-THUMP
My chest!?
My heart...
Stop...
TH-THUMP
...is going to explode!
TH-THUMP
No...
Stop...

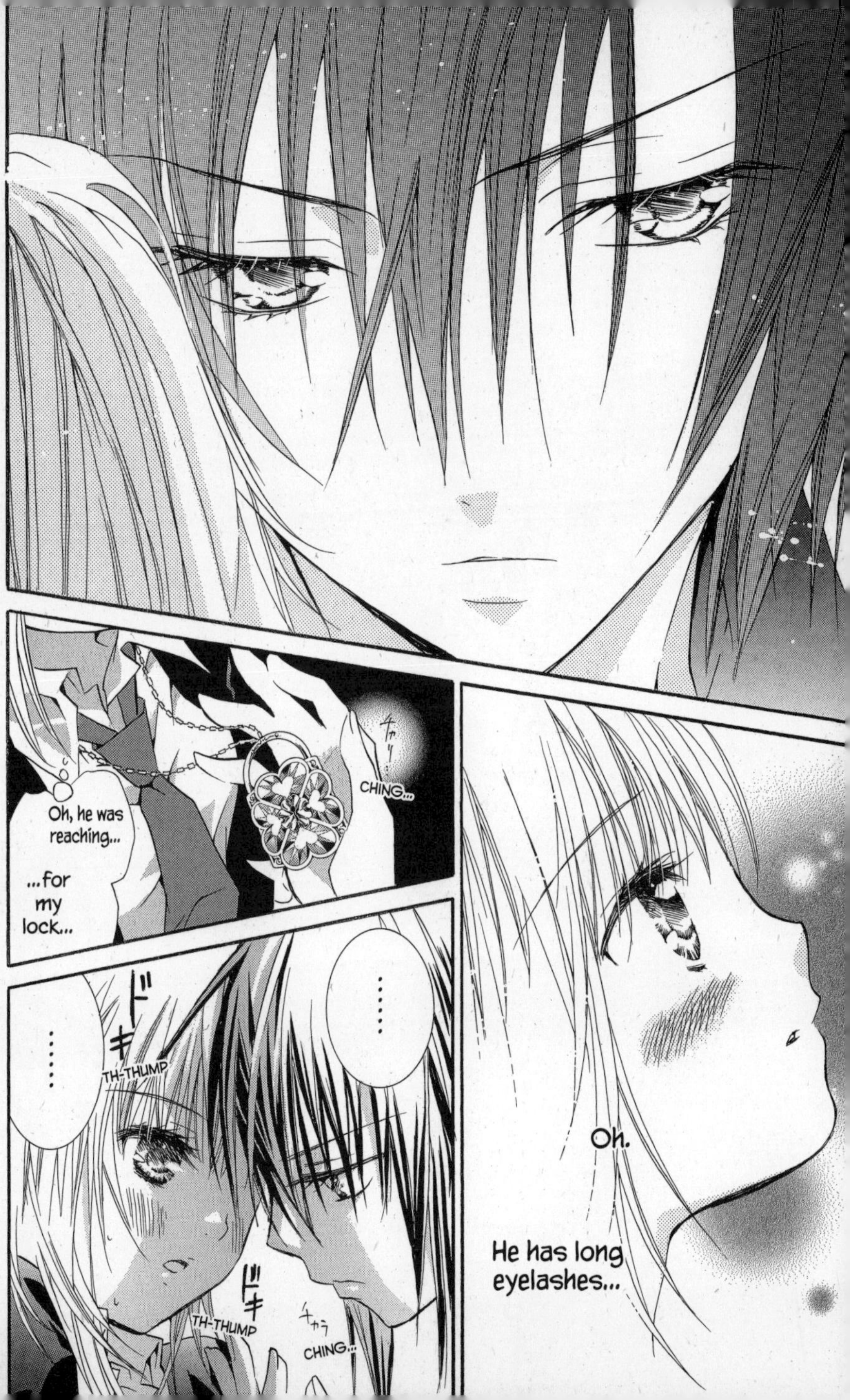
Oh.
He has long eyelashes...
CHING...
Oh, he was reaching...
...for my lock...
......
......
TH-THUMP
TH-THUMP
CHING...

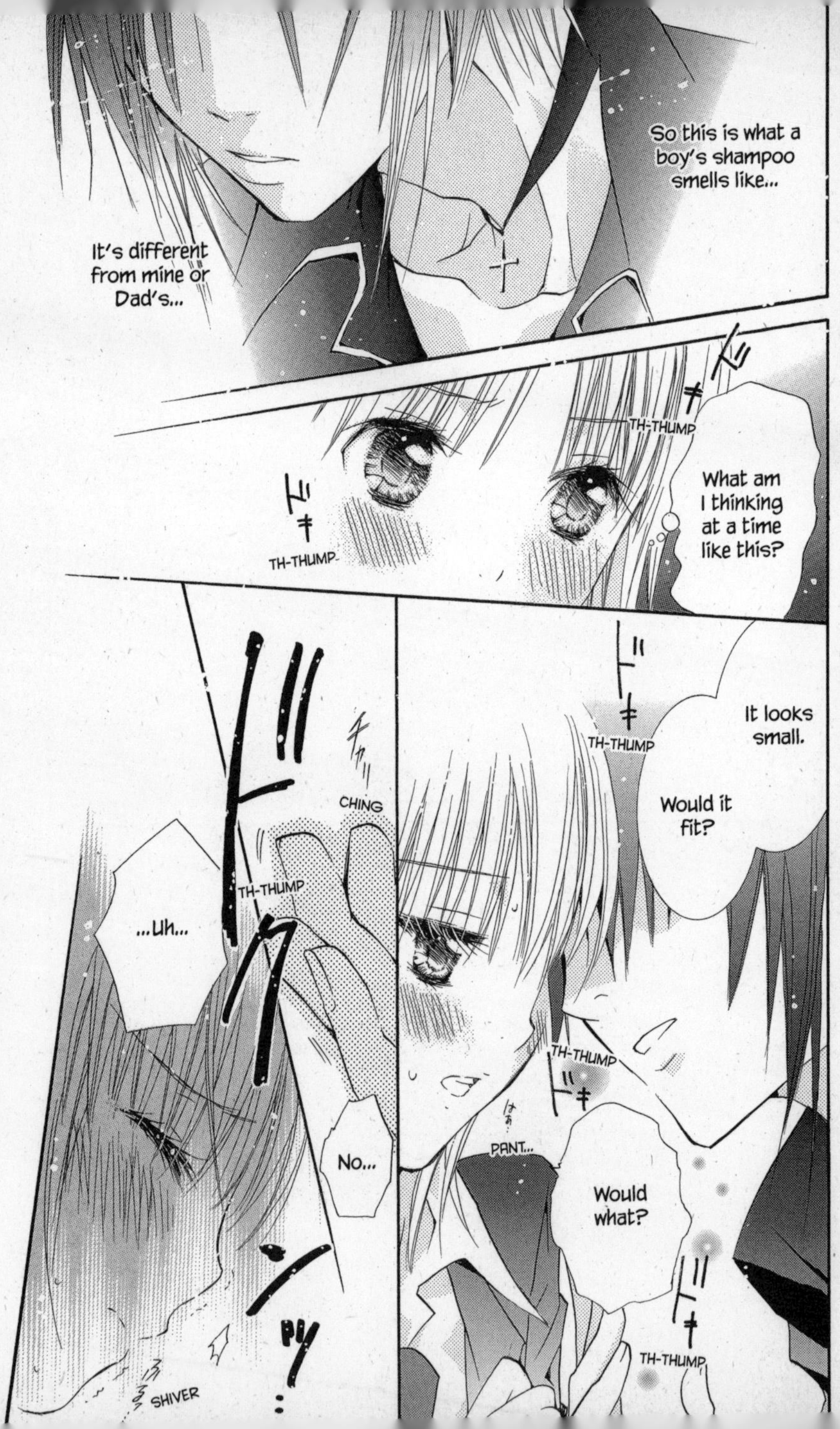
So this is what a boy's shampoo smells like...
It's different from mine or Dad's...
TH-THUMP
What am I thinking at a time like this?
TH-THUMP
TH-THUMP
It looks small.
Would it fit?
TH-THUMP
PANT...
Would what?
TH-THUMP
CHING
TH-THUMP
...uh...
No...
PY
SHIVER

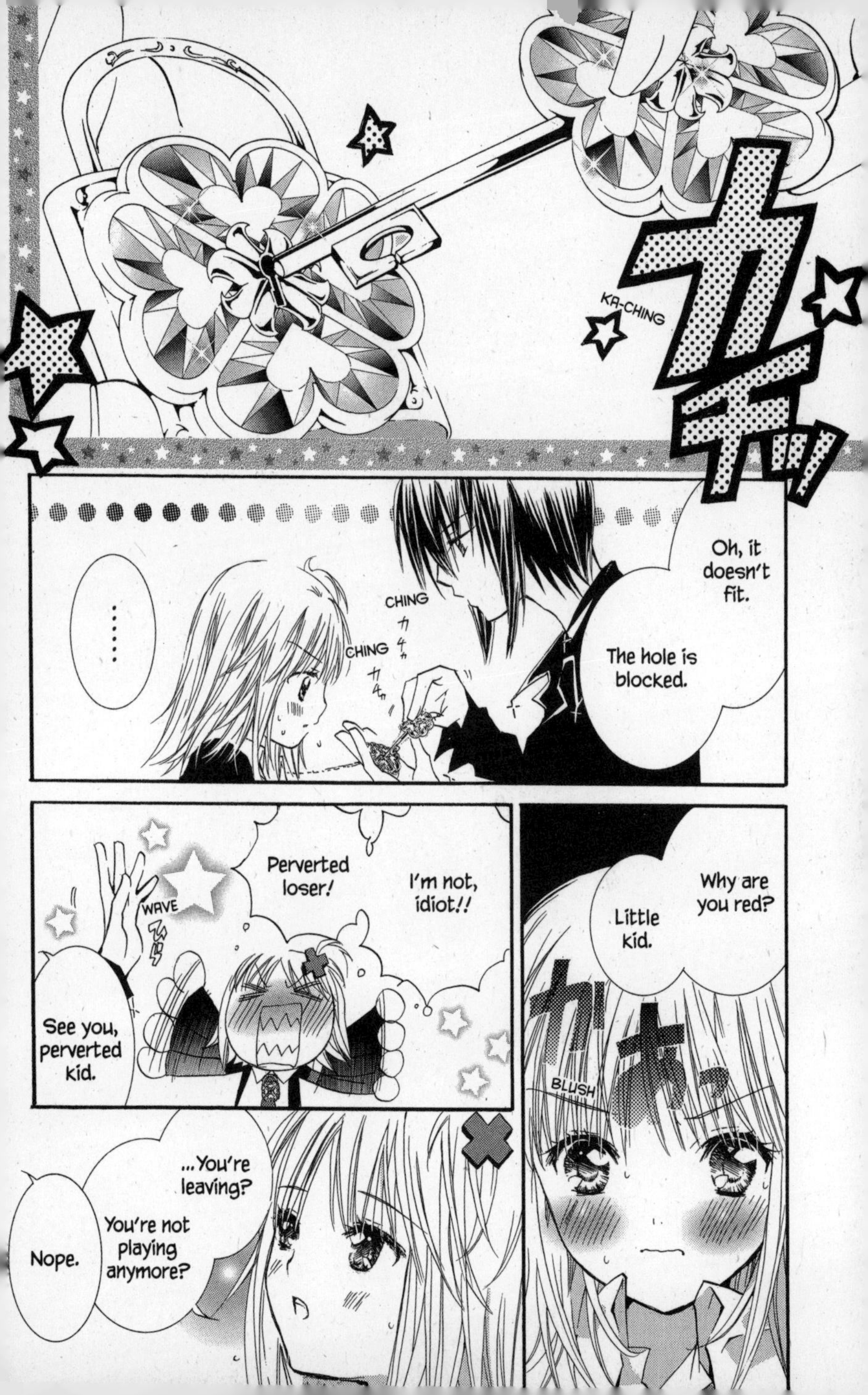
KA-CHING
Oh, it doesn't fit.
The hole is blocked.
CHING
CHING
......
Why are you red?
Little kid.
BLUSH
I'm not, idiot!!
Perverted loser!
WAVE
See you, perverted kid.
...You're leaving?
You're not playing anymore?
Nope.

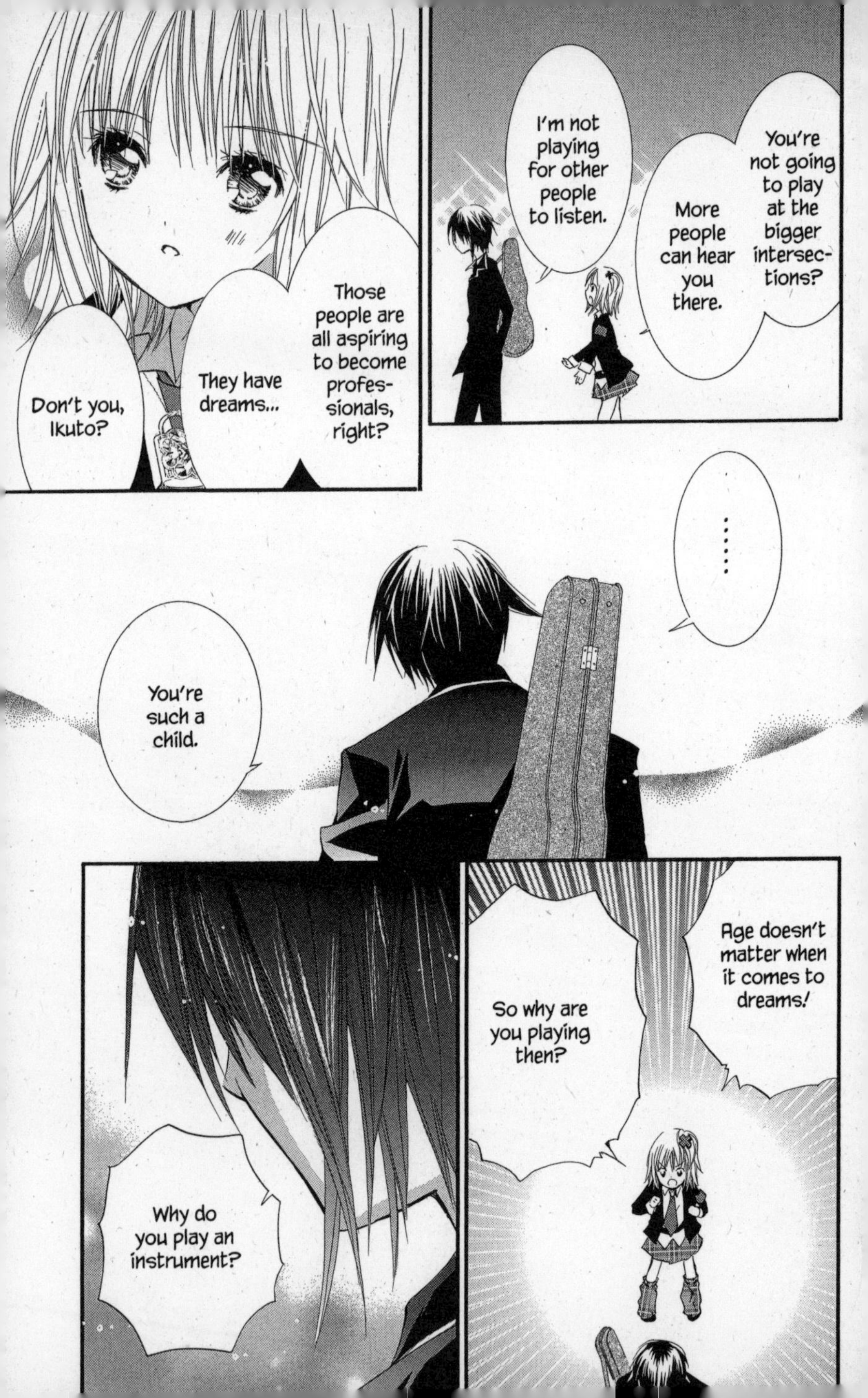
You're not going to play at the bigger intersections?
More people can hear you there.
I'm not playing for other people to listen.
Those people are all aspiring to become professionals, right?
They have dreams...
Don't you, Ikuto?
......
You're such a child.
Age doesn't matter when it comes to dreams!
So why are you playing then?
Why do you play an instrument?

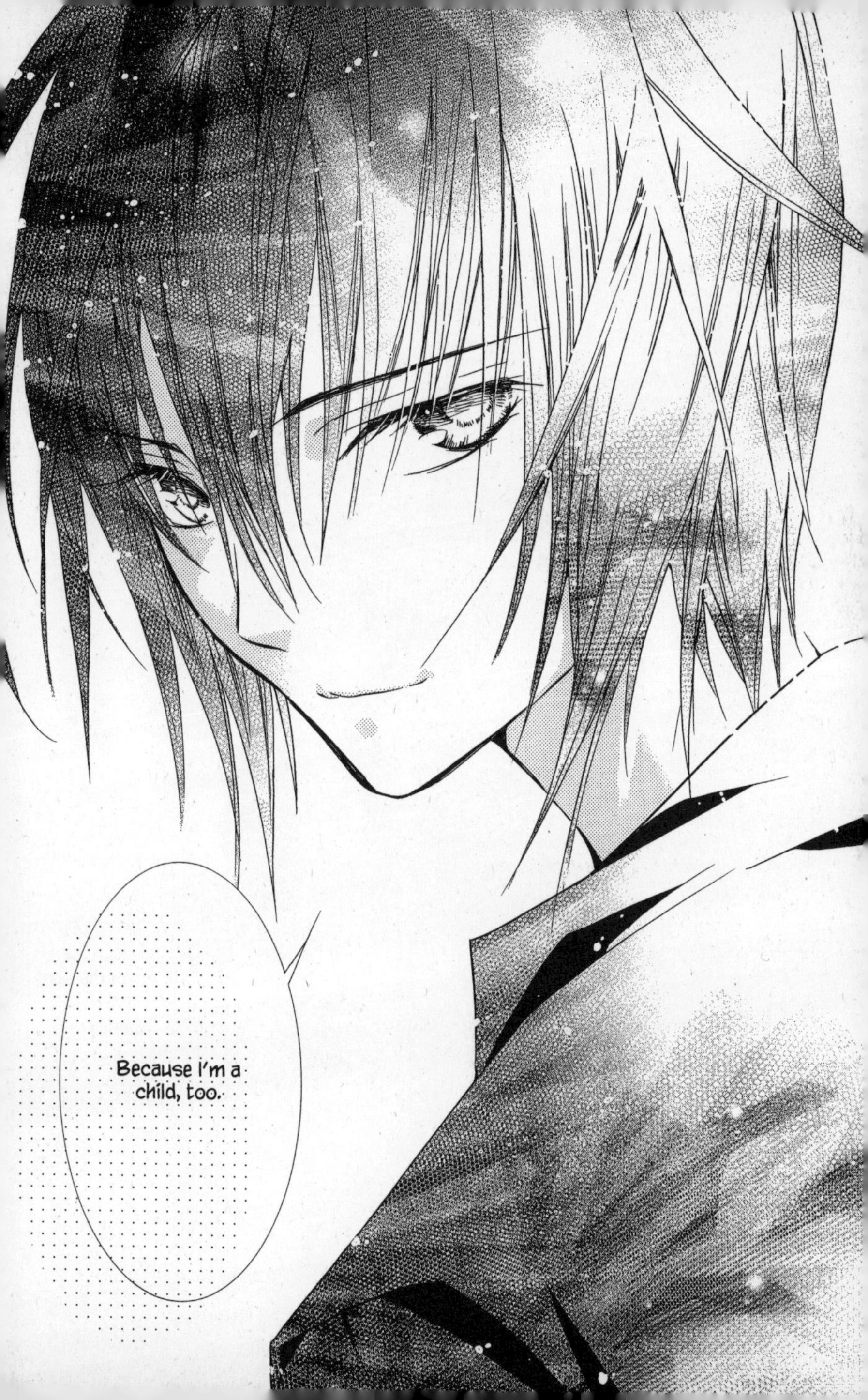
Because I'm a child, too.

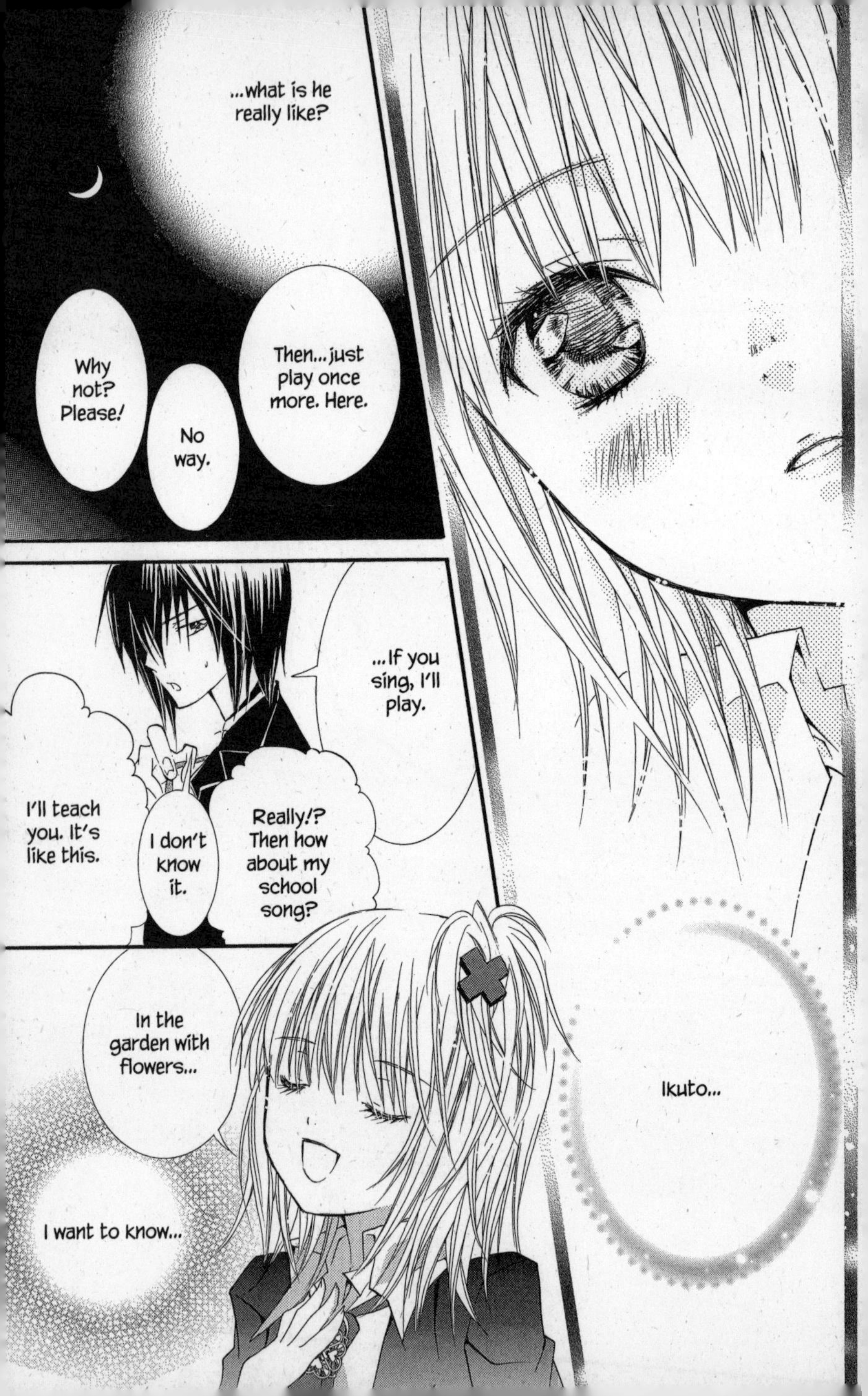
Ikuto...
...what is he really like?
Then...just play once more. Here.
No way.
Why not? Please!
...If you sing, I'll play.
Really!? Then how about my school song?
I don't know it.
I'll teach you. It's like this.
In the garden with flowers...
I want to know...

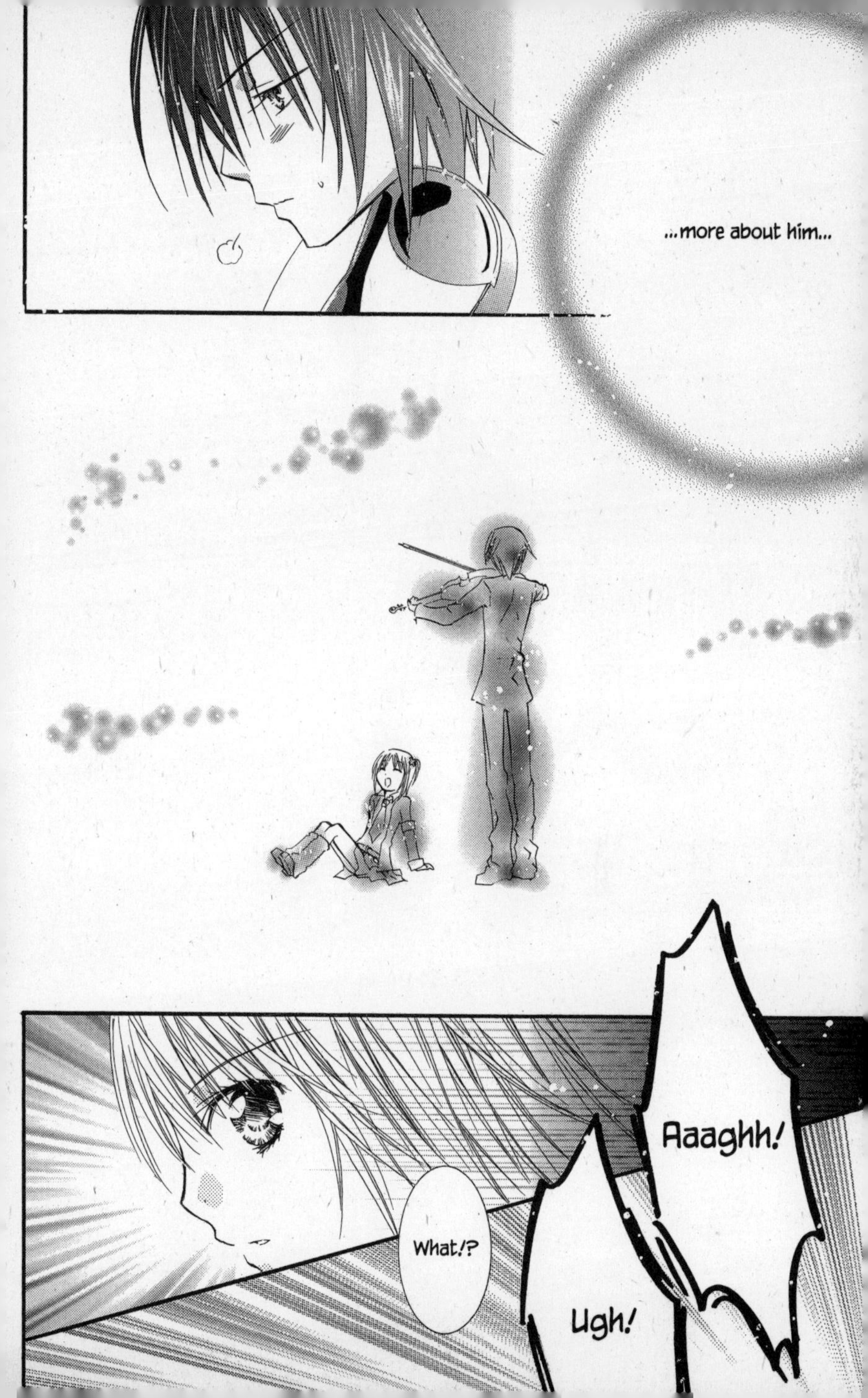
...more about him...
Aaaghh!
Ugh!
What!?

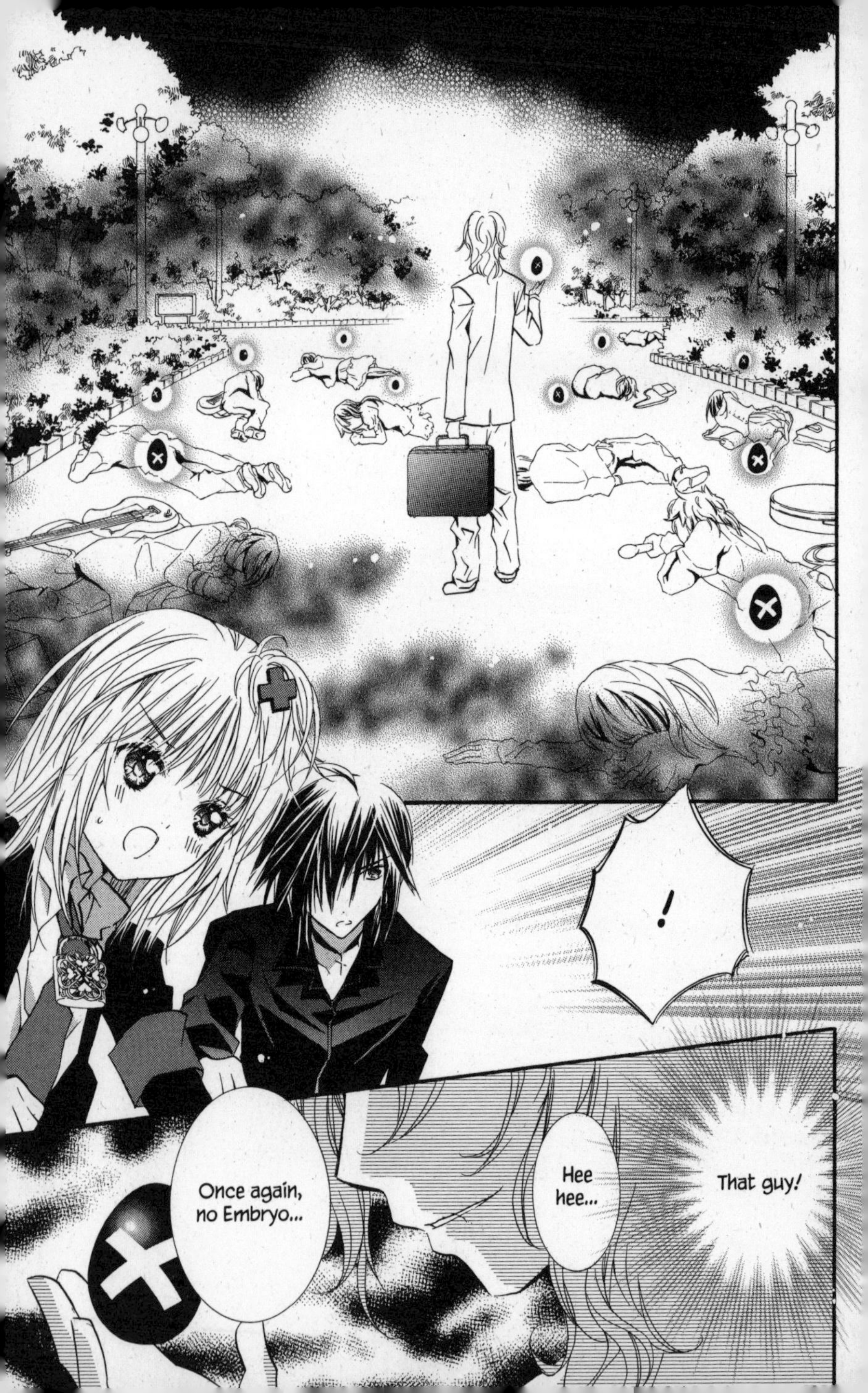
!
That guy!
Hee hee...
Once again, no Embryo...

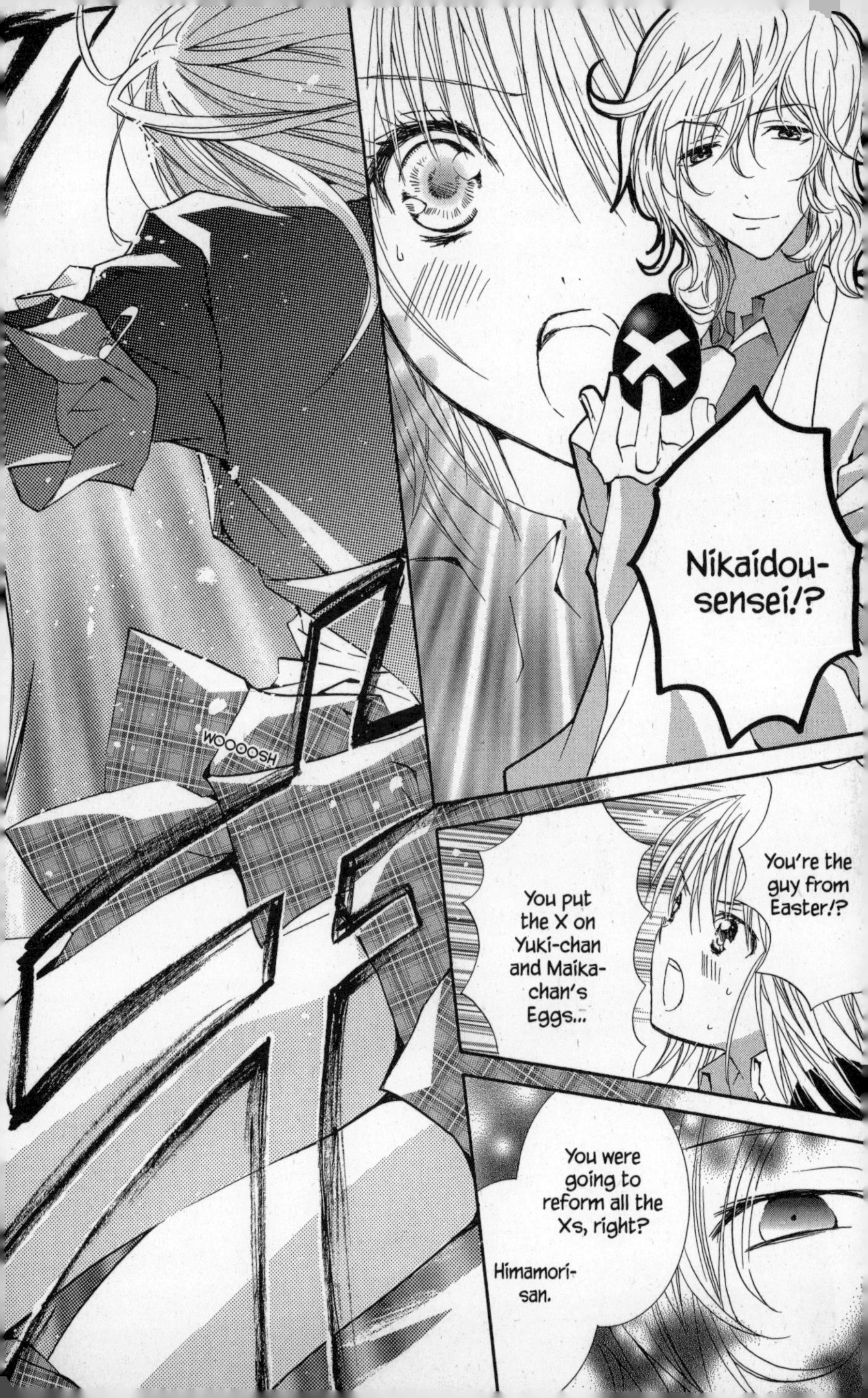
Nikaidou-sensei!?
You're the guy from Easter!?
You put the X on Yuki-chan and Maika-chan's Eggs...
You were going to reform all the Xs, right?
Himamori-san.
WOOOOSH

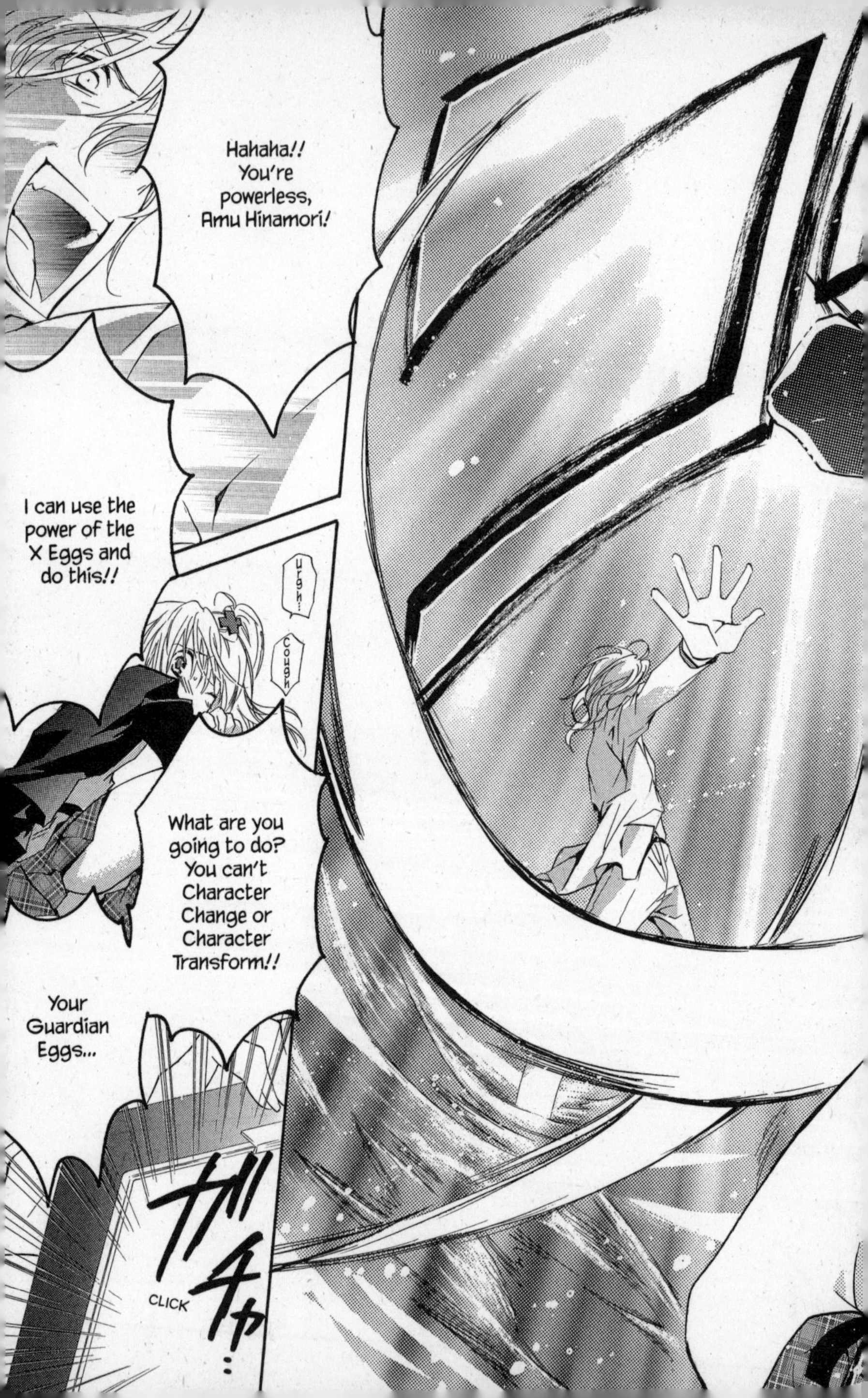
Hahaha!! You're powerless, Amu Hinamori!
I can use the power of the X Eggs and do this!!
Urgh...
Cough
What are you going to do? You can't Character Change or Character Transform!!
Your Guardian Eggs...
CLICK

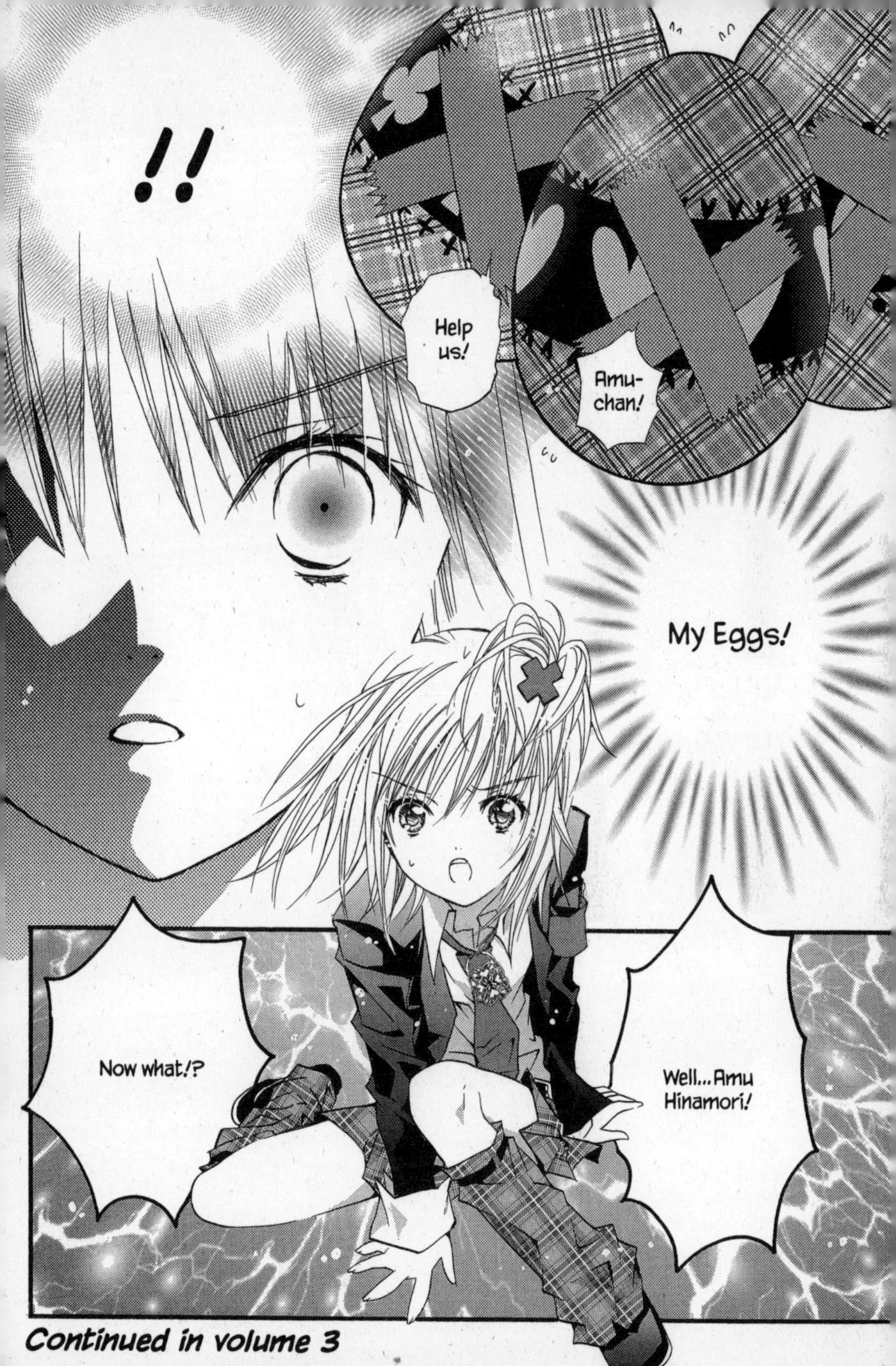
Amu-chan!
Help us!
!!
My Eggs!
Well...Amu Hinamori!
Now what!?

Continued in volume 3

Shugo Chara!

About the Creators

PEACH-PIT is:

Banri Sendo, born on June 7th

Shibuko Ebara, born on June 21st

We both are Gemini. We're a pair of manga
artists. Sendo enjoys sweets, but Ebara prefers spicy food. Our
favorite animals are cats and rabbits, and our recent hobbies are
making the ultimate *ajitama* and doing fingernail art.

Translation Notes

Japanese is a tricky language for most Westerners, and translation is often more art than science. For your edification and reading pleasure, here are notes on some of the places where we could have gone in a different direction in our translation of the work, or where a Japanese cultural reference is used.

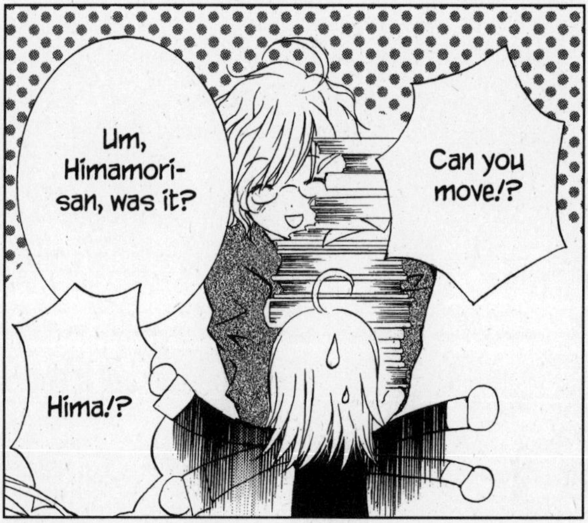
Can you move!?
Um, Himamori-san, was it?
Hima!?

Hima, page 24

This is a pun. *Hima* means "having spare time." *Hima* sounds like "Hina," the first two syllables of Amu's surname, and Yuu will continue calling her "Himamori-san" to belittle her.

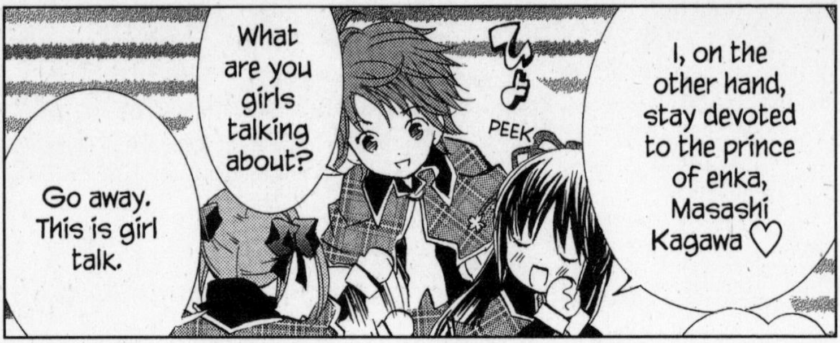
I, on the other hand, stay devoted to the prince of enka, Masashi Kagawa ♡
PEEK
What are you girls talking about?
Go away. This is girl talk.

Enka, page 46

Enka is a form of Japanese music that is similar to country music in the United States. It grew out of the democratic rights movement. When political speeches were punished in late nineteenth century Japan, political criticisms were voiced instead in the form of song. In present day, *enka* just refers to songs about certain themes such as the ocean, women, sake, tears, and goodbyes. In order to keep the Japanese style, most *enka* singers wear traditional clothing when performing.

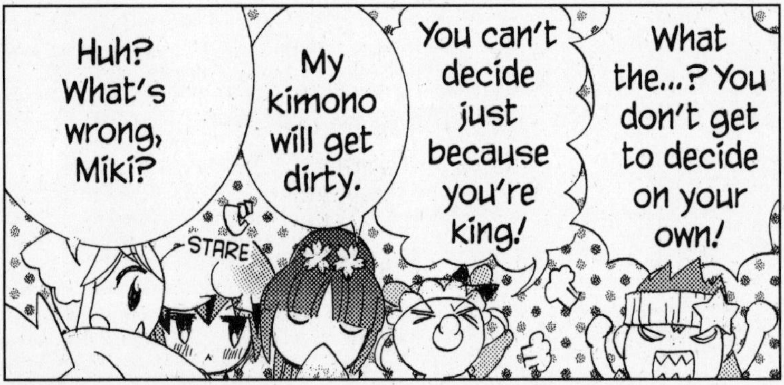
What the...? You don't get to decide on your own!
You can't decide just because you're king!
My kimono will get dirty.
STARE
Huh? What's wrong, Miki?

Kimono, page 51

A *kimono* is a piece of traditional Japanese clothing that looks like a robe. You wrap it around your body and tie a belt-like, long piece of cloth around it to keep it in place.

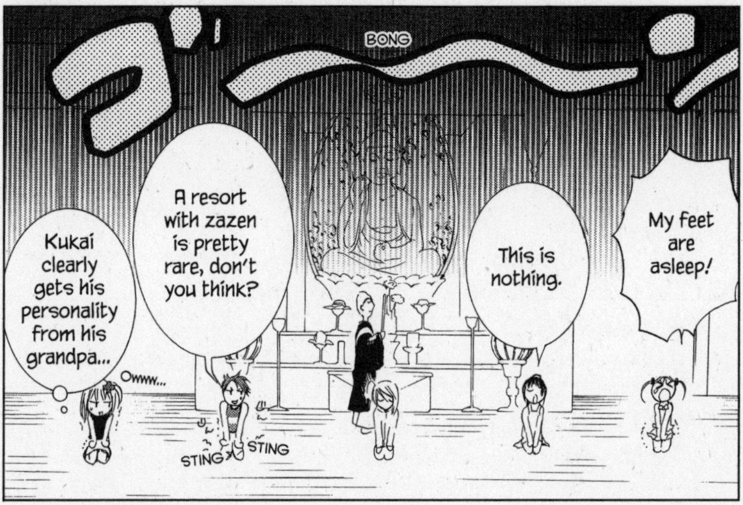
BONG
My feet are asleep!
This is nothing.
A resort with zazen is pretty rare, don't you think?
Kukai clearly gets his personality from his grandpa...
Owww...
STING
STING

***Zazen*, page 90**

Zazen is the act of sitting and opening the hand of thought. It is a Zen Buddhist practice. The term *zazen* literally means "seated meditation." It calms the body and mind to lead the meditator to enlightenment.

It's konnyaku.

Oh you guys...

You guys took so long!

Konnyaku, page 112

Konnyaku is a type of food in Japan made out of yams. It's like gelatin but much firmer, and it tastes a little like seaweed. Since it has no calories but is high in fiber, it's often eaten as diet food. Like *yaya*, many use it to scare others because in the dark a chilled *konnyaku* feels slippery and pretty gross.

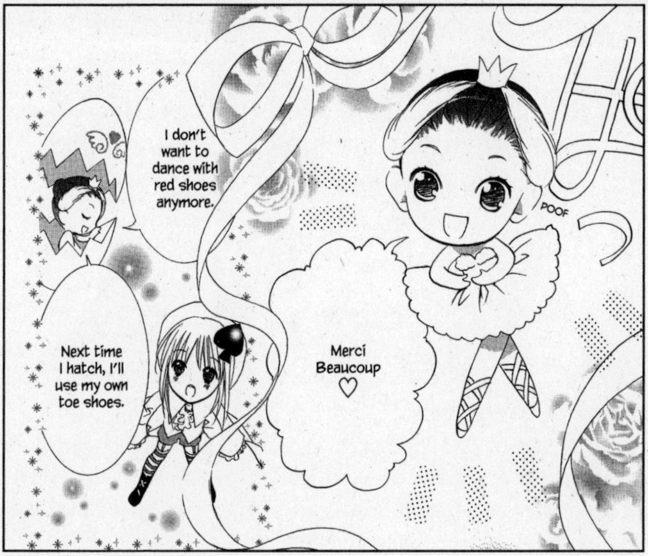
POOF
I don't want to dance with red shoes anymore.
Merci Beaucoup ♡
Next time I hatch, I'll use my own toe shoes.

Red shoes, page 154

The Character is making an allusion to *The Red Shoes* by Hans Christian Andersen. It is a story about a vain girl who was forced to dance in her red shoes until she couldn't bear it anymore and had to chop off her feet. The moral of the story is to not be so vain.

Please check our website (www.kodanshacomics.com) for information about *Shugo Chara!* volume 3. Don't miss it!

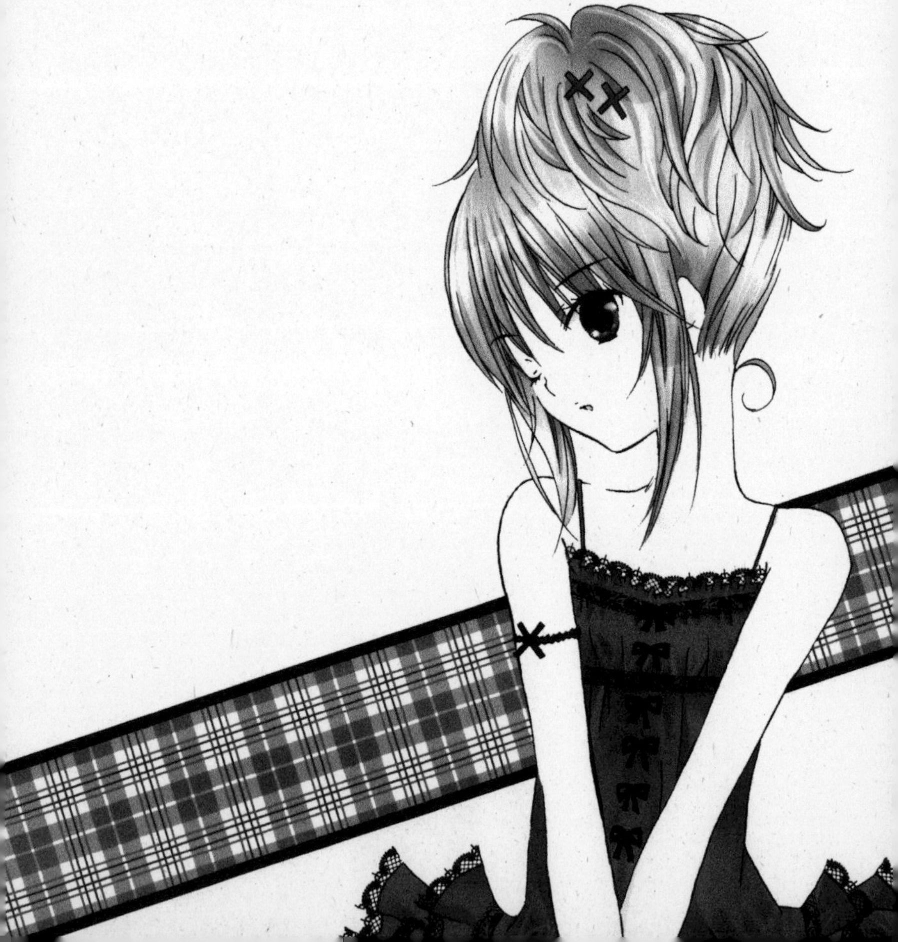

D0171750